T0332896

Trends and Applications of Text Summarization Techniques

Alessandro Fiori
Candiolo Cancer Institute – FPO, IRCCS, Italy

A volume in the Advances in Data
Mining and Database Management
(ADMDM) Book Series

Published in the United States of America by
    IGI Global
    Engineering Science Reference (an imprint of IGI Global)
    701 E. Chocolate Avenue
    Hershey PA, USA 17033
    Tel: 717-533-8845
    Fax: 717-533-8661
    E-mail: cust@igi-global.com
    Web site: http://www.igi-global.com

Library of Congress Cataloging-in-Publication Data

Names: Fiori, Alessandro, 1982- editor.
Title: Trends and applications of text summarization techniques / Alessandro
    Fiori, editor.
Description: Hershey, PA : Engineering Science Reference, [2020] | Includes
    bibliographical references.
Identifiers: LCCN 2019001873| ISBN 9781522593737 (hardcover) | ISBN
    9781522593744 (softcover) | ISBN 9781522593751 (ebook)
Subjects: LCSH: Automatic abstracting. | Electronic information
    resources--Abstracting and indexing. | Text processing (Computer science)
Classification: LCC Z695.92 .T74 2020 | DDC 025.4/10285635--dc23 LC record available at
https://lccn.loc.gov/2019001873

This book is published in the IGI Global book series Advances in Data Mining and Database
Management (ADMDM) (ISSN: 2327-1981; eISSN: 2327-199X)

British Cataloguing in Publication Data
A Cataloguing in Publication record for this book is available from the British Library.

All work contributed to this book is new, previously-unpublished material.
The views expressed in this book are those of the authors, but not necessarily of the publisher.

For electronic access to this publication, please contact: eresources@igi-global.com.

Advances in Data Mining and Database Management (ADMDM) Book Series

ISSN:2327-1981
EISSN:2327-199X

Editor-in-Chief: David Taniar, Monash University, Australia

MISSION

With the large amounts of information available to organizations in today's digital world, there is a need for continual research surrounding emerging methods and tools for collecting, analyzing, and storing data.

The **Advances in Data Mining & Database Management (ADMDM)** series aims to bring together research in information retrieval, data analysis, data warehousing, and related areas in order to become an ideal resource for those working and studying in these fields. IT professionals, software engineers, academicians and upper-level students will find titles within the ADMDM book series particularly useful for staying up-to-date on emerging research, theories, and applications in the fields of data mining and database management.

COVERAGE

- Web Mining
- Association Rule Learning
- Data Mining
- Decision Support Systems
- Information Extraction
- Data Analysis
- Database Testing
- Quantitative Structure–Activity Relationship
- Cluster Analysis
- Predictive Analysis

IGI Global is currently accepting manuscripts for publication within this series. To submit a proposal for a volume in this series, please contact our Acquisition Editors at Acquisitions@igi-global.com or visit: http://www.igi-global.com/publish/.

Titles in this Series

For a list of additional titles in this series, please visit:
https://www.igi-global.com/book-series/advances-data-mining-database-management/37146

Emerging Perspectives in Big Data Warehousing
David Taniar (Monash University, Australia) and Wenny Rahayu (La Trobe University, Australia)
Engineering Science Reference • copyright 2019 • 348pp • H/C (ISBN: 9781522555162) • US $245.00 (our price)

Emerging Technologies and Applications in Data Processing and Management
Zongmin Ma (Nanjing University of Aeronautics and Astronautics, China) and Li Yan (Nanjing University of Aeronautics and Astronautics, China)
Engineering Science Reference • copyright 2019 • 458pp • H/C (ISBN: 9781522584469) • US $265.00 (our price)

Online Survey Design and Data Analytics Emerging Research and Opportunities
Shalin Hai-Jew (Kansas State University, USA)
Engineering Science Reference • copyright 2019 • 226pp • H/C (ISBN: 9781522585633) • US $215.00 (our price)

Handbook of Research on Big Data and the IoT
Gurjit Kaur (Delhi Technological University, India) and Pradeep Tomar (Gautam Buddha University, India)
Engineering Science Reference • copyright 2019 • 568pp • H/C (ISBN: 9781522574323) • US $295.00 (our price)

Managerial Perspectives on Intelligent Big Data Analytics
Zhaohao Sun (Papua New Guinea University of Technology, Papua New Guinea)
Engineering Science Reference • copyright 2019 • 335pp • H/C (ISBN: 9781522572770) • US $225.00 (our price)

Optimizing Big Data Management and Industrial Systems With Intelligent Techniques

For an entire list of titles in this series, please visit:
https://www.igi-global.com/book-series/advances-data-mining-database-management/37146

701 East Chocolate Avenue, Hershey, PA 17033, USA
Tel: 717-533-8845 x100 • Fax: 717-533-8661
E-Mail: cust@igi-global.com • www.igi-global.com

Editorial Advisory Board

Table of Contents

Section 1
Concepts and Methods

Section 2
Domain Applications

Detailed Table of Contents

Section 1
Concepts and Methods

Chapter 1
Luca Cagliero, Politecnico di Torino, Italy
Paolo Garza, Politecnico di Torino, Italy
Moreno La Quatra, Politecnico di Torino, Italy

The recent advances in multimedia and web-based applications have eased the accessibility to large collections of textual documents. To automate the process of document analysis, the research community has put relevant efforts into extracting short summaries of the document content. However, most of the early proposed summarization methods were tailored to English-written textual corpora or to collections of documents all written in the same language. More recently, the joint efforts of the machine learning and the natural language processing communities have produced more portable and flexible solutions, which can be applied to documents written in different languages. This chapter first overviews the most relevant language-specific summarization algorithms. Then, it presents the most recent advances in multi- and cross-lingual text summarization. The chapter classifies the presented methodology, highlights the main pros and cons, and discusses the perspectives of the extension of the current research towards cross-lingual summarization systems.

As the number of electronic text documents is increasing so is the need for an automatic text summarizer. The summary can be extractive, compression, or abstractive. In the former, the more important sentences are retained, more or less in their original structure, while the second one involves reducing the length of each sentence. For the latter, it requires a fusion of multiple sentences and/or paraphrasing. This chapter focuses on the abstractive text summarization (ATS) of a single text document. The study explores what ATS is. Additionally, the literature of the field of ATS is investigated. Different datasets and evaluation techniques used in assessing the summarizers are discussed. The fact is that ATS is much more challenging than its extractive counterpart, and as such, there are a few works in this area for all the languages.

In this chapter, the authors study text mining technologies such as knowledge extraction and summarization on scientific and technical literature. First, they analyze the needs of scientific information services and intelligence analysis on massive scientific and technical literature. Second, terminology recognition and relation extraction are important tasks of knowledge extraction. Third, they study knowledge extraction based on terminology recognition and relation extraction. Fourth, based on terminology and relational network, they study the text summarization techniques and applications. Last, they give comments on current research and applications on text summarization and give their viewpoints for the possible research directions in the future.

Chapter 4

Due to the great growth of data on the web, mining to extract the most informative data as a conceptual brief would be beneficial for certain users. Therefore, there is great enthusiasm concerning the developing automatic text summary approaches. In this chapter, the authors highlight using the swarm intelligence (SI) optimization techniques for the first time in solving the problem of text summary. In addition, a convincing justification of why nature-heuristic algorithms, especially ant colony optimization (ACO), are the best algorithms for solving complicated optimization tasks is introduced. Moreover, it has been perceived that the problem of text summary had not been formalized as a multi-objective optimization (MOO) task before, despite there are many contradictory objectives in needing to be achieved. The SI has not been employed before to support the real-time tasks. Therefore, a novel framework of short text summary has been proposed to fulfill this issue. Ultimately, this chapter will enthuse researchers for further consideration for SI algorithms in solving summary tasks.

Chapter 5
Sandhya P., Vellore Institute of Technology, Chennai Campus, Tamil Nadu, India
Mahek Laxmikant Kantesaria, Vellore Institute of Technology, Chennai Campus, Tamil Nadu, India

Named entity recognition (NER) is a subtask of the information extraction. NER system reads the text and highlights the entities. NER will separate different entities according to the project. NER is the process of two steps. The steps are detection of names and classifications of them. The first step is further divided into the segmentation. The second step will consist to choose an ontology which will organize the things categorically. Document summarization is also called automatic summarization. It is a process in which the text document with the help of software will create a summary by selecting the important points of the original text. In this chapter, the authors explain how document summarization is performed using named entity recognition. They discuss about the different types of summarization techniques. They also discuss about how NER works and its applications. The libraries available for NER-based information extraction are explained. They finally explain how NER is applied into document summarization.

Section 2
Domain Applications

Chapter 6
Text Classification and Topic Modeling for Online Discussion Forums: An
Empirical Study From the Systems Modeling Community 151

Xin Zhao, University of Alabama, USA
Zhe Jiang, University of Alabama, USA
Jeff Gray, University of Alabama, USA

Online discussion forums play an important role in building and sharing domain
knowledge. An extensive amount of information can be found in online forums,
covering every aspect of life and professional discourse. This chapter introduces the
application of supervised and unsupervised machine learning techniques to analyze
forum questions. This chapter starts with supervised machine learning techniques
to classify forum posts into pre-defined topic categories. As a supporting technique,
web scraping is also discussed to gather data from an online forum. After this, this
chapter introduces unsupervised learning techniques to identify latent topics in
documents. The combination of supervised and unsupervised machine learning
approaches offers us deeper insights of the data obtained from online forums. This
chapter demonstrates these techniques through a case study on a very large online
discussion forum called LabVIEW from the systems modeling community. In the
end, the authors list future trends in applying machine learning to understand the
expertise captured in online expert communities.

Chapter 7
Summarization in the Financial and Regulatory Domain 187

Jochen L. Leidner, Refinitiv Labs, UK & University of Sheffield, UK

This chapter presents an introduction to automatic summarization techniques with
special consideration of the financial and regulatory domains. It aims to provide an
entry point to the field for readers interested in natural language processing (NLP)
who are experts in the finance and/or regulatory domain, or to NLP researchers
who would like to learn more about financial and regulatory applications. After
introducing some core summarization concepts and the two domains are considered,
some key methods and systems are described. Evaluation and quality concerns are
also summarized. To conclude, some pointers for future reading are provided.

Chapter 8
Opinion Mining and Product Review Summarization in E-Commerce 216

Enakshi Jana, Pondicherry University, India
V. Uma, Pondicherry University, India

With the immense increase of the number of users of the internet and simultaneously
the massive expansion of the e-commerce platform, millions of products are sold
online. To improve user experience and satisfaction, online shopping platform

enables every user to give their reviews for each and every product that they buy online. Reviews are long and contain only a few sentences which are related to a particular feature of that product. It becomes very difficult for the user to understand other customer views about different features of the product. So, we need accurate opinion-based review summarization which will help both customers and product manufacture to understand and focus on a particular aspect of the product. In this chapter, the authors discuss the abstractive document summarization method to summarize e-commerce product reviews. This chapter has an in-depth explanation about different types of document summarization and how that can be applied to e-commerce product reviews.

This chapter describes the evolution of a real, multi-document, multilingual news summarization methodology and application, named NewSum, the research problems behind it, as well as the steps taken to solve these problems. The system uses the representation of n-gram graphs to perform sentence selection and redundancy removal towards summary generation. In addition, it tackles problems related to topic and subtopic detection (via clustering), demonstrates multi-lingual applicability, and—through recent advances—scalability to big data. Furthermore, recent developments over the algorithm allow it to utilize semantic information to better identify and outline events, so as to offer an overall improvement over the base approach.

Foreword

With the advent of new technologies, we assisted in the explosion of the production and disclosure of a huge number of documents. Textual information in the form of digital documents quickly accumulates to huge amounts of data. Since this information is unstructured and sparse, the internet-age readers lose a lot of time in searching and reading several resources to identify and extract few concepts or news of interest. Therefore, the capability of summarizing these huge and heterogenous text collections to provide short texts focused on the reader's interests, is becoming a pressing need and a challenging task. Summarization techniques proposed in the last years are focused on automatically produce a succinct overview of the most important concepts covered by one or more documents. This book provides a valuable and in-depth overview of state-of-art automated document summarization techniques.

The development of new methods and algorithms in the fields of Natural Language Processing (NLP), machine learning and text mining, allowed the researchers in producing new summarization approaches with an overall improvement in the quality of resulting summaries. The book chapters introduce several approaches to document summarization, together with methods to assess the quality of the generated summaries. They provide a good overview of the exploitation of these techniques in the document summarization research area and some suggestions to apply the new tools in specific domains.

Indeed, summarization techniques could be applied in several domains. The book covers a selection of the most relevant application domains, ranging from biomedical analysis to finance. A challenging issue, covered in the book but still to be explored, is addressing the different languages in which documents are available and produce summaries in another language different from those of the input documents.

Silvia Chiusano
Politecnico di Torino, Italy

Preface

Written documents have been always used by people to communicate relevant information, opinions and sentiments. With the advent of new technologies, the production of documents increased exponentially. Every day a huge mass of messages, product reviews, news articles and scientific documents are produced and published over the web on social networks, marketplaces, production platforms and web sites. This unstructured information can be very useful, but many times can be verbose for the readers. Summarization has been exploited to provide a concise representation of most relevant information and focus the reader only on the most important concepts. The development of text mining, machine learning, and natural language processing techniques opened the new frontier of automatic text summarization. By means of these approaches, it is possible to automatically produce summaries typically containing either the most relevant sentences, or the most prominent keywords, in the document or in the collection. Extracting a succinct and informative description of single document and/or a collection is fundamental to allowing users to quickly familiarize themselves with the information of interest. For example, the summary of a collection of news documents regarding the same topic may provide a synthetic overview of the most relevant news facets. Differently, the summarization of social network data can support the identification of relevant information about a specific event, and the inference of user and community interests and opinions.

During the last years, several automated summarization methods have been proposed. Summarization approaches may be classified in two main categories: (1) sentence-based, if they partition documents into sentences and select the most informative ones for inclusion in the summary, or (2) keyword-based, if they detect salient keywords that summarize the document content. All these approaches usually exploit statistical metrics, text mining algorithms, machine leaning and/or Natural Language Processing (NLP) methods. For instance, clustering-based approaches, probabilistic or co-occurrence-based strategies, graph-based algorithms and itemset-based methods have been proposed. Since the language of input documents affects how the documents should be processed, more recent works have been focused on the development of summarization approaches that adapt their analysis and the resulting summaries according to the language. Even the topic domain treated by the documents can be relevant for the analysis. The usage on ontologies and POS tagging techniques have been introduced in the most recent works to overcome this issue. Another significant hurdle is the evaluation of summaries produced by different approaches in order to identify the best method in the context of interest. For this reason, the definition of automatic evaluation systems for text summaries is still an open research task.

This book provides a comprehensive discussion of the state of the art in document summarization field. The reader will find in-depth discussion of several approaches exploiting machine learning, natural language processing and data mining techniques both for single and multi-document summarization task. Moreover, the exploitation of summarization approaches in several application fields, such as financial, e-commerce and biomedical, are also provided.

This book is aimed at people who are interested in automatic summarization algorithms: PhD students, researchers, engineers, linguists, practitioners of information technology, computer scientists, bioinformatics mathematicians and specialists in business. Developers and consumers will be interested in discovering how the document summarization can improve their productivity in real applications, while researchers and students can learn more about the main concepts of the state-of-art document summarization approaches. Far from being exhaustive, this book aims to provide an overview of state-of-art automatic summarization methods, the main concepts exploited by these approaches and possible applications. Through predictions of future trends, examinations of techniques and technologies, and focuses on real application scenarios, the reader can find interesting suggestions for developing new document summarization instruments to apply in different application fields.

The book comprises nine chapters and is organized as follows.

Section 1 "Concepts and Methods", consisting of five chapters, provides a good overview of the state-of-art summarization methods and the exploitation of text mining, machine learning and natural language processing techniques to improve the quality of resulting summaries.

Chapter 1, "Combining Machine Learning and Natural Language Processing for Language-Specific, Multi-Lingual, and Cross-Lingual Text Summarization: A Wide-Ranging Overview", overviews the most recent approaches to cross-lingual document summarization. The authors introduce the traditional summarization problem and briefly describe the state-of-the-art approaches to language-specific and multi-lingual document summarization. A detailed discussion of the key issues and prospects related to the extension of the state-of-the-art methods towards the cross-lingual domain are also provided. State-of-the-art approaches to extractive and abstractive cross-lingual summarization are thoroughly described.

Chapter 2, "The Development of Single-Document Abstractive Text Summarizer During the Last Decade", is focused on the state-of-the-art works on abstractive text summarization systems for single documents, regardless of the target language of the input document. Indeed, abstractive text summarization is very challenging with respect to the extractive counterpart, and as such there are few works in this area in all the languages. The authors explore several methods developed during the last decade and identifying their limitations. Finally, the chapter discusses how summarization systems are evaluated and which datasets have been used.

Chapter 3, "Mining Scientific and Technical Literature: from Knowledge Extraction to Summarization", presents text mining technologies such as knowledge extraction and summarization on scientific and technical literature. Firstly, the authors analyze the needs of scientific information services and intelligence analysis on massive scientific and technical literature. Then, they introduce the terminology recognition and relation extraction which are important tasks of knowledge extraction are introduced. Based on terminology and relational network, the chapter discusses text summarization techniques and applications, focused on the scientific literature.

Chapter 4, "Data Text Mining Based on Swarm Intelligence Techniques: Review of Text Summarization Systems", analyzes the exploitation of the swarm intelligence (SI) optimization techniques to extract text summaries. In particular, the authors discuss why nature-heuristic algorithms, especially Ant Colony Optimization (ACO), are the most promising algorithms for solving complicated optimization tasks. Indeed, it has been perceived that the problem of text summary had not been formalized as a multi-objective optimization (MOO) task before, despite there are many contradictory objectives in needing to be achieved. For these reasons, the authors propose a novel framework of short text summary to support the real-time tasks.

Chapter 5, "Named Entity Recognition in Document Summarization", introduces the main concepts of document summarization and Named-entity Recognition (NER). Since NER is very useful for the content extraction and automatic annotation from unstructured text, it is application in document summarization can be very relevant to produce high quality summaries. Case studies showing how NER is applied to document summarization are presented to provide to the reader some possible exploitations of these approaches in real-world applications.

Section 2, "Domain Applications", consisting of four chapters, illustrates the application and the usefulness of text summarization approaches in different fields and scenarios. Real use cases and applications are presented to the reader in order to provide also a starting point to develop new methodologies and useful suggestions to improve the productivity in different fields.

Chapter 6, "Text Classification and Topic Modeling for Online Discussion Forums: An Empirical Study From the Systems Modeling Community", introduces the application of supervised and unsupervised machine learning techniques to analyze forum questions. The chapter presents supervised machine learning techniques to classify forum posts into pre-defined topic categories. As a supporting technique, web scraping is also discussed to gather data from online forum. Differently, the exploitation of unsupervised learning techniques to identify latent topics in documents is analyzed. The combination of supervised and unsupervised machine learning approaches offers deeper insights of the data obtained from online forums. The authors demonstrate these techniques through a case study on a very large online discussion forum called LabVIEW from the systems modeling community. Finally, future trends in applying machine learning to understand the expertise capture in online expert communities, such as discussion forums, are presented.

Chapter 7, "Summarization in the Financial and Regulatory Domains", starts explaining the particular properties of the financial and regulatory domains. Then, the authors survey quality criteria that mark good summaries and outlines some common ways to evaluate summarization methods quantitatively. An overview of some state-of-art general purpose methods, and of some implemented summarization systems, in particular those relevant to financial, risk and regulatory, is introduced. Finally, the chapter provides some reflections, suggestions for future work and pointers for further reading.

Chapter 8, "Opinion Mining and Product Review Summarization in E-Commerce", discusses on aspect and opinion identification and extraction from product reviews. The authors explain different methods used for opinion identification and extraction. A categorization of document summarization methods and an overview of different evaluation metrics are also presented. Finally, the chapter discusses how deep learning can be used for abstractive summarization in the field of e-commerce product review

Chapter 9, "Scaling and Semantically Enriching Language-Agnostic Summarization", describes the evolution of a real, multi-document, multilingual news summarization methodology and application, named NewSum. The system exploits the representation of n-gram graphs to perform sentence selection and redundancy removal towards summary generation. In addition, the issue related to topic and subtopic detection is tackled by means of clustering algorithm. The author demonstrates the applicability of their approach to multi-lingual document collections, and – through recent advances - the scalability to big data. Moreover, recent developments over the algorithm allow the exploitation of semantic information to better identify and outline events, so as to offer an overall improvement over the base approach.

Document summarization is an appealing research field focused on extracting relevant information from large volumes of unstructured data contained in document collections. Summarization systems can help in acquiring knowledge about a specific domain (e.g., biology, finance) quickly and without redundancy, in improving the quality of existing platforms such as marketplaces and biomedical tools removing irrelevant information. Indexing of web documents also can benefit of automatic summaries to improve the user experience. The objective of this work is to provide a clear and consolidated view of state-of-art summarization methods and their application to real use cases. We seek to explore new methods to model text data, extract the relevant information according to the user interests and evaluate the quality and usefulness of the extracted summaries. We believe that a considerable research effort will be required in the future to improve the quality of these systems, for instance, in terms of computational load and readability of the summary. Different application domains might also benefit from summarization techniques and allow scientists enhance their works. We also believe that semantic-based approaches will be the next generation of summarization systems.

We are confident that researchers and professionals in the fields of text mining, natural language processing, text summarization and social network analysis will be able to use this book to learn more about the ways in which summarization techniques can prove useful in different environments. The students can use this book as starting point for their future professional activities that involve the management and the analysis of unstructured text data.

Acknowledgment

This book would not have been possible without the cooperation of many people: the authors, the reviewers, my colleagues, the staff at IGI Global, and my family.

To the authors who have each spent a lot of time and energies writing, editing, and rewriting their chapters over the last year, without you there would be no book. To the reviewers, many of whom were also authors and therefore did double duty, your constructive feedback has made each and every chapter the best it can be. We appreciate the time you spent reading and discerning the chapters.

To all my colleagues not directly involved with the writing or reviewing of chapters, without your ideas, discussions, and support, this book would have remained just an idea. A special thank to my colleague Andrea Mignone who helped me many times during the last year in reviewing chapters and organizing the work. Thanks a lot also to Prof Silvia Chiusano who support me in the research field in the last years and wrote the foreword of this book

To all of the staff at IGI Global, in particular Jordan Tepper, I thank you for your continued support, advice, and assistance with all aspects of the project from its initial proposal up through the final publication approvals.

To my son Francesco, my wife Maria and my dog Sophie, without your love and support, there would be no book. This book is devoted to you!

Section 1
Concepts and Methods

Chapter 1
Combining Machine Learning and Natural Language Processing for Language-Specific, Multi-Lingual, and Cross-Lingual Text Summarization:
A Wide-Ranging Overview

Luca Cagliero
Politecnico di Torino, Italy

Paolo Garza
Politecnico di Torino, Italy

Moreno La Quatra
Politecnico di Torino, Italy

ABSTRACT

The recent advances in multimedia and web-based applications have eased the accessibility to large collections of textual documents. To automate the process of document analysis, the research community has put relevant efforts into extracting short summaries of the document content. However, most of the early proposed summarization methods were tailored to English-written textual corpora or to collections of documents all written in the same language. More recently, the joint efforts of the machine learning and the natural language processing communities have produced more portable and flexible solutions, which can be applied to documents written in different languages. This chapter first overviews the most relevant language-specific summarization algorithms. Then, it presents the most recent advances in multi- and cross-lingual text summarization. The chapter classifies the presented methodology, highlights the main pros and cons, and discusses the perspectives of the extension of the current research towards cross-lingual summarization systems.

DOI: 10.4018/978-1-5225-9373-7.ch001

INTRODUCTION

In recent years, accomplice the recent advances of Web-based applications, the number of textual documents produced and made available in electronic form has steadily increased. To peruse potentially large collections of textual documents, domain experts often need for the aid of automatic compression tools, namely the document summarizers. These systems are able to produce informative yet succinct summaries by filtering out irrelevant or redundant content and by selecting the most salient parts of the text.

Text summarization is an established branch of research, whose main goal is to study and develop summarization tools which are able to extract high-quality information from large document collections (Tan et al., 2006). Plenty of approaches to document summarization have been proposed in literature. They commonly rely on Natural Language Processing (NLP), Information Retrieval (IR), or text mining techniques (Nazari & Mahdavi, 2019). Automated summarization systems have found application in industrial and research domains, e.g., content curation for medical applications (Zitnik et al., 2019), news recommendation (Tang et al., 2009), disaster management (Li et al., 2010), and learning analytics (Cagliero et al., 2019, Baralis & Cagliero, 2018).

The text summarization process commonly entails the following steps:

1. Filter the content of the input documents and transform it using ad hoc textual data representations.
2. Identify the key concepts mentioned in the text and extract significant descriptions of these concepts in textual form.
3. Generate summaries of the original document content that cover all of the salient concepts with minimal redundancy.

Statistics- and semantics-based text analyses are commonly applied in order to detect the most significant concepts and their descriptions in the text (Conroy et al., 2004). Most of them rely on the hypothesis that the content of all the original documents is written in the same language. This simplifies both the models used to capture in the text, which are usually language- and domain-specific, and the computation of text similarity measures, which usually rely on frequency-based term analyses. Hereafter, they will denote as "language-specific" summarizers all the systems that cannot be applied to documents written in different languages.

The rapid growth of Internet worldwide has produced a huge mass of textual documents written in a variety of different languages. Accessing the information contained in documents written in different languages has become a relevant yet compelling research issue (Wang et al., 2018). For instance, the findings described in scientific articles and reports written in languages other than English are, in most cases, not easily accessible by foreign researchers. This limits the accessibility of the achieved results. Similarly, the news articles published on national newspapers in the local languages cannot be easily explored unless adopting language-dependent text analysis tools. The knowledge provided by documents written in foreign languages is valuable for driving experts' decisions in several domains, among which finance, medicine, transportation, and publishing industry (Wan et al., 2010). However, in practice, most researchers, practitioners, and entrepreneurs explore only small documents written in English or in their native language. Therefore, the information hidden in the documents written in foreign languages is either not considered at all or underused to a large extent.

Multi-lingual summarization entails creating summarization models that are portable to collections of documents written in different languages. Since many Information Retrieval and Data Mining techniques are independent of the language of the input documents (e.g., clustering, graph ranking, Latent Semantic Analysis), they can be directly applied to documents written in different languages (Mihalcea et al., 2004). Since the data distributions may change from one language to another, the summarization models are trained separately per language. Hence, the input of the summarizer is a collection of documents that are all written in the same language.

To overcome the limitation of multilingual summarizers, cross-lingual summarization is the task of extracting summaries of collections of textual documents written in different languages (Pontes et al., 2018). Due to its inherent complexity, the cross-lingual problem cannot be addressed by directly applying traditional summarization algorithms. In fact, most of the traditional models are unable to capture interesting correlations between portions of text written in different language. Therefore, coping with document collections written in a variety of different languages poses relevant research issues that need to be addressed by the research community.

Machine translation tools, such as Google Translate[1] and Microsoft Translator[2], provide efficient support to users who are interested in generating translated version of the original documents in their native language. However, the translation process is often time-consuming and prone to errors. Therefore, ad hoc cross-lingual summarization methods need to be designed and tested in order to overcome the limitation of traditional approaches.

This chapter overviews the most recent approaches to cross-lingual document summarization. Firstly, it introduces the traditional summarization problem and briefly describes the state-of-the-art approaches to language-specific and multi-lingual document summarization (see Sections "The text summarization problem" and "An overview of language-specific and multi-lingual summarization approaches", respectively). Then, it clarifies the key issues and prospects related to the extension of the state-of-the-art methods towards the cross-lingual domain. State-of-the-art approaches to extractive and abstractive cross-lingual summarization are thoroughly described (see Section "Cross-lingual summarization"). Finally, it draws conclusions and discusses the future perspectives of the current research (see Sections "Future research directions" and "Conclusion").

THE TEXT SUMMARIZATION PROBLEM

Text summarization aims at generating a concise summary of a collection of textual documents (Tan et al., 2006). According to the characteristics of the analyzed data, the output type, and the temporal constraints enforced during the summarization process, various formulations of the traditional text summarization problem have been proposed in literature. A thorough description of the main summarization tasks is given below.

Problem Statement

The input data of the summarization process usually consists of a collection of textual documents. The goal is to produce a summary of the input collection consisting of the most salient content. Various specializations of the original problem have been considered. Figure 1 graphically summarizes the main cases, which are thoroughly described below.

Figure 1. The text summarization problem

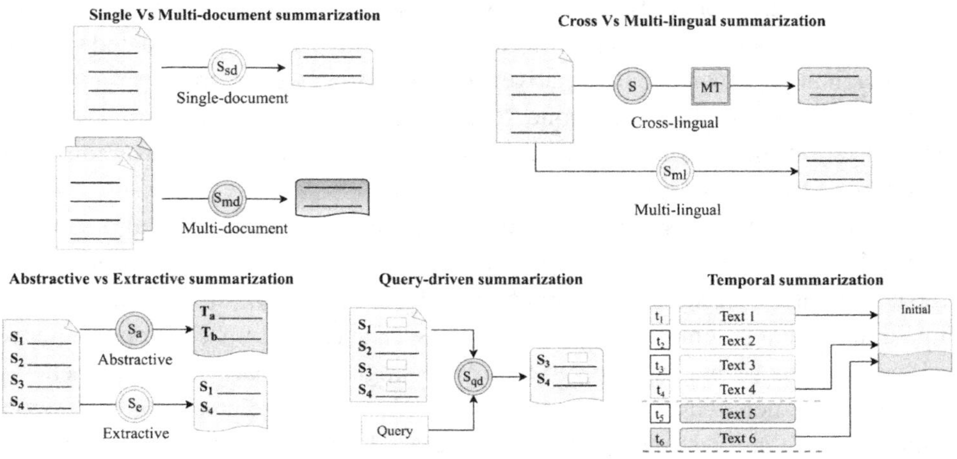

Document Cardinality

The number of documents in the analyzed collection has a relevant impact on the design of the summarization system. The summarization task is usually classified as

- *multi-document,* if the output summary is extracted from a set of input documents, or
- *single-document,* otherwise.

A popular multi-document summarization problem is the *news summarization task*, where the goal is to summarize a set of news articles published on various newspapers and ranging over the same topics. The summary should cover all the news facets with minimal redundancy (Giannakopoulos et al., 2011). An example of single-document summarization task is the automatic generation of an abstract of a scientific report. The abstract should include all the salient concepts mentioned in the report, independently of their relative position in the text.

Language

The language in which the input documents are written relevantly affects the characteristics and the usability of the summarization systems. To deeply exploit the characteristics of the natural language, several language-specific summarization systems have been proposed. In particular, due to its worldwide diffusion, the majority of the language-specific summarization systems have been designed for coping with English-written documents. However, many of the proposed approaches rely on language-independent techniques thus they can be applied to collections written in different languages.

The summarization algorithms can be classified as

- *language-specific,* if they are able to cope with input documents that are all written in the same language (typically, in English) and the output is produced in the same language as well, or
- *multi-lingual,* if they can be applied to collections written in different languages. All the documents in the collection and the output summary are assumed to be written in the same language, or
- *cross-lingual*, if the document collections are written in one language (or even in more than one), but the output summary is written in another language (different from those of the input documents).

In the cross-lingual summarization scenario, a machine translation step is commonly applied to the input documents in order to produce a set of homogeneous documents in terms of language. According to the used algorithm, the machine translation method can either tightly integrated into the summarization workflow or considered as an external module.

This chapter mainly overviews the summarization techniques proposed for tackling the multi-lingual and cross-lingual summarization tasks.

Purpose

The summarization process can be either general-purpose or driven by specific user requirements. The summarization task can be categorized as

- *query-driven,* if the output summary should reflect the content of a (user-specified) query, or
- *general-purpose,* otherwise.

Examples of query-driven summarization systems are the content curation platforms (Stanoevska-Slabeva et al., 2012), where users can visualize the summaries extracted from various news article collections. Each summary is tailored to a specific topic, whose description corresponds to the input query.

Output Type

The summary content can be either generated from scratch or extracted from the existing content. The approaches proposed to address the summarization task can be

- *abstractive*, if their aim is to generate *new* content by capturing the essence of the input text, or
- *extractive*, if their goal is to select part of the *existing* content of the input documents.

The former approaches combine words in order to reliably form grammatical sentences or key phrases, while the latter are inherently simpler because they just focus on extracting part of the original text.

Based on the type of selected content, extractive methods can be further classified as

- *Sentence-based*, if the goal is to extract a subset of document sentences, or
- *Keyword-* or *keyphrase-based*, if the goal is to extract a subset of keywords or keyphrases, respectively.

Temporal Changes in Data

Since the collections of documents may change over time, the traditional summarization problem can be extended in order to capture the updates of the content of the original documents (i.e., the *update summarization* task). Summarization models can be *incrementally* adapted in order to tailor their output summaries to the characteristics of the new data.

A related issue is the extraction of the most relevant information from a textual data stream as soon as it becomes available. More specifically, *temporal news summarization* is an extension of the original summarization task, where the aim is to select a subset of sentences from a news stream to issue as updates to the user, summarizing that event over time. Unlike the traditional summarization task, the time at which a relevant sentence is picked from the news stream matters.

Evaluation Methods

Evaluate the quality of the output summaries is crucial for assessing the effectiveness of automated summarization systems. Several methods to quantitatively and qualitatively evaluate the quality of the summarization system have been proposed. They can be classified as intrinsic or extrinsic evaluation metrics. Intrinsic evaluators assess the quality of a summary against a reference summary or based on the feedbacks provided by a domain expert who manually evaluates the output summaries. Conversely, extrinsic evaluation metrics measure the effectiveness of a summarization method in accomplishing a given task. This latter type of measures is commonly used in Information Retrieval (Blair, 1990). A description of the most popular intrinsic evaluation metrics is reported below.

Rouge

The Rouge score is among the most established intrinsic evaluation metrics (Lin, 2004). It measures the unit overlaps between the text of the reference (golden) summary, i.e., the ground truth, and text contained in the automatically generated summary. According to the unit type, the following Rouge scores have been defined:

- **Rouge-N**: it measures the overlap between the N-grams. Unigram and bigrams are mostly used (Rouge-1, Rouge-2, respectively).
- **Rouge-L**: it measures the overlap between the *longest common subsequence* of words.
- **Rouge-W**: it is a variation of the Rouge-L metric that gives higher importance to subsequent matching sequences. If there exist multiple long-sentence

matchings, it gives more importance to the summaries that tend to get them closer.

- **Rouge-S**: it considers skip-bigrams as units of text. Skip-grams are pairs of words in the sentence with arbitrary gaps. It measures the overlap between the skip-grams in the automatic and golden summaries.
- **Rouge-SU**: it is a variation of the Rouge-S metric which takes into account also the co-occurrence of unigrams in the summary text.

The performance of most of the summarization systems presented in this survey have been assessed according to the Rouge scores. Based on the selected metric, the preferred summaries have different characteristics. For example, using the Rouge-1/2 metrics the preferred summaries tend to include most of the significant words or pairs of words, while using ROUGE-L/W the preferred summaries tend to be most similar with the golden summary at the sentence level.

While the basic version of the Rouge toolkit was designed for coping with English-written text, the JRouge version of the evaluation tool[3] has been specifically designed for coping with Non-European languages.

Mean Reciprocal Rank

The Mean Reciprocal Rank (MRR) is an established quality measure used in Information Retrieval (Blair, 1990). Given the set of sentences included in the input documents, the summary consists of a subset of the top ranked ones. For each correctly identified sentence, the MRR is computed as the inverse of the rank of each of the selected sentences. In Figure 2 an example of MRR computation is given.

Specifically, in the MRR formula reported in Figure 2, N indicates the number of sentences included in the summary while $rank_i$ is the rank of the ith sentence. The final score is computed by averaging the inverse of the ranks of all the correctly identified sentences. Notice that for all the sentences that have not been included in the reference summary, the corresponding rank is set to 0 by construction.

Expert-Driven Validation

The aim of automatic text summarization is to produce informative and fluent summaries in order to support domain experts in gaining insights into the analyzed documents. Whenever available, humanly generated feedbacks are particularly useful for assessing the pertinence, conciseness, and readability of the produced summary. Usually, a double-blind assessment procedure is conducted with the help of a set of domain experts. In the cases of multi- or cross-lingual summarization, domain experts should be proficient in all the language considered in the input collection.

Figure 2. Example of evaluation of an extractive summarization algorithm using MRR metric

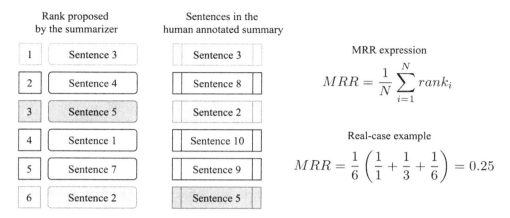

Each evaluator gives a score to each candidate summary. Then, the final score of a summarization algorithm is computed by averaging its corresponding evaluation scores. Although a manual exploration of the generated summaries provides more insights into the quality of the automated systems, it is commonly unfeasible in the research community due to the lack of domain experts.

Benchmark Data

To allow the reproducibility of the achieved results, summarization systems should be tested on benchmark data. For language-specific and multi-lingual summarization, most of the proposed benchmark datasets include both the input document collections and the golden summaries (i.e., the ground truth) written in a specific language. Conversely, for cross-lingual summarization the benchmark datasets include the output summaries for all the supported languages.

A non-exhaustive list of benchmark collection for document summarization is given below.

1. **Document Understanding Conference 2001**[4]: The benchmark collection was created for tackling both single- and multi-document summarization task. It consists of 60 collections of documents which have been partitioned into training and test sets. For each document set the reference summary of each document and those of the whole collection are given. Per-document summaries can be exploited to assess the performance of single-document summarizers,

9

while per-collections summaries are used to evaluate the effectiveness of multi-document approaches.

2. **Document Understanding Conference 2004**[5]: it is a variant of the DUC 2001 dataset. It contains an additional collection of news articles which have been automatically translated from English to Arabic. The data source can be used to explore the performance of multi-document summarization algorithms on noisy data.

3. **Document Understanding Conference 2007**[6]: it is another variant of the DUC dataset. It includes data needed for assessing the update summarization task.

4. **MultiLing Pilot 2011** (Giannakopoulos et al., 2011): this dataset was designed for testing multi-lingual summarization algorithms. It contains a set of WikiNews documents translated in Arabic, Czech, English, French, Greek, Hebrew and Hindi by native speakers. Each article belongs to one of the 10 topics under consideration and for each topic at least 3 reference summaries are provided.

5. **Text REtrieval Conference 2013** (Aslam et al., 2013): this dataset was designed to address the temporal summarization task. It consists of a collection of news articles, which have been chronologically ordered to simulate a stream of news articles ranging over a set of events. The tasks allowed for this dataset are (i) *filtering and summarization,* which entails, for a specific input topic, the retrieval of the related news articles and their summarization and (ii) *summarization only,* which entails considering a prefiltered subset of news and performing only the summarization task. More recent variants of the same dataset were proposed in years 2014 and 2015. The structure of the datasets remained unchanged.

Despite not intended for cross-lingual tasks, the DUC benchmark collections (released from 2001 to 2007) have also been adapted for this purpose by manually translating the reference summaries.

AN OVERVIEW OF LANGUAGE-SPECIFIC AND MULTI-LINGUAL SUMMARIZATION APPROACHES

A large body of work has been devoted to extracting summaries from documents written in the same language. Language-specific approaches to text summarization deeply exploit the properties of the language in order to understand the semantics behind the text. They commonly make use of dictionaries, controlled vocabulary, and ontologies to filter the content of the documents and extract significant concepts. For example, ontologies are widely used semantic models that formally represent the characteristics of the entities within a specific domain and the relationships between them. Ontologies have found application in document summarization to (i) identify the most salient concepts in the source documents and to measure their coherence with a user-provided query (Kogilavani & Balasubramanie, 2009; Ping et al., 2006), (ii) contextualize the content of a query used to drive the summarization process (Nastase, 2008), or (iii) adapt the content of the output summary to a specific context of use (Li et al., 2010, Wu & Liu, 2003). Lexical chains are a notable example of textual structure representing key information hidden in the text. They can be trained from a collection of annotated sentences. Several summarization algorithms have applied lexical chains to improve the quality of the generated summary, e.g., Pourvali & Abadeh (2012), Atkinson and Munoz (2013). However, similar to ontology-based approaches, these summarization models are tailored to a specific language and they are not easily portable to documents written in other languages.

Multi-lingual summarization approaches apply general-purpose machine learning or information retrieval techniques. Unlike language-specific methods, these algorithms do not rely on language-dependent knowledge bases (e.g., dictionaries, ontologies, controlled vocabularies). Hence, they can be directly applied to collections written in different languages. For example, *clustering techniques* (e.g., Wang & Li, 2010; Wang et al., 2011) have already been applied to group similar sentences together. The output summary consists of a selection of the best representatives per group.

Graph-based approaches to document summarization aim at modelling the textual information at different granularity levels in a graph structure. For example, in TextRank (Mihalcea et al., 2004) the authors proposed a generalization of the popular PageRank algorithm (Page et al., 1999) to measure sentence importance within the document collection. Specifically, a graph G (V, E) is created, where each vertex $v \in V$ is a sentence, while an edge $e \in E$ links two sentences and is weighted by score indicating the content overlap between two sentences. The PageRank algorithm is run on the created graph in order to measure sentence relevance. The top ranked sentences are included in the output summary. Erkan et al. (2004) proposed a similar approach, where pairwise sentence similarity is computed using the cosine similarity between the corresponding Bag-Of-Words.

More recently, Fang et al. (2017) proposed an alternative method to combine graph-based models with word-sentence relationships. The word-sentence score is computed starting from the assumption that (i) a sentence containing keywords should be ranked first, (ii) the number of sentences containing a word determine its importance.

Latent Semantic Analysis is an established text mining technique aimed at transforming textual data in a new space where document terms that are most likely to represent the same concept are grouped together. It relies on the Singular

Value Decomposition. Several attempts to apply LSA in order to drive document summarization have been made, e.g., Steinberger et al. (2011), Gong & Liu (2001), Steinberger & Jezek (2009), Patil & Bhole (2015). They combine sentences and terms using a matricial representation in order to apply the SVD decomposition. Then, the sentences including the most relevant terms are selected. In parallel, similar decomposition (e.g., the QR decomposition) have also been considered (Conroy et al. 2006).

Itemset mining techniques (Agrawal et al., 1993) has been profitably applied to data from various domains with the aim at automatically extracting co-occurrences of items or events. In the last years, frequent itemsets have also been used also for supporting the multilingual and multi-document summarization task (Baralis et al., 2012, Baralis et al., 2015 and Cagliero et al., 2019). They represent recurrent word co-occurrences in the document collection, showing a significant correlation in specific documents. In the proposed approaches, the mined itemsets are exploited to drive the process of sentence selection. Specifically, Baralis et al. (2012) applied an entropy-based approach (Mampaey et al., 2011) in order to select a non-redundant yet informative subset of itemsets. Then, the sentences covering the itemset selection are considered. Baralis et al. (2015) proposed a multilingual summarization algorithm, namely MWI-Sum. It discovers weighted itemsets, which represent word combinations with significantly high frequency of occurrence and relevance. Since each itemset potentially represents a relevant "concept" within the news collection, itemsets are used to drive the sentence selection procedure. A sentence is selected if it covers frequent itemsets that are not already covered by previously selected sentences. A generic sentence covers a frequent itemset if it contains all the words occurring in the itemset. Hence, the proposed selection procedure picks the document sentences covering significant "concepts" yet not covered by any other sentence. A limited use of basic NLP operations (i.e., stemming, stop word removal) makes the proposed approach portable to languages other than English. Notice that stemming and stop word removal are available for almost all languages. More recently, in Cagliero et al. (2019) the authors proposed a more accurate frequent itemset-based algorithm, namely ELSA, which combines frequent itemsets and latent semantic analysis (LSA). Specifically, frequent itemsets are used as input features, instead of single words, to obtain a more semantically expressive representation of the input data, while the LSA approach is used to filter out data redundancy. The joint use of frequent itemsets and LSA has significantly improved the quality of both state-of-the-art itemset- and LSA-based approaches.

Optimization-based methods have already been used to select the sentences in the document collection that maximize a given objective function (Lin & Bilmes, 2011, Gillick et al., 2008, Litvak et al., 2010). For example, Litvak et al. (2010) proposed a multi-lingual summarizer that selects, from a set of 31 features, the most relevant ones to rank sentences from a source text. Given the complexity of the exploration of all the possible combination of features, after an initialization step, genetic algorithms proceed with the selection and reproduction stage. The *selection* step filters out bad-performing solutions while during *reproduction* new combinations are proposed adding or removing specific features. The feature-set is composed of a mix of graph, word, sentence and structure-based metrics.

More recently, the same authors proposed MUSE, a supervised genetic approach to multilingual single-document summarization (Litvak & Last, 2013a). A genetic supervised model is trained on an annotated set of documents (i.e., for each document in the training set the corresponding summary is known in advance). The summary of a new document, which is assumed to be pertinent to training set, is generated by applying a weighted function based on a set of decision variables. The weight assigned to each variable is derived from the training set. The main limitations of MUSE are (i) the need for an ad-hoc training set, which often unavailable in most real contexts, and (ii) the inability to filter out redundant content (several sentences may cover the same "concept").

CROSS-LINGUAL SUMMARIZATION

The digitalization of most of the countries worldwide has bring to the explosion of text produced in different languages. Combining data from different countries and cultures allows practitioners, researchers, and entrepreneurs to get access to new domain-specific data thus extending the potential of Big Data analytics and Machine Learning techniques.

The cross-lingual summarization task entails analyzing collections of documents written in any language to produce a summary written in a different language. For example, given a collection of documents in Chinese, the goal is to generate an English-written summary. The main challenge in cross-lingual summarization is that general-purpose, multi-lingual extractive approaches cannot be applied directly, because the models are unable to extract existing content written in a different language. Coping with documents written in different languages entails analyzing textual data with different distributions. The frequency of occurrence of the analyzed words strongly depends on the underlying language. Furthermore, the same word in different language could have radically different meanings. In summary, the main challenges while coping with cross-lingual document collections are enumerated below.

- Frequency-based text analyses cannot be applied to the whole document collections, because the frequencies of occurrence of the same word in different languages are not comparable with each other.
- Semantics-based models are intrinsically language-dependent. Combining multi-lingual semantics models is potentially challenging.
- The distances between words in a document/term space are meaningful only under the assumption that all the documents/terms in the space are written in the same language.
- The structure of the text radically changes based upon the language in which the document is written.
- Translating text from one language to another entails abstracting both semantics and context of use. Depending on the target language, the complexity of the translation process significantly changes.

Addressing the cross-lingual problem entails creating a framework that combine the summarization approach with a machine translation method. While the older approaches rely on simple translation of the sentences in the summary, the most recent ones embed translation-quality metrics to produce fluent output in the target language. According to those frameworks, the translation phase, previously seen as possible source of mistakes, could be employed as a tool that contributes to the refinement of the summary's fluency. In summary,

- Machine translation allows filling the gap between the documents written in different languages. However, the quality of the summarization process is subject to an effective machine translation from the source to the target language.
- Word embedding are vector-based text representations that allow mapping words in a vector space where semantically related words are relatively close with each other. Notice that since the vector spaces are trained from language-specific training sets, an alignment phase is needed in order to map words in the source and the target languages. Alignment can be performed using bilingual lexicons.

It is possible to define a list of steps that should be undertaken to produce the final summary in the target language. Hereafter, a description of the process of cross-lingual document summarization and an overview of the recently proposed strategies are given.

The Summarization Workflow

The main steps of the cross-lingual summarization process can be summarized as follows:

- **Traditional document summarization**: The input documents are summarized using traditional language-specific or multi-lingual approaches. The intermediate summary generated at this stage is written in the language of the input documents.
- **Machine translation**: The intermediate summaries are translated in the target language using automated tools.
- **Sentence compression**: The content of the translated summary is compressed to convey as much information as possible in a restricted space.

The most straightforward approach to cross-lingual summarization is to combine multi-lingual approaches with an automated machine translator, e.g., translate the intermediate version of the summary from Chinese to English. This approach is called *late translation*. However, many variants of the original problem have been proposed as well. For example, instead of performing late translation (after the summarization process), the summarization algorithm may perform *early translation* (i.e., translate first and then summarize).

The number of languages considered in the input document collection can be variable (single language, bilingual, etc.). In case the input collection contains documents written in more than one language, multiple intermediate summaries (one per language) are first generated and then translated.

Moreover, the sentences included in the output summary can be either the raw translation of the sentences in the intermediate summary or a compressed version (leaving room for extra content under the same space limit). Sentence compression can be enabled or disabled according to the users' needs.

Notice that in the abstractive summarization context the information retrieved from the input text is further reformulated in order to create fluent and grammatically-correct sentences in the target language (see Section "Abstractive cross-lingual summarization").

Recently Proposed Approaches to Cross-Lingual Summarization

An early example of real-world cross-lingual summarizer was provided by *Columbia Newsblaster*[7]. Evans et al., 2004 presented a system based on 34 language-independent textual features, among which the position of each sentence, the sentence length, and the presence of special characters. The summarization method is integrated with a machine translation system in order to make the provided information accessible by users from all over the world.

Wan et al. (2010) proposed the integration of a translation quality score and the informativeness score to enhance the quality of the generated summaries. For each sentence, the informativeness score is computed using the sentence position in the document, its first-sentence similarity and a centroid-based weight. The translation quality instead, is predicted using ε-support vector regressors trained on a set of features (supervised learning). Only the selected sentences are translated using translation services. Hence, the proposed approach relies on supervised learning and can be classified as a *late translation* method.

More recently, the work by Wan et al. (2018) addressed the problem of optimizing the quality of the result of the cross-lingual summarization process. It ranks candidate summaries extracted using various techniques, configuration settings, and translation methods. A Ranking SVM model is trained and applied to assign a score to each candidate summary in terms of content readability and relevance. The per-summary quality metrics were computed by using different features extracted at different granularity levels (single word, sentence or entire summary).

In (Wan, 2011) the authors considered the case in which a bilingual corpus, including English- and Chinese-written documents, need to be summarized. The goal is to combine information provided by the documents written in both languages. Two complementary graph-based methodologies have been proposed. The former method, namely SimFusion, combines the pairwise sentence scores (local to each language) to get a unified sentence rank. The latter approach, namely CoRank, creates a unified graph containing also bilingual links. Specifically, nodes represent sentence while edges link sentences and are weighted by ad hoc similarity scores. The main advantage of CoRank is the use of bilingual connections to compute the final sentence score.

Boudin et al. (2011) proposed another graph-based approach to cross-language multi-document summarization. It relies on early translation. Sentences are initially translated from the source language (i.e., the language of the input multi-document collection) to the target language (i.e., the language of the generated summary) and a quality score for each translation is predicted by using an SVR regression model trained on a subset of annotated sentences (i.e. sentences for which the quality of the translation is known). Then, sentence similarities are represented using a graph-based model. The weights of the graph edges indicate pairwise sentence similarity. They are computed by combining a similarity measure between sentences and the quality of the translations. Since low quality translations are characterized by lowly weighted-connections with the other sentences they are less likely to be selected. Sentences are finally ranked by the PageRank score to select the best representatives.

As a drawback, significant sentences in the original collection could be discarded in case of low-quality translation. Similarly, Wan et al. (2010) proposed a cross-lingual document summarization algorithm that takes the quality of the translation into account to select the output sentences. Unlike (Boudin et al., 2011), it applies a late translation approach. Specifically, it selects the most relevant sentences from the source documents and generates a summary written in the source language. Then, it generates the output summary by translating the sentences of the summary in the source language. The summarization algorithm assigns a relevance score to each of the sentences in the input document collection by combining various relevance scores as well as by considering the quality of its translation in the target language. This overcomes the limitations of the approach presented by Boudin et al. (2011) due to the accident elimination of relevant sentences with low-quality translation.

Litvak et al. (2013) proposed a cross-lingual version of their multi-lingual MUSE algorithm for single-document summarization based on early translation. It first translates all the sentences from the input annotated source to the target language and then uses the standard version of MUSE to generate the summary in the target language. Since the proposed approach does not consider the quality of the translation it could potentially select sentences relevant for the original collection, but associated with an incorrect translation.

Sentence compression has been considered as additional step of the cross-lingual process. For example, Yao et al. (2015) proposed a sentence scoring method combined with a compression approach to maximize a gain-cost function. The aim is to maximize the information provided by the summary while minimizing its length. The sentence compression method iteratively expands a given text until the sentence with the maximum density compression is found. Compressive algorithms for multi-document summarization have also been proposed by Pontes et al. (2019). The authors extended their previous analysis on bilingual corpus (Pontes et al., 2018). During the preprocessing step they automatically translate sentences in the target language and performed a syntactical analysis to detect relevant sentence patterns. In the compression phase, they (i) create clusters of sentences using both source and target language similarity and then for each cluster, (ii) create a graph using keyword as nodes and word-cohesion metric to weight edges. Finally, they define a target function to be minimized in order to extract the best compressed sentence. Furthermore, the authors extended the approach (Pontes et al., 2019) applying the compressive cross-lingual algorithm to the output of a speech-to-text system. They demonstrate how their compression method is able to robustly address different transcription errors and produce fluent summaries.

Abstractive Cross-Lingual Summarization

Unlike extractive summarization approaches, abstractive algorithms aim at miming the human behavior generating new text that provides both the coverage of relevant information and grammatical correctness. Hence, an additional sentence generation step needs to be introduced. This add new complexity to the system, which not only has to select the most relevant content but also to rephrase it as best as it can. In recent years, thanks to the great advancement both in the field of *neural networks* and in *NLP*, an increasing body of work has focused on training neural networks architectures to address the abstractive summarization task. A selection of the most relevant abstractive approaches to cross-lingual summarization is given below.

Zhang et al. (2016) proposed a cross-lingual abstractive summarization technique consisting of three main steps. Firstly, the source text is automatically translated in the target language (I.e., early translation); next, the key concepts are extracted in both languages using bilingual information. Finally, an Integer Linear Programming optimization approach is used to fuse together the concept by maximizing salience and translation quality measures. Ouyang et al. (2019) proposed an alternative abstractive method able to efficiently remove the badly translated sentences, as they could degrade the quality of the overall summary. New sentences are recommended to replace the incorrect ones.

Abstractive summarization methods can be focused on generating headlines of news article rather than producing content summaries. The approach proposed by Shen et al. (2018) aims at producing the headlines in a cross-lingual context in order to maximize the accessibility of the related content. The proposed approach is based on Neural Machine Translation (NMT) and Neural Headline Generation (NHG) models, which are jointly used to translate the news article content and generate the output headline in the target language.

FRAMEWORKS FOR MULTI- AND CROSS-LINGUAL SUMMARIZATION

To disseminate the knowledge on multi- and cross-lingual summarization algorithms, various repositories of summarization algorithms, datasets, and evaluation tools have been presented in literature.

- **MUSEEC**[8] (Litvak et al., 2016): it is a Web-based application including several summarization algorithms, among which

○ *MUSE* (Litvak et al., 2013): it is a supervised learning algorithm based on genetic models. By optimizing a specific cost function, it proposes a rank for the sentences in the source text. The top ranked sentences are then included into the output summary.

○ *WECOM* (Litvak et al., 2016): it is an unsupervised learning algorithm that performs sentence compression on the source text in order to produce the output summary. By optimizing the weighting function that retain content relevance, the proposed heuristics iterates on the sentence content by removing the least ranked elementary discourse units.

○ *POLY* (Litvak et al., 2013): it is an unsupervised linear programming-based algorithm. According to the maximum coverage principle, it selects the best subset of sentences complying with the maximum length constraint. Each sentence is modelled as a hyperplane whose intersections can be used to identify the subset of most representative sentences.

All the approaches implemented for MUSEEC can be easily adapted to cope with cross-lingual documents.

- **Cross-Lingual Summarization ToolKit (CLSTK)**[9] *(Jhaveri et al., 2019)*: it is a collection of summarization algorithms implemented in the Python language and specifically designed for coping with cross-lingual data. The framework includes also the implementation of the Rouge evaluation tooltik (Lin, 2004). The algorithms that are currently provided in the framework are briefly described below.

○ *linBilmes* (Lin et al., 2011): multi-lingual summarization method based on set of submodular functions, which incorporate the requirement of representativeness and diversity of the output summary. A unique cost function is used to reward the sentences with maximal coverage of the input document, while penalizing those including redundant content.

○ *SimFusion* (Wan, 2011): cross-lingual summarization method based on a bilingual corpus. It combines the information extracted in both languages in order to improve the quality of the output summary. For both languages a similarity graph is computed, where nodes represent sentences while edges are weighted by pairwise similarity scores. An established graph ranking strategy, i.e., PageRank (Brin et al., 1998), is applied to evaluate sentence relevance.

○ *CoRank* (Wan, 2011): Similar to SimFusion, the proposed approach merges bilingual information in order to produce high-quality summaries.

Unlike SimFusion, the bilingual information is directly integrated into a unique graph including sentences written in both languages.

The CLSTK library integrates also a late-translation method relying on an established machine translation service.

- **SUMY**[10]: it is a general-purpose summarization library implemented in Python. It integrates different methods to extract summaries both from plain-text or directly from HTML pages. Despite this library is not specialized on cross- or multi-lingual data, the language independence of most of the implemented methods makes it usable for multi- and cross-lingual summarization purposes. The supported methods are enumerated below.

  - *Luhn, 1958*: it is a classic summarization algorithm that makes use of different word frequency and distribution heuristics to produce a summary for a given source of text. Those data are combined to obtain sentence-level score and thus to select the most relevant for the automatic synopsis. This algorithm is language independent, thus it can be used to test multi-lingual summarization approaches.
  - *Edmundson, 1969*: it is another classic approach that extends the one proposed by Luhn, 1958 by considering additional features (e.g., position of the sentence in the document, cue words, title and headings) to compute sentence relevance,
  - *LSA-based summarizer (Steinberger et al., 2004)*: it is a generic text summarization algorithm based on Latent Semantic Analysis in order to measure the importance of the sentences in the source text.
  - *SumBasic (Nenkova et al., 2005)*: it is a classical summarization algorithm, which is based on the idea that words that appear frequently in source text are likely to appear in the summary. It proceeds iteratively assigning to each sentence a score that depends to the probability that it contains a given word. This process is repeated for each word in the sentence. At the end of each cycle the top scored sentence is selected until a maximum summary length is reached
  - *KL-Sum (Haghighi et al., 2009)*: it is a summarization system that applies a greedy algorithm to search for sentences that decrease the KL-divergence score (Kullback et al., 1951) between the current summary and the source text. This stopping condition is integrated with the constraint on the length of the summary to produce desired-size output.
  - *Reduction:* it is a simple graph-based summarization method. The graph and the similarity between sentences are computed following the same

method proposed by TextRank (Mihalcea et al., 2004). The sentence importance is computed, for each node, as the sum of the weight of the connected edges.

- ○ *TextRank (Mihalcea et al., 2004) and LexRank (Erkan et al., 2004):* graph-based summarization algorithms.

FUTURE RESEARCH DIRECTIONS

Over the last years, the research interest in the domain of cross- and multi-lingual summarization has grown as result of the popularity of the Internet. Web-based applications have eased the accessibility of textual data sources in various domains ranging from journalism, economy, education, and medicine. For example, online newspapers are nowadays a huge yet invaluable source of information, which is hard to manage due to the heterogeneity of the generated data. Getting rid of redundant or misleading news data is so hard that automated summarization systems are playing an increasingly important role. Despite the great advances in the study and development of document summarization, there is still room for further improvements, especially in multi- and cross-lingual contexts where data is quite heterogeneous and hard to explore without the help of domain experts.

Graph-based algorithms have become one of the most established multi-lingual summarization techniques. The key component of these methods is the construction of similarity graphs represents the key associations among different textual units. The latest ground-breaking results obtained by Neural Networks in different NLP tasks (e.g., analogy detection, translation) can inspire researchers in finding new metrics representing not only syntactical and word-based similarity but also hidden features that cannot be trivially inferred from text. In the near future, this class of summarization algorithms will combine Natural Language Understanding approaches with deep graph analysis in order to support more advanced knowledge extraction processes.

The use of multi-lingual summarization algorithms prevents from using language-specific semantic information. However, the dissemination of knowledge over the Web has enabled the creation of ontologies written in multiple languages. Some efforts have already been devoted to combining ontologies in different languages into a unified knowledge base (Fu et al., 2010; Dragoni, 2015; McCrae et al., 2017). Integrating multi-lingual ontologies into the multi- and cross-lingual summarization systems is an appealing future research direction.

Due to the intrinsic complexity of the abstractive summarization problem, few attempts to extend existing approaches towards the cross-lingual domain have been made. Since extractive summarization techniques are more flexible, a stronger effort has already been devoted to cross-lingual summarization while assuming that the content of the input documents remains unchanged. However, a tight integration between abstractive techniques and machine translation approach can be performed. Specifically, the machine translation algorithms could exploit abstraction methods to combine sequences of concepts into a single sentence written in the target language.

The increasing amount of textual data opens interesting scenarios of application of cross-lingual summarization tools in new application domains. e.g., the summarization of social data, books, financial reports, and legal documents.

Finally, most of the sub-task of general summarization problem can be addressed in the cross-lingual context as well. On the one hand, this significantly increases the complexity to the summarization task, but, on the other hand, it leverages the interest of the research community towards these very relevant problem, which are still far from being completely solved.

CONCLUSION

This chapter gives a wide-ranging overview of the existing approaches to tackle the document summarization problem. More specifically, it pays a particular attention to the applicability of the presented techniques to the multi- and cross-lingual domains. This survey of summarization techniques could be helpful for researchers and practitioners who are approaching the issue of coping large collections of documents written in a variety of different language. The key issue that is tackled by cross-lingual summarizer is to combine textual information written in different language into a unified model able to capture the most significant concepts.

The first part of the chapter is mainly intended to support readers who are approaching the document summarization problem for the first time, while the core of the chapter is focused on a detailed analysis of the portability of different techniques towards the cross-lingual domain.

The takeaways of this work can be summarized as follows:

- Pushing the semantics into the summarization process entails limiting the portability of the proposed approaches toward multi- and cross-lingual domains,
- Machine learning and Natural Language Processing techniques are particularly effective in modelling the textual correlations hidden in large collections of documents written in the same language,
- Combining models generated from collections written in different languages is feasible under the following conditions: (i) an accurate supervised learning model can be trained on annotated data, (ii) an effective machine translation

system can be integrated, (iii) the models can be mapped to a common knowledge base.

REFERENCES

Agrawal, R., Imieliński, T., & Swami, A. (1993). Mining association rules between sets of items in large databases. *SIGMOD Record*, *22*(2), 207–216. doi:10.1145/170036.170072

Aslam, J. A., Ekstrand-Abueg, M., Pavlu, V., Diaz, F., & Sakai, T. (2013, November). TREC 2013 Temporal Summarization. TREC.

Baralis, E., & Cagliero, L. (2018). Highlighter: Automatic Highlighting of Electronic Learning Documents. *IEEE Transactions on Emerging Topics in Computing*, *6*(1), 7–19. doi:10.1109/TETC.2017.2681655

Baralis, E., Cagliero, L., Fiori, A., & Garza, P. (2015). Mwi-sum: A multilingual summarizer based on frequent weighted itemsets. *ACM Transactions on Information Systems*, *34*(1), 5. doi:10.1145/2809786

Baralis, E., Cagliero, L., Jabeen, S., & Fiori, A. (2012). *Multi-document summarization exploiting frequent itemsets*. SAC. doi:10.1145/2245276.2245427

Baralis, E., Cagliero, L., Jabeen, S., Fiori, A., & Shah, S. (2013). Multi-document summarization based on the Yago ontology. *Expert Systems with Applications*, *40*(17), 6976–6984. doi:10.1016/j.eswa.2013.06.047

Blair, D. C. (1990). *Language and Representation in Information Retrieval*. New York: Elsevier North-Holland, Inc.

Boudin, F., Huet, S., & Torres-Moreno, J. M. (2011). A graph-based approach to cross-language multi-document summarization. *Polibits*, *43*, 113–118. doi:10.17562/PB-43-16

Brin, S., & Page, L. (1998) The Anatomy of a Large-Scale Hypertextual Web Search Engine. In *Seventh International World-Wide Web Conference (WWW 1998)*, Brisbane, Australia. 10.1016/S0169-7552(98)00110-X

Cagliero, L., Farinetti, L., & Baralis, E. (2019). Recommending Personalized Summaries of Teaching Materials. *IEEE Access: Practical Innovations, Open Solutions*, *7*, 22729–22739. doi:10.1109/ACCESS.2019.2899655

Cagliero, L., Garza, P., & Baralis, E. (2019). ELSA: A Multilingual Document Summarization Algorithm Based on Frequent Itemsets and Latent Semantic Analysis. *ACM Transactions on Information Systems*, *37*(2), 21. doi:10.1145/3298987

Conroy, J. M., Schlesinger, J. D., Goldstein, J., & O'leary, D. P. (2004). Left-brain/right-brain multi-document summarization. *Proceedings of the Document Understanding Conference*.

Conroy, J. M., Schlesinger, J. D., & O'Leary, D. P. (2006). *Topic-Focused Multi-Document Summarization Using an Approximate Oracle Score*. ACL. doi:10.3115/1273073.1273093

Dang, H. T. (2005, October). Overview of DUC 2005. In *Proceedings of the document understanding conference* (*Vol. 2005*, pp. 1-12). Academic Press.

Dragoni, M. (2015, April). Exploiting multilinguality for creating mappings between thesauri. In *Proceedings of the 30th Annual ACM Symposium on Applied Computing* (pp. 382-387). ACM. 10.1145/2695664.2695768

Edmundson, H. P. (1969). New methods in automatic extracting. *Journal of the Association for Computing Machinery*, *16*(2), 264–285. doi:10.1145/321510.321519

Elhadad, M., Miranda-Jiménez, S., Steinberger, J., & Giannakopoulos, G. (2013). Multi-document multilingual summarization corpus preparation, part 2: Czech, hebrew and spanish. In *Proceedings of the MultiLing 2013 Workshop on Multilingual Multi-document Summarization* (pp. 13-19). Academic Press.

Erkan, G., & Radev, D. R. (2004). Lexrank: Graph-based lexical centrality as salience in text summarization. *Journal of Artificial Intelligence Research*, *22*, 457–479. doi:10.1613/jair.1523

Evans, D. K., Klavans, J. L., & McKeown, K. (2004). *Columbia Newsblaster: Multilingual News Summarization on the Web*. HLT-NAACL. doi:10.3115/1614025.1614026

Fang, C., Mu, D., Deng, Z., & Wu, Z. (2017). Word-sentence co-ranking for automatic extractive text summarization. *Expert Systems with Applications*, *72*, 189–195. doi:10.1016/j.eswa.2016.12.021

Filatova, E., & Hatzivassiloglou, V. (2004). A formal model for information selection in multi-sentence text extraction. *Proceedings of the 20th international conference on Computational Linguistics*, 397. 10.3115/1220355.1220412

Fu, B., Brennan, R., & O'sullivan, D. (2010). Cross-Lingual Ontology Mapping and Its Use on the Multilingual Semantic Web. *MSW*, *571*, 13–20.

Giannakopoulos, G., El-Haj, M., Favre, B., Litvak, M., Steinberger, J., & Varma, V. (2011). *TAC 2011 MultiLing pilot overview*. Academic Press.

Gillick, D., Favre, B., & Hakkani-Tür, D. Z. (2008). *The ICSI Summarization System at TAC 2008*. TAC.

Goldstein, J., Mittal, V., Carbonell, J., & Kantrowitz, M. (2000). Multi-Document Summarization By Sentence Extraction. *Proceedings of the ANLP/NAACL Workshop on Automatic Summarization*, 40-48.

Gong, Y., & Liu, X. (2001). *Generic Text Summarization Using Relevance Measure and Latent Semantic Analysis*. SIGIR. doi:10.1145/383952.383955

Haghighi, A., & Vanderwende, L. (2009, May). Exploring content models for multi-document summarization. In *Proceedings of Human Language Technologies: The 2009 Annual Conference of the North American Chapter of the Association for Computational Linguistics* (pp. 362-370). Association for Computational Linguistics. 10.3115/1620754.1620807

Jhaveri, N., Gupta, M., & Varma, V. (2018). A Workbench for Rapid Generation of Cross-Lingual Summaries. *Proceedings of the Eleventh International Conference on Language Resources and Evaluation (LREC-2018)*.

Jhaveri, N., Gupta, M., & Varma, V. (2019, January). clstk: The Cross-Lingual Summarization Tool-Kit. In *Proceedings of the Twelfth ACM International Conference on Web Search and Data Mining* (pp. 766-769). ACM. 10.1145/3289600.3290614

Kullback, S., & Leibler, R. A. (1951). On information and sufficiency. *Annals of Mathematical Statistics*, *22*(1), 79–86. doi:10.1214/aoms/1177729694

Li, L., Forascu, C., El-Haj, M., & Giannakopoulos, G. (2013). *Multi-document multilingual summarization corpus preparation, part 1: Arabic, english, greek, chinese, romanian*. Association for Computational Linguistics.

Li, L., Wang, D., Shen, C., & Li, T. (2010). Ontology-enriched multi-document summarization in disaster management. *Proceeding of the 33rd international ACM SIGIR conference on Research and development in information retrieval*, 819-820.

Lin, C., & Hovy, E. (2003). Automatic evaluation of summaries using N-gram co-occurrence statistics. *Proceedings of the Conference of the North American Chapter of the Association for Computational Linguistics on Human Language Technology*, *1*, 71-78. 10.3115/1073445.1073465

Lin, C. Y. (2004). *Rouge: A package for automatic evaluation of summaries*. Text Summarization Branches Out.

Lin, H., & Bilmes, J. (2011, June). A class of submodular functions for document summarization. In *Proceedings of the 49th Annual Meeting of the Association for Computational Linguistics: Human Language Technologies-Volume 1* (pp. 510-520). Association for Computational Linguistics.

Linhares Pontes, E., González-Gallardo, C., Torres-Moreno, J., & Huet, S. (2019). *Cross-lingual speech-to-text summarization.* doi:10.1007/978-3-319-98678-4_39

Litvak, M., & Last, M. (2013a). Multilingual single-document summarization with muse. In *Proceedings of the MultiLing 2013 Workshop on Multilingual Multi-document Summarization* (pp. 77-81). Academic Press.

Litvak, M., & Last, M. (2013b). Cross-lingual training of summarization systems using annotated corpora in a foreign language. *Information Retrieval, 16*(5), 629–656. doi:10.100710791-012-9210-3

Litvak, M., Last, M., & Friedman, M. (2010). A new approach to improving multilingual summarization using a genetic algorithm. In *Proceedings of the 48th annual meeting of the association for computational linguistics* (pp. 927-936). Association for Computational Linguistics.

Litvak, M., & Vanetik, N. (2013). Mining the gaps: Towards polynomial summarization. In *Proceedings of the Sixth International Joint Conference on Natural Language Processing* (pp. 655-660). Academic Press.

Litvak, M., Vanetik, N., Last, M., & Churkin, E. (2016). Museec: A multilingual text summarization tool. *Proceedings of ACL-2016 System Demonstrations*, 73-78. 10.18653/v1/P16-4013

Luhn, H. P. (1958). The automatic creation of literature abstracts. *IBM Journal of Research and Development, 2*(2), 159–165. doi:10.1147/rd.22.0159

Mampaey, M., Tatti, N., & Vreeken, J. (2011). Tell me what I need to know: succinctly summarizing data with itemsets. *Proceedings of the 17th ACM SIGKDD Conference on Knowledge Discovery and Data Mining.*

McCrae, J. P., Arcan, M., & Buitelaar, P. (2017). *Linking knowledge graphs across languages with semantic.* Academic Press.

Mihalcea, R., & Tarau, P. (2004). Textrank: Bringing order into text. *Proceedings of the 2004 conference on empirical methods in natural language processing.*

Nazari, N., & Mahdavi, M. (2019). A survey on Automatic Text Summarization. *Journal of Artificial Intelligence and Data Mining, 7*(1), 121–135. doi:10.22044/jadm.2018.6139.1726

Nenkova, A., & Vanderwende, L. (2005). *The impact of frequency on summarization*. Microsoft Research. Tech. Rep. MSR-TR-2005, 101.

Ouyang, J., Song, B., & McKeown, K. (2019, June). A Robust Abstractive System for Cross-Lingual Summarization. *Proceedings of the 2019 Conference of the North American Chapter of the Association for Computational Linguistics: Human Language Technologies*, 1, 2025-2031.

Page, L., Brin, S., Motwani, R., & Winograd, T. (1999). *The PageRank citation ranking: Bringing order to the web*. Stanford InfoLab.

Patel, A., Siddiqui, T.J., & Tiwary, U.S. (2007). *A language independent approach to multilingual text summarization*. Academic Press.

Patil, S.B., & Bhole, A.T. (2015). *Multi-document English Text Summarization using Latent Semantic Analysis*. Academic Press.

Pontes, E. L., Huet, S., & Torres-Moreno, J. M. (2018, October). A Multilingual Study of Compressive Cross-Language Text Summarization. In *Mexican International Conference on Artificial Intelligence* (pp. 109-118). Springer. 10.1007/978-3-030-04497-8_9

Pontes, E. L., Huet, S., Torres-Moreno, J. M., & Linhares, A. C. (2018, June). Cross-language text summarization using sentence and multi-sentence compression. In *International Conference on Applications of Natural Language to Information Systems* (pp. 467-479). Springer.

Radev, D., Teufel, S., Saggion, H., Lam, W., Blitzer, J., Celebi, A., & Liu, D. (2002). *Evaluation of text summarization in a cross-lingual information retrieval framework. Center for Language and Speech Processing, Johns Hopkins University*. Baltimore, MD: Tech. Rep.

Saggion, H., Torres-Moreno, J. M., Cunha, I. D., & SanJuan, E. (2010, August). Multilingual summarization evaluation without human models. In *Proceedings of the 23rd International Conference on Computational Linguistics: Posters* (pp. 1059-1067). Association for Computational Linguistics.

Shen, S. Q., Chen, Y., Yang, C., Liu, Z. Y., & Sun, M. S. (2018). Zero-Shot Cross-Lingual Neural Headline Generation. IEEE/ACM Transactions on Audio. *Speech and Language Processing*, *26*(12), 2319–2327.

Stanoevska-Slabeva, K., Sacco, V., & Giardina, M. (2012). *Content Curation: a new form of gatewatching for social media?* Retrieved from https://pdfs.semanticscholar.org/89e2/06cdb4f36ff9b0b69b3244b3be4c883d1f4e.pdf

Steinberger, J., & Jezek, K. (2004). Using latent semantic analysis in text summarization and summary evaluation. *Proc. ISIM, 4*, 93-100.

Steinberger, J., Kabadjov, M. A., Steinberger, R., Tanev, H., Turchi, M., & Zavarella, V. (2011). *JRC's Participation at TAC 2011: Guided and MultiLingual Summarization Tasks*. TAC.

Takamura, H., & Okumura, M. (2009a). Text summarization model based on maximum coverage problem and its variant. *Proceedings of the 12th Conference of the European Chapter of the Association for Computational Linguistics*, 781-789. 10.3115/1609067.1609154

Takamura, H., & Okumura, M. (2009b). Text summarization model based on the budgeted median problem. *Proceeding of the 18th ACM conference on Information and knowledge management*, 1589-1592. 10.1145/1645953.1646179

Tan, P. N., Steinbach, M., & Kumar, V. (2006). *Introduction to data mining*. Pearson Addison Wesley Boston.

Tang, J., Yao, L., & Chen, D. (2009). Multi-topic-based query-oriented summarization. *SIAM International Conference Data Mining*.

Wan, X. (2011, June). Using bilingual information for cross-language document summarization. In *Proceedings of the 49th Annual Meeting of the Association for Computational Linguistics: Human Language Technologies-Volume 1* (pp. 1546-1555). Association for Computational Linguistics.

Wan, X., Li, H., & Xiao, J. (2010, July). Cross-language document summarization based on machine translation quality prediction. In *Proceedings of the 48th Annual Meeting of the Association for Computational Linguistics* (pp. 917-926). Association for Computational Linguistics.

Wan, X., Luo, F., Sun, X., Huang, S., & Yao, J. G. (2018). Cross-language document summarization via extraction and ranking of multiple summaries. *Knowledge and Information Systems*, 1–19.

Wan, X., & Yang, J. (2006). Improved affinity graph based multi-document summarization. *Proceedings of the Human Language Technology Conference of the NAACL*, 181-184.

Wang, D., & Li, T. (2010). Document update summarization using incremental hierarchical clustering. *Proceedings of the 19th ACM international conference on Information and knowledge management*, 279–288. 10.1145/1871437.1871476

Wang, D., Zhu, S., Li, T., Chi, Y., & Gong, Y. (2011). Integrating Document Clustering and Multidocument Summarization. *ACM Transactions on Knowledge Discovery from Data*, 5(3), 14. doi:10.1145/1993077.1993078

Yao, J. G., Wan, X., & Xiao, J. (2015). Phrase-based compressive cross-language summarization. In *Proceedings of the 2015 conference on empirical methods in natural language processing* (pp. 118-127). Academic Press. 10.18653/v1/D15-1012

Zhang, J., Zhou, Y., & Zong, C. (2016). Abstractive cross-language summarization via translation model enhanced predicate argument structure fusing. *IEEE/ACM Transactions on Audio. Speech, and Language Processing*, 24(10), 1842–1853.

Zitnik, M., Nguyen, F., Wang, B., Leskovec, J., Goldenberg, A., & Hoffman, M. M. (2019). Machine learning for integrating data in biology and medicine: Principles, practice, and opportunities. *Information Fusion*, 50, 71–91. doi:10.1016/j. inffus.2018.09.012 PMID:30467459

ADDITIONAL READING

Brin, S., & Page, L. (1998). The anatomy of a large-scale hypertextual Web search engine. *Proceedings of the seventh international conference on World Wide Web 7*, 107-117. 10.1016/S0169-7552(98)00110-X

Campr, M., & Ježek, K. (2015, September). Comparing semantic models for evaluating automatic document summarization. In *International Conference on Text, Speech, and Dialogue* (pp. 252-260). Springer, Cham. 10.1007/978-3-319-24033-6_29

Gong, Y., & Liu, X. (2001). Generic Text Summarization Using Relevance Measure and Latent Semantic Analysis. *Proceedings of the 24th Annual International ACM SIGIR Conference on Research and Development in Information Retrieval*. 10.1145/383952.383955

Gupta, V., & Lehal, G. S. (2010). A Survey of Text Summarization Extractive Techniques. *Journal of Emerging Technologies in Web Intelligence*, 2(3). doi:10.4304/jetwi.2.3.258-268

Jauua, M., & Hamadou, A. B. (2003). Automatic Text Summarization of Scientific Articles Based on Classification of Extract's Population. *Proceedings of the 4th international conference on Computational linguistics and intelligent text processing*, 623-634. 10.1007/3-540-36456-0_70

Mikolov, T., Chen, K., Corrado, G., & Dean, J. (2013). Efficient estimation of word representations in vector space. *arXiv preprint arXiv:1301.3781.*

Nomoto, T., & Matsumoto, Y. (2001). A new approach to unsupervised text summarization. *Proceedings of the 24th annual international ACM SIGIR conference on Research and development in information retrieval,* 26-34. 10.1145/383952.383956

Pham, H., Luong, T., & Manning, C. (2015). Learning distributed representations for multilingual text sequences. In *Proceedings of the 1st Workshop on Vector Space Modeling for Natural Language Processing* (pp. 88-94). 10.3115/v1/W15-1512

Rajaraman, A., & Ullman, J. D. (2011). *Mining of Massive Datasets.* New York, NY, USA: Cambridge University Press. doi:10.1017/CBO9781139058452

Rambow, O., Shrestha, L., Chen, J., & Lauridsen, C. (2004). Summarizing email threads. *Proceedings of the Human Language Technology Conference of the NAACL,* 105-108.

Schwarz, G. (1978). Estimating the dimension of a Model. *Annals of Statistics, 6*(2), 461–464. doi:10.1214/aos/1176344136

KEY TERMS AND DEFINITIONS

Abstractive-Based Summarization: The process of generating a summary by means of new content and new sentences automatically generated by capturing the essence of the input document.

Cross-Lingual Language Model: Machine learning model representing relations between words in different languages.

Document Summarization: The process of conveying the most representative content of either a single document or a document collection to a concise summary.

Extractive-Based Summarization: The process of generating a representative summary by selecting the most relevant sentences from the input documents.

Frequent Itemset Mining: Frequent itemset mining is a widely exploratory technique to discover relevant recurrences hidden in the analyzed data.

Knowledge Discovery From Data (KDD): The process of extracting hidden information from data. It includes the tasks of data selection, preprocessing, transformation, mining, and evaluation.

Machine Translation: Automatic translation of sentences or documents from a source language to a target language by means of automatic algorithms.

Multi-Document Summarization: The process of generating a representative summary from a collection of input documents.

Natural Language Processing: Subfield of computer science that concerns the processing of large amounts of natural language data by means of automated systems.

Single-Document Summarization: The process of generating a representative summary from a single input document.

Text Analytics: Techniques to derive high-quality information from textual data.

Word Embeddings: Feature learning techniques aimed to map words or phrases from a vocabulary to vectors of real numbers. The vector space allows analysts to identify semantic similarities between linguistic items based on their distributional properties in large textual corpora.

ENDNOTES

[1]   https://translate.google.com/
[2]   https://translator.microsoft.com/
[3]   https://github.com/kavgan/ROUGE-2.0
[4]   https://www-nlpir.nist.gov/projects/duc/guidelines/2001.html
[5]   https://duc.nist.gov/duc2004/
[6]   https://duc.nist.gov/duc2007/tasks.html
[7]   http://newsblaster.cs.columbia.edu/
[8]   https://gitlab.com/SCEMUSEEC
[9]   https://github.com/nisargjhaveri/clstk
[10]   https://github.com/miso-belica/sumy

Chapter 2

The Development of Single–Document Abstractive Text Summarizer During the Last Decade

Amal M. Al-Numai
King Saud University, Saudi Arabia

Aqil M. Azmi
King Saud University, Saudi Arabia

ABSTRACT

As the number of electronic text documents is increasing so is the need for an automatic text summarizer. The summary can be extractive, compression, or abstractive. In the former, the more important sentences are retained, more or less in their original structure, while the second one involves reducing the length of each sentence. For the latter, it requires a fusion of multiple sentences and/or paraphrasing. This chapter focuses on the abstractive text summarization (ATS) of a single text document. The study explores what ATS is. Additionally, the literature of the field of ATS is investigated. Different datasets and evaluation techniques used in assessing the summarizers are discussed. The fact is that ATS is much more challenging than its extractive counterpart, and as such, there are a few works in this area for all the languages.

DOI: 10.4018/978-1-5225-9373-7.ch002

INTRODUCTION

The digital world has become more complex and crowded with massive volumes of digital data. In 2018, the size of the indexed World Wide Web is over 5.22 billion pages (Kunder, 2018, Dec 15), spread over 1.8 billion websites (Fowler, 2018, Feb 20). As the number of electronic text documents is growing so is the need for an automatic text summarizer. It is difficult to read and gain knowledge from vast number of texts. In some fields, reading and understanding long texts consume time and effort. Consequently, automatic text summarization can be seen as a viable solution which is used in different domains and applications. It can decrease the time taken to summarize huge texts in many areas and media. It extracts and identifies the important information from a text; which can provide concise information with less effort and time. In addition, it can solve the information storage problem by reducing the document's size. Text summarization can support different applications and usage such as news feed, reports abstract, meeting, email and email threads, digest web pages and blogs, recap large amount of web opinions, helping doctors to get an overview about their patients' medical history. Also, students can use the summarization as a helping tool for quick overviewing their studying materials. Web crawler bots can be used to browse the web systematically according to a specific field; news for example, and summarize their contents in a meaningful way. Text summarization can be used in various stand-alone applications or combined with other systems, such as information retrieval, text clustering, data mining applications, web documents and pages, tweet, and opinion summarization.

Automatic text summarization is not a new idea, but there is a huge room for improvement. Simulating how human summaries texts lead to a major innovation in the field of artificial intelligence, abstractive text summarization becomes a necessity in the field of Natural Language Processing. It needs multiple tools to run together in order to extract knowledge and generate a new text. Many researchers have focused on extractive method due to its simplicity. Even though the extractive summarization is quite advanced, there are still researchers working on single document summarization, and those working on multi-document summarization. Now, the abstractive summarization itself is a challenging area. There are few research studies about abstractive summarization in different languages which are still immature due to the difficulties and the challenges of the natural language generation. More effort is necessary to advance this important research field.

In the literature, abstractive text summarization has been applied on several languages; such as English, Arabic, Hindi, Kannada, Malayalam, Telugu, and Vietnamese. Different methods have been conducted to achieve abstractive summary; such as discourse structure, graph-base, semantic-base, linguistic-based, information extraction rules, statistical model, machine learning techniques which include deep learning methods, and hybrid methods. Some of abstractive text summarization systems use the output of extractive summarization systems as a middleware to produce an abstractive summary such as (Kallimani, Srinivasa, & Eswara Reddy, 2011) and (Lloret, Romá-Ferri, & Palomar, 2013). Another troubling issue is the lack of automated assessment tool. For extractive summaries, researchers have developed different metrics to automatically assess the quality of the summary. However, for abstractive summaries, it is mainly human judgment. This is an expensive and time-consuming method for assessing the summary, and probably one of the main contributor to slow pace of development of abstractive summarizers.

This chapter will focus on the state-of-the-art work on abstractive text summarization systems for single documents, regardless of the target language of the input document, with a research has been published in English. To give room for in-depth look, the authors decided to limit the review to those developed during the last decade (covering the period 2008-2018), exploring the methods used in this subject and identifying their limitations. Furthermore, the chapter will show how these systems are evaluated and which datasets have been used. The fact is, abstractive text summarization is much more challenging than its extractive counterpart, and as such there are a few works in this area in all the languages.

BACKGROUND

Definition

Before addressing the concept of abstract summarization, the authors will investigate the denotative meaning of the words "summary" and "abstract". Oxford (Summary, 1989) dictionary defines the word "summary" as "A brief statement or account of the main points of something." Merriam-Webster (Summary, 1828) defines the word as "a brief statement that gives the most important information about something." Cambridge (Summary, 1995) dictionary: "a short, clear description that gives the main facts or ideas about something."

In addition, the word "abstract" as a noun is defined according to Cambridge dictionary (Abstract, 1995) as: "a short form of a speech, article, book, etc., giving only the most important facts or ideas" in British English, and as: "a few sentences that give the main ideas in an article or a scientific paper" in American English. Moreover, Merriam-Webster (Abstract, 1828) defines the word as "a brief written statement of the main points or facts in a longer report, speech, etc." Oxford dictionary (Abstract, 1989) defines it as "A summary of the contents of a book, article, or speech."

What Is Text Summarization

Text summarization is the process of transforming text to a shorter length, while retaining the main and important ideas of the original text. The length of the summarized text may vary from 10% to 50% of the original's, though typically it is 30%. So, the text is rewritten to form a reduced text with few words or sentences while preserving the gist of the written text. According to (Jones, 1999), a text document can be summarized automatically by following three phases; interpretation, transformation, and generation. Figure 1 shows the flow of these phases. That means interpreting the source text to get a representation. This source representation is transformed; by different techniques, to summary representation in order to generate a summary. To participate in this process, researchers use set of features. These features are extracted from the text. Some of the more common ones are: title words, number of title words, sentence length, sentence position, total number of sentences, weight of words according to their position, their relevance to the title words, or using TF-IDF, keywords, and synonyms.

The main characteristics of text summarization are: preserving main and important information, producing short summary length, and grammatically and syntactically correct (Moawad & Aref, 2012). Automatic text summarization can be used in various stand-alone applications such as summarizing meetings (Siddhartha Banerjee, Mitra, & Sugiyama, 2015; Liu & Liu, 2009), news, email and email threads (Torres-Moreno, 2014), web documents and pages (Korabu & Ingale, 2013), social media tweets, and opinions (Ganesan, Zhai, & Han, 2010). Furthermore, automatic text summarization can be combined with other systems; such as information retrieval, text clustering, and data mining applications (Embar, Deshpande, Vaishnavi, Jain, & Kallimani, 2013).

Types of Summarization

Automatic summarization can be categorized into various classes according to different aspects. In the case of *number of documents*, the summary can be done on a single document or heterogeneous/homogeneous multi-documents. Furthermore, the *summary type* can be extractive, compression, or abstractive. For the first type,

Figure 1. Automatic summarization phases

the main important sentences are extracted as they are, while the second one involves reducing the length of each sentence. Whereas the third type requires a fusion of multiple sentences and/or paraphrasing. According to *the context*, the summary can be user driven; in which a user asks to get a summary based on his/her query, or generic; that does not require any user query (Torres-Moreno, 2014).

Abstractive and Extractive Text Summarization

As mentioned in the previous section, automatic text summarization methods are extractive, abstractive, and sentence compression. The following will be more closely to the first two types as they are the most common types in the state-of-the-art systems, considering their definitions, comparing them, and exploring their pros and cons.

Extractive summarization is defined by (Kleinbauer & Murray, 2012) as: "generating a summary by identifying the most salient parts of the source and concatenating these parts to form the actual summary," and by (Torres-Moreno, 2014) as: "Extraction consists of selecting units of text (sentences, segments of sentences, paragraphs or passages), deemed to contain a document's essential information and of assembling these units in an adequate way." Moreover, Rush et al. (Rush, Chopra, & Weston, 2015) defined extractive summary as: "crop out and stitch together portions of the text to produce a condensed version."

On the other hand, abstractive summary is defined by (Kleinbauer & Murray, 2012) as: "generating a summary document by representing what the source document actually means, in some kind of semantic representation using natural language understanding (NLU)." Or as "produce a bottom-up summary, aspects of which may not appear as part of the original" (Rush et al., 2015). Additionally, (Torres-Moreno, 2014) stated that abstractive summary is: "produce summaries based on text understanding and seek to generate a grammatically correct, concise and coherent text."

Based on process phases suggested by (Jones, 1999), (Kleinbauer & Murray, 2012) did a comparison between abstractive and extractive text summarization as listed in Table 1.

Advantages and Disadvantages of Extractive and Abstractive Summarization

Extractive text summarization is easy to generate summary in the sense that it does not need deep understanding of the original text. It often outputs the summary in a short time (Kleinbauer & Murray, 2012). However, the textual coherence is not guaranteed since it does not pay attention on co-reference relationships and it does

Table 1. Comparison of the interpretation(I), transformation(T), and generation(G) phases for abstractive and extractive summarization

	Abstractive Summarization	Extractive Summarization
I	Use NLU to create symbolic representation of contents.	Extract features for every unit of text.
T	Transform source representation into summary representation.	Extract units based on evaluating features.
G	Use NLG to create text from summary representation.	Smoothing and post-processing.

(Kleinbauer & Murray, 2012)

not care about the correlation between sentences (Lloret et al., 2013). Redundant phrases are highly expected in the summary (Le & Le, 2013).

On the other hand, abstractive text summarization carrying out NLP techniques to process the text or the output of extractive summarizers. It exerts great effort on sentence truncation, aggregation, generalization, reference adjustment and rewording (Le & Le, 2013). It generates a concise and succinct summary (Embar et al., 2013), planning to create a syntactically correct summary (Das & Martins, 2007).

It is still a major challenge for NLP community despite some work on sub-sentential modification (Le & Le, 2013). It is more complex than extractive summarization and difficult to deal with, since it needs powerful text generation techniques and extensive natural language processing (Gambhir & Gupta, 2016).

ABSTRACTIVE TEXT SUMMARIZERS

In the literature, the abstractive text summarization systems are limited due to the difficulties on natural language processing. It attracts the attention of researchers to devote more effort on. Different methods have been conducted to achieve abstractive summary; such as graph-base, semantic-base, machine learning techniques, discourse structure, linguistic-based, and hybrid methods. The followings discuss each of them.

Graph-Based

Opinosis (Ganesan et al., 2010) is an abstractive summarization framework to build summaries of redundant opinions using graphs. It does not require domain knowledge and uses shallow NLP. The idea is to use a graph data structure to represent the text and then finding the appropriate path to generate a summary. The graph node represents a unique word in the document and annotated with part-of-speech (POS). The directed edges between nodes specify the sentence structure. POS helps in identifying valid paths which, in turns, are scored to select the high scores. The summary is accomplished by ranking the scored paths and eliminating duplicated ones by using similarity measure. The next step is to select a set of top paths to represent the summary according to a predefined summary size. The system evaluation was conducted by humans in order to compare their summaries with the automatically generated ones. ROUGE and a readability test are used for the assessment process. The system could generate readable, concise and well-formed summary. Since it does not depend on knowledge, it is a language independent and can be used to summarize non-English text documents.

COMPENDIUM (Lloret et al., 2013); a hybrid approach for combining extractive and abstractive sentences in the biomedical domain, used the output of an extractive summarization model to generate new sentences in one of these forms: either a compressed version of a longer sentence, or a new sentence containing information from two individual ones. The inputs were represented as a weighted direction word graph, where the nodes and edges are representing the words and adjacency relation between two words, respectively. Moreover, the inverse frequency of co-occurrence of two words were considered as the edge's weight, taken into account the importance of the nodes they link, through the PageRank algorithm.

After the creation of word graph, the shortest path between nodes is used to create new sentences starting from the first word of each sentence. These new sentences are subject to filtering and all incorrect sentences are removed based on set of pre-defined rules. Then, cosine similarity was used to measure the similarity between the extractive sentence and the abstractive one to decide which one to consider in the final summary. The experiments showed that their extractive model performed better than the abstractive one for most of the ROUGE metrics. The reason behind this is relying on the reduction of the sentences and no additional information was provided, so the recall will not be higher than the extractive model. Generating sentences from the original text instead of the relevant ones may solve this issue. On the other hand, according to user satisfaction, the abstractive model outperformed the extractive one. No specific patterns, nor learning the structure of a text in order to generate its summary.

Furthermore, (Kumar, Srinathan, & Varma, 2013) identified the important words by using bigrams model with some statistics in order to compute the significance of these bigrams. The importance was measured according to bigrams frequency, their position in the document, and the position of the sentences acquiring them. Sentences that share similar topic were grouped by using Average Agglomerative Clustering, and the clusters were ranked according to their sentences significance measure. These steps were outset for designing an abstractive summarization system for single document written in English. The system based on vertex constrained shortest path scheme that depends on weighted minimum vertex cover (WMVC). The idea behind WMVC is to represent the words for each sentence as a node in a directed graph. Then, the path length between vertices was calculated to obtain the shortest paths, which is considered as abstractive sentence summary. There is no sentence paraphrasing or rewriting the sentence using synonyms as the system merges the sentences by eliminating some words and do grammar checking.

Additionally, an abstractive conversation summarizer was developed by (Mehdad, Carenini, & Ng, 2014) and based on a user query. The summarizer consists of three phases. In the first one, an extractor summarization system was utilized to detect the most related sentences to a user query. The log-likelihood ratio was used to identify the important terms (signature terms) in a chat log that will assist in finding the relevant sentences in a document. These terms have been weighted according to (Lin & Hovy, 2000). Additionally, the user query terms were expanded via WordNet noun synsets and weighted as 1. Each utterance scored according to the combination of query terms and signature terms weights. Next phase, the top ranked utterances are processed by removing redundant meaning in sentences by building entailment graph as in (Mehdad, Carenini, Ng, & Joty, 2013). The last phase focused on generating abstract sentences by following three steps: grouping similar sentences using K-mean clustering algorithm, constructing a word graph for each cluster, and ranking each group path according to different aspects: the appearance of the query term, the more grammatically correct paths, and the path weight that depends on the frequency of each nodes (words) and the distance between two words in the path. For each cluster, the best path is selected as a summary sentence. The model has been evaluated manually by scoring the overall quality and the relatedness to the query, and automatically via ROUGE-1 and ROUGE-2 precision, recall, and F1 scores. However, there were no comparison is done with other abstractive models. Instead, the evaluation was conducted by comparing the proposed model with other extractive summarization models, which outperform them in the manual evaluation and ROUGE-1 precision.

Semantic-Graph

The proposed framework of (Greenbacker, 2011) enables the generation of abstractive summaries from unified semantic models, regardless of the original format of the information sources. He contended that this framework is more akin to the human process of conceptual integration and regeneration in writing an abstract, as compared to the traditional NLP techniques of rating and extracting sentences to form a summary. Furthermore, the approach enables the generation of summary sentences about the information collected from graphical formats, for which there were no sentences available for extraction, and helps avoiding the issues of coherence and ambiguity that tend to affect extraction-based summaries (Nenkova, 2006). This work shares similarities with the knowledge-based text condensation model of (Reimer & Hahn,

1988) as well as with (Rau, Jacobs, & Zernik, 1989), who developed an information extraction approach for conceptual information summarization.

The approach consists of the following steps: building the semantic model, rating the informational content, and generating a summary. The semantic model was constructed in a knowledge representation based on typed, structured objects organized under a foundational ontology (McDonald, 2000). To analyze the text, they used Sparser, a linguistically-sound, phrase structure-based chart parser with an extensive and extendible semantic grammar (McDonald, 1992). They assumed a relatively complete semantic grammar exists for the domain of documents to be summarized. So, they manually extended an existing grammar on an as- needed basis, with plans for large-scale learning of new rules and ontology definitions as future work.

In the second step; rating content, the concepts containing the most information and having the most connections to other important concepts in the model should be conveyed in the summary. An information density metric (ID) was proposed to rate a concept's importance based on a number of factors: the completeness of the concept's attributes, number of connections with other concepts and the importance of these connected concepts, and document and rhetorical structure, that take into account the location of a concept within a document and the juxtaposition. After computing the ID of each concept, the graph-based ranking algorithm (Demir, Carberry, & McCoy, 2010) was applied to select items for the summary. This algorithm is based on PageRank (Page, Brin, Motwani, & Winograd, 1999) with some changes. The algorithm iteratively selects concepts one at a time, re-ranking the remaining items by increasing the weight of related concepts and discounting redundant ones. The last step is expressing these elements as sentences following the generation technique of (McDonald & Greenbacker, 2010).

(Moawad & Aref, 2012) generated an abstractive summary automatically for the input text using a semantic graph reducing technique. This approach exploits a new semantic graph called Rich Semantic Graph (RSG). RSG is an ontology-based representation developed to be used as an intermediate representation for Natural Language Processing (NLP) applications. The new approach consists of three phases: creating a rich semantic graph for the source document, reducing the generated rich semantic graph to more abstracted graph, and finally generate the abstractive summary from the abstracted rich semantic graph. Additionally, RSG was used for Arabic text representation (S. Ismail, Moawd, & Aref, 2013; S. S. Ismail, Aref, & Moawad, 2013) by the same authors on an ongoing work for Arabic summarization (Saad, Moawad, & Aref, 2011). Moreover, another work has used this technique for summarizing Hindi texts (Subramaniam & Dalal, 2015). The model uses Domain Ontology and Hindi WordNet to select different synonyms for generating the summary. There are no mentioned experiment results.

Moreover, (Le & Le, 2013) proposed an abstractive text summarization for Vietnamese language based on extractive summarization model. The approach is different from (Ganesan et al., 2010) and (Lloret & Palomar, 2011) in which anaphora resolution is used in the extractive model. The anaphora resolution has solved the problem of getting different words/phrases for the same concept, which are represented in different nodes in the graph. Once the extractive summarization is complete, the output is used as an input to the abstractive model that involved two stages. The first one is the sentence reduction; that aims to remove unimportant and redundant clauses from the beginning of a sentence using RST, and prebuilt syntactic rules to complete the end of the reduced sentence. The objective of the second stage is to use word graph to represent the relations between words, clauses and sentences, then combine multiple sentences to generate new ones based on three pre-defined cases.

Regarding Arabic contributions, (Azmi & Altmami, 2018) built the first abstractive summarizer system based on a modified version of the extractive summarizer created by (Azmi & Al-Thanyyan, 2009). The system segments the text into topics using sliding window and bag-of-word (Harrag, Hamdi-Cherif, & Al-Salman, 2010), then generates a title for each segment using TF-IDF. Rhetorical Structure Theory (RST) is used to generate the extractive summary. Subsequently, the abstractive summary is produced by removing some words such as position names, days, and sub-sentence; resulting in a reduced sentence length. However, there is no paraphrasing and thus leads to non-coherent summary.

Another work has been done on Malayalam language (Kabeer & Idicula, 2014). It used statistical and semantic strategies. The statistical model is used to extract the top-ranked sentences that are considered as important ones. The model scores each sentence depending on set of features such as keywords and their frequency in the document, title words, sentences location, etc. After identifying the related sentences, these sentences are used in a semantic graph model to generate abstractive summary. To construct the semantic graph, the POS tagging is identified; so the triple Subject, Object, and Predicate are extracted. The Subject and Object are considered as graph nodes. Node connection edges represent the relationship between the subject and object via predicate. Each edge is weighted by calculating set of features such as sentence location, triple location, in-degree and out-degree of connected nodes, and others. To reduce the semantic graph, each edge having less than the edges' average weight is removed. As a result, all non-connected nodes are also deleted. Moreover, summary sentences are generated by representing the remaining nodes as subject-object-predicate. A collection of 25 news documents was used to evaluate the models. The experiments are measured by human and ROUGE metric. The results show that the extractive model gives better outcome than abstractive ones.

On the other hand, there is in-progress work toward abstractive summarization based on transformations of semantic representations such as Abstract Meaning Representation (AMR) (Banarescu et al., 2013). The objective is to represent the sentences to individual AMR graphs, combining and transforming those graphs into a single summary AMR graph, then generating text from the summary graph (Liu, Flanigan, Thomson, Sadeh, & Smith, 2015).

Linguistic-Based

Additionally, there is an effort toward abstractive summarization in other than English. sArAmsha system proposed by (Embar et al., 2013) used guided summarization for Kannada; an Indian language. It is based on lexical analysis, Information Extraction (IE) rules that were created manually, and domain templets for generating sentences. The function of IE rules is to extract relevant information after performing POS, NER, and other lexical analysis techniques. Moreover, the category of the document is identified by using Term Frequency (TF). After these steps, the best template is chosen to form sentences. As a result, the system produces short and concise summary. Similar work has been done with Telugu language (Kallimani et al., 2011).

Neural Network and Deep Learning

Neural Attention-Based Summarization model (ABS) (Rush et al., 2015) was the first model that employed neural network to solve ATS, It generated abstractive summary based on the concept of feed forward neural network language model (NNLM) (Bengio, Ducharme, Vincent, & Janvin, 2003). It also took advantage of the attention-based model of (Bahdanau, Cho, & Bengio, 2014). The model is sentence-level summarization for headline generation. It encoded a sentence then decoded it to generate a summary. Attention-Based Encoder was used as the encoder, and beam-search for the decoder. The generated summary is with fixed words length and with the same vocabulary as the source text. The model is considered as data-driven approach as it mainly uses a combination of document-summary pair to train the model, and it doesn't impose more linguistic structure. This model summarizes each sentence separately. Both (Cohn & Lapata, 2008) and (Woodsend, Feng, & Lapata, 2010) approaches differ from this in that they directly use the syntax of the input/output sentences. The results showed that it outperforms the baseline models. However, words reordering yields incorrect syntactic sentence. There is an absence of fusion multiple sentences, and no dynamic summary length.

Posteriorly, a Recurrent Attention Summarizer (RAS) (Chopra, Auli, & Rush, 2016) is an improvement version of (Rush et al., 2015) model. The refinement was done by aggregating the words' position with their word-embeddings representation.

Additionally, a recurrent NN was used for generating a summary instead of feed forward NNLM. These improvements overcome the problem of word ordering issued in (Rush et al., 2015) models. Two versions of RNN were utilized; Elman RNN and LSTM RNN, where the prior had better result than the later one in term of perplexity and F1 ROUGE scores.

Another work in deep learning based model is by (Nallapati, Zhou, Gulcehre, & Xiang, 2016). They applied the encoder-decoder RNN model developed by (Bahdanau et al., 2014). The encoder is a bi-directional GRU RNN and the decoder is uni-directional GRU RNN; each one has the same hidden state size. They adopted the Encoder-Decoder RNN with attention mechanism and employing the Large Vocabulary Trick (LVT) proposed by (Jean, Cho, Memisevic, & Bengio, 2014). They also build another model called Feature-rich Encoder to capture the problem of how to identify key concepts and key entities in the document being processed. This was done by using word-embedding representation for each word document and adding linguistic features such as POS tags, NE tags, and TF and IDF. Another issue in RNN model is sometimes keywords or important words appear in test dataset and not in training dataset. These out-of-vocabulary (OOV) words had been handled by developing a switching generator-pointer model that uses a sigmoid activation function to decide when to switch on to generate a word from its target vocabulary, and when to switch off to point to a word position in the source text. Moreover, specifying which sentence that engage in generating a summary is not obvious way especially for long documents. To overcome this issue, they incorporated the concept of hierarchical attention structure with RNN by adapting the encoder to be two bi-directional RNN; one at the word-level and the other at sentence-level. Positional embedding is also concatenated with the hidden state of the sentence-level RNN. The word-level attention is re-scaled by the corresponding sentence-level attention weights. The attention weighted context vector is then computed using the new rescaled attention; which in turns is fed to the hidden state of the decoder as an input. The experiments on Gigaword dataset showed that the model with LVT outperformed the result of ABS+ model (Rush et al., 2015) and the one of (Chopra et al., 2016); where all were trained on the first sentence of a document. This improvement might be due to capturing more contextual information in the word embeddings. Whereas, there were no significant important when using DUC dataset. To extend the tests for generating multiple summary sentences, they built a dataset from CNN and Daily Mail websites. The findings showed the hierarchical model outperforms the first model. However, they all generate repetitive phrases. Temporal Attention model (Sankaran, Mi, Al-Onaizan, & Ittycheriah, 2016) is used to remedy this issue. Nevertheless, there are repetitive sentences even it beats the other models.

The preceding models were focused on headline generation or one sentence summary. In contrast, (See, Liu, & Manning, 2017) designed a pointer-generation network model with and without coverage property to generate multi-sentence summaries. They combined a pointer network (Vinyals, Fortunato, & Jaitly, 2015) to a baseline model similar to (Nallapati et al., 2016). However, the model learn when to use a pointer or generate a word at any timestep, whereas in (Nallapati et al., 2016) the pointer decision is accomplished only when encountering a OOV word. This updated version improved handling the OOV words. In addition to the OOV issue, they altered the coverage model (Tu, Lu, Liu, Liu, & Li, 2016) to resolve the phrase repetition issue. This is done by adding a vector of the sum of attention distributions for every previous decoder timestep to the attention mechanism of the next timestep. Furthermore, a coverage loss is defined to penalize the frequently attend to the same word's position. This technique beat the Temporal Attention model that has been used in (Nallapati et al., 2016) for solving this issue. CNN and Daily Mail dataset is used to test and train the model. ROUGE and METEOR are used to evaluate the model, and there was a noticeable improvement tends to the pointer-generator network model with coverage property.

Furthermore, (Paulus, Xiong, & Socher, 2017) built a neural intra-attention model depending on RNN, where the encoder is a bi-directional LSTM and the decoder is a uni-directional LSTM. They deal with the phrases' repetition by using an intra-temporal attention function for each decoding step as (Nallapati et al., 2016). Even though, there is a repetition especially for long document. To control, an intra-decoder attention (IA) mechanism is defined; which takes into account the prior decoded sequences. Additionally, while testing, the decoder is prevented from generating any trigram sequence that has been output before. The previous RNN models train their models by minimization a maximum-likelihood (ML) loss function. (Paulus et al., 2017) argue that minimizing ML dose not perpetually guaranty the best evaluation result with discreate metric such as ROUGE. So, a reinforcement learning (RL); self-critical policy gradient (Rennie, Marcheret, Mroueh, Ross, & Goel, 2017), is used in the training loss function. The experiment results show that ML model with and without IA, RL with IA, and hybrid ML&RL with IA gain higher ROUGE scores than the intra-temporal attention model by (Nallapati et al., 2016) on the CNN/Daily Mail dataset. Although RL with IA gain higher ROUGE score than the hybrid ML&RL with IA, human evaluation showed that the later generates more readable and relevance summary than RL.

Recently, (Chang, Huang, & Hsu, 2018) applied (Rush et al., 2015) model on LCSTS Chinese dataset. For language specification, the input encoder representation is word-embeddings, whereas the input decoder representation is character-embedding. Following this strategy of representation results in an improvement on ROUGE-F1 scores against Chinese models such as (Chen, Zhu, Ling, Wei, & Jiang, 2016) and (Li, Lam, Bing, & Wang, 2017).

Fuzzy Logic

A hybrid system based on knowledge base and fuzzy logic has been implemented by Dania (Sagheer & Sukkar, 2017). The system was applied on specific domain Arabic text. Related domain concepts is pre-defined, and a knowledge-based is used to identify the concepts from the input text and to extract the semantic relations between concepts. The generated sentence is composed of three parts: subject, verb, and object. After generating multiple sentences from the concepts and their relations, a fuzzy logic system is used. It computes the fuzzy value for each word in a sentence, apply fuzzy rules, and do defuzzification in order to sort the summary sentences in descending order according on their fuzzy value. The system is experimented on texts of Essex Arabic Summaries Corpus. No evaluation method was used to test and compare the system with other techniques.

Table 2 lists abstractive summarization systems, considering the used methods and the evaluation techniques.

DATASETS

Any summarization system requires data to test it. Choosing which dataset to use for experiments depends on the scope of the summarizer; if it is a single-document or a multi-documents, if it is for headline generation or multiple sentences, and which language is being processed. The followings are the most common datasets that have been used in single-document abstractive text summarization systems.

Gigaword

It comes in multiple forms depending on the language and the additional features to each version. The most common used dataset in summarization are: English Gigaword corpus (Graff, Kong, Chen, & Maeda, 2003) and Annotated English Gigaword (Napoles, Gormley, & Van Durme, 2012).

Document Understanding Conferences (DUC)

DUC dataset (Over, Dang, & Harman, 2007) also has variants and the experiments were mostly done on DUC 2003 and DUC 2004. It includes documents, their manual and automatic summaries, and evaluation results.

Table 2. Abstractive summarization systems and their methods and evaluations

Paper	Year	Summary Scope	Method	Pre-Extractive Model	Language	Corpus-Dataset	Accuracy	Precision	Recall	F-measure	Evaluation method
(Ganesan et al., 2010)	2010	Opinions	Graph-Based	No	English	Reviews collected from Tripadvisor.co, Amazon.com, and Edmunds.com	-	ROUGE-1: 44.82 ROUGE-2: 14.16 ROUGE-SU4: 22.61	ROUGE-1: 28.31 ROUGE-2: 8.53 ROUGE-SU4: 8.51	ROUGE-1: 32.71 ROUGE-2: 9.98 ROUGE-SU4: 10.27	ROUGE and human
(Greenbacker, 2011)	2011	Multimodal-document	Semantic-graph	No	English	-	-	-	-	-	Human (accuracy, clarity, completeness)
(Kallimani et al., 2011)	2011	Single-document	Semantic-Syntax	Yes	Telugu	-	-	-	-	-	-
(Moawad & Aref, 2012)	2012	Single-document	Semantic- graph	No	English	-	-	-	-	-	-
(Le & Le, 2013)	2013	Single-document	Semantic (RST)-graph	Yes	Vietnamese	50 documents collected from newspapers	Sentence correct syntax: 95% Complete in meaning: 72%	-	-	ROUGE-1: 25.13 ROUGE-2: 13.44	ROUGE and human
(Lloret et al., 2013)	2013	Single-document	Graph-Based	Yes	English	50 medical research articles	-	ROUGE-1: 41.81 ROUGE-2: 12.63 ROUGE-L: 28.01 ROUGE-SU4: 16.95	ROUGE-1: 38.66 ROUGE-2: 11.49 ROUGE-L: 25.95 ROUGE-SU4: 15.6	ROUGE-1: 40.20 ROUGE-2: 12.03 ROUGE-L: 26.94 ROUGE-SU4: 16.24	ROUGE and qualitative: degree of reflecting important information, knowing the topic, validity according to the original abstract.

continued on following page

Table 2. Continued

Paper	Year	Summary Scope	Method	Pre-Extractive Model	Language	Corpus-Dataset	Accuracy	Precision	Recall	F-measure	Evaluation method
(Embar et al., 2013)	2013	Single-document	Linguistic-based, Information Extraction rules	No	Kannada; an Indian language	-	-	-	-	-	Compression Ratio; automatic and manually (human)
(Kumar et al., 2013)	2013	Single-document	Graph-Based	Yes	English	DUC-2001, DUC-2002	-	-	DUC-2001 ROUGE-1: 0.49152 ROUGE-2: 0.18461 ROUGE-W: 0.15445 DUC-2002 ROUGE-1: 0.52002 ROUGE-2: 0.23402 ROUGE-W: 0.17756		ROUGE and human (scores for grammar)
(Kabeer & Idicula, 2014)	2014	Single-document	Statistical + Semantic- graph	Yes	Malayalam	Newspaper	-	Human: 0.455 ROUGE-L: 0.466	Human: 0.4968 ROUGE-L: 0.667	Human: 04623 ROUGE-L: 0.400	ROUGE and human
(Mehdad et al., 2014)	2014	Multimodal-document	Statistical + Graph-Based	Yes	English	GNUe Traffic archive	-	ROUGE-1: 40 ROUGE-2: 20	ROUGE-1: 56 ROUGE-2: 25	ROUGE-1: 42 ROUGE-2: 22	ROUGE, and human (scores for overall quality, relatedness, preference, grammar)

continued on following page

47

Table 2. Continued

Paper	Year	Summary Scope	Method	Pre-Extractive Model	Language	Corpus-Dataset	Accuracy	Precision	Recall	F-measure	Evaluation method
(Rush et al., 2015)	2015	Sentence-level	Feed-forward neural network language model, bag-of-words	No	English	Gigaword for training & testing, DUC-2004 for testing	–	–	DUC-2004 ROUGE-1: 26.55 ROUGE-2: 7.06 ROUGE-L: 22.05 Gigaword ROUGE-1: 30.88 ROUGE-2: 12.22 ROUGE-L: 27.77	–	ROUGE, Perplexity, percentage of summary's words relying on the source
(Subramaniam & Dalal, 2015)	2015	Single-document	Semantic- graph	No	Hindi	–	–	–	–	–	–
(Liu et al., 2015)	2015	Single-document	semantic-graph	Yes	English	AMR bank based on Gigaword	–	ROUGE-1: 87.5	ROUGE-1: 43.7	ROUGE-1: 57.8	Number of nodes and edges. ROUGE
(Chopra et al., 2016)	2016	Sentence-level	Deep Learning	No	English	Gigaword, DUC-2004	–	–	DUC-2004 (RAS-Elmam) ROUGE-1: 28.97 ROUGE-2: 8.26 ROUGE-L: 24.06	Gigaword (RAS-Elmam) ROUGE-1: 33.78 ROUGE-2: 15.97 ROUGE-L: 31.15	ROUGE, Perplexity

continued on following page

Table 2. Continued

Paper	Year	Summary Scope	Method	Pre-Extractive Model	Language	Corpus-Dataset	Accuracy	Precision	Recall	F-measure	Evaluation method
(Nallapati et al., 2016)	2016	Single-document	Deep Learning	No	English	Gigaword, DUC-2004, CNN/Daily Mail	–	–	DUC (words-1vt5k-1sent) ROUGE-1: 28.61 ROUGE-2: 9.42 ROUGE-L: 25.24	Gigaword (words-1vt5k-1sent) ROUGE-1: 35.3 ROUGE-2: 16.64 ROUGE-L: 32.62 CNN/Daily Mail ROUGE-1: 35.46 ROUGE-2: 13.3 ROUGE-L: 32.65	ROUGE, percentage of summary's words relying on the source
(Sagheer & Sukkar, 2017)	2017	Single-document	Fuzzy logic + Knowledge Base	No	Arabic	EASC	–	–	–	–	–
(See et al., 2017)	2017	Single-document	Deep Learning	No	English	CNN/Daily Mail	–	–	–	ROUGE-1: 39.53 ROUGE-2: 17.28 ROUGE-L: 36.38 METEOR: Exact match:17.32 Full mode:18.72	ROUGE, METEOR

continued on following page

Table 2. Continued

Paper	Year	Summary Scope	Method	Pre-Extractive Model	Language	Corpus-Dataset	Accuracy	Precision	Recall	F-measure	Evaluation method
(Paulus et al., 2017)	2017	Single-document	Deep Learning	No	English	CNN/Daily Mail, New York Times (NYT)	–	–	–	CNN/ Daily Mail (RL with IA) ROUGE-1: 41.16 ROUGE-2: 15.75 ROUGE-L: 39.08 CNN/ Daily Mail (ML+RL with IA) ROUGE-1: 39.87 ROUGE-2: 15.75 ROUGE-L: 36.9 NYT (RL) ROUGE-1: 47.22 ROUGE-2: 30.51 ROUGE-L: 39.27 NYT (ML+RL) ROUGE-1: 47.03 ROUGE-2: 30.72 ROUGE-L: 43.10	ROUGE, human (scores for relevance and readability)

continued on following page

Table 2. Continued

Paper	Year	Summary Scope	Method	Pre-Extractive Model	Language	Corpus-Dataset	Accuracy	Precision	Recall	F-measure	Evaluation method
(Azmi & Altmami, 2018)	2018	Single-document	Semantic (RST) - graph	Yes	Arabic	Newspaper (Saudi, Egyptian, and Lebanese)	Quality of summary of length 50%: 90.6, length 40%: 76.4, length 30%: 58.4, length 20%: 38.4	–	–	–	Human
(Chang et al., 2018)	2018	Single-document	Deep Learning	No	Chinese	Large scale Chinese Short Text Summarization (LCSTS)	–	–	–	ROUGE-1: 46.1 ROUGE-2: 33.61 ROUGE-L: 43.46	ROUGE

CNN/Daily Mail Corpus

Multiple-sentence summaries have been generated by (Nallapati et al., 2016).

Essex Arabic Summaries Corpus (EASC)

It is an Arabic dataset, that includes set of articles and their extractive summaries and human summaries (El-Haj, Kruschwitz, & Fox).

EVALUATIONS

Any system has to be evaluated to measure its performance and quality, and to test its effectiveness. Previous studies on abstractive text summarization for single document measured the quality of a summary by variant techniques. ROUGE (Recall-Oriented Understudy for Gisting Evaluation) (Lin, 2004) is the most common automatic evaluation technique. It compares a generated summary with a reference one according to a set of metrics; ROUGE-1 compares each word between the automatic and reference summaries, ROUGE-2 compares bigrams between them, ROUGE-L compares the longest words sequence between them, and ROUGE-SU skip-bigram that counts unigrams and any pair of words between them. Another automatic evaluation strategy is by measuring the percentage of automatic generated summary's words relying on the original source text. Additionally, METEOR (Metric for Evaluation of Translation with Explicit ORdering) (Satanjeev Banerjee & Lavie, 2005) measures the alignment between the generated summary and the reference one based on unigram tokens; including stem words and synonym. Due to the naturality of ATS, automatic evaluations are still not sufficient techniques to assess a system, since their evaluations are based on word-level. In contrast, manual evaluation is the most convinced assessment, and at the same time is not a feasible technique to evaluate a system. Human experts are conducted to assess a summary based on variant metrics. The quality of a summary is mainly assessed manually by considering the coherency, grammatical structure, non-redundant phrases, and relatedness. However, the present limitation on evaluating ATS requires more research to discover and develop novel automatic assessment methods.

DISCUSSION AND FUTURE RESEARCH DIRECTIONS

Automatic text summarization became one of the most trending NLP application in the current decade. Many companies pay attention of text summarization especially the abstractive; such as IBM (Nallapati et al., 2016), Facebook (Chopra et al., 2016; Rush et al., 2015), Google (See et al., 2017), and Salesforce (Paulus et al., 2017). Most ATS systems were built using graphs, linguistics, semantic techniques, machine learning algorithms, or hybrid methods. The current literature focuses on using graphs or deep learning approaches. Nevertheless, no previous study has investigated the use of swarm intelligence (SI) algorithms – to the best of our knowledge – to solve abstractive summarization, though it has been successful in solving other NLP problems. There are a number of researches that utilized SI algorithms in extractive summarization, such as Ant Colony Optimization (ACO) (Mosa, Hamouda, & Marei, 2017), Particle swarm optimization (PSO) (Binwahlan, Salim, & Suanmali, 2009), and Cat Swarm Optimization (CSO) (Rautray & Balabantaray, 2017).

One of the problems is the lack of standard metric to measure/assess the quality of abstractive summary. The metrics used to assess the extractive summaries are not suitable for abstractive summaries, since the latter summaries no longer retain their original structure. Alternately, we may resort to manual evaluation. But, as the manual evaluation differs from one person to another, means we need to rely on more than one person to do the evaluation and then take the average. This is a costly endeavor. This calls for investing in future research to assess the quality of ATS.

Data plays an important role in building and evaluating any system. However, there are a limited number of datasets that are ready to participate in evaluating ATS, and most of them have short-length sentences. Experimenting on limited functionality datasets creates difficulties for the researchers to examine their methods. Also, the lack of resources slows down the direction toward designing new systems.

CONCLUSION

This chapter sets out to discover the literature of abstractive text summarization systems for single document. It has been shown that ATS system is more challenging than extractive one. ATS is still not mature and needs more helping tools to assist the paraphrasing sentences and generating new words. Number of datasets that have been used in the literature are presented. Furthermore, the main evaluation measures are discussed. As also recommended above, future research should find out feasible automatic assessment metrics.

REFERENCES

Abstract. (1828). In *Merriam Webster*. Retrieved from http://www.merriam-webster.com/dictionary/abstract

Abstract. (1989). In *Oxford Dictionaries* Retrieved from http://www.oxforddictionaries.com/definition/english/abstract

Abstract. (1995). In *Cambridge Dictionary*. Retrieved from http://dictionary.cambridge.org/dictionary/english/abstract

Azmi, A., & Al-Thanyyan, S. (2009). *Ikhtasir—A user selected compression ratio Arabic text summarization system*. Paper presented at the Natural Language Processing and Knowledge Engineering, 2009. NLP-KE 2009. International Conference on.

Azmi, A. M., & Altmami, N. I. (2018). An abstractive Arabic text summarizer with user controlled granularity. *Information Processing & Management, 54*(6), 903–921. doi:10.1016/j.ipm.2018.06.002

Bahdanau, D., Cho, K., & Bengio, Y. (2014). *Neural Machine Translation by Jointly Learning to Align and Translate*. CoRR, abs/1409.0473

Banarescu, L., Bonial, C., Cai, S., Georgescu, M., Griffitt, K., Hermjakob, U., . . . Schneider, N. (2013). *Abstract Meaning Representation for Sembanking*. Academic Press.

Banerjee, S., & Lavie, A. (2005). METEOR: An automatic metric for MT evaluation with improved correlation with human judgments. *Proceedings of the acl workshop on intrinsic and extrinsic evaluation measures for machine translation and/or summarization.*

Banerjee, S., Mitra, P., & Sugiyama, K. (2015). Generating abstractive summaries from meeting transcripts. *Proceedings of the 2015 ACM Symposium on Document Engineering.* 10.1145/2682571.2797061

Bengio, Y., Ducharme, R., Vincent, P., & Janvin, C. (2003). A neural probabilistic language model. *Journal of Machine Learning Research, 3,* 1137–1155.

Binwahlan, M. S., Salim, N., & Suanmali, L. (2009). Swarm Based Text Summarization. *Proceedings of the 2009 International Association of Computer Science and Information Technology-Spring Conference.* 10.1109/IACSIT-SC.2009.61

Chang, C.-T., Huang, C.-C., & Hsu, J. Y.-j. (2018). *A Hybrid Word-Character Model for Abstractive Summarization.* CoRR, abs/1802.09968

Chen, Q., Zhu, X., Ling, Z., Wei, S., & Jiang, H. (2016). Distraction-based neural networks for modeling documents. *Proceedings of the Twenty-Fifth International Joint Conference on Artificial Intelligence.*

Chopra, S., Auli, M., & Rush, A. M. (2016). Abstractive sentence summarization with attentive recurrent neural networks. *Proceedings of NAACL-HLT*. 10.18653/v1/N16-1012

Cohn, T., & Lapata, M. (2008). Sentence compression beyond word deletion. *Proceedings of the 22nd International Conference on Computational Linguistics*.

Das, D., & Martins, A. F. (2007). A survey on automatic text summarization. *Literature Survey for the Language and Statistics II course at CMU, 4*, 192-195.

Demir, S., Carberry, S., & McCoy, K. F. (2010). A discourse-aware graph-based content-selection framework. *Proceedings of the 6th International Natural Language Generation Conference*.

El-Haj, M., Kruschwitz, U., & Fox, C. *Using Mechanical Turk to Create a Corpus of Arabic Summaries.* Paper presented at the Editors & Workshop Chairs.

Embar, V. R., Deshpande, S. R., Vaishnavi, A., Jain, V., & Kallimani, J. S. (2013). *sArAmsha-A Kannada abstractive summarizer.* Paper presented at the Advances in Computing, Communications and Informatics (ICACCI), 2013 International Conference on.

Fowler, D. S. (2018, Feb 20). *How Many Websites Are There In The World?* Retrieved from https://tekeye.uk/computing/how-many-websites-are-there

Gambhir, M., & Gupta, V. (2016). Recent automatic text summarization techniques: A survey. *Artificial Intelligence Review*, 1–66.

Ganesan, K., Zhai, C., & Han, J. (2010). Opinosis: a graph-based approach to abstractive summarization of highly redundant opinions. *Proceedings of the 23rd international conference on computational linguistics*.

Graff, D., Kong, J., Chen, K., & Maeda, K. (2003). English gigaword. Linguistic Data Consortium, 4(1), 34.

Greenbacker, C. F. (2011). Towards a framework for abstractive summarization of multimodal documents. *Proceedings of the ACL 2011 Student Session*.

Harrag, F., Hamdi-Cherif, A., & Salman Al-Salman, A. (2010). Comparative study of topic segmentation algorithms based on lexical cohesion: Experimental results on Arabic language. *Arabian Journal for Science and Engineering, 35*(2), 183.

Ismail, S., Moawd, I., & Aref, M. (2013). Arabic text representation using rich semantic graph: A case study. *Proceedings of the 4th European conference of computer science (ECCS'13)*.

Ismail, S. S., Aref, M., & Moawad, I. (2013). *Rich semantic graph: A new semantic text representation approach for arabic language.* Paper presented at the 17th WSEAS European Computing Conference (ECC'13).

Jean, S., Cho, K., Memisevic, R., & Bengio, Y. (2014). *On Using Very Large Target Vocabulary for Neural Machine Translation.* CoRR, abs/1412.2007

Jones, K. S. (1999). Automatic summarizing: factors and directions. *Advances in Automatic Text Summarization*, 1-12.

Kabeer, R., & Idicula, S. M. (2014). *Text summarization for Malayalam documents— An experience.* Paper presented at the Data Science & Engineering (ICDSE), 2014 International Conference on.

Kallimani, J. S., Srinivasa, K., & Eswara Reddy, B. (2011). *Information extraction by an abstractive text summarization for an Indian regional language.* Paper presented at the Natural Language Processing andKnowledge Engineering (NLP-KE), 2011 7th International Conference on. 10.1109/NLPKE.2011.6138217

Kleinbauer, T., & Murray, G. (2012). Summarization. In A. Popescu-Belis, H. Bourlard, J. Carletta, & S. Renals (Eds.), *Multimodal Signal Processing: Human Interactions in Meetings* (pp. 170–192). Cambridge, UK: Cambridge University Press. doi:10.1017/CBO9781139136310.010

Korabu, K., & Ingale, M. S. V. (2013). Semantic Summarization Of Web Documents. *International Journal of Computer Science & Communication Networks*, *3*(3), 173.

Kumar, N., Srinathan, K., & Varma, V. (2013). A knowledge induced graph-theoretical model for extract and abstract single document summarization. In *Computational Linguistics and Intelligent Text Processing* (pp. 408–423). Springer. doi:10.1007/978-3-642-37256-8_34

Kunder, M. d. (2018, Dec 15). *The size of the World Wide Web (The Internet).* Retrieved from https://www.worldwidewebsize.com

Le, H. T., & Le, T. M. (2013). *An approach to abstractive text summarization.* Paper presented at the Soft Computing and Pattern Recognition (SoCPaR), 2013 International Conference of. 10.1109/SOCPAR.2013.7054161

Li, P., Lam, W., Bing, L., & Wang, Z. (2017). Deep Recurrent Generative Decoder for Abstractive Text Summarization. *Proceedings of the 2017 Conference on Empirical Methods in Natural Language Processing.* 10.18653/v1/D17-1222

Lin, C.-Y. (2004). ROUGE: A Package for Automatic Evaluation of Summaries. *Text Summarization Branches Out: Proceedings of the ACL-04 Workshop.*

Lin, C.-Y., & Hovy, E. (2000). *The Automated Acquisition of Topic Signatures for Text Summarization.* Paper presented at the COLING 2000 Volume 1: The 18th International Conference on Computational Linguistics. 10.3115/990820.990892

Liu, F., Flanigan, J., Thomson, S., Sadeh, N., & Smith, N. A. (2015). *Toward abstractive summarization using semantic representations.* Academic Press.

Liu, F., & Liu, Y. (2009). From extractive to abstractive meeting summaries: Can it be done by sentence compression? *Proceedings of the ACL-IJCNLP 2009 Conference Short Papers.* 10.3115/1667583.1667664

Lloret, E., & Palomar, M. (2011). Analyzing the use of word graphs for abstractive text summarization. *Proceedings of the First International Conference on Advances in Information Mining and Management.*

Lloret, E., Romá-Ferri, M. T., & Palomar, M. (2013). COMPENDIUM: A text summarization system for generating abstracts of research papers. *Data & Knowledge Engineering, 88,* 164–175. doi:10.1016/j.datak.2013.08.005

McDonald, D. D. (1992). An efficient chart-based algorithm for partial-parsing of unrestricted texts. *Proceedings of the third conference on Applied natural language processing.* 10.3115/974499.974534

McDonald, D. D. (2000). Issues in the representation of real texts: the design of KRISP. *Natural language processing and knowledge representation, 77-110.*

McDonald, D. D., & Greenbacker, C. F. (2010). 'If you've heard it, you can say it': towards an account of expressibility. *Proceedings of the 6th International Natural Language Generation Conference.*

Mehdad, Y., Carenini, G., & Ng, R. T. (2014). Abstractive summarization of spoken and written conversations based on phrasal queries. *Proceedings of the 52nd Annual Meeting of the Association for Computational Linguistics.* 10.3115/v1/P14-1115

Mehdad, Y., Carenini, G., Ng, R. T., & Joty, S. (2013). Towards Topic Labeling with Phrase Entailment and Aggregation. *Proceedings of NAACL-HLT.*

Moawad, I. F., & Aref, M. (2012). *Semantic graph reduction approach for abstractive Text Summarization.* Paper presented at the Computer Engineering & Systems (ICCES), 2012 Seventh International Conference on. 10.1109/ICCES.2012.6408498

Mosa, M. A., Hamouda, A., & Marei, M. (2017). Graph coloring and ACO based summarization for social networks. *Expert Systems with Applications, 74,* 115–126. doi:10.1016/j.eswa.2017.01.010

Nallapati, R., Zhou, B., Gulcehre, C., & Xiang, B. (2016). *Abstractive Text Summarization Using Sequence-to-Sequence RNNs and Beyond.* arXiv preprint arXiv:1602.06023

Napoles, C., Gormley, M., & Van Durme, B. (2012). Annotated gigaword. *Proceedings of the Joint Workshop on Automatic Knowledge Base Construction and Web-scale Knowledge Extraction.*

Nenkova, A. (2006). *Understanding the process of multi-document summarization: Content selection, rewriting and evaluation.* Columbia University.

Over, P., Dang, H., & Harman, D. (2007). DUC in context. *Information Processing & Management, 43*(6), 1506–1520.

Page, L., Brin, S., Motwani, R., & Winograd, T. (1999). *The PageRank citation ranking: bringing order to the Web.* Academic Press.

Paulus, R., Xiong, C., & Socher, R. (2017). *A Deep Reinforced Model for Abstractive Summarization.* CoRR, abs/1705.04304

Rau, L. F., Jacobs, P. S., & Zernik, U. (1989). Information extraction and text summarization using linguistic knowledge acquisition. *Information Processing & Management, 25*(4), 419–428. doi:10.1016/0306-4573(89)90069-1

Rautray, R., & Balabantaray, R. C. (2017). Cat swarm optimization based evolutionary framework for multi document summarization. *Physica A, 477,* 174–186. doi:10.1016/j.physa.2017.02.056

Reimer, U., & Hahn, U. (1988). Text condensation as knowledge base abstraction. *Artificial Intelligence Applications, 1988., Proceedings of the Fourth Conference on.*

Rennie, S. J., Marcheret, E., Mroueh, Y., Ross, J., & Goel, V. (2017). *Self-Critical Sequence Training for Image Captioning.* Paper presented at the 2017 IEEE Conference on Computer Vision and Pattern Recognition (CVPR). 10.1109/CVPR.2017.131

Rush, A. M., Chopra, S., & Weston, J. (2015). *A neural attention model for abstractive sentence summarization.* arXiv preprint arXiv:1509.00685

Saad, S., Moawad, I., & Aref, M. (2011). Ontology-Based Approach for Arabic Text Summarization. *Proceeding of International Conference on Intelligent Computing and Information Systems (ICICIS).*

Sagheer, D., & Sukkar, F. (2017). A Hybrid Intelligent System for Abstractive Summarization. *International Journal of Computers and Applications, 168*(9).

Sankaran, B., Mi, H., Al-Onaizan, Y., & Ittycheriah, A. (2016). *Temporal Attention Model for Neural Machine Translation.* CoRR, abs/1608.02927

See, A., Liu, P. J., & Manning, C. D. (2017). Get To The Point: Summarization with Pointer-Generator Networks. *Proceedings of the 55th Annual Meeting of the Association for Computational Linguistics.* 10.18653/v1/P17-1099

Subramaniam, M., & Dalal, V. (2015). *Test Model for Rich Semantic Graph Representation for Hindi Text using Abstractive Method.* Academic Press.

Summary. (1828). In *Merriam Webster.* Retrieved from http://www.merriam-webster.com/dictionary/summary

Summary. (1989). In *Oxford Dictionaries* Retrieved from https://en.oxforddictionaries.com/definition/summary

Summary. (1995). In *Cambridge Dictionary.* Retrieved from http://dictionary.cambridge.org/dictionary/english/summary

Torres-Moreno, J.-M. (2014). *Automatic text summarization.* John Wiley & Sons. doi:10.1002/9781119004752

Tu, Z., Lu, Z., Liu, Y., Liu, X., & Li, H. (2016). Modeling Coverage for Neural Machine Translation. *Proceedings of the 54th Annual Meeting of the Association for Computational Linguistics.* 10.18653/v1/P16-1008

Vinyals, O., Fortunato, M., & Jaitly, N. (2015). Pointer networks. *Proceedings of the 28th International Conference on Neural Information Processing Systems.*

Woodsend, K., Feng, Y., & Lapata, M. (2010). Generation with quasi-synchronous grammar. *Proceedings of the 2010 Conference on Empirical Methods in Natural Language Processing.*

ADDITIONAL READING

Indurkhya, N., & Damerau, F. J. (2010). *Handbook of natural language processing* (Vol. 2). CRC Press.

Jo, T. (2019). Text Summarization. In *Text Mining* (pp. 271–294). Springer. doi:10.1007/978-3-319-91815-0_13

Kirmani, M., Hakak, N. M., Mohd, M., & Mohd, M. (2019). Hybrid Text Summarization: A Survey. In Soft Computing: Theories and Applications (pp. 63-73): Springer. doi:10.1007/978-981-13-0589-4_7

Marcu, D. (2000). *The theory and practice of discourse parsing and summarization.*

Mihalcea, R., & Radev, D. (2011). *Graph-based natural language processing and information retrieval.* Cambridge university press. doi:10.1017/CBO9780511976247

Poibeau, T., Saggion, H., Piskorski, J., & Yangarber, R. (2012). *Multi-source, multilingual information extraction and summarization.* Springer Science & Business Media.

Pustejovsky, J., & Stubbs, A. (2012). *Natural Language Annotation for Machine Learning: A guide to corpus-building for applications.* O'Reilly Media, Inc.

Raphal, N., Duwarah, H., & Daniel, P. (2018, 3-5 April 2018). *Survey on Abstractive Text Summarization.* Paper presented at the 2018 International Conference on Communication and Signal Processing (ICCSP). 10.1109/ICCSP.2018.8524532

KEY TERMS AND DEFINITIONS

Machine Learning: The study of building systems that learn from itself and are adopted by the environment.

Natural Language Processing: A discipline that is concerned with the interaction between the human natural language and computers.

Rhetorical Structure Theory: Analyzing texts based on relations linking parts of the text.

Semantic Graph: A graph representation of the concepts and their semantic meaning.

Summarizer: A system that reduces the length of a document while preserving its information.

Swarm Intelligence: The study of the behavior and the interaction of agents with each other and with their environment, simulating the nature system.

TF-IDF: Stands for term frequency-inverse document frequency. It measures the frequency of a term in a document and its importance.

Chapter 3
Mining Scientific and Technical Literature:
From Knowledge Extraction to Summarization

Junsheng Zhang
Institute of Scientific and Technical Information of China, China

Wen Zeng
Institute of Scientific and Technical Information of China, China

ABSTRACT

In this chapter, the authors study text mining technologies such as knowledge extraction and summarization on scientific and technical literature. First, they analyze the needs of scientific information services and intelligence analysis on massive scientific and technical literature. Second, terminology recognition and relation extraction are important tasks of knowledge extraction. Third, they study knowledge extraction based on terminology recognition and relation extraction. Fourth, based on terminology and relational network, they study the text summarization techniques and applications. Last, they give comments on current research and applications on text summarization and give their viewpoints for the possible research directions in the future.

DOI: 10.4018/978-1-5225-9373-7.ch003

INTRODUCTION

With the quick development of Internet and social media technologies, we have entered the era of information explosion. Online texts such as news, books, scientific and technical literature, microblogs, blog and production comments have generated and propagated quickly, which has formulate a huge corpus in the Web (Resnik and Smith, 2006). Massive texts make convenience for users to acquire information conveniently; however, information overloading becomes a new challenging problem. Although search engines such Google and Baidu have help users to search information quickly by providing a list of documents as the result, users still have to spend more time to browse and read the returned documents for seeking specific information and understanding the content, for example, the development of a specific event or the tracking of a specific object such as a person and an organization. How to provide brief and enough information for users becomes an urgent problem in big data era. Automatic summarization is a research direction for solving the information overloading problem.

Automatic summarization is to analyze one or more documents by machine and extract important information which is organized into a short and readable text (Gambhir and Gupta, 2017). Summarization is to compress the content of original documents and with the important content left. Users can grasp necessary information by reading the short summary generated by machine and save reading time. There are two ways of summarization generation, one is extractive summarization and the other is abstractive summarization (Gupta and Gupta, 2018).

Extractive summarization is to select important sentences from documents without changing the components of original sentences (Alguliyev et. al, 2018), while abstractive summarization is to generate new sentences based on understanding the content of documents. For extractive summarization, texts of documents have different information units such as section, paragraph, sentences, phrases and words. Extractive summarization approach assigns different weights to different information units via different weighting algorithms, and then select information units with high weights.

Abstractive summarization requires understanding of the text and produce summaries which fuse information from multiple sources effectively. Abstractive summarization needs syntactic and semantic analysis on texts, and then makes information fusion for generating sentences with natural language processing technologies.

Currently, most summarization systems adopt extractive summarization approach, and abstractive summarization technologies are harder than extracting sentences from texts. However, summarization research area has been gaining momentum with the shift towards semantic processing in recent years. An important distinction between abstractive techniques and extractive techniques is that abstractive summarization can use words or phrases that were not present in the original text, while extractive summarization use orginal sentences in the original text. Furthermore, abstractive summaries do not suffer from issues such as redundancy, which is commonly seen in extractive summaries. To overcome problems associated with template-based abstractive summarization techniques, it is important to design data-driven techniques for abstractive summarization such that manual intervention for summary generation can be minimized or completely avoided. Summarization has been applied by researchers using textual data from several domains such as news and social media data. Each of the domains pose different set of challenges.

Besides of extractive summarization and abstractive summarization, there are many classification standards for automatic summarization systems. According to the working objects of automatic summarization systems, there are two types of document summarization, that is, single document summarization and multiple document summarization (Tao et. al, 2008 & Wang et. al, 2011 & Cagliero, Garza, and Baralis, 2019). According to the languages of documents, automatic summarization could be classified into mono-lingual summarization, multilingual summarization (Saggion et. al, 2010) and cross-lingual summarization (Litvak and Last, 2013). According to the functions, automatic summarization systems could be classified into generic and query-focused (Gong and Liu, 2001 & Ouyang et. al, 2011). Researches on automatic text summarization aim to discover approaches and realize the automatic summarization system with high efficiency. Many approaches have been proposed to solve various kinds of problems. Search engines such as Google and Baidu have aggregated search results into a short summary for users to judge the relevance.

Automatic summarization needs to select key points from documents. How to select the key points is the basis of successful automatic summary systems. The research problems are as follows:

- How to represent the *meaning* of documents? There are different information units in documents including word, phrase, sentence, paragraph, section and so on. Various associations exist among different units, and connect information units into a semantically linked network (graph) (Zhang, Sun, and Jara, 2015). The meaning of a document can be represented by a multidimensional vector, a topic set (Harabagiu and Lacatusu, 2005) or a semantic graph (Baralis et. al, 2013).

- How to evaluate the *importance* of information units? The importance of different information units are closely related, that is, important sections include important paragraphs, important paragraphs include important sentences, important sentences include important phrases and words. So it is necessary to study the importance evaluation methods for different units, which is shown as the weight calculating algorithms.

After important information units are identified, automatic summarization systems need to combine the selected information units into a cohesive summary. The generated summary needs good cover rate and readability, and it also needs to satisfy the limitation of length.

Extractive summarization can ensure the readability of sentences but the connections between sentences may be incoherent. Abstractive summarization could generate the compressed sentences, but the coherence is also uncertain. There are some hybrid approaches by combining the extractive summarization and abstractive summarization. Abstractive text summarization can be generated by incorporating reader comments (Gao et. al, 2018).

Evaluation on readability is also important indicator for automatic summarization. The readability has considerable influence on the user experience. The readability considers not only the single sentence but also the cohesion between sentences. However, there is no definite evaluation method for the readability of single sentence and sentence set yet.

The summarization has requirements on coverage and novelty. Novelty needs to reduce redundancy. MMR approach (Maximal Marginal Relevance) is suggested for reducing redundancy (Carbonell and Goldstein, 1998). How to make balance between different requirements are decided by different summarization tasks.

OVERVIEW OF SCIENTIFIC INFORMATION SERVICES AND INTELLIGENCE ANALYSIS

Study on automatic summarization is active in research areas such as library and natural language processing. Library needs to generate abstracts for massive literature, and manual summarization is with low-efficiency. Therefore, automatic summarization is proposed to generate summarization by machines instead of human beings. Usually, scientific research papers have abstracts written by authors. However, it is necessary to generate summary for multi-documents, and sometimes the documents are multilingual. With the development of automatic summarization research, there are many famous summarization systems including *NeATS* of ISI (Lin and Hovy, 2001), *NewsBlaster* from Columbia University (Evans, Klavans, and McKeown, 2004), and *NewsInEssence* from Michigan University (Radey et. al, 2005).

Recent years, information service on information resources has changed from document unit to knowledge unit, from resource providing to content analysis, and from grammatical level to semantic level or pragmatic level. Information resources are classified and organized, which are searched according the query requirements of users. Intelligence analysis, which originates from information, also needs the deepening of intelligence and information content. Scientific and technological intelligence is closely related to strategy and planning of the development of science and technology.

Research and Application on Knowledge Extraction and Document Summarization

Knowledge service needs to extract the knowledge points from the scientific and technical literature first. Knowledge extraction is closely related to knowledge recognition. Knowledge points are recognized from documents with template-based method or machine learning method. Associations exist among knowledge points, and knowledge extraction is to extract knowledge points and establish the associations between these knowledge points.

Knowledge extraction mainly studies how to extract factual knowledge from document content without considering semantic information to formulate the ontology or knowledge graph, while document summarization focuses on how to consolidate single (multiple) document information and solve the problem of information overloading. Knowledge extraction is to extract structured knowledge points from the unstructured documents. Knowledge points are organized into the network structure such as knowledge graph. After knowledge extraction, knowledge points are organized into triple structure such as entity-attribute-value and entity-relation-entity in knowledge graph.

The value of scientific and technical documents is determined by the knowledge implied in the documents. Knowledge in scientific and technical documents may be shown as discovery, fact, method, problem and result. Knowledge extraction aims to extract them from documents by machines automatically. Before knowledge are extracted from documents, extracting rules are necessary which are written by experts or learned by machine learning algorithms. Document summarization is to represent the meaning of one or more documents with short text. According to the set of scientific and technical documents, it is necessary to formulate the summarization from multiple and multi-lingual literature.

Demand for Scientific and Technical Literature Information and Knowledge Service

With the development of information technology, different types and sources of scientific and technical literature resources are increasing, but how to obtain essential knowledge from the complex big data and achieve effective provision of scientific and technical information and knowledge services is a long-term research work. There is an urgent need to extract knowledge from a large number of scientific and technical literature and to provide users with short text using text summarization technology.

Scientific and technical literature records the discovery of human knowledge and the process of technical invention and innovation. Terminologies make different scientific and technical literature from the general documents, which represent the concept and content of science and technology research. Terminologies in scientific and technical literature are gradually formed with the continuous exploration and study of various research fields. Concepts accumulated during the process are defined as terminologies, and terminology is the important objects of information analysis and knowledge extraction. Terminology recognition and relationship extraction are indispensable in the process of scientific and technical literature analysis.

With the quick development of science and technology, scientific and technical literature is generated more quickly than before. With the growth of scientific and technical literature, scientific and technical researchers on the one hand benefit from the convenience and richness of scientific and technical information; on the other hand, they are troubled by the problem of "information overloading". How to retrieve resources more efficiently, analyze and mine semantic information from scientific and technical literature resources, and provide more abundant and diverse information presentation methods are important ways to improve the utilization of scientific and technical literature resources and solve researchers' suffering from information overloading.

While news has received far more attention than scientific literature in the multidocument summarization community, scientific literature represents a challenging and important domain. Generally, scientific literature is more difficult and time-consuming to summarize by hand than news articles. Very few up-to-date, manually generated summaries exist for many areas of scientific research. The creation of such manually generated summaries is so difficult that it often results in publication in the form of a surveys or book chapters. These manually generated summaries are then outdated within a few years. So it is urgent to study the automatic summarization techniques for scientific literature.

Hierarchical summaries for scientific topics could be especially beneficial to fresh researchers and students who are interested in persuing a new topic, but lack guidance on the overarching problems and approaches. Hierarchical summaries could give such researchers and students the basic ideas of the topic and allow them to explore in more detail the areas. Hierarchical summarization mimics how a user with a general interest would interact with a human expert (Christensen, 2015). It first starts with a general overview summary, and then users can click on sentences to learn more about areas of interest. Hierarchical summarization allows for structured output, custom output length, personalization, and interaction.

Figure 1 shows the schematic diagram of the summarization system for scientific and technical literature. Users submit their requirements, and then scientific and technical literature are searched and acquired from digital library and Internet. Data processing is necessary including changing the scientific and technical literature into texts and storing them in database. Terms recognition and relation extraction are

Figure 1. Schematic diagram of the summarization system for scientific and technical literature

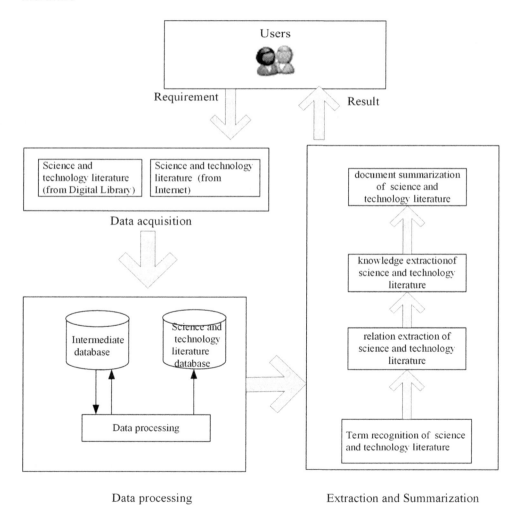

carried out for knowledge extraction. Based on the result of knowledge extraction, document summarization is generated and returned to users.

TERMINOLOGY RECOGNITION AND RELATION EXTRACTION FOR SCIENTIFIC AND TECHNICAL LITERATURE

It is necessary to study the technology of terminology recognition from massive scientific and technical literature. If terminology recognition and relation extraction are operated manually by human, it will reduce the efficiency of terminology acquisition, and cannot meet the requirements of information analysis. Therefore, it is necessary to study automatic terminology recognition and relational extraction techniques with high accuracy and adaptability in different research domains.

Terminology Recognition

There is no unified and standard definition for terminology. Many researchers have put forward their own definitions for terminology. Generally, terminology refers to the collection of terms used to express concepts in the professional research fields, which is closely related to knowledge and concepts in these research fields. Generally speaking, terminology only circulates in one or several fixed research fields. It is only used by researchers in the specific research fields, while common vocabularies are used by researchers from different research fields.

Terminology recognition has been widely used in many research fields, such as information retrieval, machine translation, domain ontology construction (Meijer, Frasincar, and Hogenboom, 2014 & Qu et. al, 2016), automatic text categorization and automatic summarization. Researchers have done many researches on automatic recognition of terminology (Sui, Chen, and Wei, 2003 & Zheng, Zhao, and Yang, 2009).

Currently, the main research methods of term recognition are based on linguistic rules or statistics rules. The method based on linguistic rules is to generate rules according to lexical patterns and semantic information of professional terms and then extract terms from corpus according to these rules. While the statistical method is to use statistical strategies such as mutual information, word frequency, TF-IDF and left-right entropy to make statistics on the features of terminology. In essence, the statistical method is based on linguistic rules implied in the scientific and technical texts.

Statistical-based terminology recognition methods have both advantages and disadvantages. Matching strategy for rule-based terminology recognition is faster than statistical-based terminology recognition approach, while the disadvantage of linguistic rules method is that the rule defined by human is hard to cover the rules to recognize complex terminology, especially the new terminology. Besides, the consistency of rules is difficult to maintain when more and more rules are generated. The statistical-based terminology recognition approach does not depends on specific expertise or domain specific resources, so it is portable or transferable for different research domains, but the process of statistical calculation depends on the large-scale corpus. The single use of linguistic rule-based method or statistics-based method cannot meet the need of high accuracy of automatic terminology extraction, so the combination of the two methods is the main direction in current research.

Terminology recognition system automatically calculates the word frequency of vocabulary in corpus, determines the accuracy of vocabulary extraction through expert verification, and re-imports the modified word frequency results into the system. In addition, the co-occurrence of vocabulary in corpus is calculated so that when the user increases the correlation of the entries, and words with high co-occurrences can be recommended to the user.

Taking term extraction from patents for example, a term bears the following features:

1. A term is a noun phrase.
2. A term does not contain stop words.
3. The length of a term is tow to four words. The length of a candidate term is set according to evaluations by information analysis specialists. If longer terms are allowed, they will introduce too much noise.

In a patent record, three bibliographic sections can be used to extract terms. They are title, abstract, and claims. Claims can be divided into first claim, dependent claim, and independent claim. As the patent records that we have contain only first claim, we discuss first-claim section only in the remaining part of the paper. Figure 2 shows an example of title, abstract, and first claim in a patent record, and we focus on the abstract and first-claim sections for term extraction.

During term extraction, we have the assumption that *if a candidate string appears in both abstract and first claim of the same patent record, it is a candidate term.* After we obtain the candidate term with the assumption, a weighting process is necessary to rank the candidate terms. We calculate the TF-IDF and MI of candidate terms separately. If the TF-IDF or MI value of a candidate term is above the given threshold, it is kept; otherwise, it will be removed from the result set. We do not combine the two values in the paper and represent two separate ranked lists in the experiment part. TF-IDF is a typical weighting method to evaluate the importance of a term from single document and collection perspectives. MI is a commonly used index to evaluate the importance of a term w.r.t. a given class. MI is used because

Figure 2. An example of a patent record

US6664692

TITLE: Electrical machine

ABSTRACT: A slow moving electrical machine includes an annular set of windings on iron cores of laminated sheets or pressed iron powder and a corresponding annular set of permanent magnets the windings being concentrated and the iron cores having windings being arranged alternatingly with iron cores without windings. The machine has a number of grooves between the cores which is different from a number of poles of the permanent magnets the number of grooves s and the number of poles p being defined by $|s - p| = 2 * m$ and $s = 12 * n * m$ where n and m are natural numbers. The machine is constructed and arranged for three phase operation with serial connection of adjacent windings within a group with $2 * m$ groups of windings per phase and with serial or parallel connection of groups of windings.

FIRST CLAIM: Slow moving electrical machine, comprising an annular set of windings on iron cores of laminated sheets or pressed iron powder, and a corresponding annular set of permanent magnets, the windings being concentrated and the machine having a number of grooves between the cores which is different from a number of poles of the permanent magnets, the number of grooves s and the number of poles p being defined by $|s - p| = 2 * m$ and $s = 12 * n * m$, where n and m are natural numbers, the iron cores being arranged such that iron cores having windings alternate with iron cores without windings, the cores being disposed in groups corresponding to three phase operation of the machine with $2 * m$ groups of windings per phase, with adjacent wound cores within a group being connected in series, and groups of cores being connected in series or in parallel.

---

there is class-related information in our patent collection, that is, the five categories provided by information analysis specialist, and MI is able to provide weighting results on class level. We have found there are little differences between MI and chi-squared, and the paper thus reports MI result only.

Figure 3 shows the flowchart to extract patent terms using abstract and first claim. The steps are as follows:

1. After we obtain the three sections, we tag the collection and give every word/ string a Part-of-Speech tag with GENIA Tagger. The Part-of-Speech tag is used to identify noun phrases in the following step.
2. Remove numbers, punctuation marks, and stop words. If a stop word is removed, a blank ('//' in Figure 3) is left. The blank is used for identifying candidate string boundary in the following step.
3. During the process, if a three-word-length string, for example, 'moving electrical machine', is identified, the original two-word-length string 'electrical machine' will be eliminated.
4. Remove candidate phrases (strings) that are not noun phrases.
5. Select candidate terms according to the above assumption.

Figure 3. The flowchart to extract patent terms using abstract and claim

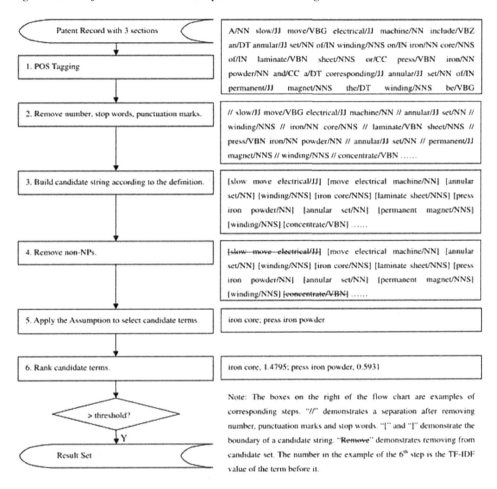

Relation Extraction

The development of the relation extraction method has experienced three stages: (1) Rule Based method. Before the statistical machine learning method be used, the relation extraction task is same as many NLP tasks in the past which developed by experts in a particular field, and extracted by computer. The rule based extraction system developed by experts is highly dependent on the rule itself, which has poor generalization performance, and is too simple or complex to produce an ideal effect. So the rule based relation extraction method is not popular for a long time. (2) Traditional machine learning method. With the rapid development of machine learning, many NLP fields, including relation extraction, have begun to use the machine learning algorithm actively. At the beginning, there are only a small amount of machine learning based systems. But soon it found that machine learning based system are good to the traditional rule based system in precision,generalization performance and running efficiency. So the machine learning method became the main method of relation extraction in a very short time. (3) Open information extraction. With the development of the Internet, the text information on the Internet has become the main target of relation extracting. The Internet contains massive and complex data, how to make use of these un-labeled texts and improve the generalization of the relation extraction system on the large scale is the main challenge of relation extraction task. In such environment, a lot of unsupervised and semi-supervised methods have been proposed. In addition, the distance supervised method based on knowledge bases like Freebase, Wiki is also worthy of attention.

- Traditional machine learning method

The basic idea of the traditional machine learning method is to transform the relation extraction problem into a binary classification problem, and then training the supervised system with labeled text. Further, the supervised methods of relation extraction are divided into features based method and kernel method. Feature based method is needed to manually set the feature matrix of text, and the kernel method dose not. The Feature based method may have better results in some specific areas.

The process of dealing with the problem of relation extraction with machine learning method is divided into the following steps:

1. Find sentences that contain relation entity in the texts. Giving a sentence S = $group_1$ (ws_1 e_1 ws_2 e_2 ws_3 R), $group_2$ (ws_1 e_1 ws_2 e_2 ws_3 R) ..., where e_1 and e_2 are the entities, ws_1, ws_2 and ws_3 are the word sequences around the entities.
2. Transform the relation groups into corresponding feature matrix, F(group).
3. Set a hypothesis h(F(group)), if the value of h() is positive means that the group have relation R, otherwise have not.

In this way, we transform the task of extracting relation into the task that identifies a specific relation in sentence. We use a number of text with positive and negative labels as the training data, and construct the supervised relation extraction system using SVM, Logistic or other binary classifiers.

- Open information relation extraction

Modern relation extraction system mostly using traditional supervised learning method to extract relations. The main problem of this system is difficult to be obtained with a large number of labeled training data. ACE conference provides 17000 training data for relation extraction problem; however, such a small number of training samples in the extraction of a variety of complex type of relation is very difficult to get a good result. In the face of the requirement of Internet information extraction application, scholars begin to transfer the research object from the traditional limited texts to the open information on the Internet. The goal is to use the massive, redundant, unstructured texts on the Internet which contains a lot of noise to train the relation extraction model, so we can use the system to extract new unstructured texts. Open information relation extraction system has the following features compared to the traditional relation extraction system.

1. A variety of text types, the extracting object is not limited to a single text field, such as newspaper text, but directly deal with multiple types of text on the Internet.
2. A variety of relation types, transform the "relation identification" which can only deal with a single relation in the past to "relation extraction" which can deal with a variety of relation types.
3. A variety of characters, we can use entities, relationships, time and other semantic element to identify and extract relations.

However, it is hard to directly use these unstructured data which contain a lot of noise as the training sample. so people put forward a variety of unsupervised and semi-supervised machine learning methods to try to extracting relations from the big data. In addition, there is a distant supervised learning method which would like to use the open knowledge base with millions of relation samples, such as Freebase and Wikipedia, to train relation extraction model. For example, each concept on Wiki has some manual labeled information in InfoBox. The basic assume is that the description text of wiki concept contain some relations in potential, so we can use the relation type written in InfoBox to automatically label the description text, thereby solving the problem of insufficient training data. The WOE relation extraction system, which is developed by University of Washington, is based on the Wikipedia as the goal, to extract the relations. Next, we will discuss some semi-supervised methods, they have gradually become the common algorithm of relation extraction field.

Most of existing research on relation extraction of terminology from scientific literature mainly focuses on the acquisition of hierarchical relations of mono-lingual terminologies. In China, the research on acquisition of hierarchical relations of terms is less. Most of this kind of research work can only deal with existing words. Hierarchical relationship between terminologies obtained by clustering method cannot be automatically obtained because the number of clustering hierarchies needs to be determined manually. The main methods for acquiring hierarchical relationships of monolingual terminologies mainly are as follows:

1. Utilizing linguistic knowledge method is to use existing linguistic knowledge or semantic resources, extract terminology and internal relationship through knowledge matching. This method includes dictionary matching method and lexical-syntactic pattern recognition method. The lexicon-based approach is to find broader terms of a given terminology by mining the regularity of the definition of terminology in a dictionary, while the lexical-syntactic approach is to automatically find the broader terms from given documents. The disadvantage of this method is that it often neglects the relationship between new terminologies, because the predefined semantic resources are limited, and templates need to be manually formulated. The acquisition of patterns has a great impact on the acquisition effect, and the domain extensibility is not good.
2. The idea of co-occurrence analysis is that if two terminologies often appear in the same document, paragraph or sentence, there may be a relationship between the two terminologies. This method based on co-occurrence analysis has a good effect in judging whether there is a relationship between terminologies, and it is the basis for acquiring deep semantic relations.
3. Using the method of distribution hypothesis. Distribution hypothesis is also called Harris hypothesis. The main idea of distribution hypothesis is that if the context of two words is similar, then the two words are similar. The two methods to acquire terminology hierarchy based on distribution hypothesis are hierarchical clustering method and Formal Concept Analysis (FCA) method. Hierarchical clustering method is difficult to obtain clustering labels, while FCA method is difficult to deal with the situation of many terminologies in the documents.
4. Hybrid method integrates the above three methods, namely, obtaining hierarchical relations by hierarchical clustering or formal conceptual analysis, and combining linguistic methods, such as referring to matching dictionaries or syntactic patterns to obtain hierarchical labels.

KNOWLEDGE EXTRACTIONS FOR SCIENTIFIC AND TECHNICAL LITERATURE

In scientific and technical activities, the reading, analysis and reference of scientific and technical literature is an important part of scientific and technical research. Nowadays, with the expansion and richness of literature, in-depth knowledge mining and extraction from massive scientific and technical literature by computers automatically can provide better information support for scientific researchers, which is of great significance to the development of science and technology.

Knowledge Extraction Methods Based Terminology

Terminology has become an essential tool for researchers to carry out scientific and technical exchanges and academic research. Terminology acts as a starting point to study and elaborate the methods and techniques from knowledge description, knowledge organization to knowledge extraction. Current knowledge extraction methods are basically based on vocabulary. Vocabulary, as the most illustrative and key vocabulary representing the content characteristics of data resources, is the basis for effective and fast retrieval of data resources. Taking thesaurus as an example, thesaurus achieves the indexing and organization of data information resources by establishing a glossary of terms, as well as the relationships among use, generation, subordination, division and reference of terms. Knowledge extraction is based on the terminology structure, and relationships between terminologies.

Terminological Structural Framework Design

- *Vocabulary*: Core Word, Foundation Word.
- *Definition*: On average, each core vocabulary has one definition.
- *Relations*: Synonym relation is symmetrical and transitive; genera are asymmetrical and they are transitive under the same father-class; correlation relations is symmetrical and generally non-transitive.
- *Classification mapping*: Multidimensional classification mapping can be set according to the related classification method settings.
- *Attribute*: According to the specific field and knowledge service requirements.

Design of Relationship Between Terminologies

- *Synonymy*: synonymy, antonym.
- *Hierarchical*: genera, partOf, cases.
- *Correlation*

Semantic Relation Expression and Semantic Promotion of Terminologies

The semantic description of terminology is equivalent to the description of knowledge, including vocabulary, vocabulary definition and the relationship between vocabularies.

However, for comprehensive, multi-domain knowledge extraction, it is necessary to establish unified standards and norms for knowledge organization semantics and interoperability implementation, so as to enhance and realize the ability of data sharing among systems to be understood at the level of fully defined domain concepts, specifically involving the expression mode of vocabulary concepts and synonymous concepts attribution. And with the semantic standardization, ambiguity concepts processing and other technical means.

Relation Extraction

Message Understanding Conferences (MUC) was held by the U.S. Defense Advanced Research Projects Agency (DARPA) for the information extraction and data mining task. MUC from 1987 to 1998 for a total of 7 times, mainly discussed and evaluated five text extraction problems (Grishman and Sundheim, 1996), which are Named Entity Recognition, co-reference eliminating, template element filling (like entity extracting), template relation filling, scenario template filling (like event extracting). The template relation filling task introduced in 1998 is similar to the current relation extraction task. After 1998, the evaluation task of the information extraction is transferred to ACE (Automatic Content Extraction) meeting, ACE meeting defined the task of relation extraction for relation detection and recognition (RDR) and provided some corpus for training and testing. In the past 30 years, many of the ideas and methods of relation extraction are proposed and discussed at the two meetings, which promote the rapid development of this research field.

The development of the relation extraction method has experienced three stages: (1) Rule-based method. Before the statistical machine learning method be used, the relation extraction task is same as many NLP tasks in the past which developed by experts in a particular field, and extracted by computer. The rule based extraction system developed by experts (Zelenko, Aone, and Richardella, 2003), is highly dependent on the rule itself, which has poor generalization performance, and is too simple or complex to produce an ideal effect. So the rule-based relation extraction method is not popular for a long time. (2) Traditional machine learning method. With the rapid development of machine learning, many NLP fields, including relation extraction, have begun to use the machine learning algorithm actively. At the beginning, there are only a small amount of machine learning based systems (Vogt and Miller, 1998). But soon it was found that machine learning based system are better than traditional rule-based system in precision, generalization performance and running efficiency. So the machine learning method became the popular method of relation extraction. (3) Open information extraction. With the development of the Internet, the text information on the Internet has become the main target of relation extracting. The Internet contains massive and complex data, how to make use of these un-labeled texts and improve the generalization of the relation extraction system on the large scale is the main challenge of relation extraction task. In such environment, a lot of unsupervised and semi supervised methods have been proposed. In addition, the distance supervised method based on knowledge bases like Freebase, Wiki is also worthy of attention.

Application of Knowledge Extraction Technology in Scientific and Technical Literature

There are many types of scientific and technological documents, and the characteristics of texts are different. The specific methods of knowledge extraction will be different. This section introduces a knowledge extraction method for scientific and technical policy text data, which mainly refers to terminology extraction and terminology-based scientific and technical policy text content extraction (Zeng, Yao, and Li, 2017). Typical features of terminology in the field of scientific and technical policy are as follows:

1. Headwords are ubiquitous. The headword refers to the basic terminology frequently appearing in scientific and technical policy texts. Most non-singular terminologies are noun structures or predicate structures composed of headwords.
2. Connection structure. In terms of scientific and technical policy, there are some special terminologies which are connected by symbols between morphemes.
3. Data is sparse. Because of the size of the corpus, many terms appear only once or a few times.
4. The phenomenon of terminology nesting is obvious. A terminology consisting of multiple words is a combination of a single terminology, which makes these terminologies nested.

The technical process of terminology extraction is as follows:

1. Text preprocessing includes word segmentation and stop word deletion.
2. Rule filtering is to filter candidate terms by setting word collocation rules and remove words that do not meet the conditions.
3. C-VALUE calculates terminology degree. Terminology degree is a measure of the degree of relevance of a word to the field, and is a statistical metric characteristic of a term. The candidate terms filtered by word collocation rules in the previous step are added to the personal dictionary of NLPIR word segmentation system. The C-VALUE method is used to calculate the

terminology degree of candidate terms, and then a threshold is set to screen candidate terms through this threshold.

To measure the weight of each terminology in a sentence, this is because the sentence contains not only actual meaningful words, but also some stop words and meaningless function words. Terminology is a collection of professional concepts in the field. In theory, the terminology in a sentence contains the main idea of a sentence. In this section, we use TF-IDF to measure the weight of words. The calculation method of TF is to calculate the frequency of each terminology appearing in the whole document. The calculation method of IDF is to divide the total number of sentences by the number of sentences containing the term and then take logarithm. Content-based sentence weight calculation methods are as follows:

$$S_c\left(S_i\right) = \frac{\sum_{j=1}^{n} w\left(t_j\right)}{Len\left(S_i\right)}$$

Len (Si) denotes the number of terms in a sentence. w (t_j) is the TF-IDF value of terminologies in a sentence. This formula calculates and sums the TF-IDF value of each terminology t_j in the sentence S_i, divides it by the number of terminologies in the sentence, and the result is the mean value, so the calculation shows that the importance value of the sentence is irrelevant to the length of the sentence.

Similarity is calculated based on vector space model. Vector space model (VSM) is the most commonly used sentence and document similarity measurement model. Its advantage is that it uses statistical methods to solve semantic problems based on linear model, and its calculation method is simple and efficient. Based on the principle of VSM, each sentence and title is segmented by a dictionary formed by a terminology library, and the sentence and title are represented by the vector of the word it contains, that is, the feature item. After each sentence and its corresponding title are represented by the vector of the feature item, the angle between the vector of the sentence and its corresponding title is calculated. The smaller the angle between the vector, the higher the similarity between the title and the sentence. The cosine theorem can be used to calculate the similarity between sentences and titles as follows:

$$Sim\left(S_i, T\right) = \frac{S_i * T}{S_i * T}$$

Here, S_i refers to the vector of the sentence and T refers to the vector of the title.

GENERATION OF TEXT SUMMARIZATION FOR SCIENTIFIC AND TECHNICAL LITERATURE

According to the characteristics of scientific and technical literature, this section studies the technology and algorithm of automatic summarization, mine knowledge, and explore the organization and presentation of knowledge.

Text Summarization of Documents

Text summarization is a kind of information extraction technology. It aims to analyze the structure and content of text, model the dependencies of different text units (such as sentences or words), mine salient or representative text units, and reorganize them into more refined and representative summaries. Text summarization requires that the newly generated summary meets three requirements: high coverage, strong representativeness and low redundancy.

Automatic text summarization technology is to automatically extract abstracts from natural language texts by computer. Abstracts are concise and representative sentences, which contain the core content of the text or the content that users are interested in. More valuable sentences can be used as abstractive sentences in summarization, but the method of automatic abstraction is complex. In order to make the abstractive sentences output in the way of semantic coherence, we consider not only whether the sentences are more valuable and can express the central meaning of the text, but also the generality, length and relevance of the sentences.

The segmented document has a certain structure, which is generally divided into hierarchical structure including chapter, section, paragraph and sentence. For the processing of structured semi-structured documents, we mainly use segmentation procedures to segment documents according to the organizational order. For example, taking sections, paragraphs and sentences as examples, we can divide a document into sections, one section contains several paragraphs, and each paragraph is divided into several sentences. When sentences are extracted, we first need to define a set of feature templates to extract possible candidate words for expressing text fragments according to these features. The setting of the feature template mainly refers to the following factors:

1. The title of the document, chapter, section and paragraph, and the words in the title window will generally give a general description of the content of the whole text, chapter and paragraph.
2. The beginning and end of each structural segment, and the beginning and end of the paragraph generally describe the main content of this paragraph.

3. Substantive words. The words in the entity word window may contain the characteristics of expressing the content of the paragraph.
4. Special symbol intervals. Structured articles of some textbook categories will divide a separate paragraph before the beginning of the paragraph and generalize the content described in this paragraph into words with special symbols such as brackets.

For knowledge-intensive text fragments, the description of knowledge in a single-text document is limited. Although the structure of content representation is hierarchical and conceptually inclusive, it is still unable to avoid the limitations of knowledge description in a single document and to reflect the latest description of knowledge in the whole domain. Generally, people rely on a lot of manual work to classify, edit and organize knowledge. There is no effective knowledge description and feature extraction mechanism for knowledge-intensive text fragments. The renewal of knowledge mainly depends on manual work, which cannot meet the needs of a large number of knowledge-intensive text fragments for the renewal of knowledge representation.

Application of Text Summarization Technology

Automatic text summarization has four steps: content representation, weight calculating, content selection and content organization. Each sentence contains many words, and the weight of the sentences is determined by the weights of the words in this sentence. The frequency of a word is related to the weight of the word. TF-IDF is used to calculate the weight of words in a document or corpus. After the weights of words are calculated, the vectors of sentences are constructed which use all the words as the dimensions of the sentence vectors. The vectors of sentences are used to calculate the similarities between sentences. Cosine similarity is often used to measure the similarity between sentences. Each sentence acts as a node, similarity between two sentences acts as an edge, and then the similarity graph is formulated. Furthermore, the weights of sentences are calculated in the similar graph by iterative algorithm. Sentences with high weights are selected from the semantic linked network of sentences and ordered with the sequence in the original documents to formulate the summarization.

Event-based summarization of scientific literature has been studied (Zhang, Li, and Yao, 2018). Each scientific and technical literature is regarded as a scientific research event, whose elements are distributed in the full text of scientific literature. Scientific research event elements include 5W1H: *when, where, who, what, how* and *why*. When, where, who and what are corresponding to publication time, publication venue, authors and title which are essential parts of metadata of scientific and technical literature. Why are represented by research problems that implies the research motivation, and how is represented by methods and results. Research problem, method and result need to be extracted from full text of scientific and technical literature. Scientific research events could be constructed into a semantic link network for intelligence analysis (Zhang, Sun, and Yao, 2017 & Zhang et. al, 2016). To extract why and how, it is necessary to classify sentences into four classes: problem, method, result and others. Problem typed sentence explains the research problem of the scientific literature; Method typed sentence explains the research method(s) during the research; Result typed sentence explains the results of the research; and other types sentences contain all the sentences that are not problem, method or result typed sentences.

Figure 4 shows the process to generate the event-based summarization for scientific and technical literature.

TextRank algorithm is used to calculate the weights of sentences. Each sentence in scientific and technical literature has an event element type. The top-k weighted sentences in the same event element type are selected as the candidate sentences in automatic summary. k is the number of sentences in automatic summary.

Figure 5 shows the comparing results including original abstracts in the paper and the automatic summary extracted from the full text. The event-based summary includes elements such as authors, publication venue, publication time, problem, method and result. The structured event-based summary could help users to know the contents with more details quickly with different event elements.

Figure 4. The process to generate the event-based summarization

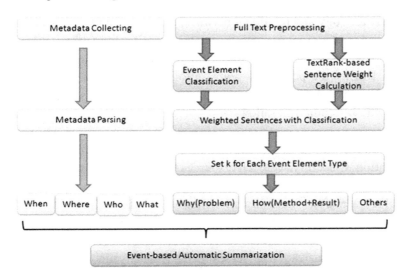

Figure 5. Comparison between automatic summary and manual abstract (in Chinese)

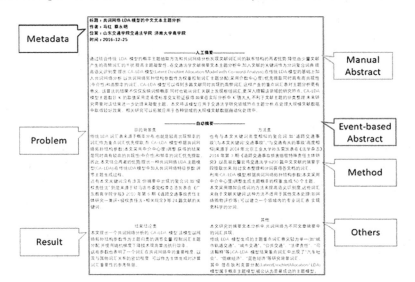

CONCLUSION AND FUTURE WORK

In this chapter, we study text mining technologies such as knowledge extraction and summarization on scientific and technical literature. First, we analyze the needs of scientific information services and intelligence analysis on massive scientific and technical literature. Second, we introduce terminology recognition and relation extraction which are important tasks of knowledge extraction. Third, we study knowledge extraction based on terminology recognition and relation extraction. Based on terminology and relational network, we study on the text summarization techniques and applications, especially on the scientific literature.

Automatic summarization is an important research direction in natural language processing. During the past sixty years, automatic summarization research have achieved many research development; however, there are some key outbreak technologies to be studied as follows:

1.   Multilingual corpus construction for automatic summarization training and evaluation. Currently, research resources for automatic summarization are not enough including data, tools and systems. Evaluation data set provided by DUC and TAC are in English and with little scale. This will have influence on the accuracy, and it is far from the requirement for statistical learning especially for the deep learning. For other languages, the learning and evaluation resources for automatic summarization are less, which has greatly hindered the development

of automatic summarization in these languages. Therefore, the research field needs more input to construct the multi-lingual automatic summarization resources.

2. The automatic evaluation method for automatic summarization. Evaluation methods of automatic summarization need further improvement, especially the automatic evaluation. Although n-gram based Rouge evaluation method has been widely used, it has continuous voices of doubt. Therefore, automatic summarization research needs more reasonable evaluation method, which will satisfy personalized requirements for automatic summarization.

3. Natural language based summarization generation. Summarization generation needs to satisfy the manual abstract by human being. However, automatic generation like human being will be the ultimate of automatic summarization. Current summarization methods select important sentences according to the statistical information or positions of sentences in documents, which are shallow information. Semantics between sentences and the cohesive structure of sentences need more attractions during automatic summarization, which will lead to the abstractive summarization generation.

4. Automatic survey generation is a special type of automatic summarization, which can be used in news report, literature review of scholarly publication, public opinion on the web. Comparing with the typical automatic summarization, the automatic survey is longer, and systematic logic and local cohesion are considered. Automatic survey generation will be prosperous and widely used in different applications.

5. Cross-lingual automatic summarization is a type of automatic summarization in multi-lingual scenarios. Cross-lingual automatic summarization depends on the quality of machine translation systems. Commonly used language could be used as the axis language to solve the sparsity of language resources of minor type of languages. Cross-lingual, mono-lingual and multi-lingual automatic summarization are frequently used in the scenarios of multilingual information analysis such as scientific and technological intelligence studies.

6. Multimodal summarization is to formulate summarization from information resources in multimodal formats such as texts, images, videos and audios. Deep learning has achieved great success in speech recognition, image recognition and computer vision. Therefore, multimodal summarization will become attracting applications in the near future.

7. Question-Answer oriented automatic summarization. Keyword based search engines have been becoming natural language based search engine. For the questions focusing on why and how, it is hard to answer with a phrase or a sentence. These kinds of questions need to extract and integrate information

from single-document or multiple-documents together with the event-based summarization.

8.   Viewpoint oriented automatic summarization will become a type summarization with the sentimental analysis and human-machine dialogue.

With the development of semantic analysis, discourse analysis and deep learning technologies, automatic summarization will make great process in the near future and it will combine with more intelligent Internet applications.

REFERENCES

Alguliyev, R. M., Aliguliyev, R. M., Isazade, N. R., Abdi, A., & Idris, N. (2018). COSUM: Text summarization based on clustering and optimization. *Expert Systems: International Journal of Knowledge Engineering and Neural Networks*.

Baralis, E., Cagliero, L., Mahoto, N., & Fiori, A. (2013). GRAPHSUM: Discovering correlations among multiple terms for graph-based summarization. *Information Sciences*, *249*, 96–109. doi:10.1016/j.ins.2013.06.046

Cagliero, L., Garza, P., & Baralis, E. (2019). ELSA: A Multilingual Document Summarization Algorithm Based on Frequent Itemsets and Latent Semantic Analysis. *ACM Transactions on Information Systems*, *37*(2), 21. doi:10.1145/3298987

Carbonell, J., & Goldstein, J. (1998, August). The use of MMR, diversity-based reranking for reordering documents and producing summaries. In *Proceedings of the 21st annual international ACM SIGIR conference on Research and development in information retrieval* (pp. 335-336). ACM. 10.1145/290941.291025

Christensen, J. M. (2015). *Towards large scale summarization* (Doctoral dissertation). University of Washington.

Evans, D. K., Klavans, J. L., & McKeown, K. R. (2004, May). Columbia newsblaster: Multilingual news summarization on the web. In *Demonstration Papers at HLT-NAACL 2004* (pp. 1–4). Association for Computational Linguistics. doi:10.3115/1614025.1614026

Gambhir, M., & Gupta, V. (2017). Recent automatic text summarization techniques: A survey. *Artificial Intelligence Review*, *47*(1), 1–66. doi:10.100710462-016-9475-9

Gao, S., Chen, X., Li, P., Ren, Z., Bing, L., Zhao, D., & Yan, R. (2018). *Abstractive Text Summarization by Incorporating Reader Comments*. arXiv preprint arXiv:1812.05407.

Gong, Y., & Liu, X. (2001) Generic text summarization using relevance measure and latent semantic analysis. *Proceedings of the 24st annual international ACM SIGIR conference on research and development in information retrieval*, 19–25. 10.1145/383952.383955

Grishman, R., & Sundheim, B. (1996, August). Message Understanding Conference-6: A Brief History. In COLING (Vol. 96, pp. 466-471). Academic Press.

Gupta, S., & Gupta, S. K. (2018). Abstractive Summarization: An Overview of the State of the Art. *Expert Systems with Applications*, *121*, 49–65. doi:10.1016/j.eswa.2018.12.011

Harabagiu, S., & Lacatusu, F. (2005, August). Topic themes for multi-document summarization. In *Proceedings of the 28th annual international ACM SIGIR conference on Research and development in information retrieval* (pp. 202-209). ACM.

Lin, C. Y., & Hovy, E. (2001, August). Neats: A multidocument summarizer. *Proceedings of the Document Understanding Workshop.*

Litvak, M., & Last, M. (2013). Cross-lingual training of summarization systems using annotated corpora in a foreign language. *Information Retrieval*, *16*(5), 629–656. doi:10.100710791-012-9210-3

Meijer, K., Frasincar, F., & Hogenboom, F. (2014). A semantic approach for extracting domain taxonomies from text. *Decision Support Systems*, *62*, 78–93. doi:10.1016/j.dss.2014.03.006

Ouyang, Y., Li, W., Li, S., & Lu, Q. (2011). Applying regression models to query-focused multi-document summarization. *Information Processing & Management*, *47*(2), 227–237. doi:10.1016/j.ipm.2010.03.005

Qu, P., Zhang, J., Yao, C., & Zeng, W. (2016). Identifying long tail term from large-scale candidate pairs for big data-oriented patent analysis. *Concurrency and Computation*, *28*(15), 4194–4208. doi:10.1002/cpe.3792

Radev, D., Otterbacher, J., Winkel, A., & Blair-Goldensohn, S. (2005). NewsInEssence: Summarizing online news topics. *Communications of the ACM*, *48*(10), 95–98. doi:10.1145/1089107.1089111

Resnik, P., & Smith, N. A. (2006). The web as a parallel corpus. *Computational Linguistics*, *29*(3), 349–380. doi:10.1162/089120103322711578

Saggion, H., Torres-Moreno, J. M., Cunha, I. D., & SanJuan, E. (2010, August). Multilingual summarization evaluation without human models. In *Proceedings of the 23rd International Conference on Computational Linguistics*: Posters (pp. 1059-1067). Association for Computational Linguistics.

Sui, Z., Chen, Y., & Wei, Z. (2003, October). Automatic recognition of Chinese scientific and technological terms using integrated linguistic knowledge. In *Natural Language Processing and Knowledge Engineering, 2003. Proceedings. 2003 International Conference on* (pp. 444-451). IEEE.

Tao, Y., Zhou, S., Lam, W., & Guan, J. (2008) Towards more text summarization based on textual association networks. *Proceedings of the 2008 fourth international conference on semantics, knowledge and grid*, 235–240. 10.1109/SKG.2008.17

Vogt, P. F., & Miller, M. J. (1998). Development and applications of amino acid-derived chiral acylnitroso hetero Diels-Alder reactions. *Tetrahedron*, *54*(8), 1317–1348. doi:10.1016/S0040-4020(97)10072-2

Wang, D., Zhu, S., Li, T., Chi, Y., & Gong, Y. (2011). Integrating document clustering and multidocument summarization. *ACM Transactions on Knowledge Discovery from Data*, *5*(3), 1–26. doi:10.1145/1993077.1993078

Zelenko, D., Aone, C., & Richardella, A. (2003). Kernel methods for relation extraction. *Journal of Machine Learning Research*, *3*(Feb), 1083–1106.

Zeng, W., Yao, C., & Li, H. (2017). The exploration of information extraction and analysis about science and technology policy in China. *The Electronic Library*, *35*(4), 709–723. doi:10.1108/EL-10-2016-0235

Zhang, J., Li, K., & Yao, C. (2018). Event-based Summarization for Scientific Literature in Chinese. *Procedia Computer Science*, *129*, 88–92. doi:10.1016/j. procs.2018.03.052

Zhang, J., Sun, Y., & Jara, A. J. (2015). Towards semantically linked multilingual corpus. *International Journal of Information Management*, *35*(3), 387–395. doi:10.1016/j.ijinfomgt.2015.01.004

Zhang, J., Sun, Y., & Yao, C. (2017). Semantically linking events for massive scientific literature research. *The Electronic Library*, *35*(4), 724–744. doi:10.1108/ EL-09-2016-0198

Zhang, J., Yao, C., Sun, Y., & Fang, Z. (2016). Building text-based temporally linked event network for scientific big data analytics. *Personal and Ubiquitous Computing*, *20*(5), 743–755. doi:10.100700779-016-0940-x

Zheng, D., Zhao, T., & Yang, J. (2009, March). Research on domain term extraction based on conditional random fields. In *International Conference on Computer Processing of Oriental Languages* (pp. 290-296). Springer. 10.1007/978-3-642-00831-3_27

Chapter 4
Data Text Mining Based on Swarm Intelligence Techniques:
Review of Text Summarization Systems

Mohamed Atef Mosa
Institute of Public Administration, Department of Information Technology, Riyadh, Saudi Arabia
National Authority for Remote Sensing and Space Sciences, Cairo, Egypt

ABSTRACT

Due to the great growth of data on the web, mining to extract the most informative data as a conceptual brief would be beneficial for certain users. Therefore, there is great enthusiasm concerning the developing automatic text summary approaches. In this chapter, the authors highlight using the swarm intelligence (SI) optimization techniques for the first time in solving the problem of text summary. In addition, a convincing justification of why nature-heuristic algorithms, especially ant colony optimization (ACO), are the best algorithms for solving complicated optimization tasks is introduced. Moreover, it has been perceived that the problem of text summary had not been formalized as a multi-objective optimization (MOO) task before, despite there are many contradictory objectives in needing to be achieved. The SI has not been employed before to support the real-time tasks. Therefore, a novel framework of short text summary has been proposed to fulfill this issue. Ultimately, this chapter will enthuse researchers for further consideration for SI algorithms in solving summary tasks.

DOI: 10.4018/978-1-5225-9373-7.ch004

INTRODUCTION

The need for text summarization has often evolved with the growth of information and publishing on the web. An immense amount of data is being produced day by day as a result of the interactions and interchange of knowledge among users on internet platforms. Which makes it an extremely difficult process to nominate the most relevant, important information. To outdo the problems of information explosion, automatic text summary has become a necessity. The task of summarization minimizes the exertion time required to highlight the most informative sentences. Generally, a summary can be characterized as a text that is generated from one or more texts that reveals the important information in the original text while being short. The field of automatic summarization is over fifty years of age[1].

Since the summarization issue had been introduced a long time ago, it was solved by several algorithms. Nonetheless, few researchers have been persisted for solving text summarization using swarm intelligence (SI) algorithms. This chapter aims to motivate swarm intelligence techniques to be employed in the future for solving summarization tasks which have proven their effectiveness in other several areas. In addition, the authors have highlighted the state-of-the-art papers that have been used in summarizing the content of social media effectively (Mosa, Hamouda, &Marei, 2017a; Gambhir & Gupta, 2017).

On the other hand, as far as we know, there is not any reviews or surveys about automatic summarization using SI techniques presented antecedently. Only some surveys have reviewed some of the approaches that have presented summarization tasks based on other conventional techniques except SI4, 5. It intends to show a general figure of an automatic summary of text by investigating many existing studies that have been developed based on SI techniques. Additionally, the authors have been addressed the utilized evaluation strategies, the outcomes, and the differently related corpora. Besides, they suggested a generic framework for future work.

TYPES OF TEXT SUMMARIZATION

Single/multi-documents and short text are the three important categories of the summary. The task of generating a brief from many documents is more complicated than the extraction the information from the single document. The main problem appears in summarizing several documents together, particularly in a huge amount of short text. Some researchers suggested with regard to the redundancy to pick the sentences that are at the beginning of the paragraph and then measuring the similarity with the later sentences to select the best one (Sarkar, 2019). Therefore, the Maximal Marginal Relevance approach (MMR) is proposed by (Mosa, Hamouda, & Marei,

2017b) to reduce the redundancy. To produce the optimal results in multi-document and short text summarization, several researchers have investigated diverse systems and algorithms to generate an optimal summary (Mosa et al., 2017a; Gambhir & Gupta, 2017; Liu, Chen, & Tseng, 2015; Al-Dhelaan, 2015).

Besides, the summarization task can also be categorized as an abstractive or extractive task. An extractive summary is a process of how to select the most important sentences from the original text based on the length of the summary. Some good features and scores are assigned to sentences in the original text and then the sentences that have the highest score are chosen to constitute the final summary. Whereas an abstractive summary is a task of producing new other derived words that do not appear within the original text after the paraphrasing process. Therefore, it is more complicated than extractive type. Additionally, summarization can also be classified into two types: generic-summary or query-summary (Ouyang, Li, Li, & Lu, 2011).

On the other hand, summarization can be unsupervised or supervised task (Fattah & Ren, 2009; Riedhammer, Fav, & Hakkani-Tur, 2010). A supervised system needs the training data for selecting the most important content. In the training phase, the algorithm needs a large amount of annotated data for learning. These approaches are labelled to positive and negative samples according to an occurrence of the sentence in the summary or not (Mosa et al., 2017a; Chali & Hasan, 2012). Some popular classification methods are employed to accomplish sentence classification tasks, such as decision tree (DT) 14, support vector machine (SVM) (Ouyang et al., 2011) and neural networks[10] (Fattah & Ren, 2009). In contrast, unsupervised systems do not demand any training data. The final output of the summary is just generated by accessing only the original text. Thus, they are more suitable for any newly observed data lacking any sophisticated adjustments. Some systems apply swarm and heuristic rules to extract highly relevant summary (Gambhir & Gupta, 2017; Fattah & Ren, 2009; Binwahlan & Suanmali, 2009a, 2009b, 2009c, 2009d).

On the other hand, concerning language, there are three kinds of summaries: monolingual, multilingual and cross-lingual summaries (Franco-Salvador, Rosso, & Montes-y-Gómez, 2016). If the language of the original source and the summary document is the same, it's a monolingual summarization system. When the document has more than one language like Arabic and English, the summary finally has just one language, then it is named as a multilingual summarization system. But when the original document is in the English language and the summary is in Arabic or any other language except for the English, then it is named as a cross-lingual summarization system.

SWARM INTELLIGENCE OVERVIEW

A swarm is a vast number of homogenous, simple agents interplaying locally between themselves, and their environment, with no centric control to permit a global interesting behaviour to emerge. SI algorithms have recently emerged from a family of nature-inspired, population methods that are capable of producing robust solutions for many complex problems (Panigrahi, Shi, & Lim, 2011). SI can, therefore, be defined as a relatively new branch of Artificial Intelligence (AI) that is employed to model the collective behaving of societal swarms in nature, for example, honey bees, ant colonies, and bird flocks. Despite these (bugs or swarm individuals) are mildly silly with restricted capacities on their own, they are interacting with each other to cooperatively accomplish tasks necessary for their survival. The social connections among swarm individuals can be either direct or indirect (Belal, Gaber, El-Sayed, & Almojel, 2006).

Decades ago, researchers and scholars have examined the behaviour of social insects due to the astounding efficiency of these systems. In the late-80s, computer researchers have proposed the scientific perceptions of these natural swarm systems in the field of AI. In 1989, the articulation "Swarm Intelligence" was first presented by Beni G. and Wang J (1993) in the worldwide optimization structure as a set of algorithms for controlling robotic swarm. In 1991, Ant Colony Optimization (ACO) (Dorigo, Maniezzo, & Colorni, 1991; 1992) was proposed and partners as a novel nature-enlivened meta-heuristic for the arrangement of hard combinatorial optimization problems (CO). In 1995, particle swarm optimization was advanced by Kennedy J. and Eberhart R. C. (1995), Eberhart, R., and Kennedy, J. (1995) and was first designed for simulating bird flocking social behaviour. By the late-90s, these two most widespread SI algorithms started to go beyond a purely scientific interest and to enter the domains of real-world applications. It is perhaps worth mentioning here that a number of years later, precisely in 2005, Artificial Bee Colony Algorithm was proposed by Karaboga, D (2005). Since the computational modelling of swarms was proposed, there has been a steady increase in the number of articles employing the outstanding application of SI algorithms in several optimization tasks.

SI principles have been successfully applied at a variety of problem areas including function optimization problems, scheduling, structural optimization, finding optimal routes, and image/data analysis (Van den Bergh & Engelbrecht, 2002). Computational modelling of swarms has been further applied to an extensive variety of different areas, including machine learning, dynamical approaches, and operations research, bioinformatics and medical informatics, and they even applied in business and finance.

In this chapter, we will highlight just on the most two important and famous algorithms of the swarm intelligence, ACO and particle swarm optimization PSO.

Later, a convinced justification of why the nature-heuristic is effective techniques for solving text summarization tasks.

Ant Colony Optimization Algorithm

ACO is based on the set pheromone tracing behaviour of real ants that help find the shortest route between a food source and their nest. ACO was employed to solve several optimization problems such as scheduling, sequential ordering, probabilistic and Travelling Salesman Problem (TSP). The major idea is to model the problem to be solved as a search for an optimal solution in a weighted graph, called the construction graph, and to use artificial ants to search for major paths. A construction graph is a graph on which the ants iteratively deposit pheromone trails to support select the graph nodes of goodness paths that correspond to solution components. The manner of real artificial ants behaviour are simulated in several ways: (1) they deposit pheromone trails on the high-quality nodes of paths to strengthen the most promising paths components of the construction graph, (2) artificial ants synthesize solutions by moving through the construction graph and select their paths concerning probabilities, which rely on the pre-deposited pheromone trails, and (3) at each iteration artificial pheromone trails decrease enough rapidly to simulate the evaporation pheromone in real ants slowly. The key point in the development of ACO model is to decide the fitness function on the basis of which components of a problem's construction graph will be allegoric with a high pheromone trail and to determine how ants will exploit these promising elements when constructing new solutions. The fitness function (FF) of ACO is most probably implicitly formulated as cost minimization of its solution.

It is worth mentioning that the searching habits of ant algorithms can be distinguished by two main features: exploration, and exploitation. Exploration is the possibility of the algorithm to broadly search through the space area when exploitation is the ability of the algorithm of searching thoroughly in the local neighbourhood where best solutions have before been captured. Higher exploitation is reflected in the quick convergence of the system to a suboptimal solution, whereas higher exploration leads to best solutions at a higher computational cost due to the tardy convergence of the algorithm. In the ant colony algorithm, an appropriate trade-off between exploitation and exploration has been adapted. Pseudo code for the ACO algorithm is shown in Algorithm 1.

After initialization, the ACO algorithm repeats the three main step: at each iteration, a number of solutions are constructed using the ants; then change these solutions for the better over a local search (optional), and finally, the evaporation and update pheromone is constructed. The selection of a solution component is guided by a stochastic technique, which is based on the amount of pheromone associated with

Algorithm 1. Algorithmic of ACO

Initialize the pheromone trails and other parameters, and calculate heuristic information;
    1. While (termination conditions are not met)
2. For each ant i Do
    3. Construct ant solutions from each ant's walk on the construction graph by pheromone trails according to Equation 1.
    4. Apply local search (optional) and evaluate the exit criteria based on the FF.
    5. Evaporate and update pheromones.
    6. End

each of the elements and the heuristic information. At each iteration, the calculating probability of movement is accounted as shown:

$$\rho_{ij}^{k}(t) = \begin{cases} \dfrac{\left[\tau_{ij}(t)\right]^{\alpha} \cdot \left[\eta_{ij}\right]^{\beta}}{\sum_{l \in \mathcal{N}_i^k}\left[\tau_{il}(t)\right]^{\alpha} \cdot \left[\eta_{il}\right]^{\beta}} & if\ l \in j_k(i) \\ 0 & otherwise \end{cases} \tag{1}$$

Where k is an ant appearing at the node τ_i within the iteration t to determine the successor node τ_j from its neighborhoods of unvisited nodes $\mathcal{N}_i^k$. τ_{ij} is a pheromone trail associated with the edge from $node_i$ to $node_j$. η_{ij} represents the greedy heuristic information. α and β represent the weights of pheromone and heuristic information respectively. $j_k(i)$ represents the accumulation of possible candidate successor nodes of τ_i.

Particle Swarm Optimization Algorithm

The original particle swarm optimization PSO was designed as a global version of the algorithm, that is, in the original PSO algorithm, each particle globally compares its fitness to the entire swarm population and adapts its velocity towards the swarm's global optimal particle. PSO follows a random optimization method using Swarm Intelligence (SI). The constitutional idea is that each particle acts a potential solution which it changes and updates depending on its own experience and that of neighbours. The original version of the PSO mechanism is essentially presented by the following two simple equations, shown in (2) and (3) respectively.

Algorithm 2. Algorithmic of POS

1. Initialize a population of particles with random positions and velocities in the search space.
2. While (termination conditions are not met)
3. Evaluate the desired fitness function to be optimized for each particle's position.
4. For each particle i Do
5. Update the position and the velocity of particle i according to Equations 2 and 3.
6. Map the position of particle i in the solution space and evaluate the exit criteria based on the FF.
7. Update $pbest_i(t)$, $gbest_i(t)$ if necessary using Equations 4 and 5.
8. End

$$x_i(t+1) = x_i(t) + v_i(t) \tag{2}$$

$$v_i(t+1) = \omega v_i(t) + c_1 r_1 \left(pbest_i(t) - x_i(t) \right) + c_2 r_2 \left(gbest_i(t) - x_i(t) \right) \tag{3}$$

Where $x_i(t)$ is the position of particle i at time t, $v_i(t)$ is the velocity of particle i at time t, $pbest_i(t)$ is the best position by particle itself, $gbest_i(t)$ is the best position caught by the whole swarm up to now, The inertia weight ω plays a role in balancing the local and global search. c_1, c_2 are two positive acceleration coefficients that scale the influence of the best position and the best global position, and r_1, r_2 is a uniform random number in (0, 1). Update $pbest_i(t)$, $gbest_i(t)$ at time t is presented as follow:

$$pbest_i(t+1) = \begin{cases} pbest_i(t) & if\ f\left(pbest_i(t) \right) \leq x_i(t+1) \\ x_i(t+1) & if\ f\left(pbest_i(t) \right) > x_i(t+1) \end{cases} \tag{4}$$

$$gbest_i(t+1) = \min\left[f(y), f\left(gbest_i(t) \right) \right] where\, y \in \left\{ pbest_0(t) \ldots pbest_s(t) \right\} \tag{5}$$

According to the algorithm of POS, there are three main terms in Equation 3, the current speed of the particle, which denotes its present state and has the potentiality to balance the entire search process. The cognition term is to give a powerful ability to avoid a local minimum during the search task. The social term is leading the particles toward knowing the best solutions. By a good employing the three terms, the particles can find the best position. On the other hand, two main approaches to PSO exist according to the interpretation of the based on particle fitness information, one particle is appointed as the best particle. Then, all the other particles are accelerated in its direction, meanwhile, in the direction of their own best previously faced solutions. The PSO algorithm is very rapid, naive and easy to understand and implement. PSO finds the optimum value, but it becomes so slow near global optimum if the solution space is as high as its convergence speed. Besides, it shows poor quality performance when dealing with the large and complicated data set. But there are several PSO variants have been developed to get over such problem.

Why Nature Algorithms Are the Best for Solving Text Summary Task

All optimization algorithms have common goals to achieve a minimum or maximum of the objective function. Besides, optimization methods such a function can be divided into two basic classes: numerical methods and nature inspired methods. Özgür Yeniay30 showed a comparison between two popular heuristic methods with two commonly used gradient-based methods, namely Generalized Reduced Gradient (GRG) and Sequential Quadratic Programming (SQP), to obtain optimal conditions. The results of the comparison denoted that the traditional methods have not outperformed the heuristic methods on the majority of the problems. Moreover, it is more reliable, robust and more efficient than the other methods. The nature algorithms showed noticeable achievement when solving the Economic Load Dispatch (ELD) problem compared with the classical optimization algorithms (Santra, Mondal, & Mukherjee, 2016).

A critical analysis of these SI-based algorithms was carried out by analysing their ways to mimic evolutionary operators, the ways of achieving exploration and exploitation in algorithms by using mutation, crossover, and selection by (Yang & Xin-She, 2014). They finally stated that SI-based algorithms can have some advantages over traditional algorithms.

On the other hand, the main consecration of the ACO is the best algorithm among other meta-heuristic and SI algorithms like a firefly algorithm, genetic algorithm, tabu search, simulated annealing, ABC, and CSO, etc., are: Firstly, the function of ACO in solving optimization tasks proved to be highly strong and could be easily understood. In addition, it is a meta–heuristic framework that can be adapted to many different problems, typically are represented as a weighted graph. Secondly, the convergence of ACO had been analytically proved by Gutjahr (2000) whereas the convergence of most other meta-heuristic algorithms has not yet proven using mathematical models, the results are only based- experimentation. Thirdly, it is evident from the literature that ACO outperforms other meta-heuristic and SI algorithms. though different in terms of their vocabulary is almost analogous in the work implementation of ACO (Prakasam & Savarimuthu, 2016). Thus, all these motives were the support for using of ACO other than optimization methods. Finally, we can notice that in table 1, the mean success ratio of traditional and nature-heuristic techniques in terms of time complexity, accuracy/efficiency, convergence, and stability are compared. In contrast, Table 1 shows the comparison between ACO and other Met-heuristic methods in terms of time Convergence, accuracy/efficiency, and reliability is performed. Subsequently, we can notice that the ACO algorithm is the best one in most put forward aspects. So, the authors recommend the ACO to be the most considerable algorithm for solving such as these issues in the future.

SWARM INTELLIGENCE METHODS FOR DIFFERENT TYPES OF SUMMARIZATION

This section presents numerous different types of summarization techniques based on the swarm intelligence algorithms, mainly to show the recent single-document, multi-document, and short text summarization approaches respectively.

Single-Document Summarization Based on Swarm Intelligence

Regarding ACO algorithms, recently a few studies employed ACO mechanism in their works. Hassan, O. F (2015) proposed an ACO based on the automatic single-document text summary to generate good abstract. After applying the text pre-processing, several features types of text have been proposed to extract the more salient sentences from the text. These features are the number of words in a title, length of sentence, and sentence position as into the text, thematic words, and numerical data. Later, the ACO starts by producing a number of ants based on features, each feature is selected randomly. Each ant goes through the graph to complete its path

Table 1. Comparison between numerical and nature inspired/meta-heuristic methods

Parameter	Time Complexity	Accuracy/ Efficiency	Convergence	Stability
Numerical	Low[23]	Low[22, 24]	Unsecured[30]	Low[22, 24]
nature / meta-heuristic	High[23]	High[22, 24]	Just from experimentations[34]	High[22, 24]
ACO	High[23]	High[22, 24]	analytically proved [25]	High[22, 24]

from the initial positions according to the probability method. The gathered subsets of the feature are assessed by the best summation of the feature subset. The algorithm is halted when an optimal summary is found, or the algorithm gets the maximum number of times to generate the final abstract. Deposition of pheromone is made. Finally, the authors used 100 documents for training from the DUC2002 data set. Each starts by pre-processing stage, then extracting the text features by scoring all document sentences as follows (Hassan, 2015).

$$Score_{\left(S_i\right)} = \sum_{j=0}^{5} s\left(f_i\right) * voop\left(i\right) \tag{6}$$

Where $Score_{\left(S_i\right)}$ is the score of the sentence S_i, $s\left(f_i\right)$ is the score of the feature and $voop\left(i\right)$ is the value of the bit in ACO. Later, the top the twenty percentage of sentences is selected as an abstract. The ROUGE-1 is employed as a fitness function to assess the quality of the summary. In addition, two of the Human-made summaries (H2-H1) is assigned as a reference. H2-H1 is compared with each other to easily evaluate how proximate the performances of the proposed systems are opposite to human performance. Moreover, some algorithms are assigned for comparisons like the genetic algorithm and PSO. The proposed systems ultimately exceeded all other algorithm.

The particle swarm optimization (PSO) is applied to choosing the most appropriate features successfully. It is used to collect a subset of features to train it using neural network and classification. According to the successes of PSO, the study (Binwahlan & Suanmali, 2009b) adapted PSO in a text summarization area that depends on the extraction of the most meaningful sentences from the original text. They introduced the PSO algorithm to evaluate the influence structure of the feature on the feature selection procedure. Most used features are combined with a linear combination to exhibit the significance of the sentence. The simply employed features were "keyword" and "first sentence similarity". In contrast, sentence centrality, word sentence score, and title feature had considered as complicated features. Later, a clustering algorithm is implemented to divide the document sentences into a number of clusters that are equal to the length of the summary. The PSO has been employed into all cluster to capture the most effective features after based on a feature score. For feature's existence representation, each bit takes one or zero as a value of. The particle position was represented as shown in Figure 1. Every bit takes the value of one or zero, which represents the case of one feature. If the bit contains zero, it means that the feature is not selected. Subsequently, the authors used a ROUGE-1 method as a fitness function. One-hundred articles from DUC-2002 were used as a

Figure 1. The structure of a particle

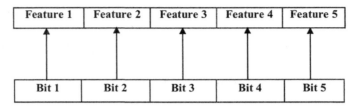

dataset for training the system. The complex features received higher weights than simple features in the result, which shows that feature structure is essential in the feature selection task.

Furthermore, in Binwahlan and Suanmali (2009b) the dataset was divided into two sections (training and testing) to calculate the features weights. The authors used 129 documents as a dataset, 99 of them were used in the training phase, and the rest were used for testing. Consequently, the selected sentences for the summary must be ranked in a descending manner. For outcomes evaluation, the summarizer of Microsoft word and the human summary have been compared with. The result of PSO outperforms the Microsoft word-summarizer and the human model. Moreover, Binwahlan and Suanmali (2009c) continued optimizing the summarization issue based on the PSO model mixed with the maximal margin importance (MMI) technique (Mosa et al., 2017b). Each sentences cluster is represented as one binary tree or more. The sentences in the binary tree are ordered according to the scores as shown in Equations 7, and 8.

$$Score_{BT}\left(S_i\right) = impr\left(S_i\right) + \left(1 - \left(impr\left(S_i\right) * frindsNO\left(S_i\right)\right)\right) \tag{7}$$

$$impr\left(S_i\right) = avg\left(WSS\left(S_i\right) + SC\left(S_i\right) + SS_{NG(S_i)} + sim_{fsd(S_i)} + kwrd\left(S_i\right)\right) \tag{8}$$

Where WSS : the score of the word, SC : sentence centrality, SS_{NG} : the average of similarity features, the similarity of the sentence S_i with the first calculated sentence in the document depending on a cosine similarity metric, and $kwrd$ is the keyword feature. $Score_{BT}\left(S_i\right)$ is the sentence S_i score in the binary tree, $impr\left(S_i\right)$ is the average of the signification sentence S_i and $frindsNO\left(S_i\right)$ is the number of the closest sentences. The main idea behind that work is to prevent the likely redundancy by selecting a sentence that has low relevance to previously selected sentences in the summary, at the same time, is largely relevant to the topic. Finally, the results are evaluated using ROUGE-1, ROUGE-2, and ROUGE-L respectively.

On the other hand, Binwahlan, Salim, & Suanmali (2009d) proposed an automatic text summarization system from an abundance of text sources. A fuzzy logic incorporated with the swarm intelligence system has been mixed to accomplish this task. Initially, the weights of sentences have been obtained from the swarm module. Later, these weights had been used as inputs for the fuzzy system. The fuzzy logic has the advantage of training and developing in such problems, so the rules are completely understandable and simple to modify, add, and remove rules. The main objective of employing PSO for fabricating the features weights in accordance with the importance, which played a meaningful role in the discrimination between features significance. The score of each sentence S_i in the document is calculated as shown (Binwahlan, Salim, & Suanmali, 2009d).

$$swarm\_import\left(S_i\right) = \sum_{j=1}^{5} \omega_j * score f_j\left(S_i\right) \tag{9}$$

In the fuzzy logic, a trapezoidal membership function is employed to determine the degree to be the input values pertain to the adequate fuzzy sets. High, medium and low are three fuzzy sets are used. Later, obtaining all the phrases scores that have been produced by the fuzzy inference system, the phrases are re-ranked depending on those scores. The top n sentences are picked to be the brief. A proposed system is generated in two forms. Where the variety does not dominate the behaviour of the model and it works such as the fuzzy swarm-based method. In the second form, the behaviour of the system is a variety dominated. In addition, for removing the redundant sentences, various selection as implemented to gives the high performance as well. Combining all these mechanisms gives better performance than each one individually. Finally, the score of the sentence is accounted according to their scores for finally constitute the summary. The experiments conducted based on the DUC 2002 document sets for assessment of the proposed method. The swarm approach and benchmarks (MS-Word / H2-H1) used the average F-measure with ROUGE-1, ROUGE-2, and ROUGE-L. It was shown that the incorporation between the fuzzy logic with a swarm approach has achieved a noticeable performance. Moreover, the results showed when the fuzzy model was mixed higher performance than the swarm model.

What is more, Asgari, Masoumi, & Sheijani (2014) proposed a novel approach for text summarization using multi-agent particle swarm optimization. First, the pre-processing performed containing separation of sentences, stop words removing, and steaming task. Then, some feature has been calculated as an adapt TF-IDF method (Asgari et al., 2014).

$$G(T_{ij}) = \log \frac{N}{n_j} + 1 \tag{10}$$

Where N is the total number of the sentences, and n_j is the number of sentences that possess the word j. After calculating the weight of sentences, the similarity matrix had been obtained deepening on the cosine metric. Subsequently, a MAPSO algorithm is applied the extraction of pivot sentences as a summary. Then initialized MAPSO parameters, a random number of sentences are assigned to each particle agent. The cost of each particle is calculated according to the dependency of sentences with each other. Moreover, the readability factor denotes that the gathered summary has a high degree of similarity. Calculate the cost of each agent and select the best sentences. This method has been examined with a set of DUC 2002 standard documents and the summaries had been evaluated using ROUGE against other methods.

Regarding the Turkish language, a new hybrid of artificial bee colony algorithm mixed with the semantic features is proposed in Güran, Nilgün, and Mustafa (2013) to extract summary. The system used five semantic features are joined based on their weights using two new approaches. The first utilizes the process of analytical hierarchical, which is based on several human judgments. Secondly, the ABC algorithm is employed to determine the real weights of the features. To obtain the optimal weights, the used corpus was 100 documents, it is split into 88 documents for training and the rest for testing using five-fold cross-validation. Finally, the experimental results showed that exploiting the features with each other gave a better performance than exploiting each feature individually.

On the other hand, other SI algorithms like the bacterial foraging and cuckoo algorithms were employed for solving a summary task in (Nikoo, Faraahi, Hashemi, & Erfani, 2012; Mirshojaeo & Masoomi, 2015). Used cuckoo search optimization algorithm (CSOA) (Mirshojaei & Masoomi, 2015) to enhance the performance of the summary task. Important sentences are extracted from the text by the CSOA algorithm based on the cost function.

$$CF_s = \frac{\log\left(C * 9 + 1\right)}{\log\left(M * 9 + 1\right)} \tag{11}$$

Where CF_s is the sentences' coherence factor, C is the average distance of the available sentences, and M is the maximum weight of the sentences. Eventually, extraction of the summary is based on 1) human judgments, 2) matching sentences together, 3) matching words together. The experiments used the DUC 2002 document sets for evaluation based on the F-measure method. Analysing of obtained results indicated reliability and better performance of the proposed approach.

Moreover, Nikoo et al (2012) introduced a new approach for automatic text summarization based on bacterial foraging optimization. A bit string is used to represent the corresponding words. Each bit can take only 1 or 0. Secondly, the weight of sentences is determined by summing the total weights of their words. Rouge-1 is employed to evaluate each candidate summary text.

Multi-Document Summarization Based on Swarm Intelligence

Regarding the multi-document summarization (MDS), Donis-Díaz, Rafael, & Janusz (2015) has identified a new model for linguistic summarization of numerical data (LDS) based on ACO. The ACO-LDS algorithm used the Max-Min ant system. The frequency of using the term F_u is basic for a heuristic information mechanism. Where F_u is the number of times, $u_{v_{ij}}$ that node v_{ij} has been used in the summary as follows (Donis-Díaz et al., 2015).

$$F_u = 1 - \left(u_{v_{ij}} / p \right)^e \tag{12}$$

Term p represents the number of propositions added up till now to the partial summary and e is a parameter in 0, 1 to graduate the "power" of the influence of F_u.

Later, the local search is applied to all constructed solutions after each iteration to enhance the produced summaries. According to the value of fitness function, the best summary is updated. Finally, the exit criteria terminate the algorithm when the stagnation condition appears, or the algorithm reaches the maximum number of iterations. Finally, the ACO-LDS algorithm was good in extracting the summary but fails to enhance diversity.

On the other hand, Yadav and Sugandha (2016) also presented a hybridized algorithm using the combination of PSO and fuzzy C-Means. The approach used PSO mixed with Fuzzy-C-Means and K-means for partitioning the text into a number of clusters. The used dataset documents were 1504, and the number of clusters, not more than five and not less than two. Entropy, F-Measure, and similarity distance are three methods used to evaluate cluster result. Finally, the quality of the FCPSO cluster has achieved performance better than that KPSO.

Besides, additional work related to MDS is applied. Some researchers Bazghandi et al. (2012), Aliguliyev (2010) suggested a hybrid system by mixing the PSO algorithm with the mutation mechanism in the genetic algorithm. A set of document summarization system has been prepared as an input of the system (Bazghandi et al., 2012) including the relevant/irrelevant information to the main topic of the text. The sentences had been clustered using the PSO algorithm, the sentences within a cluster shall be dissimilar from the sentences in other clusters. A group of sports news was chosen from the ISNA (Iranian Students News Agency) as the experimental corpus. Eight subsets have been administered for assessments and tests. PSO and K-means algorithms are used in comparison with the proposed method. In Aliguliyev (2010) another generic multi-document summarization approach using sentences clustering is introduced. But in this method, if the two terms appear in the same text, that means they are semantically relatives. Moreover, a new sentence extractive method is developed using calculation the mean weight of a sentence with respect to the cluster, which they are assigned to. Finally, DUC-2007 and DUC-2005 corpus are used in experimental based on ROUGE-2 and ROUGE-SU4 metric.

A multi-document summarization system based a clustering, semantic labeling, and PSO are developed to rank sentences in each cluster (Khan, Salim, & Kumar, 2015). First, divide the document into the separated sentences. Next, a semantic role parser is employed to obtain PAS from sentence collection set. Jiang's similarity method is used for calculating the semantic similarity. Subsequently, the hierarchical clustering algorithm is applied. PSO is employed in the features selection to capture the optimal weights into each cluster for selection. Eventually, the Experiment of this approach has been performed on DUC-2002 and evaluated against the benchmark summarization systems using F-measure. Experimental results affirm that the proposed approach yields better results than other comparison summarization systems.

Furthermore, a successful model of honey bees searching follows for nectar in a field of summarization[45] (Peyrard & Eckle-Kohler, 2016). The Jensen-Shannon (JS) divergence method in this approach was considered as a similarity metric for comparing the summary content and the original multi-documents. The framework has been developed based on two approaches; one is based on a genetic algorithm, the second is based on an ABC algorithm. DUC-2002 and DUC-2003 are used in the experiments using ROUGE-1 and ROUGE-2 evaluation methods based on human evaluation. Finally, the proposed algorithm has been compared with four known algorithms as TF-IDF weighting, LexRank, and KL-div Greedy (Haghighi & Vanderwende, 2009). The evaluation has shown a competitive performance of the proposed approach.

In addition, another novel multi-document summarization technique is presented based on ABC optimization (Chakraborti & Dey, 2015). It is used by companies for extracting significant facts about the specific product from their competitors' news to strategic business decision making. Initially, the system creates a bag-of-words vector space, runs the latent semantic analysis, uses just top 5%, represents the documents, runs the self-organizing map, and employs the K-Means algorithm to cluster the provided data. Later, the ABC algorithm is applied to generate the final summary. The corpus consists of news items about multiple products of the company. So, the news items about specific categories of products will be clustered according to each product. Finally, the results presented based on collecting news items for an appointed consumer electronics company from authentic news sites. In terms of F-measure and ROUGE performance evaluation, the ABC algorithm outperformed the MEAD algorithm in several aspects.

On the other hand, a novel Cat Swarm Optimization (CSO) based multi-document summarizer is proposed to address this problem (Rautray & Balabantaray, 2017). The system applied firstly the pre-processing operations that containing: segmentation of sentences, tokenization, remove stop words and stemming. Subsequently, the authors have tried to build summaries from document sets with multiple objectives as non-redundancy, content coverage, cohesion, and readability, which are explained as follows (Rautray & Balabantaray, 2017).

$$f(S) = f_{\text{cov}}(S) + f_{coh}(S) + f_{read}(S) \tag{8}$$

$$f_{\text{cov}}(S) = sim(S_i, O); i = 1, 2, \ldots, n \tag{9}$$

$$f_{coh}(S) = 1 - sim(S_i, S_j), where\, i \neq j; i, j = 1, 2, \ldots, n \tag{10}$$

$$f_{read}(S) = sim(S_i, O); i = 1, 2, \ldots, n \tag{11}$$

Where O is the center of the main content collection of sentences. The coverage content of each sentence in the summary $f_{cov}(S)$ represents as a similarity between S_i and O. That means, higher similarity values correspond to high content coverage. Likewise, the great value of $f_{coh}(S)$ specifies the high connection between sentences and vice versa. $f_{read}(S)$ Measures the similarity among sentences for specifying higher popular ones in the summary. The cat's positions are applied according to the fitness function as shown in equation (8). Save *gbest* as the best cat position/ summary. Finally, *gbest* is the vector of candidate sentences that constitute the summary when the exit criteria are satisfied. In terms of the experiment, the performance had been evaluated using F-score, ROUGE methods based on a benchmarks DUC 2006 and DUC 2007. Finally, in most cases, CSO showed better performance.

Short Text Summarization Base on Swarm Intelligence

On the other work, with regard to the short text of social network, (Mosa et al., 2017a) proposed recently and for the first time, short text summarization task based on ACO algorithm. The system has been introduced a novel method to summarize an Arabic short text on Facebook posts, specifically Egyptian slang, by selecting a list of comments associated with a certain post. The algorithm begins as shown in figure 2 by applying the natural language processing (NLP) phase to generate the list of vectors, by removing any foreign language, redundant character, and symbols. Later, convert the slang words into modern standard Arabic (MSA) and steaming processes are developed. Subsequently, a Simi-graph is constructed by isolating lengthy comments and more similar comments based on a predefined threshold. Accordingly, comments represent the nodes and directed edges designate the possible candidate comments based on the similarity. Two celebrated metrics are employed to measure the similarity: 1) Jaccard similarity, 2) Cosine similarity. The Cosine similarity is defined as shown (Mosa et al., 2017a).

$$Cosine_{(C_i,C_j)} = \frac{\sum_{i=1}^{n} A_i.B_i}{\sqrt{\sum_{i=1}^{n} A_i^2} \sqrt{\sum_{i=1}^{n} B_i^2}} \tag{12}$$

The cosine similarity approach is applied in text matching when the attribute vectors A_i and B_i are usually the term frequency vectors of the comments C_i and C_j. The second method is the Jaccard similarity that is presented as follow.

$$Jaccard_{(C_i,C_j)} = C_i.C_j / C_i \cup C_j \tag{13}$$

Figure 2. ACO based user-contributed summarization framework

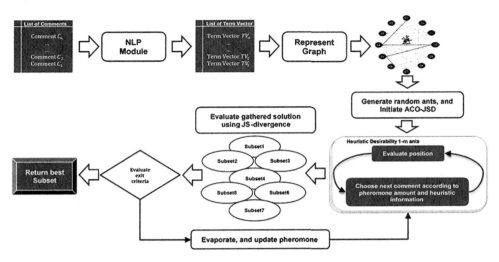

The Jaccard method measures the similarity between the finite sample sets. Subsequently, the number of ants is set on randomly the number of nodes. Each ant applies an arbitrary probability depend on three features associated with two limitations, to make a clever decision which node should be visited later. Some of the effective features are selected to make the desirable heuristic information, as TF-IDF, (El-Fishawy, Hamouda, Attiya, & Atef, 2014), PageRank, and a number of (likes, mentions, and replies) to constitute effective heuristic information as shown (Mosa et al., 2017a)

$$\eta_{ij} = \frac{\lambda \cdot PR\left(C_i\right) + \theta \cdot TF - IDF\left(C_i\right) + \gamma \cdot ISU\left(C_i\right)}{\omega \cdot \sum_{w_i \in C_i} w_i + \upsilon \cdot Maxsimi\left(C_i, C_{ps}\right)} \tag{14}$$

Where the PageRank algorithm $PR\left(C_i\right)$ is used to select the more popular comments based on the similarity (Khabiri, Caverlee, & Hsu, 2011). TF-IDF is defined as follows, $tf\left(w_i\right)$ is the number the term w_i appears in the comments. $idf\left(w_i\right)$ is the logarithm of the number of comments. $ISU\left(C_i\right)$ is the number of likes, replies, mentions, and any other emotion that the comment had possessed.

Afterward, the algorithm picks the feasible comment which has the highest probability and pheromone. After each iteration, visited paths is selected for depositing pheromone. Finally, when there is no additional improvement for several iterations or the algorithm reaches the maximum number of iterations, the algorithm halts. The JS-Divergence method is employed as a fitness function to measure the divergence between the numerical representation ratio of the words in the summary and original text as follow (Gambhir & Gupta, 2017).

$$RRI = \frac{information\ ratio\ in\ the\ summary}{information\ ratio\ in\ the\ list\ of\ comments} \tag{15}$$

To determine the best values of ACO parameters, the weights of heuristic information features and the parameters of ACO are varied among candidate values except for one parameter that keeps unchanged to determine the suitable one. Ultimately, in terms of the corpus, two benchmarks are used. They have been collected from the Egyptian and Arabic news pages on Facebook (Alaa El-Dine, El-Zahraa, El-Taher, 2012) Four volunteers have been invited to assess the goodness of the generated summary against other traditional algorithms. Twenty comment streams are used as a length of the summary. The F-measures mechanism is employed in the evaluation phase based on the human summary. The result showed that the system's performance was superior to all of the other systems.

Occasionally, the list of original comments in social media may exceed 30 000 comments and the ants may fall into local optimum if the number of alternative selection is numerous or the weights of candidate comments are approximate. Therefore, Mosa et al. (2017a) hypothesized dividing the list of comments into small similar versions of the original one. The paper opens up an inventor field of short text summarization using a hybrid ant colony optimization, mixed with a graph coloring and local search methods. Initially, the graph coloring algorithm has been utilised to constitute small lists, whereas each color has just dissimilar important comments. At the same time, each color should retain a higher ratio of retaining information based on Tri-vergence of probability distributions (TPD) (Cabrera-Diego, Torres-Moreno, & Durette, 2016). The same comment may be appended to several colors. Later, the final summary will be extracted from just the best color, unlike the clustering mechanism. Subsequently, activating ACO mixed with the local search to constitute the summary.

SUMMARY EVALUATION

Evaluation item is an exceedingly important part of automatic text summarization; still, it represents a challenging problem in this field (Lloret & Palomar, 2012). There are several factors behind the challenges and obstacles of summary systems evaluation. One motive is that to assess summary contents, a comparison is made

Figure 3. ACO problem representation for user-contributed summarization

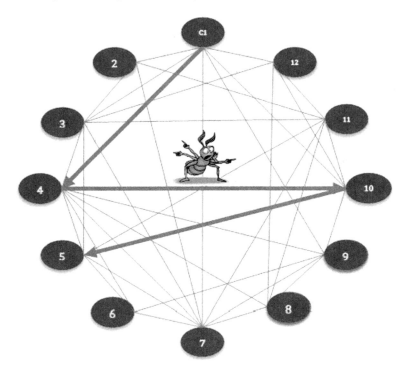

with reference summaries (Lloret & Paalomar, 2012). The problem with making such a corpus is no ideal 'unique' summary (El-Haj, Kruschwitz, & Fox, 2011) whereas several summaries can be adequate for the same document, and even using unlike phrases, can create many versions of the same summary. Furthermore, the generation of reference summaries based on human experts and time-consuming task is a costly task. It is not facilitated for humans to know what kind of data should show up in the summary. On other words, information changes depending on the target of the summary and to pick this information automatically is a very complicated issue. Generally, two ways for specifying the performance of a summarization task (El-Haj et al., 2011) (1) extrinsic evaluation: the quality of summarization relies on how it affects other issues as information retrieval, Text classification, and question answering. (2) Intrinsic evaluation: the determined summary quality depends on the coverage ratio between the human-summary and machine-summary. Retention of the information is the important aspects on the basis of which a summary is good. But how to know which parts of the document are relevant and which are not, it is still a problem with this task.

Evaluation Corpora

Many workshops addressing the area of summarization twenty years ago, such as SUMMAC, DUC, and TAC. These workshops powerfully avail the summarization field in many aspects. For instance, document Understanding conferences (DUCs) where a significant series of conferences that addressed the subjects of automatic summarization and were turned by the US department of commerce's national institute of standards and technology (NIST). Gambhir & Gupta (2017) compared and evaluated their results using DUC's benchmark. In 2008, DUC turned into a summarization path at the Text Analysis Conference (TAC). It is also entertains a sequencing of evaluation workshops that provide many tracks addressing different areas of NLP. The summarization issue was included from 2008 to 2014. Additionally, in some cases, authors have used their own corpus (see Table 2), and for this reason, it is not possible to compare the results of all these studies. Although DUC 2001, 2002, 2003, 2005, 2007, and ISNA, in addition to the used languages are different including English, Persian, Arabic, and Turkish.

Evaluation Methods

To evaluate the quality of the summary, there are many numbers of methods used for summary evaluation like Pyramid method, ROUGE (Lin, 2004) etc.

This section shows the various evaluation methods which had been used in this chapter. Table 3 shows the different types of summary evaluation. ROUGE is a popular and widely used set of automatic evaluation metric. It consists of a package that automatically evaluates summaries and has been used by most of the surveyed systems such as Binwahlan (2009a), Binwahlan, Salim, & Suanmali (2009d), Gambhir & Gupta (2017), Nikoo et al. (2012), Mirshojaei & Masoomi (2015), Rautray & Blabantaray, (2017), Chakraborti & Dey (2015), Bazghandi, Tabrizi, Jahan, & Mashahd (2012), Hassan (2015). In the ROUGE method, the number of common terms between a specific summary and a selected reference. Thus, it supports to evaluate the summary issue automatically. Besides, ROUGE containing: ROUGE-L, ROUGE-N, ROUGE-W, ROUGE-SU, and ROUGE-S as follows.

- ROUGE-L calculates the ratio between the size of two summaries' longest common subsequence and size of reference summary.
- ROUGE-N quantifies the common N-gram units among a specific summary and a collection of reference summaries, where N determines the length of N-Grams.
- ROUGE-S evaluates the proportion of common skip bigrams among a specific summary and a collection of summaries.

Table 2. Types of corpus produced by the surveyed literature and their summarization approach

Reference	Corpus
Binwahlan M. et al[18]	DUC-2002
Binwahlan M. et al[15]	DUC-2002
Peyrard, M., and Eckle-Kohler, J[45]	DUC-2002 and DUC-2003
Mosa, M. A. et al, 2017a[2]	Authors' corpus
Mosa, M. A. et al, 2017b[3]	Authors' corpus
HASSAN, O. F. 2015[35]	DUC-2002
(Güran, A, 2013)	Authors' corpus
Chakraborti, S., and Dey, S. 2015[47]	Authors' corpus
Binwahlan M. et al[18]	DUC-2002
Binwahlan M. et al[15]	DUC-2002
Asgari, H, 2014[36]	DUC-2002
Bazghandi, M., et al, 2012[42]	ISNA (Iranian Students News Agency)
Aliguliyev, R. M., 2010[43]	DUC-2005 and DUC-2007
Khan, A., et al, 2015[44]	DUC-2002
Nikoo, M. D., et al, 2012[38]	DUC-2002
Mirshojaei, S. H., and Masoomi, B. 2015[39]	DUC-2002
Rautray, R., and Balabantaray, R. C. 2017[48]	DUC-2006 and DUC-2007

- ROUGE-W It's the optimization over the simple longest common subsequence approach.
- ROUGE-SU is the average score between ROUGE-S and ROUGE-1 and it extends ROUGE-S with a counting term as unigram.

For example, ROUGE-N is a recall measure that evaluates the summary by computing the n-gram recall between the set of references summaries and the summary itself as follows (Lin, 2004).

$$ROUGE - N = \frac{\sum_{s \in MS} \sum_{n-gram \in S} Match\left(n - gram\right)}{\sum_{s \in MS} \sum_{n-gram \in S} Count\left(n - gram\right)} \tag{16}$$

Furthermore, although some ROUGE measures correlate well with human evaluations based on DUC's human evaluation methods of English corpora at 2001, 2002 and 2003 conferences (Lin, 2004), the same assumption may not be correct with other methods of human evaluation or with other corpora in other languages, such as Arabic.

On the other hand, the summary process evaluates based on other celebrated metrics which are precision, recall, and f-measure. They are also predicting the coverage area between generated machine-summaries and human-summary. It is common information retrieval metric (Nenkova, 2006) have been used by some studies such as Mosa et al. (2017a), Bazghandi et al. (2012), Binwhalan & Suanmali (2009b), Chakraborti & Dey (2015) to evaluate their generated summaries against other reference summaries automatically (Ninkova, 2006).

$$Recall = \frac{relevant\ unigrams \cap retrieved\ unigrams}{relevant\ unigrams} \qquad (17)$$

$$Precision = \frac{relevant\ unigrams \cap retrieved\ unigrams}{retrieved\ unigrams} \qquad (18)$$

Precision determines the fraction of the correct selected sentences between the system and the humans. Recall determines the ratio of relevant selected sentences. Precision/recall are antagonistic methods to one another. F-measure trades off between precision, and recall based on a parameter β (used $\beta = 1$). Thus, F-measure is defined as follows:

$$F - measure = \frac{\left(\beta^2 + 1\right) Precision * Recall}{\beta^2\ Precision + Recall} \qquad (19)$$

Although this metric has some of the drawbacks that were discussed in (Nenkova, 2006). As there is no perfect summary in using reference for comparison, which sometimes strafes the summary that possesses good phrases that are not selected by the reference. Moreover, they strafe summaries that use sentences not selected by the reference summary as well, even if they are similar to the selected sentences.

Other automatic methods were also used at short text summarization are Tri-vergence of probability distributions (TPD) (Cabera-Diego et al., 2016) and Jensen–Shannon divergence (Louis & Nenkova, 2009) (JSD). TPD and JSD mechanisms of automatic evaluation have been employed to assess the quality of the short text summarization in Mosa et al. (2017a), Gambhir & Gupta (2017), Mosa, Hamouda, & Marei, (2017c) to ensure the summary has had the gist of the original document.

They are the most attractive mechanisms used to evaluate the summary contents automatically. Expressly, these methods measure the ratio of information in the summary as for the original text. TPD theoretically allows calculating the similarity between triplets of objects. It is a statistical measure that compares three different probability distributions Q, P, and R simultaneously to ensure it captures the important retention information in the original text. The composite tri-vergence of Kullback–Leibler is defined as shown (Cabrera-Diego et al., 2016):

$$T_c\left(P\|Q\|R\right)=\sum_{\sigma\in P}p_\sigma\log\frac{p_\sigma}{\left[\sum_{\omega\in Q}q_\omega\log\frac{q_\omega}{r_\omega}\Big/N\right]} \tag{20}$$

Where Q is the original text, R is an selected summary, and P is all other picked summaries of the set excepting R. ω is the terms belonging to Q; r_ω and q_ω are the probabilities of ω to occur in 'R' and 'Q' respectively, σ is the words belonging to P; p_σ is the probabilities of σ to occur in P. N represents the normalization parameter. On the other hand, The JS-divergence between two probability distributions Q and P is given by:

$$J\left(P\|Q\right)=\frac{1}{2}\left[D\left(P\|A\right)+D\left(Q\|A\right)\right] \tag{21}$$

Where the $D\left(P\|A\right)$ is defined as follow:

$$D\left(P\|A\right)=\sum_{w}pP\left(w\right)\log_2\frac{pP\left(w\right)}{pQ\left(w\right)} \tag{22}$$

$$A=\left(P/Q\right)/2\,.$$

In text summarization task, the two distributions are the numerical distributions of words in the summary and the original text. Clearly, according to Cabrera-Diego, L. et al (2016) the analysis results showed that the tri-vergence can have a better performance, in comparison to the JS-divergence, when more than sixteen summaries are analysed.

Table 3. Different types of evaluation used in the surveyed literature

Reference	Evaluation Method
Binwahlan M. et al (2009d)	ROUGE-1, ROUGE-2, and ROUGE-L
Binwahlan M. et al (2009a)	ROUGE-1
Peyrard & Eckle-Kohler (2016)	JS-1, JS-2, ROUGE-1, and ROUGE-2
Mosa, M. A. et al (2017a)	F-measure, JSD, similarity, and lengthy
Mosa, M. A. et al (2017b)	ROUGE-1, TPD, similarity, and lengthy
HASSAN, O. F. (2015)	ROUGE-1, and ROUGE-2
Bazghandi, M., et al. (2012)	ROUGE-1, and F-measure
Chakraborti, S., and Dey, S. (2015)	ROUGE, and F-measure
Binwahlan M. et al (2009d)	ROUGE-1, ROUGE-2, ROUGE-L, and F-measure
Binwahlan M. et al (2009a)	ROUGE-1, ROUGE-2, and ROUGE-L
Asgari et al. (2014)	ROUGE-1
Aliguliyev, R. M., (2010)	ROUGE-2, and ROUGE-SU4
Khan, A., et al, (2015)	F-measure
Nikoo, M. D., et al, (2012)	ROUGE-1
Mirshojaei, S. H., and Masoomi, B. (2015)	ROUGE
Rautray, R., and Balabantaray, R. C. (2017)	ROUGE-1, ROUGE-2, F-measure, PPV, S_{svt}, S_{acc}

DISCUSSION

Few studies addressed swarm optimization based text summarization task by comparison with other traditional algorithms, such as machine learning and genetic algorithms. Nevertheless, this situation is beginning to change recently when the short text summarization process has been solved using ACO (Mosa et al., 2017a) and graph coloring combines with ACO (Gambhir & Gupta, 2017).

Mani I. (2001) divided the summarization methods depending on linguistic space levels into 1) shallow methods, in which the representation level does not emerge as the syntactic level & extractive summaries are commonly produced; 2) deeper methods, in which the representation level is leastwise at the semantic level and abstractive summaries are the output; and 3) hybrid approaches, which combine between the previous two methods. Although the syntactic-based approach is still popular in different natural language processing (NLP) tasks. NLP studies need to jump the curve (Cambria & White, 2014) by adopting extra semantic approaches instead of depending on only syntactic ones. To the best of our knowledge, there exist no abstractive summaries generated based on SI. It is anticipated that generating abstract summary will be one of the prominent challenges by using swarm intelligence algorithms.

Most of the summarization systems followed the numerical approaches, by applying a machine learning algorithm e.g. Support Vector Machine (SVM), GAs, and mathematical regression, Naïve Bayesian, GP, and ANNs (Aliguliyev, 2010). This situation can be explained by perhaps this is because the authors do not imagine completely how to model the problem of summary in the optimization problem. Until 2016, no study has ever used SI in solving the short text summarization problem. However, this situation is beginning to change especially after Mosa et al. (2017a) and Bambhir & Gupta (2017) were published.

Moreover, it is found that the SI has presented extremely successful approaches for solving the problem of the summary with the famous, widespread, different languages such as English, Arabic (Mosa et al., 2017a; Gambhir & Gupta, 2017) Persian (Bazghandhi et al., 2012) and Turkish (Güran et al., 2013) to extract the summary text. Table 4 shows the majority of summarization types systems with their types.

On the other hand, to the best of our knowledge, no summarization system had been developed using SI techniques as a multi-objective optimization (MOO) task. There is, however, an ongoing study that has begun in formalizing a multi-document summary problem into MOO problem (Rautray & Balabantaray, 2017). In addition, although Rautray & Balantaray (2017) named their approach MOO task, it is not clear from the paper if any new major contribution has been added to the summary text. Several previous studies can be adeptly formalized into MOO (Mosa et al., 2017a; Bambhir & Gupta, 2017; Binwhalan & Suanmali, 2009a; Binwhalan, Salim, & Suanmali, 2009d; Rautray & Balabantaray, 2017). To be the approach more reliable and cleverness, different maximization or minimization objectives should be employed to promote the quality of the summary. The authors in need of combines like the normal boundary intersection (NBI) (Das & Dennis, 1998) weighted sum methods with SI to capture the optimal weights of these objectives. The main purpose of using such an NBI method to determine the desired weights of the multi-objective. Consider the generic MO problem as the following (Das & Dennis, 1998):

$$MINIMUM \; or \; MAXIMUM \left(f_1\left(x\right), f_2\left(x\right), \dots, f_k\left(x\right) \right)$$

$$s.t. \, x \in X, \tag{23}$$

Table 4. Types of summaries produced by the surveyed literature and their summarization approaches

Reference	Types of Summaries	Summarization Approach
Binwahlan M. et al (2009d)	Multi-document, and mono-lingual summaries	PSO and fuzzy
Binwahlan M. et al (2009a)	Single-document, and mono-lingual summaries	PSO
Peyrard, M., and Eckle-Kohler, J (2016)	Multi-document, and mono-lingual summaries	ABC and genetic
Mosa, M. A. et al, (2017a)	Short text, and mono-lingual summaries	ACO
Mosa, M. A. et al, (2017b)	Short text, and mono-lingual summaries	ACO and graph coloring
HASSAN, O. F. (2015)	Single-document, and mono-lingual summaries	ACO
(Güran, 2013)	Single-document, and mono-lingual summaries	ABC
Chakraborti, S., and Dey, S. (2015)	Multi-document, and mono-lingual summaries	ABC
Binwahlan M. et al, (2009b)	Single-document, and mono-lingual summaries	PSO
Binwahlan M. et al, (2009c)	Single-document, and mono-lingual summaries	PSO
Asgari, H, (2014)	Single-document, and mono-lingual summaries	PSO
Bazghandi, M., et al, (2012)	Multi-document, and mono-lingual summaries	PSO and genetic mutation
Aliguliyev, R. M., (2010)	Multi-document, and mono-lingual summaries	PSO and genetic mutation
Khan, A., et al, (2015)	Multi-document, and mono-lingual summaries	PSO
Nikoo, M. D., et al, (2012)	Single-document, and mono-lingual summaries	Bacterial Foraging
Mirshojaei, S. H., and Masoomi, B. (2015)	Single-document, and mono-lingual summaries	Cuckoo Search
Rautray, R., and Balabantaray, R. C. (2017)	Multi-document, and mono-lingual summaries	CSO

Where the integer $k \geq 2$ is the number of objectives and the set X is the feasible set of decision vectors. The feasible set is typically defined by some constraint functions.

Furthermore, to the best of our knowledge, SI techniques had not proposed to support a fully incremental algorithm of summary in real-time text streams, especially, social short messages. The main key is that designing more flexible groups that can be updated effortlessly using certain criteria that can meet the real-time needs.

PROPOSAL APPROACH

In this chapter, a novel approach is proposed as shown in figure 4. To model the summary task as an extended work of summarizing STS (Mosa et al., 2017a; Gambhir & Gupta, 2017). Mosa et al (2017a) and Gambhir & Gupta (2017) could re-formulate the short text summary problem into MOO task and satisfied the real-time needs. Actually, regarding the short test summary, several features have been employed in Mosa et al (2017a) and Gambhir & Gupta (2017) can be considered objectives herein below: 1) Maximize the ratio of information (ROI) as for original text based on TPD Cabrera-Diego et al (2016). 2) Maximize the popularity of comments (POC) using PageRank method (Khabiri, Caverlee, & Hsu, 2011). 3) Maximize the more attractive comments by fans according to Equation 17. 4) Minimization of the redundancy/similarity (SIMI) between the extracted comments. 5) Minimization of the length (CR) of the summary. Moreover, the complex constraints need to be taken into account in the scheduling process such as the comment not admissible to be picked more one time in the summary, the value of the weight of each objective <=1, and the summation of weights are <=1.

In this section, the particulars of the approach are expressively showed (Mosa, Anwar, & Hamouda, 2019) . The overall process unravels to illustrative ingredients as shown in Figure 5 (Mosa, Anwar, & Hamouda, 2019). Firstly, Natural Language Processing (NLP) operations are used to just remain the important words in the original shapes. Secondly, we recommend the authors to use the ACO algorithm for solving this MOO task. In addition, it is better to shrink the solution area for protecting the ants of likely cycling. One of the best mechanism is clustering method by grouping the high similar comments together into the same cluster. To further enhance the clustering task in the real-time, a fully incremental clustering method shall be developed using the Naïve Bayes (NB). We already have several clusters/groups. NB is a straightforward algorithm for assigning newcomers comments to the closest cluster. It works on conditional probability that is the likelihood that a certain comment belongs to a certain cluster. Therefore, we can calculate the probability of an event using its prior knowledge (existing clusters) as shown below.

Figure 4. A proposed real-time framework for STS

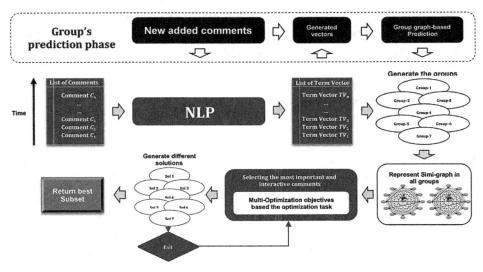

$$C_{NB} = \arg\max_{c \in C} P(C_j) \prod_{w \in W} P(w \mid C) \tag{24}$$

$$P(C_j) = \frac{N_c}{N} \tag{25}$$

$$P(w \mid c) = \frac{count(w,c) + 1}{count(c) + |V|} \tag{26}$$

Where N_c is the number of short messages in cluster c. N is the number of all short messages. $count(w,c)$ is the number of word w in the cluster c. $count(c)$ is the number of all the words in cluster c. and $|V|$ is the number of unique words.

The main target behind the clustering task is to expedite the updating task to satisfy the real-time needs and protect ants from likely cycling. The newcomer short messages are assigned to the most appropriate cluster with no need to cluster the task from the start. In this work, the ACO algorithm is then used to obtain the individual minima and maxima of various objectives we had listed. Then, NBI is utilized to resolve the variable scalar by changing the scalar values. The Pareto frontier is constructed based on the output of the algorithms. NBI and ACO are employed within all clusters to discover which subset is interactive, representative, variant, the highest ratio of information and lack redundancy.

Finally, it is predictable for the researchers at developing the proposed approach that achieve a noticeable performance. Due to the proposed approach is an extended work of STS approaches that had been introduced by Mosa et al (2017a), Mosa et al, (2017b), and Gambhir & Gupta (2017) produced results that should be compared with the previous two approaches. On the other hand, it has been noticed from this intensive survey, the ACO is one of the best algorithms of swarm intelligence with regard to the convergence, accuracy, and stability, whereas the time of complexity is high. Therefore, the authors recommend that the ACO should be further considered in the near future works along with the consideration of some smart issues to enhance the ACO complexity. Some researchers have proved and recommended some aspects to reduce the convergence time of ACO as Bazghandi et al. (2012). They stated that the convergence time could be reduced in some special cases when the number of ants is larger.

CONCLUSION

The review had been conducted in this chapter would be as enhance the starting point for the researchers interested in the summarization field. Unfortunately, this chapter has shown that usage of SI methods in the summary task is quite limited somehow, especially the developed techniques based on ACO comparing with other literature summarization techniques. Moreover, a great justification and of why swarm intelligence should be nominated for these tasks especially ACO. No summary task has been formalized before into MOO task using SI. Therefore, a proposed framework is presented to cover this insufficient work. In addition, the authors recommended ACO mixed with NBI to solve this task. Extraction of the essence of the short messages is formulated as a multi-objective optimization (MOO) task. Ultimately, Evaluation methods used corpus, and the types of summary have been presented. Indeed, there is a great opportunity for further research in summarization based on SI. Some good future work may be provided by the researchers with the help of some of the previously presented work to improve the summary generation techniques so that this research field progresses continuously.

REFERENCES

Al-Dhelaan, M. (2015). StarSum: A Simple Star Graph for Multi-document Summarization. In *Proceedings of the 38th International ACM SIGIR Conference on Research and Development in Information Retrieval*. ACM.

Al-Saleh, A. B., & Menai, M. E. B. (2016). Automatic Arabic text summarization: A survey. *Artificial Intelligence Review*, *45*(2), 203–234. doi:10.100710462-015-9442-x

Alaa El-Dine, A. H. F., & El-zahraa El-taher. (2012). Automatic Summarization of Arabic post. *The first International Conference for Faculty of Computers and Information*.

Aliguliyev, R. M. (2010). Clustering Techniques and Discrete Particle Swarm Optimization Algorithm for Multi-Document Summarization. *Computational Intelligence*, *26*(4), 420–448. doi:10.1111/j.1467-8640.2010.00365.x

Asgari, H., Masoumi, B., & Sheijani, O. S. (2014, February). Automatic text summarization based on multi-agent particle swarm optimization. In *Intelligent Systems (ICIS), 2014 Iranian Conference on* (pp. 1-5). IEEE. 10.1109/IranianCIS.2014.6802592

Bazghandi, M., Tabrizi, G. T., Jahan, M. V., & Mashahd, I. (2012). Extractive Summarization Of Farsi Documents Based On PSO Clustering. *jiA, 1*, 1.

Belal, M., Gaber, J., El-Sayed, H., & Almojel, A. (2006). Swarm Intelligence. In Handbook of Bioinspired Algorithms and Applications. Chapman & Hall.

Beni, G., & Wang, J. (1993). Swarm intelligence in cellular robotic systems. In *Robots and Biological Systems: Towards a New Bionics?* (pp. 703–712). Springer Berlin Heidelberg. doi:10.1007/978-3-642-58069-7_38

Binwahlan, M. S., Salim, N., & Suanmali, L. (2009d). *Fuzzy Swarm Based Text Summarization 1.* Academic Press.

Binwahlan, M. S. N., & Suanmali, L. (2009a). Swarm based features selection for text summarization. *International Journal of Computer Science and Network Security IJCSNS.*, *9*(1), 175–179.

Binwahlan, M. S. N., & Suanmali, L. (2009b). Swarm based text summarization. In *Computer Science and Information TechnologySpring Conference, 2009. IACSITSC'09. International Association of* (pp. 145–150). IEEE. doi:10.1109/IACSIT-SC.2009.61

Binwahlan, M. S. N., & Suanmali, L. (2009c). Swarm Diversity Based Text Summarization. In *Neural Information Processing* (pp. 216–225). Springer. doi:10.1007/978-3-642-10684-2_24

Cabrera-Diego, L. A., Torres-Moreno, J. M., & Durette, B. (2016, June). Evaluating Multiple Summaries without Human Models: A First Experiment with a Trivergent Model. In *International Conference on Applications of Natural Language to Information Systems* (pp. 91-101). Springer International Publishing. 10.1007/978-3-319-41754-7_8

Cambria, E., & White, B. (2014). Jumping nlp curves: *A review of natural language processing research review article. Comput Intell Mag I EEE*, *9*(2), 48–57. doi:10.1109/MCI.2014.2307227

Chakraborti, S., & Dey, S. (2015, October). Product news summarization for competitor intelligence using topic identification and artificial bee colony optimization. In *Proceedings of the 2015 Conference on research in adaptive and convergent systems* (pp. 1-6). ACM. 10.1145/2811411.2811465

Chali, Y., & Hasan, S. A. (2012). Query focused multi-document summarization: Automatic data annotations and supervised learning approaches. *Natural Language Engineering*, *18*(1), 109–145. doi:10.1017/S1351324911000167

Colorni, A., Dorigo, M., & Maniezzo, V. (1992, September). An Investigation of some Properties of an Ant Algorithm. In PPSN (Vol. 92, pp. 509-520). Academic Press.

Das, I., & Dennis, J. E. (1998). Normal-boundary intersection: A new method for generating the Pareto surface in nonlinear multicriteria optimization problems. *SIAM Journal on Optimization*, *8*(3), 631–657. doi:10.1137/S1052623496307510

Donis-Díaz, C. A., Rafael, B., & Janusz, K. (2014). Using ant colony optimisation and genetic algorithms for the linguistic summarization of creep data. In Intelligent Systems. Springer International Publishing.

Dorigo, M., Maniezzo, V., & Colorni, A. (1991). *The ant system: An autocatalytic optimizing process.* Academic Press.

Eberhart, R., & Kennedy, J. (1995, October). A new optimizer using particle swarm theory. In Micro Machine and Human Science. In *Proceedings of the Sixth International Symposium on* (pp. 39-43). IEEE.

El-Fishawy, N., Hamouda, A., Attiya, G. M., & Atef, M. (2014). Arabic summarization in twitter social network. *Ain Shams Engineering Journal*, *5*(2), 411–420. doi:10.1016/j.asej.2013.11.002

El-Haj, M., Kruschwitz, U., & Fox, C. (2011, December). Exploring clustering for multi-document Arabic summarisation. In *Asia Information Retrieval Symposium* (pp. 550-561). Springer Berlin Heidelberg.

Fattah, M. A., & Ren, F. (2009). GA, MR, FFNN, PNN and GMM based models for automatic text summarization. *Computer Speech & Language, 23*(1), 126–144. doi:10.1016/j.csl.2008.04.002

Franco-Salvador, M., Rosso, P., & Montes-y-Gómez, M. (2016). A systematic study of knowledge graph analysis for cross-language plagiarism detection. *Information Processing & Management, 52*(4), 550–570. doi:10.1016/j.ipm.2015.12.004

Gambhir, M., & Gupta, V. (2017). Recent automatic text summarization techniques: A survey. *Artificial Intelligence Review, 47*(1), 1–66. doi:10.100710462-016-9475-9

Güran, A., Güler Bayazit, N., & Gürbüz, M. Z. (2013). Efficient feature integration with Wikipedia-based semantic feature extraction for Turkish text summarization. *Turkish Journal of Electrical Engineering and Computer Sciences, 21*(5), 1411–1425. doi:10.3906/elk-1201-15

Gutjahr, W. J. (2000). A graph-based ant system and its convergence. *Future Generation Computer Systems, 16*(8), 873–888. doi:10.1016/S0167-739X(00)00044-3

Haghighi, A., & Vanderwende, L. (2009, May). Exploring content models for multi-document summarization. In *Proceedings of Human Language Technologies: The 2009 Annual Conference of the North American Chapter of the Association for Computational Linguistics* (pp. 362-370). Association for Computational Linguistics. 10.3115/1620754.1620807

Hassan. O. F. (2015). *Text summarization using ant colony optimization algorithm* (Doctoral dissertation). Sudan University of Science and Technology.

Karaboga, D. (2005). *An idea based on honey bee swarm for numerical optimization* (Vol. 200). Technical report-tr06, Erciyes University, Engineering Faculty, Computer Engineering Department.

Kennedy, J., & Eberhart, R. (1995). Synthetic structure of industrial plastics (Book style with paper title and editor). In *Proceeding of the 1995 IEEE International Conference on Neural Networks* (pp. 1942-1948). IEEE. 10.1109/ICNN.1995.488968

Khabiri, E., Caverlee, J., & Hsu, C. F. (2011, July). Summarizing User-Contributed Comments. ICWSM.

Khan, A., Salim, N., & Kumar, Y. J. (2015). A framework for multi-document abstractive summarization based on semantic role labelling. *Applied Soft Computing*, *30*, 737–747. doi:10.1016/j.asoc.2015.01.070

Lin, C. Y. (2004, July). Rouge: A package for automatic evaluation of summaries. In *Text summarization branches out: Proceedings of the ACL-04 workshop* (Vol. 8). Academic Press.

Liu, C. Y., Chen, M. S., & Tseng, C. Y. (2015). Incrests: Towards real-time incremental short text summarization on comment streams from social network services. *IEEE Transactions on Knowledge and Data Engineering*, *27*(11), 2986–3000. doi:10.1109/TKDE.2015.2405553

Lloret, E., & Palomar, M. (2012). Text summarisation in progress: A literature review. *Artificial Intelligence Review*, *37*(1), 1–41. doi:10.100710462-011-9216-z

Louis, A., & Nenkova, A. (2009, August). Automatically evaluating content selection in summarization without human models. In *Proceedings of the 2009 Conference on Empirical Methods in Natural Language Processing* (pp. 306-314). Association for Computational Linguistics. 10.3115/1699510.1699550

Luhn, H. P. (1958). the automatic creation of literature abstracts. *IBM Journal of Research and Development*, *2*(2), 159–165. doi:10.1147/rd.22.0159

Mani, I. (2001). *Automatic summarization* (Vol. 3). John Benjamins Publishing. doi:10.1075/nlp.3

Mirshojaei, S. H., & Masoomi, B. (2015). Text Summarization Using Cuckoo Search Optimisation Algorithm. *Journal of Computer & Robotics*, *8*(2), 19–24.

Mosa, M. A., Anwar, A. S., & Hamouda, A. (2019). A survey of multiple types of text summarization with their satellite contents based on swarm intelligence optimization algorithms. *Knowledge-Based Systems, 163*, 518-532. DOI. org/10.1016/j.knosys.2018.09.008

Mosa, M. A., Hamouda, A., & Marei, M. (2017a). Ant colony heuristic for user-contributed comments summarization. *Knowledge-Based Systems*, *118*, 105–114. doi:10.1016/j.knosys.2016.11.009

Mosa, M. A., Hamouda, A., & Marei, M. (2017b). Graph coloring and ACO based summarization for social networks. *Expert Systems with Applications*, *74*, 115–126. doi:10.1016/j.eswa.2017.01.010

Mosa, M. A., Hamouda, A., & Marei, M. (2017c). *How can Ants Extract the Essence Contents Satellite of Social Networks*. LAP Lambert Academic Publishing.

Nenkova, A. (2006). Summarization evaluation for text and speech: issues and approaches. *INTERSPEECH*.

Nikoo, M. D., Faraahi, A., Hashemi, S. M., & Erfani, S. H. (2012). A Method for Text Summarization by Bacterial Foraging Optimisation Algorithm. *IJCSI International Journal of Computer Science Issues, 9*(4), 36–40.

Ouyang, Y., Li, W., Li, S., & Lu, Q. (2011). Applying regression models to query-focused multi-document summarization. *Information Processing & Management, 47*(2), 227–237. doi:10.1016/j.ipm.2010.03.005

Panigrahi, B. K., Shi, Y., & Lim, M. H. (Eds.). (2011). *Handbook of swarm intelligence: concepts, principles and applications* (Vol. 8). Springer Science & Business Media.

Peyrard, M., & Eckle-Kohler, J. (2016). *A General Optimization Framework for Multi-Document Summarization Using Genetic Algorithms and Swarm Intelligence.* Retrieved from https://pdfs.semanticscholar.org/f744/715aedba86271000c1f49352e0bfdcaa3204.pdf

Prakasam, A., & Savarimuthu, N. (2016). Metaheuristic algorithms and probabilistic behaviour: A comprehensive analysis of Ant Colony Optimization and its variants. *Artificial Intelligence Review, 45*(1), 97–130. doi:10.100710462-015-9441-y

Rautray, R., & Balabantaray, R. C. (2017). Cat swarm optimization based evolutionary framework for multi document summarization. *Physica A, 477*, 174–186. doi:10.1016/j.physa.2017.02.056

Riedhammer, K., Favre, B., & Hakkani-Tür, D. (2010). Long story short- global unsupervised models for keyphrase based meeting summarization. *Speech Communication, 52*(10), 801–815. doi:10.1016/j.specom.2010.06.002

Santra, D., Mondal, A., & Mukherjee, A. (2016). Study of Economic Load Dispatch by Various Hybrid Optimization Techniques. In *Hybrid Soft Computing Approaches* (pp. 37–74). Springer India. doi:10.1007/978-81-322-2544-7_2

Sarkar, K. (2010). Syntactic trimming of extracted sentences for improving extractive multi-document summarization. *Journal of Computers, 2*, 177–184.

Song, W., Choi, L. C., Park, S. C., & Ding, X. F. (2011). Fuzzy evolutionary optimization modelling and its applications to unsupervised categorization and extractive summarization. *Expert Systems with Applications, 38*(8), 9112–9121. doi:10.1016/j.eswa.2010.12.102

Van den Bergh, F., & Engelbrecht, A. P. (2002, October). A new locally convergent particle swarm optimiser. In *Systems, Man and Cybernetics, 2002 IEEE International Conference on* (Vol. 3, pp. 6-pp). IEEE. 10.1109/ICSMC.2002.1176018

Yadav, R. K., & Singh, S. (2016). A New Approach to Automated Summarization based on Fuzzy Clustering and Particle Swarm Optimization. *International Journal of Computers and Applications, 148*(1).

Yang, X-S. (2014). Swarm intelligence based algorithms: A critical analysis. *Evolutionary Intelligence, 7*(1), 17-28.

Yeniay, Ö. (2014). Comparative study of algorithms for response surface optimization. *Mathematical and Computational Applications, 19*(1), 93–104. doi:10.3390/mca19010093

ADDITIONAL READING

Al-Saleh, A. B., & Menai, M. E. B. (2016). Automatic Arabic text summarization: A survey. *Artificial Intelligence Review, 45*(2), 203–234. doi:10.100710462-015-9442-x

El-Fishawy, N., Hamouda, A., Attiya, G. M., & Atef, M. (2014). Arabic summarization in twitter social network. *Ain Shams Engineering Journal, 5*(2), 411–420. doi:10.1016/j.asej.2013.11.002

Gambhir, M., & Gupta, V. (2017). Recent automatic text summarization techniques: A survey. *Artificial Intelligence Review, 47*(1), 1–66. doi:10.100710462-016-9475-9

Liu, C. Y., Chen, M. S., & Tseng, C. Y. (2015). Incrests: Towards real-time incremental short text summarization on comment streams from social network services. *IEEE Transactions on Knowledge and Data Engineering, 27*(11), 2986–3000. doi:10.1109/TKDE.2015.2405553

Mosa, M. A., Hamouda, A., & Marei, M. (2017a). Ant colony heuristic for user-contributed comments summarization. *Knowledge-Based Systems, 118*, 105–114. doi:10.1016/j.knosys.2016.11.009

Mosa, M. A., Hamouda, A., & Marei, M. (2017b). Graph coloring and ACO based summarization for social networks. *Expert Systems with Applications, 74*, 115–126. doi:10.1016/j.eswa.2017.01.010

Mosa, M. A., Hamouda, A., & Marei, M. (2017c). *How can Ants Extract the Essence Contents Satellite of Social Networks*. LAP Lambert Academic Publishing.

Sarkar, K. (2010). Syntactic trimming of extracted sentences for improving extractive multi-document summarization. *Journal of Computers*, *2*, 177–184.

KEY TERMS AND DEFINITIONS

Automatic Summarization: The process helps to reduce a huge amount of data to a short set of words that reveals the core of the full text.

Multi-Document Summarization: An automatic process target at extraction of information from multiple documents written about the same topic.

Natural Language Processing: The process concerned with the interactions between computers and different natural languages of human, in particular how to machines to process and analyze big-data of natural language.

Nature Heuristic Techniques: Techniques designed for solving complicated problems especially, optimization ones more quickly when traditional methods fail to find an exact solution.

Short Text Summarization: A process targeting to select the most important short texts written about the same topic.

Swarm Intelligence Techniques: SI systems possess typically of a population of a number of agents interacting with each other within their environment. These interactions between all agents lead to the emergence of "intelligent" global behavior, unknown to the individual agents.

Text Mining: The process of extracting and deriving high quality and important information from text.

Chapter 5
Named Entity Recognition in Document Summarization

Sandhya P.
Vellore Institute of Technology, Chennai Campus, Tamil Nadu, India

Mahek Laxmikant Kantesaria
Vellore Institute of Technology, Chennai Campus, Tamil Nadu, India

ABSTRACT

Named entity recognition (NER) is a subtask of the information extraction. NER system reads the text and highlights the entities. NER will separate different entities according to the project. NER is the process of two steps. The steps are detection of names and classifications of them. The first step is further divided into the segmentation. The second step will consist to choose an ontology which will organize the things categorically. Document summarization is also called automatic summarization. It is a process in which the text document with the help of software will create a summary by selecting the important points of the original text. In this chapter, the authors explain how document summarization is performed using named entity recognition. They discuss about the different types of summarization techniques. They also discuss about how NER works and its applications. The libraries available for NER-based information extraction are explained. They finally explain how NER is applied into document summarization.

DOI: 10.4018/978-1-5225-9373-7.ch005

INTRODUCTION

Named-entity Recognition (NER) is the process in which the entities are extracted for searching, sorting and storing textual information into the categories such as names of organizations, places, persons, expressions of time, quantities or any other measurable quantity. NER system extracts from the plain text in English language or in any other language. NER is also called as entity extraction or entity identification. NER finds the entities from the raw and unstructured data and then define them into different categories. NER reacts differently with different systems. Hence output of one project may not be the same as the output of another project. Although the required outputs of two different systems will be different.

NER is the subtask of the information extraction. It is also a significant component of natural language processing applications. Part-of-Speech tagging, semantic parsers and thematic meaning representations will all outperform when NER is integrated. NER plays a vital role in systems like question answers system, textual entailment, automatic forwarding and news and document searching. NER provides proper and good analytical results. NER is carried out based on different learning methods according to the systems it is being used in. There are three learning methods: Supervised Learning (SL), unsupervised learning (UL) and semi-supervised learning (SSL) (Sekine & Ranchhod, 2007). Supervised learning needs a large dataset. As there is shortage of such datasets, the other two methods are preferred over supervised learning.

Document summarization is a process by which the text is automatically condensed to a summary with the most important information. In general for a human it is required to read the documents and then summarize it. Hence we can extract vital information, we can use them in the use cases such as; dates from feedback system, famous product or model of an item and reviews about the locations. There are many ways to identify the phrases from the text. The simplest method for text identification is by using the dictionary of words.

NER can also be used to process the document. It will extract the words, which are called as entities. These entities will be categorized like persons, organizations, places, time and measurement, and many more. The most important words will then be selected. These words would work as summary for the given document.

In this chapter we explain how document summarization is performed using Named Entity Recognition. First, we discuss about the Named-entity recognition. Then we explain document summarization. The evaluation techniques for text summarization are explained. We then explain how NER works practically with its applications. Then we have mentioned about applying NER to document summarization and issues with it. Then recent advances are explained.

Named Entity Recognition

Named Entity Recognition (NER) is a subtask of the Information Extraction. Information Extraction(IE) is the process in which the structured data is extracted from the unstructured and/or semi-structured data. NER is very useful for the content extraction and automatic annotation from the multi-media documentary. The human approach is satisfied with the Natural Language Processing(NLP) which will solve the problem of automatic machine understandable data into the human language processing. IE will have a set of documents which will be matched to the preprocessed templates. The manner of the text will be the same, but the data will differ (Bhandari et al., 2017). For example, the template of the topic on terrorism will have the information for perpetrator, victim, weapons, terrorist groups and more. Hence this will try to make us understand the information about the corresponding slots for information retrieval.

NER systems are the type of state-of-the-art intelligence systems which almost match to the human efficiency. This system is trained in such manner that it can find the entities from the unstructured data and categorize them efficiently. This system reads the text and highlights the entities. NER will separate different entities according to the project. Hence NER is a domain sensitive concept. Also, NER for one project may not be useful for the other.

NER have named entities divided into the different categories like organizations, person names, medical terms, time expressions, locations, money values, quantities, percentages and many more. Let us take an example of an unannotated block of text:

Ram bought 500 shares of TATA in 2010.

Now, annotating the text it will be like:

[Ram]$_{Person}$ bought 500 shares of [TATA]$_{Organization}$ in [2010]$_{Time}$.

The named entity refers to the rigid names which are defined by Kripke (Kripke, Saul. 1982). It will not stand for the phrases or the words that are somewhat referable. But in practice the NER agrees to have many other names and referents which are not rigid. For example, the famous automotive company established by Henry Ford can be referred as 'Ford Motor Company' or 'Ford'. But 'Ford' also refers to other meaning like crossing a water body at shallow place. The rules in NER includes the proper name and medical terms but excludes the pronouns (such as 'it').

NER process involves two steps. The steps are detection of names and classifying them. The first step further involves segmentation. Continuous words are considered as tokens and nesting is not allowed. This will be helpful in identifying the named entities like 'Bank of India' as the single entity, although we know that the word 'India' itself can act as a named entity. The second step is to choose an ontology which will organize the things categorically.

Numerical expressions like money, percentage and time are also considered as named entity in NER. For example, 'in the year 2001' is a rigid designator. A term is said to be a rigid designator when it designates the same thing in all possible worlds in which that thing exists. Here, 2001 is the rigid reference to the Gregorian calendar. However, 'I will go on a trip in June' is loosely quantified since June may refer to the month of current year, next year or after 5 years.

As the technology is increasing the need for hierarchical entity is demanded. Recently BBN (originally Bolt, Beranek and Newman) Technologies in 2002, proposed 29 types and 200 sub-types for Question Answering. Recently, Ritter in 2011, used Freebase entity types in social media texts.

There are basically three learning methods in NER; which are Supervised learning, Semi-Supervised learning and unsupervised learning (Nadeau D. & Sekine S., 2007). Supervised learning (SL) method is the most dominant method among all. Supervised learning includes techniques like Hidden Markov Models, Decision Trees, Maximum Entropy Models, Support Vector Machine and Conditional Random Fields. The systems implementing these techniques will have to read a large annotated dataset. It will go through the whole list and remember the entities from the dataset. Then it will create unambiguous rules on retrieved features. The SL system will tag the test corpus words from studying the annotated entities from training dataset. The second method is semi-supervised learning (SSL) method which is newer than SL. The technique SSL uses is bootstrapping. For example, a system which needs to identify names of disease needs a small dataset with example names. By using this dataset system tries to find the sentences with these entities. Again, then system finds other sentences with related disease names. The process continues till a large context is gathered. The third method is unsupervised learning method. The most obvious technique used is clustering. We can find named entities from already clustered groups of text on the basis of similarity. This will indeed rely on lexical resources, lexical patterns and statistics of large unannotated dataset.

For evaluation of output of NER system, many measures are considered. Accuracy is defined on the token level. Simultaneously it has problems like: many tokens of real world text are not resided in the defined entity names, so baseline accuracy is much higher than expected; and misreading of the full name occurs which is not penalized properly, like person's full name is ½ accuracy defined. In the CoNLL (*Conference* on Natural Language Learning) conference has defined F1 score (Goutte C.& Gaussier E., 2005) as below:

- Precision is the number of the predicted entities which are exactly as the gold standards evaluation data, i.e. when [$_{Person}$ Harry] [$_{Person}$ Blick] is predicted, but [$_{Person}$ Harry Blick] is not predicted. So, the precision for the predicted text is zero. Precision is average of all predicted text.
- Recall is the number of the names in gold standard that are exactly at the same locations as in predictions.
- F1 score is equal to the harmonic mean of the above two measures.

NER systems uses linguistic technique of grammar-based and statistical methods of machine learning. Grammar-based techniques are most reliable with better precision and low recall and with the hard work of experienced computational linguists. While statistical systems require the manually annotated data in a large amount. Machine learning NER systems are mostly based on conditional random fields.

NER systems are very fragile, as they are developed for one domain and does not perform well for the other. So, the same effort is required to make it perform well in other domains. This is very true for both statistical and rule-based systems. In early stages of NER systems in 1990s, it was mainly focused on journalistic documents. Then the focus changed to military documents and reports. Later, the automatic content extraction (ACE) (Doddington et al., 2004) included many styles of informal texts such as weblogs, conversational text scripts, etc. Since 1998, the entities are very interestingly identified from medical domain. The most interesting sub-domain is the gene names. The same is for the chemical entities and names of the drugs. In medical domain, the text is written in the native language. So first the English vocabularies are translated into the native language and then NER approach is applied.

There are many use cases (Sanjana Kamath & Rupali Wagh, 2017) where the named entity recognition is applied. Some of them are as follows.

1. Discretion of the news content

The publishing and news houses will have to generate a very large amount of the online content every day. Hence to manage them it will need an extra effort as they must get the most from all content. NER systems can automatically scan all the content and tell the most important information from it. Having the knowledge of the predefined tags we can automatically categories the articles according to the categories and enable easy discovery. There are many NER APIs available on internet for free to perform this task.

2. Effectual search algorithms

Imagine you are developing an application for internal searching from the documents. Now one query will be fired and will search through all the documents, taking more time. The efficient way for this problem is by using NER. NER can be run on the documents and the entities from each document are stored in one document. Now when the query is run, it will be matched only with the document stored with entities. This will lead to faster searching technique.

3.   Fueling Content Recommendations

Recommendation systems are having very useful in today's world. Netflix is the best example of the recommendation system. Recommendation system can do wonders for the media specific company by showing more engaging and addictive contents. For news writers, using NER will tell them the similar content articles. This is done by extracting the entities from one article and recommending other articles which has the most similarity between them. The media industry appropriately uses the content recommendations.

4.   Customer service support

There are many techniques by which we can handle the customer feedback system. Suppose a person is handling a customer feedback store of a clothing line which has many branches in world. So, daily he has to handle many customer feedbacks of the company named Blue Cloud. Suppose a customer has commented on social media saying that "@blue_cloud please train Bangalore staff for current trending fashion clothes ". Now the NER API would get the company name and location entity as Blue Cloud and Bangalore as their values. This is categorizing the complaint. This is very easy way to handle feedbacks.

5.   Research Papers

Scholastic papers and research papers is one of the biggest dataset available with online publication. There could be innumerable papers of one topic with the slightest modification. Querying through the documents will take a lot of time for specific information. Separating the papers through the entities will help to save the trouble of finding through all the documents. Hence from then the system will glance only through the important named entities and check for that document. So, giving the specified words will only search through the required documents.

Document Summarization

Document summarization is also called as automatic summarization. It is a process in which the text document with the help of software will create a summary by selecting the important points of the original text. Document summarization is fragment of data mining and machine learning. The core idea is to find the subset of document which will summarize the whole document. Nowadays summarization is very useful. Search engines are a good example of systems using summarization. Other examples are media types like video and image collections. Document summarization creates a summary of the entire document by using the important sentences and image summarization finds the most suitable image from the group of images. This is very helpful in the type of the surveillance videos to find out the most important information (Babar S., 2013).

The most common approach of summarization is; extraction and abstraction. Extraction is the method in which the existing words from the document are selected and presented as the summary. While abstractive method builds the semantically meaningful summary and it uses natural language processing for the human touch to it. Mainly research consists of the extractive methods (Hahn U. & Mani I. 2000). Now elaborating all the techniques very briefly as follows:

1.   Extraction-based summarization

In this type of system, it extracts the words or objects from the entire documents. It also does not modify any of the content. Key phrase extraction is the example in which it selects the phrases that will give summary of the document. In document summarization the main aim is to select the words from the document and create a summary for it. In image collection summarization the main aim is to extract the most relevant image from the group.

2.   Abstraction-based summarization

Abstraction is the method in which it involves paraphrasing of the document. Hence it condenses the document more efficiently than extraction. The system uses the natural language processing which is difficult to explore. There are very few works done in abstractive methods in comparison to extractive summarization.

3.   Aided summarization:

Machine learning is used for document summarization with text mining or information retrieval. So, Machine Aided Human Summarization will help with summarization and there is Human Aided Machine Summarization which will require the post human help.

Recently Deep Learning is showing good results in document summarization. The approach is proposed as the sequence-to-sequence problem. This acts as abstractive methods and it will generate the whole new summary by creating new language model for source texts. Results obtained from the deep learning methods are not so as expected to the results of the extractive methods. However, they are impressive for the news articles headlines. Here the main advantage of this type of system is that it does not include any preprocessing of the data and does not require the special vocabulary. As these models are completely data driven (Munot N. & Govilkar S. 2014).

Systems for Document Summarization

There are two types of extractive summarization methods; generic summarization and query relevant summarization. Generic summarization refers to the method in which the summary is given for collection of documents, videos or images. Query-based summarization is a process which summarizes object specific to a query.

Keyphrase Extraction

Consider extracting keywords or keyphrases from the given article. In process of providing manually, one may lack considering pre-existing keyphrases. The keyphrases are directly pulled from the text. While abstractive keyphrase will internalize the content and generate keyphrases which don't appear in original text. In supervised learning method, each example of unigram, bigram and trigram are found from text (Turney P. 2002). Based on known features, we assign the class of keyphrases as positive and negative. This is called as binary classification. The unsupervised technique consists of TextRank. TextRank algorithm searches the text itself and decides onto keyphrases that appear central to the text. TextRank doesn't rely on previous training data. TextRank is a generalize graph-based ranking algorithm. For keyphrase extraction, it will build some text units as vertices. Edges are created by co-occurrence of words. In short co-occurrence graph will have dense part which has terms that appear often.

Document Summarization

Document summarization has a goal for identifying summary of a text. Supervised text summarization method has a collection of documents and human generated summaries. These features are learned and applied. The main drawback is that manually created summary doesn't exactly match up with the sentences in the summary. In a workshop, system for multi-document summarization for news domain was developed. It had naïve Bayes classifier with statistical language models. The researchers explored effectiveness of maximum entropy classifier for summarization against feature dependencies. LexRank is an algorithm which uses eigen vector centrality and random walks to have importance of sentences. In both LexRank and TextRank were creating a graph for each document. the edges have semantic similarity or content overlap. LexRank uses cosine similarity of TF-IDF. It combines LexRank score with sentence position and length with user-specified or automatically given weights. TextRank uses single document summarization while LexRank is for multi document summarization.

Multi document summarization is applied to the more than one document for summarization (Hahn U. & Mani I. 2000). The size may vary from bytes to gigabytes. Hence approach depends on the sizes. The approach involves analyzing one document and then applying the same across all documents in transformation and synthesis phases. The method of summarization has steps; elimination, aggregation and generalization operations, on sentences of all documents. Concatenating the summaries of all documents is not appropriate because there could be many summaries which are having redundancy, and this could be ambiguous. Summaries could help to find similarities and differences between the documents. For example, two different news of terrorist attack could have same summary although both occurred at different locations.

Multi lingual summarization can be performed across many languages. It can be applied on languages like Arabic, Czech, Greek, Hindi, Hebrew, Chinese, English, Romanian, French and Spanish (Li et al. 2013). Summarization tool has been developed for these languages to have their summaries.

Issues With Document Summarization

There are issues with the text summarization with single document and multi-documents. These issues could be with grouping documents, identifying most related sentences, reducing redundancy, document ranking, sentence ranking, categorizing sentences, summary accuracy and user interactive interface Shodhaganga (2000). Below mentioned are all issues described in detail.

- Clustering: The system should be able to group the similar documents and sentences.
- Coverage: The ability to find the related sentences across all documents.
- Anti-redundancy: The ability to decrease redundancy between sentences in summary.

- Summary cohesion criteria: The ability to combine the related sentences in a meaningful manner. This includes:
  - Document ordering: Arranging all related and similar sentences at highest position and then the next highest scored sentences are kept.
  - Rank ordering: This will present the most similar information and most dissimilar information first, so that user gets the maximum content.
  - Topic-cohesion: This will categorize sentences by topic clustering using sentence similarity and sentence ranking.
  - Occurrence ordering: Documents or sentences ordering done based on occurrences in search engine retrieval.
- Coherence: Readable summaries are generated and should be helpful to scholars.
- Effective user interface: Easy access to source document or select or eliminate documents.

Evaluation Techniques

Evaluating the techniques of text summarization is very important for the system to build itself to perfection. There are two types of measures; intrinsic and extrinsic. Intrinsic measures involve the evaluation methods using human evaluation and extrinsic measures involve task-based measure of the performance of the system. By evaluation we get to know the truthfulness and usefulness of the system. Measuring readability, comprehensibility and coherence is a tough task to perform. Manual evaluation known as gold standard is also performed by experts. Based on this the qualitative measure is performed. It is achieved by counting the phrases opted by system to the gold standard. The quantitative measurement is done with help of a tool for three measures; recall, precision and F-score.

Extrinsic method checks impact of summarization tasks like information retrieval, classification, or any on the completion of other tasks like reading and relevance assessment. Intrinsic method determines the impact on itself. It checks the quality between automatically generated summary and human made summary. The most important evaluation method is ROUGE (recall oriented understudy of gisting evaluation). It was introduced by Lin (2004). Steinberger J and Jezek K (2009) explained that it is score for similarity of words between human based summary and machine generated summary. This helps to evaluate the summary. It based on similarity of n-grams. The ROUGE-n is calculated as

$$ROUGE-n = \frac{\Sigma C \in RSS \Sigma gram_n \in C \, Count_{match}\left(gram_n\right)}{\Sigma C \in RSS \Sigma gram_n \in C \, Count_{match}\left(gram_n\right)}$$

where $\text{Count}_{match}(\text{gram}_n)$ is the maximum number of n-grams co-occurring in a candidate summary and a reference summary and $\text{Count}(\text{gram}_n)$ is the number of n-grams in the reference summary.

Background Information

NE is the lowest of task performed in Information Extraction. Nobata et. al. (2002) in their paper discusses the system having Named Entity trying to identify the proper nouns like names of location, persons, organizations, expressions and quantity measures. They used sentence extraction technique for text summarization. Various cues were used for this. Statistics like word frequency and document frequency was used to get sentence significance. Linguistics cues were used for the sentence structure.

Mulani N. & Dhamal, S. (2018) has performed text summarization on many languages. To perform text summarization in English, three phases are executed. The first phase is pre-processing, which consists of tokenization, stop word removal and stemmer removal. Here extractive method of NER is used to obtain better stability. Extractive summarization means creating summaries by reusing portions of input text verbatim. The second phase is feature extraction which will create the feature matrix for all sentences. Third step is generating summary by analyzing the score of each sentence. The result is shown in graph format.

Hassel, M. (2004) has performed text summarization for Swedish language. For NER, SweNam (Dalianis and Astrom 2001) is used. It is a preprocessor for SweSum (SweSum is the first automatic text summarizer for Swedish language.) and classifies all entities into names of persons, companies, locations, products, brands and time stamps. Then this summary, which is generated by SweSum is then compared to the gold standard. With NER and gold standard had 33.9% sentences in common. While without NER, summary had 57.2% sentences matched with gold standard. This surely tells that how SweNum is reliable as it mimics the human selection tool.

Munot, N. & Govilkar, S. (2015) have developed a system that takes input as document and build rich semantic graph giving output as summary. The first step is generating rich semantic graph from the input document. This graph is then reduced to semantic graph. The last step is to get the abstractive summary from this reduced semantic graph. NER is used for locating the atomic elements and classifying them to categories. Here they have used Stanford NER tool. An abstractive summarization technique generates summary by re-phrasing the input text.

In the paper presented by G. Veena et. al (2016) Singular Value decomposition and NER is used to extract important sentences from the document. SVD is used to identify the relationships in document. Here multi-document SVD is applied and term-document matrix is created. By SVD they identified the important paragraph from the document. Using NER important entities are identified. This will improve the accuracy of document.

Jhalani, R. & Meena, Y. (2016) has explained the three phases; text analysis, information extraction and sentence generation in their paper. Text analysis summarizes document by using Stanford NLP toolkit. Second phase information extraction will use domain knowledge, extraction rules and heuristics on analyzed text and get the important content. The third phase will generate the summary.

Kallimani J. et. al (2016) explains how abstractive summarization involves collecting information from the document itself. This will generate abstractive summary by unified model with attribute-based information extraction rules and class-based templates. Document is classified with the help of term frequency/ inverse document frequency (TF/IDF) rules. Templates are used to generate intensive summaries. Java API is used for the implementation.

Megala S. et al (2014) uses lexical analysis and data dictionary for this work. Extraction techniques in summarization uses features like indicators cue phrases, NER, local feature, legal vocabulary, state transition feature and 5 more. There are in total 10 features to utilize feature technique for the most accurate summary.

Jiang R. et al (2016) explains how different tools are available for NER. They are using the publicly available tools. Then the outputs are compared with Wikipedia gold standard and self-annotated documents. The best NER tool is applied to the interested domain.

Large clinical records are written in natural language. Aramaki E. et al (2009) presented how to extract information from clinical records. To solve this problem, they convert text into a tabular format. The core steps followed are; medical event recognition modules and negative event identification to check whether an event occurred or not. This proposes SVM-based classifier using NER.

Examples of NER Used for Document Summarization

Pennington J et al. (2014) have developed their own system called as GloVe which is global vectors for word representation. They model necessary properties to have linear directions and said that global log bilinear regression models are most appropriate to do so. They proposed the specified weighted least squares model that was trained on global word-word co-occurrence counts. This model produced word vector space with efficiency of 75% of accuracy. Their method outperformed other methods. Now discussing about the system, first they establish notations. Let X denote word-word co-occurrence matrix. X_{ij} is number of times word j occurs in context of word i. Let $P_{ij} = P(j|i) = X_{ij} / X_i$ be probability that word j appears in word i. for example take $i = ice$ and $j = steam$. The ratio of their co-occurrence with k is measured. For words which are related to ice and not steam like $k = solid$, denotes that P_{ik} / P_{jk} will be large. While words related to steam and not ice, like $k = gas$ will have smaller ratio. Finally, for words like *water* or *computer,* which are related to either both or none will have ratio approximately one. The ratio P_{ik}/P_{jk} depends on three depends on three words *i, j* and *k* with function $F(w_i, w_j, w_k) = Pik/Pjk$. To restrict this function on two words as target we have $F(w_i\text{-}w_j, w_k) = P_{ik}/P_{jk}$. F could be parameterized for neural network $F((w_i\text{-}w_j)^T w_k) = P_{ik}/P_{jk}$. Main drawback is that weights are equally distributed. Such rare co-occurrences are noisy and carry information than the more frequent ones. Some evaluation methods consist of word analogies. Word analogy task has semantic questions like "Athens is to Greece as Berlin is to __?". Another is word similarity where it tests for vector space substructure. They also evaluate their model on word similarity. Another method is Named- entity recognition, where dataset is annotated into four categories: person, location, organization and miscellaneous. Coming to results, GloVe performs very much better than baseline models even with smaller vector size and smaller corpus.

Mulani N. and Dhamak S. (2018) have performed graph-based text summarization by using NER and Part-of-Speech tagger in English language which could be extended to other Indian regional languages. NER is used for better stability of model. They have represented data in graph form. The first step of system is preprocessing module. Here it analyses the input text. Further mentioned are the steps involved in it. First is sentence segmentation, which is breaking text into words with word count. Second is tokenization. Tokenization means splitting into words with help of comma, spaces and special symbols. And last is stop word removal. It removes all unnecessary words which have no importance in sentence. The second step of system is Feature Extraction module. This module accepts preprocessed sentences and generates NER and POS for next module. Vector feature terms are used for every sentence to check statistically and linguistically. Each sentence gets a score which ranges between 0 to 1. NER label words as entities. POS tagger assigns parts of speech to words. The last module is summarized module. Each sentence has weight based on feature terms. There are many features which are described one by one. First is average TF-ISF, which says that term frequency is distribution of each word over document. Inverse sentence frequency is measure which says that a term occurs in few sentences which are more important than others. Third is sentence length; it filters out short and long sentences. Fourth is sentence position which means that beginning sentences are thematic and end sentences are conclusion. Fifth is numerical data feature which insists that numerical data should be included in summary. Sixth is sentence to sentence similarity. Seventh is title feature which consists of words that signifies gist of summary. Eighth feature is SVO qualification. The sentence has an order of <subject><verb><object> in English. The sentences are arranged in descending order by how summary is generated. Summarized graph is created.

Sripada S. et al. have presented a paper with multi-document summarization by extraction method. They have given three techniques by which summarization occurs in a collection of documents. The first technique is to select sentences with maximum importance score to have summary. Instead of selfishly picking sentences on scores, they build algorithm of stack decoder which close to optimal solution. It close to optimal and not optimal because stack sizes are limited in algorithm to prevent exponential blowup. In the second technique, they cluster using the semantic scores of K-means clustering algorithm. The centroid from clusters is placed in summary. The third technique is graph based where generating summary is converted to problem of finding cliques in sentence distance graph. A clique in graph means a strongly connected component which is formed by subset of vertices. These cliques are added to form summary, based on importance score. Dataset consists of 60 sets of 10 documents each. Generalized abstract 100 words or lesser was created. There are many features considered to score a sentence. Similarity scores are Jaccard similarity, Cosine similarity and TF-IDF similarity. The Jaccard similarity is said to be amount of word overlap normalized by union of sets of the words in two sentences. Cosine similarity is defined by cosine of an angle between vectors represented by the word-frequency vectors of two sentences. TF-IDF is vector-based model. Each sentence is given an important score. These scores are used to order sentences and find most important ones. Higher the score, higher is the probability of sentence being in the summary. Each sentence is measured against a set of features. The score is defined as weighted sum of individual feature values. The features are TF-IDF sum, sentence length, named entities count, top-k important words, sentence position, numerical literal count, upper case letters count, nouns count, verbs count and adjectives count. These features are generated for training data and then employed to documents. Some of the features are normalized. TF-IDF sum, top-k important words, upper case letters, named entities count, numerical literals count and POS tag counts are normalized by dividing with sentence length.

Hassel M (2003) have performed text summarization in Swedish language. SweSum is proposed for Swedish newspaper. It has many topic identification schemes for itself. Sentences are beginning of document are scored high. A sentence with keyword is also scored high. A keyword could be defined as word with high term frequency. For named entities SweNam is used. SweNam will identify the entities and categorized them into names of persons, companies, locations and time stamps. SweNam will give this input to SweSum. All entities are at equal weights. With help of this, SweSum will generate a summary for document. Two sets of text each with ten texts are given for creating gold standard. Two evaluate these groups, a system was devised to gather manual extracts from group. There is a low agreement among human extractors as to which sentences form a good summary. Then extracted summary with SweSum is compared to the gold standard. They found out that summaries with using NER was having 33.9% similarity to the gold standard. While the summary without using NER had 57.2% similarity to the gold standard. This only tells us that how well SweSum objectifies human selection. Different runs with SweSum is incorporated to get the summary. When named entities are given no weights they will get extracted as there are large amount of common words. This gives high cohesion in summary but rarely will have condensed redundancy. Another drawback was that named entities having weights seemed repetitive in summary.

Applying NER Into Document Summarization

Earlier days document summarization was just some tedious task. Now with the help of NER it will be easily handled. NER helps to label the sequence of words which will further be used for creating summary. NER labels the nouns which will fetch the words which are in categories of names of persons, locations, organizations and expressions of quantity. This is very helpful for the summary. Now if we apply word frequency on it we will get the most important words from the document. This is how NER helped text summarization.

HR department is facing a very big time-consuming task of segregating the resumes of applied candidates and more tedious is fetch the real gems from a big pile of resumes. To add this many resume are flooding with information, half of it which turns out to be unimportant. Through NER model the resumes can be evaluated very quickly. This will decrease the burden of professionals.

First the main task is to create an annotated dataset to train the model. Almost 220 resumes were taken for this task. They could be downloaded from online jobs platform. Dataturks is the platform where resumes are automatically annotated and were manually annotated too. The tool is very helpful to create annotations of entities and generate a JSON formatted data. This is called as training data. These resumes Cn b downloaded from here (https://dataturks.com/projects/abhishek.narayanan/ Entity%20Recognition%20in%20Resumes).

Here training dataset consists of 200 resumes and test dataset has 20 resumes.

Here we are using spaCy to train the model. A sample of JSON file which is generated is

spaCy's model are very efficient in tagging the entities. They use prediction technique that whether a word is a named entity. These predictions are based on the training dataset which trained model. By giving the test data, predictions are made. As annotators know the answers correctly, they can give the feedback in the form of the error gradient of loss function. This function tells that if the difference in gradient is more, then more updating is required to model.

The model should be generalized. Like for word 'Amazon', it comes with many meaning. It could be a company name or a river name. But here in this context it

Figure 1. Interface of NER system
(https://dataturks.com/projects/abhishek.narayanan/Entity%20Recognition%20in%20Resumes)

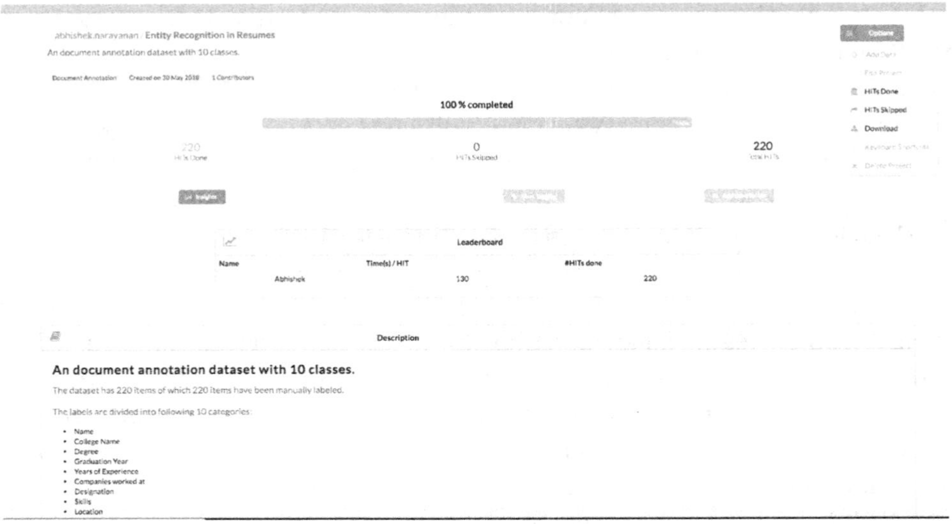

Figure 2. Entities searched and highlighted
(https://dataturks.com/projects/abhishek.narayanan/Entity%20Recognition%20in%20Resumes)

Figure 3. Snippet of annotated resume

```
[
  {
    "label": [
      "Email Address"
    ],
    "points": [
      {
        "start": 998,
        "end": 1037,
        "text": "indeed.com/r/Pavithra-M/26f392ec8251143b"
      }
    ]
  },
  {
    "label": [
      "Skills"
    ],
    "points": [
      {
        "start": 611,
        "end": 983,
        "text": "ADOBE PHOTOSHOP (Less than 1 year), ANDROID (Less than 1 year), APPLICA
          :\n\n█ Programing Languages: C, C++ and JAVA.\n\n█ Databases: MySQL, SQL serve
      }
    ]
}
```

will act as a company name. So, get highest accuracy, small batches of the data is taken into consideration. Train for many iterations so that accuracy is achieved. Another important measure is dropout rate. It is rate at which a model drops the features randomly. For example, if the dropout rate is 0.3 then each feature has 30% possibility to get dropped.

The test dataset is of 20 resumes. The accuracy is measured by recall, precision and f-score. An overall score is generated on the test data. The entity-wise result is shown in Table 1.

Table 1. Comparison of entities by the evaluation factors in spaCy method

Recognized Entity	Precision	Recall	F1-Score
College Name	100%	100%	100%
Location	99.28%	99.27%	99.27%
Designation	100%	98.78%	99.39%
Email Address	100%	99.43%	99.71%
Name	97.83%	97.83%	97.83%
Skills	94.30%	98.40%	96.32%

(https://towardsdatascience.com/a-review-of-named-entity-recognition-ner-using-automatic-summarization-of-resumes-5248a75de175)

The entities will get the data like as follows:

- Degree: Bachelor of Computer Science
- Designation: Java Developer
- Graduation Year: 2016
- Name: Raj Mehta
- Companies worked at: Wipro
- Email: green.com/r/raj-mehta/4632947
- Location: Bengaluru
- Skills: Java (less than 1 year), REST API (less than 1 year), Spring Framework (less than 1 year), UI Technologies

Using Stanford NER in Java model to train data. Every line has word-label pair, where world and label are separated by '\t'. Documents are tokenized into words. Stanford CoreNLP have a properties file which will state all the required parameters to build a model. The same accuracy is measured and output of all measures is shown in Table 2.

Table 3 compares both the models with their ultimate evaluating measures.

Issues With Document Summarization Using NER

Document summarization has the input of document and output as the summary of the text. Now applying the concept of NER to document summarization, we get the

Table 2. Comparison of entities by evaluation measures in Stanford NER method

Recognized Entity	Precision	Recall	F1-Score
College Name	100%	100%	100%
Location	100%	97.78%	98.88%
Designation	100%	100%	100%
Email Address	95.83%	100%	97.87%
Name	100%	100%	100%
Skills	96.36%	96.36%	96.36%
Years of Experience	100%	100%	100%
Graduation Year	96.55%	87.50%	91.80%
Degree	100%	100%	100%
Companies worked at	98.08%	100%	99.03%

(https://towardsdatascience.com/a-review-of-named-entity-recognition-ner-using-automatic-summarization-of-resumes-5248a75de175)

Table 3. Comparing both methods

Recognized Entity	F-Score for spaCy	F-Score for Stanford NER
College Name	100%	100%
Location	98.97%	98.88%
Designation	99.39%	100%
Email Address	99.71%	97.87%
Name	99.81%	100%
Skills	100%	96.36%
MEAN	99.64%	98.85%

(https://towardsdatascience.com/a-review-of-named-entity-recognition-ner-using-automatic-summarization-of-resumes-5248a75de175)

entities which are processed phrases from which the most important ones will be forming summary in the end. The technology always comes with its pros and cons.

First problem with using NER in document summarization is selecting the most relevant information from the source document (Hahn U. & Mani I., 2000). The second problem is to know whether the summary is correctly shown. These problems are so open that sometimes it is difficult to find the solutions. The importance of the information depends on the readers of that document.

Assigning weights for the named-entity is sometimes very poor. It will prioritize the elaborative sentences over introductory and will go into the serious loss. Elaborative sentences have more importance than the introductory because the introductory sentences focuses on something newly introduced in the document.

The toughest of all is that what should be included in the summary and what is to be extracted from the document. The relevant features are derived as the solution for the first document and all other documents too (Mani 2001). This will be further used to have scoring the sentences or paragraphs. Now select the top ranked sentences/ paragraphs and will result into summary. Scoring is the measure of the probability of the likelihood of the closeness of it to the summary. But the main thing is that there are many ways of having the features. The simplest of all, having the summary is concatenation strategy, which is simple order of selected sentences from document (Paice 1990).

Recent Advances in Document Summarization Using NER

Many new approaches have been developed since the first discovery. The state-of-the-art approaches consists of the diverse techniques. It talks about the improved concept coverage, information diversity, content coherence and summarization frameworks that integrate sentence compression. The new abstractive systems are now being able to produce new sentences. This will also solve the problem of closeness of the output summary to the actual required one (Yao J. et al. 2017).

CONCLUSION

Here applying NER to the unstructured data we can get the relationships between the entities. These entities could be a type of name of person, organization, location, time & quantity measure expressions and many more. The important entities can be extracted from the document. These entities are then categorized. After categorizing they form into a phrase which will in turn be the summary of the data. So, this is a very new way to obtain document summarization.

FUTURE ENHANCEMENT

The work in the field of document summarization is now growing ever since the new technologies were introduced. The advent of machine learning has given a whole new lot of aspect. Now divide the document summarization into the problem specific and algorithm specific. Then in problem specific we could say that document summarization could be enhance to the version of multi domain summarization and cross language multi documents summarization (source and summary both in different language). In algorithm specific some new approaches could be added to it like RNN, LSTM, Reinforcement Learning and Generative Adversarial Networks.

REFERENCES

Automatic summarization. (2019, June 19). Retrieved from https://en.wikipedia.org/wiki/Automatic_summarization

Babar, S. (2013). *Text Summarization: An Overview*. Retrieved from https://www.researchgate.net/publication/257947528_Text_SummarizationAn_Overview

Bengfort, B. (2013, April 17). *An Introduction to Named Entity Recognition in Natural Language Processing - Part 1*. Retrieved from http://www.datacommunitydc.org/blog/2013/04/a-survey-of-stochastic-and-gazetteer-based-approaches-for-named-entity-recognition

Bhandari, N., Chowdri, R., Singh, H., & Qureshi, S. R. (2017). Resolving Ambiguities in Named Entity Recognition Using Machine Learning. *Next Generation Computing and Information Systems (ICNGCIS) 2017 International Conference on*, 159-163.

Complete guide to build your own Named Entity Recognizer with Python. (2018, April 29). Retrieved from https://nlpforhackers.io/named-entity-extraction/

DistrictDataLabs. (2017, December 27). *Named Entity Recognition and Classification for Entity Extraction*. Retrieved from https://medium.com/district-data-labs/named-entity-recognition-and-classification-for-entity-extraction-6f23342aa7c5

Doddington, G., Mitchell, A., Przybocki, M., Ramshaw, L., Strassel, S., & Weischedel, R. (2004). The Automatic Content Extraction (ACE) program-tasks, data, and evaluation. *Proceedings of LREC*. 2.

Eiji, A., Miura, Y. T. M., Tomoko, O., Hiroshi, M., & Kazuhiko, O. (2009). TEXT2TABLE: Medical Text Summarization System Based on Named Entity Recognition and Modality Identification. *Proceedings of the BioNLP 2009 Workshop, 2009, Association for Computational Linguistics*, 185-192.

Entity extraction: How does it work? (2016, July 7). Retrieved from https://www.expertsystem.com/entity-extraction-work/

Goutte, C., & Gaussier, E. (2005). A Probabilistic Interpretation of Precision, Recall and *F*-Score, with Implication for Evaluation. In D. E. Losada & J. M. Fernández-Luna (Eds.), Lecture Notes in Computer Science: Vol. 3408. *Advances in Information Retrieval. ECIR 2005*. Berlin: Springer. doi:10.1007/978-3-540-31865-1_25

Hahn, U., & Mani, I. (2000). The Challenges of Automatic Summarization. *Computer, 33*(11), 29–36. doi:10.1109/2.881692

Hassel, M. (2003). Exploitation of Named Entities in Automatic Text Summarization for Swedish. *Proceedings of NODALIDA'03 – 14th Nordic Conferenceon Computational Linguistics*.

Hassel, M. (2004). Evaluation of Automatic Text Summarization, A practical implementation. *Licentiate Thesis Stockholm*, 59-67.

Jagadish, S. (2016, January). Statistical and analytical study of guided abstractive text summarization. *Research Communications. Current Science, 110*(1), 10.

Jhalani & Meena. (2017). An Abstractive Approach For Text Summarization. *International Journal of Advanced Computational Engineering and Networking, 5*(1), 5-10.

Jiang, R., & Banchs, E. (2016). Evaluating and Combining Name Entity Recognition Systems. Academic Press. doi:10.18653/v1/W16-2703

Josef & Karel. (2009). Evaluation Measures For Text Summarization. Computing and Informatics, 28, 1001–1026.

Kamath & Wagh. (2017). Named Entity Recognition Approaches and Challenges. *International Journal of Advanced Research in Computer and Communication Engineering, 6*(2).

Kripke, S. (1982). *Naming and Necessity*. Boston: Harvard University Press.

KumarP. (2013, November 22). *Document Summarization*. Retrieved from https://www.slideshare.net/pratikkumarshanu/document-summarization

Li, Forascu, El-Haj, & Giannakopoulos. (2013). Multi-document multilingual summarization corpus preparation, Part 1: Arabic, English, Greek, Chinese, Romanian. *MultiLing 2013: Multilingual Multi-document Summarization Proceedings of the Workshop.*

Li, S., & Li, S. (2018, August 17). *Named Entity Recognition with NLTK and SpaCy*. Retrieved from https://towardsdatascience.com/named-entity-recognition-with-nltk-and-spacy-8c4a7d88e7da

Lin, C.-Y. (2004). ROUGE: A Package for Automatic Evaluation of summaries. *Proceedings of the ACL Workshop: Text Summarization Braches Out.*

Loper, E., & Bird, S. (2002). NLTK: The Natural Language Toolkit. In *Proceedings of the ACL Workshop on Effective Tools and Methodologies for Teaching Natural Language Processing and Computational Linguistics*. Philadelphia: Association for Computational Linguistics. 10.3115/1118108.1118117

Minkov, E., Wang, R., & Cohen, W. (2005). Extracting Personal Names from Email: Applying Named Entity Recognition to Informal Text. *Conference: HLT/EMNLP 2005, Human Language Technology Conference and Conference on Empirical Methods in Natural Language Processing, Proceedings of the Conference.*

Molĺa, D., van Zaanen, M., & Smith, D. (2006). Named Entity Recognition for Question Answering. *Proceedings of the 2006 Australasian Language Technology Workshop (ALTW2006)*, 51–58.

Multi-document summarization. (2018, February 8). Retrieved from https://en.wikipedia.org/wiki/Multi-document_summarization

Munot & Govilkar. (2014). Comparative Study of Text Summarization Methods. *International Journal of Computer Applications, 102*(12).

Munot, N., & Govilkar, S. S. (2015, February). Conceptual Framework For Abstractive Text Summarization. *International Journal on Natural Language Computing, 4*(1), 39–50. doi:10.5121/ijnlc.2015.4104

Nadeau, D., & Sekine, S. (2007). A Survey of Named Entity Recognition and Classification. *Lingvisticae Investigationes., 30*. doi:10.1075/li.30.1.03nad

Nilofar, M. S. D. (2018). Graph Based Text Summarization using NER and POS. *International Journal for Scientific Research & Development, 5*(12), 85–87.

Nobata, C., Sekine, S., Isahara, H., & Grishman, R. (2002). Summarization System Integrated with Named Entity Tagging and IE pattern Discovery. *The Third International Conference on Language Resources and Evaluation.*

Paice, D. (1990). Constructing Literature Abstracts by Computer: Techniques and Prospects. *Information Processing & Management, 26*(1), 171–186. doi:10.1016/0306-4573(90)90014-S

Pennington, J., Socher, R., & Manning, C. (2014). GloVe: Global Vectors for Word Representation. *Proceedings of the 2014 Conference on Empirical Methods in Natural Language Processing (EMNLP)*, 1532–1543. 10.3115/v1/D14-1162

Recognition, N. E. (2018, February 6). *Applications and Use Cases.* Retrieved from https://towardsdatascience.com/named-entity-recognition-applications-and-use-cases-acdbf57d595e

Santhana Megala, S. (2014). Enriching Text Summarization using Fuzzy Logic. *International Journal of Computer Science and Information Technologies, 5*(1), 863–867.

Sekine, S., & Ranchhod, E. (2007). Named Entities: Recognition, classification and use cases. *Lingvisticæ Investigationes, 30*(1), 3–26. doi:10.1075/li.30.1.03nad

Shodhaganga. (2000). *Single and Multi-document Summarization. Optimized Summarization Of Research Papers Using Data Mining Strategies.* SVKM's MPSTME, NMIMS.

Sripada, S., Kasturi, V., & Parai, G. (n.d.). *Multi-document extraction based Summarization.* CS 224N: Final Project, Stanford University.

Sripada, S., Kasturi, V. G., & Parai, G. K. (2010). *Multi-document extraction based Summarization*. Retrieved from https://nlp.stanford.edu/courses/cs224n/2010/reports/

Sulaiman, Abdul Wahid, Sarkawi, & Omar. (2017). Using Stanford NER and Illinois NER to Detect Malay Named Entity Recognition. *International Journal of Computer Theory and Engineering, 9*(2).

Turney, P. D. (2002). Learning Algorithms for Keyphrase Extraction. *Information Retrieval, 2*(4), 303–336. arXiv:cs/0212020

Veena, G., Gupta, D., Jaganadh, J., & Nithya Sreekumar, S. (2016, December). A Graph Based Conceptual Mining Model for Abstractive Text Summarization. *Indian Journal of Science and Technology, 9*(S1). doi:10.17485/ijst/2016/v9iS1/99876

Yao, Wan, & Xiao. (2017). Recent advances in document summarization. *Knowledge and Information Systems, 53,* 1-40. doi:10.100710115-017-1042-4

KEY TERMS AND DEFINITIONS

Abstraction-Based Summary: Abstractive methods build an internal semantic representation and then use natural language generation techniques to create a summary that is closer to what a human might express.

Document Summarization: Automatic summarization is the process of shortening a text document with software, to create a summary with the major points of the original document.

Extraction-Based Summarization: In extraction-based summarization an extract is constructed by selecting pieces of text (words, phrases, sentences, paragraphs) from the original source and organizing them in a way to produce a coherent summary.

Information Extraction: Information extraction is the task of automatically extracting structured information from unstructured and/or semi-structured machine-readable documents.

Named-Entity Recognition: Named-entity recognition is a subtask of information extraction that seeks to locate and classify named entity mentions in unstructured text into pre-defined categories such as the person names, organizations, locations, medical codes, time expressions, quantities, monetary values, percentages, etc.

Natural Language Processing: Natural language processing is a subfield of computer science, information engineering, and artificial intelligence concerned with the interactions between computers and human languages, how to program computers to process and analyze large amounts of natural language data.

ROUGE: ROUGE, or recall-oriented understudy for gisting evaluation, is a set of metrics and a software package used for evaluating automatic summarization and machine translation software in natural language processing.

Section 2
Domain Applications

Chapter 6

Text Classification and Topic Modeling for Online Discussion Forums:
An Empirical Study From the Systems Modeling Community

Xin Zhao
University of Alabama, USA

Zhe Jiang
University of Alabama, USA

Jeff Gray
University of Alabama, USA

ABSTRACT

Online discussion forums play an important role in building and sharing domain knowledge. An extensive amount of information can be found in online forums, covering every aspect of life and professional discourse. This chapter introduces the application of supervised and unsupervised machine learning techniques to analyze forum questions. This chapter starts with supervised machine learning techniques to classify forum posts into pre-defined topic categories. As a supporting technique, web scraping is also discussed to gather data from an online forum. After this, this chapter introduces unsupervised learning techniques to identify latent topics in documents. The combination of supervised and unsupervised machine learning approaches offers us deeper insights of the data obtained from online forums. This chapter demonstrates these techniques through a case study on a very large online discussion forum called LabVIEW from the systems modeling community. In the end, the authors list future trends in applying machine learning to understand the expertise captured in online expert communities.

DOI: 10.4018/978-1-5225-9373-7.ch006

1. INTRODUCTION AND BACKGROUND

Systems modeling is the process of developing abstract models that represent multiple perspectives (e.g., structural, behavioral) of a system. Such models also provide a popular way to explore, update, and communicate system aspects to stakeholders, while significantly reducing or eliminating dependence on traditional text documents. There are several popular systems modeling tools, such as Simulink (MathWorks, 2019) and LabVIEW (National Instruments, 2019).

Laboratory Virtual Instrument Engineering Workbench (LabVIEW) is a system-design platform and development environment for a visual programming language from National Instruments. LabVIEW offers a graphical programming approach that helps users visualize every aspect of the system, including hardware configuration, measurement data, and debugging. The visualization makes it simple to integrate measurement hardware from any vendor, represent complex logic on the diagram, develop data analysis algorithms, and design custom engineering user interfaces. LabVIEW is widely used in both academia (Ertugrul, 2000, 2002) and industry, such as Subaru Motor (Morita, 2018) and Bell Helicopter (Blake, 2015). There are more than 35,000 LabVIEW customers worldwide (Falcon, 2017).

Text summarization refers to the technique of extracting information from a large corpus of data and represents a common application area of machine learning and natural language processing. With the increasing production and consumption of date in all aspects of our lives, text summarization helps to reduce the time to digest and analyze information by extracting the most valuable and pertinent information from a very large dataset.

There are two main types of text summarization: extractive text summarization and abstractive text summarization. Extractive text summarization is a technique that pulls keywords or key phrases from a source document to infer the key points from original documents. Abstractive text summarization refers to the creation of a new document for summarizing the original document. The result of abstractive text summarization may include new words or phrases not in the original documents.

To understand the current best practices and tool-feature needs of the LabVIEW community, we collected user posts from the LabVIEW online discussion forum. An online discussion forum is a website where various individuals from different backgrounds can discuss common topics of interest in the form of posted messages. Online discussion forums are useful resources for sharing domain knowledge. The discussion forums can be used for many purposes, such as sharing challenges and ideas, promoting the development of community, and giving/receiving support from peers and experts. Several researchers have identified benefits of online discussion forums from different aspects, such as education (Jorczak, 2014), individual and society development (Pendry & Salvatore, 2015) and socialization (Akcaoglu & Lee,

2016). The LabVIEW discussion forum has very rich resources for text summarization because most of the user-generated content in the forums is text-based. We applied text classification based on supervised machine learning techniques and topic modeling based on unsupervised machine learning techniques to the large collection of LabVIEW forum posts. After downloading all the post questions through web scraping, we first used supervised machine learning to classify all the questions into four categories (i.e., "program", "hardware", "tools and support" and "others"). We compared three popular methods, including Multinomial Naive Bayes, Support Vector Machine and Random forest. After this, we applied unsupervised machine learning techniques to delve into the largest category ("program") to find subtopics. In this chapter, we examine three unsupervised machine learning approaches: K-means clustering, hierarchical clustering and Latent Dirichlet Allocation (LDA). We use the LabVIEW discussion forum as our case study with empirical results.

The contributions of this chapter are two-fold. First, we demonstrate how text summarization techniques can be used to extract online discussion forum key information. Second, we describe future trends and research directions based on the analyses of text summarization results, which give direction toward future areas of investigation for the text summarization research community.

This chapter is structured as follows: In Section 2, we first introduce the process and technical details of supervised machine learning techniques in the context of text classification. After this, we use the LabVIEW discussion forum as a case study to introduce our empirical experiment that demonstrates how to apply supervised machine learning techniques to classify posts with predefined categories for the LabVIEW posts. In Section 3, unsupervised machine learning algorithms are first presented, followed by the empirical application of unsupervised machine learning technique in gaining subtopics of LabVIEW posts in a specific category. Future trends in this area represented by this paper are summarized in Section 4 and concluding remarks are offered in Section 5.

2. TEXT CLASSIFICATION

Text classification is the process of assigning a set of predefined categories to text. Text classification is the heart of many applications, such as spam filtering (Kumar, et al., 2016), sentiment analysis (Cambria, 2016) and readability assessment (Miltsakaki & Troutt, 2008).

Text classification has been a popular research topic over the past decade. Nenkova and Mckeown (2012) surveyed several text summarization techniques from the perspective of different phases involved in the summarization. A newer and complete summarization work is described by Altınel and Ganiz (2018). In their work, they divided text summarization into two major categories: traditional text summarization and semantic text summarization.

- **Traditional text classification:** Traditional text summarization is based on the concept of Bag-of-Words (BOG, Salton & Yang, 1973). This classification technique separates document into individual words and it only considers their corresponding frequencies in a document. The information of word locations are discarded during the processing of classification.
- **Semantic text classification:** Semantic text classification tries to overcome the shortcoming in traditional text classification techniques by including semantic relations between words. Altınel and Ganiz summarized five categories for semantic text summarization:
  - domain knowledge based approaches: a technique that classifies documents based on common knowledge bases (such as Wikipedia, Suganya and Gomathi, 2013);
  - corpus-based approaches: similar to domain knowledge based approaches, but based on a training corpus instead of knowledge (Deerwester et al., 1990);
  - deep learning based approaches: text classification based on deep learning methodologies (we will give a more detailed explanation on semantic text classification in Section 4);
  - word/character sequence enhanced approaches: In this method, string-matching techniques are applied to find string sequences in a document (Razon & Barnden, 2015); and
  - linguistic enriched approaches: lexical and syntactic rules are applied to extract key information compared with other approaches (Abbasi et al., 2011).

In this chapter, we focus on text classification analysis based on an existing corpus. We applied machine learning techniques to analyze a corpus to predict new documents. In general, text classification based on machine learning techniques includes four steps:

Step 1: Data Pre-processing
Step 2: Feature Extraction
Step 3: Model Training
Step 4: Model Evaluation

With the help of the model we obtain from Step 3, predictions on new data can be achieved. In this section, we first describe these four steps in detail. At the end of this section, the case study from the modeling community is introduced as an example application of how these techniques are applied in a real scenario.

2.1 Data Pre-Processing

The first step is to refine the text data in the dataset to remove noise and errors. In the text that is mined from a discussion forum, there are several characters (such as '[' and '/') and words (such as 'I' and 'we') that are meaningless and not important for extracting the key information. To remove these characters, a common approach is to convert these characters into their corresponding Unicode characters. These Unicode characters will be removed when they are recognized. After removing meaningless characters, tokenization, a technique for breaking sentences into pieces (these pieces are called tokens) is applied to the text data. Tokens can be individual words or phrases. Usually, tokens are individual words. In this step, two operations are needed: stemming (e.g., converting words into common bases, such as 'windows' to 'window') and filtering (e.g., dropping stop words like 'a', 'an' and 'the').

2.2 Feature Extraction

After data cleaning, each document consists of a sequence of tokens (or symbols). In order to apply machine learning algorithms to these documents, we need to represent the sequence of tokens in each document as a numeric feature vector, which is recognizable for machines. One simple way to extract features is to use a word-document frequency matrix (also called bag-of-words) (Zhang, Jin, & Zhou, 2010). In this approach, the frequency of occurrence of each word is used as a feature for training a classifier. A more prevalent approach is TF-IDF (Sparks Jones, 1972), which is a measure that adopts two statistical methods - Term Frequency (TF) and Inverse Document Frequency (IDF). TF is the total number of times a given term appears in the text, and IDF measures the weight of a given word in the entire text. It is a measure of how much information the word provides. TF-IDF is the product of term frequency and inverse document frequency. There are several schemes for calculating TF and IDF (Manning, Raghavan, & Schütze, 2008). Recently, Word2Vec (Lilleberg, Zhu, & Zhang, 2015) based on deep learning has become increasingly popular. In this section, we discuss the bag-of-words model and TF-IDF model.

2.2.1 Bag-of-Words Model

A bag-of-words model (BoW) is a simple way to extract features from text for use. It is a representation of text that describes the occurrence of words in a document. The name "bag" comes from the fact that in the document, the order or the structure of words are irrelevant. BoW model is primarily concerned with whether known words occur in the document. If one word exists, the frequency of occurrence of this word is used as a feature for training a classifier. If one word does not exist, the feature of this word is simply marked as 0. Consider a simple example showing how to build a BoW model from existing documents: imagine we have text documents containing three posts (abstracted here for example purposes, CompactRIO is a controller made by National Instruments for industrial control systems):

- **Post 1:** "LabVIEW is easy to use. It is popular, too."
- **Post 2:** "CompactRIO is a hardware supported by LabVIEW."
- **Post 3:** "How can you debug a program?"

The first step is to build a vocabulary vector for the document. The length of the vocabulary is equal to the number of unique words in the documents. In this example:

```
Vocabulary = ['LabVIEW', 'is', 'easy', 'to', 'use', 'it',
'popular', 'too', 'CompactRIO', 'a', 'hardware',
            'supported', 'by', 'how', 'can', 'you', 'debug',
'program']
```

Each word in the document is compared with words in the vocabulary. If a word appears in the vocabulary, the frequency counter for that word is incremented. For example, in Post 2, the third word is 'a,' we look up the dictionary and find out word 'a' exists and its position is 10. So we put 1 in the Post 2 vector at position 10 (marked in red below). Applying the vocabulary to the three posts, we transfer the posts to feature vectors as follows:

- **Post 1:** [1, 2, 1, 1, 1, 1, 1, 1, 1, 0, 0, 0, 0, 0, 0, 0, 0, 0]
- **Post 2:** [1, 1, 0, 0, 0, 0, 0, 0, 1, 1, 1, 1, 1, 0, 0, 0, 0, 0]
- **Post 3:** [0, 0, 0, 0, 0, 0, 0, 0, 0, 1, 0, 0, 0, 1, 1, 1, 1, 1]

2.2.2 TF-IDF Model

TF-IDF model is a very popular Natural Language Processing (NLP) technique to transform text into vectors. It is composed of two components: TF and IDF. TF is defined as "The weight of a term that occurs in a document is simply proportional to the term frequency" (Luhn, 1957). There are several schemes to calculate TF weight, such as term frequency and log normalization. The most commonly used approach is term frequency, which is defined as:

$$TF\left(t\right) = \frac{Number\ of\ times\ term\ t\ appears\ in\ the\ document}{Total\ number\ of\ terms\ in\ the\ document}.$$

However, some common words, such as 'is' and 'the,' may appear in a document many times but have little importance. IDF measures how important a term is by weighing down the frequent terms while scaling up the rare ones. It is defined as:

$$IDF\left(t\right) = \log\frac{Total\ number\ of\ documents}{Number\ of\ times\ term\ t\ appears\ in\ all\ documents}.$$

TF-IDF is then calculated as:

$$TF - IDF\left(t\right) = TF\left(t\right) \times IDF\left(t\right).$$

For example, suppose we have two documents:

- **Document 1:** This post is related to category *program.*
- **Document 2:** This question is related to category *hardware.*

Based on the definition above, we have the TF-IDF results for each word shown in Table 1.

2.3 Model Training

The third step of the technique is to apply machine learning algorithms to train the machine to build the classification model. There are various techniques that can be used for text classification. The training process starts with a manually labeled training set, whereby each document is manually labeled into predefined categories. The machine then learns a classification model that can automatically predict the class label of a new text document. A test set of documents are often used to verify the accuracy of the classifier. In this section, we introduce three widely used algorithms for text classification: Multinomial Naive Bayes, Support Vector Machines and Random Forest. The reason why we chose these three algorithms is because they are easy to implement and have relatively good classification results.

Table 1. TF-IDF calculation example

Word Vocabulary	TF		IDF	TF ×TDF	
	Document 1	Document 2		Document 1	Document 2
the	$\dfrac{1}{7}$	$\dfrac{1}{7}$	$\log\dfrac{2}{2}=0$	0	0
post	$\dfrac{1}{7}$	0	$\log\dfrac{2}{1}=0.3$	0.043	0
question	0	$\dfrac{1}{7}$	$\log\dfrac{2}{1}=0.3$	0	0.043
is	$\dfrac{1}{7}$	$\dfrac{1}{7}$	$\log\dfrac{2}{2}=0$	0	0
related	$\dfrac{1}{7}$	$\dfrac{1}{7}$	$\log\dfrac{2}{2}=0$	0	0
to	$\dfrac{1}{7}$	$\dfrac{1}{7}$	$\log\dfrac{2}{2}=0$	0	0
category	$\dfrac{1}{7}$	$\dfrac{1}{7}$	$\log\dfrac{2}{2}=0$	0	0
program	$\dfrac{1}{7}$	0	$\log\dfrac{2}{1}=0.3$	0.043	0
hardware	0	$\dfrac{1}{7}$	$\log\dfrac{2}{1}=0.3$	0	0.043

2.3.1 Multinomial Naive Bayes

Multinomial Naive Bayes classifier is a probabilistic algorithm based on Bayes' Theorem (Bayes, 1763). It is a widely adopted algorithm in NLP, such as text classification, spam email detection, and sentiment analysis. Because of the nature of Bayes' Theorem, one precondition is assumed when applying Naive Bayes classifiers: All features are conditionally independent given the underlying class category. Bayes' Theorem states that:

$$P(C \mid X) = \frac{P(X \mid C) \times P(C)}{P(X)}$$

where C represents the category of the text and X is the feature of the text. $P(C|X)$ is called the *posterior probability*, which is the statistical probability of the category for a given document based on its numeric feature. $P(X|C)$ is called *likelihood*. It means that for a given category, the probability of a feature X occurs. $P(C)$ and $P(X)$ are called *prior probability*. $P(C)$ is the probability of the occurrence of category C in the documents and $P(X)$ is the probability of the occurrence of feature X in the document. Based on this theorem, given an instance with feature $X_1, X_2, ..., X_n$, the possibility of this instance belonging to category C_k is defined as:

$$P(C_k \mid X_1, X_2, ... X_n) = P(C_k) \times P(X_1 \mid C_k) \times P(X_2 \mid C_k) \times ... \times P(X_n \mid C_k).$$

This is known as the Bayes Classifier. We will illustrate Bayes Classifier with an example. Suppose we have a document set (treated as training set) containing three posts belonging to two categories as seen in Table 2.

A key question is to decide which category a new post (e.g., *"Test a program in LabVIEW"*) belongs to. There are 15 distinct words in the example training set: ["LabVIEW", "program", "is", "hard", "to", "debug", "share", "your", "example", "with", "others", "in", "the", "NI", "community"]. Adding the words from the new post, we have 22 distinct words: ["LabVIEW", "program", "is", "hard", "to", "debug", "CompactRIO", "cannot", "connect", "to", "share", "your", "example", "with", "others", "in", "the", "NI", "community", "test", "a", "in"]. Based on Bayes' Theorem, we have:

$$P(program \mid Test\ a\ program\ in\ LabVIEW)$$
$$= \frac{P(Test\ a\ program\ in\ LabVIEW \mid program) * P(program)}{P(Test\ a\ program\ in\ LabVIEW)} \tag{1}$$

Table 2. Example posts with their categories

Post	Category
LabVIEW program is hard to debug.	*program*
CompactRIO cannot connect to LabVIEW.	*hardware*
Share your Example Program with others in the NI community.	*program*

$$P(hardware \mid Test\ a\ program\ in\ LabVIEW)$$

$$= \frac{P(Test\ a\ program\ in\ LabVIEW \mid hardware) * P\left(hardware\right)}{P\left(Test\ a\ program\ in\ LabVIEW\right)} \quad (2)$$

Because we assume all the events are independent, for Equation (1), we have

$$P\left(Test\ a\ program\ in\ LabVIEW \mid program\right)$$
$$= P(test \mid program) * P(a \mid program) * P(program \mid program)$$
$$* P(in \mid program) * P(LabVIEW \mid program)$$

Equation 1 can be reduced to calculate the occurrence of words "test," "a," "program," "in," "LabVIEW" in the existing training set *program*. For a word that does not appear in training set *program* (such as 'test'), we apply *Laplace Smoothing* (a technique for smoothing categorical data): we first add 1 to every word count and then add the number of possible words to the divisor (so the result will never be greater than 1). Thus,

$$P(test \mid program) = \frac{0+1}{15+22}$$

$$P(a \mid program) = \frac{0+1}{15+22}$$

$$P(program \mid program) = \frac{2+1}{15+22}$$

$$P(in \mid program) = \frac{0+1}{15+22}$$

$$P(LabVIEW \mid program) = \frac{1+1}{15+22}.$$

Based on the training set, we have $P\left(program\right) = \frac{2}{3}$. (2 posts are categorized as program in total of 3 posts). Applying the same approach to Equation 2, we have

$$P\left(program \mid Test\ a\ program\ in\ LabVIEW\right) = \frac{1}{37} \times \frac{1}{37} \times \frac{3}{37} \times \frac{2}{37} \times \frac{2}{3} \approx 5.768 * 10^{-8}$$

$$P\left(hardware \mid Test\ a\ program\ in\ LabVIEW\right) = \frac{1}{27} \times \frac{1}{27} \times \frac{1}{27} \times \frac{1}{27} \times \frac{1}{3} \approx 4.646 * 10^{-8}$$

Therefore, the new post "Test a program in LabVIEW" is classified as a *program* related post. To simplify the calculation process, data preprocessing (such as removing stop words) is always performed in advance.

In Multinomial Naïve Bayes, the algorithm configuration is related to the setting of the *smoothing parameter* (which is usually called α). When α is set as 1 (also known as "*Laplase Smoothing*"), it means we add 1 to each word counting. This is shown in the example introduced above. When α is set as 0 (also known as "*Lidstone Smoothing*"), we add 0 to each word counting. In the following discussion throughout this chapter, we choose $\alpha = 1$.

2.3.2 Support Vector Machine

A Support Vector Machine (SVM) is a supervised machine learning algorithm that is widely used in classification problems. Like other machine learning algorithms, some data pre-processing is also executed in SVM, such as data cleaning and feature extraction. However, unlike calculating the frequency of each feature in the document in Multinomial Bayes, SVM plots each feature vector as an n-dimensional point (where n is the number of total features in a post) with the value of each feature corresponding to the value of a particular coordinate. Then, we perform classification by finding the **hyperplane** that separates points from the different classes ("support vectors" are the points near the boundary hyperplane). Thus, the core problem of learning a SVM classifier is to find the best separation hyperplane.

We will illustrate SVM with a simple example. Suppose we have two categories (blue triangle and orange circle) and the data has two features (x and y). Figure 1 shows this example.

There are several possible hyperplanes that can be used to separate points from these two categories (such as the dotted black line and bold black line in Figure 2). Research has shown that the hyperplane with largest margin (shown in the bold black line) is the best (Joachims, 2006). For a dataset that is inseparable in 2 dimensional space, SVM transforms the data to a higher dimension to do separation. Figure 3 shows such a situation.

Figure 1. Two categories containing different data points

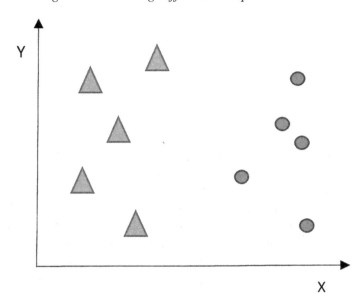

For a dataset with n features (in other words, a dataset in an n-dimension), SVM finds an n-1 dimension hyperplane to separate it. When data is not linearly separable, SVM transforms the dataset to a higher dimensional dataset where it becomes separable. However, it is almost impossible to try out all the transformations from lower dimension to higher dimension. To solve this, SVM computes the pair-wise dot products. For a given pair of vectors and a transformation into a higher-dimensional space, there exists a function (which is known as a *"kernel function"*) that can compute the dot product in the higher-dimensional space without explicit transformation. This is called *"kernel tricks,"* which saves computation and makes SVM feasible in high dimension datasets.

The algorithm configuration for SVM is much more complicated than Multinomial Naïve Bayes. There are several parameters used in SVM, such as penalty parameter C, kernel type, whether to use shrinking heuristic, and the size of kernel. In this section, we discuss the two most important parameters for SVM: C and Kernel.

Parameter C is called the penalty parameter (or complexity parameter). It shows the tolerance of error. The larger the value of C, the less tolerance for the algorithm. Overfitting is more likely to happen with higher values of C. On the contrary, a smaller C value offers more tolerance of error and under-fitting is more likely to happen. The kernel parameter refers to which kernel is to be used by the SVM engine. Common kernel functions include linear kernel, poly kernel and RFB kernel. In the experiment we conducted, we chose C = 1 and linear kernel.

Figure 2. Possible separations of two categories

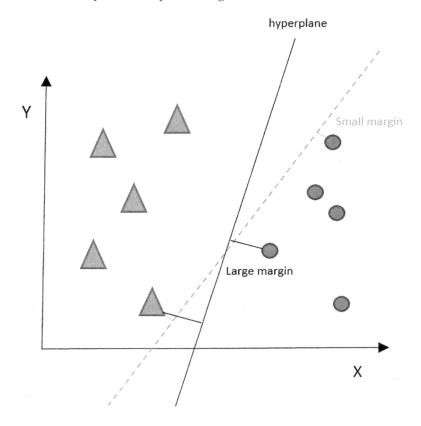

Figure 3. Data inseparable in 2D space is separable in 3D space. Example is taken from
(Deshpande, 2018)

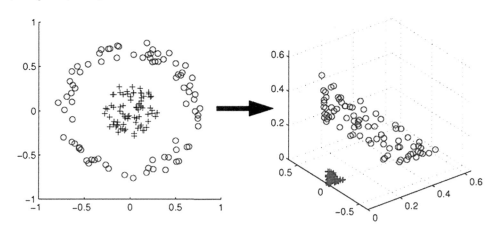

2.3.3 Random Forest

Random Forest is a supervised machine learning technique based on decision trees. A decision tree is a tree-like structure where internal nodes represent a test condition on a feature attribute. The answer for the test is binary (only "yes" or "no") or multi-way. Each leaf is a final predicted class. When using a decision tree to classify text, we start from the root, and select a sub-branch based on the test result on the root node. This decision process is repeated until a leaf node is reached, where a class is predicted. Figure 4 is a decision tree showing a simple post classification strategy (the number below each category indicates the prediction probability).

A random forest classifier is an algorithm based on the ensemble of decision trees. It involves learning a collection of decision trees to make a final prediction based on voting. The random forest algorithm first creates several decision trees randomly to evaluate the performance of each decision tree constructed and then averages the results to improve the predictive accuracy.

The algorithm configuration for random forest is closely related to the setting of random trees. In general, three parameters are crucial to the performance of random forest. First, the depth of each tree. A deep tree may increase the performance of the algorithm, but it increases the calculation time. Second, number of max features, which decides how many attributes a tree uses every time a subtree is created. The higher value this parameter holds, the more attributes a tree has. Usually, increasing this value could improve the performance of a random forest. Similarly, it also increases the running time. In our experiment, we chose unlimited tree depth and

$$\log \frac{Number\ of\ feature}{2}$$

as the max number assigned to each tree in the forest.

Figure 4. An example for decision tree based classification strategy

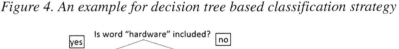
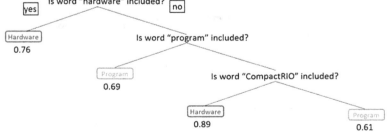

2.4 Evaluation

2.4.1 Evaluation Approaches

The most dominant way to evaluate the model built from a ML algorithm is to apply *K-fold cross validation* (Kohavi, 1995), which divides the training data into K parts equally. Suppose K = 10 and the 10 parts are labelled as *A, B, C, D, E, F, G, H, I, J*. In the first iteration, we use part *A* through part *I* as training datasets (9 parts in total) and use part *J* as a testing dataset. In the second iteration, we choose part *B* through part *J* as training datasets and use part *A* as a testing dataset. Proceeding similarly for the other permutations, we will have 10 iterations in total. We calculate the average value for these 10 iterations as the final evaluation result. The reason why we apply K-fold cross validation is because cross-validation is a good evaluation technique when there are no sufficiently large training and testing sets (Duda, Hart, & Stork, 2012).

2.4.2 Evaluation Metrics

There are several evaluation metrics in the context of text classification problems. The most basic and simple one is *accuracy*, which can be defined as:

$$accuracy = \frac{Number\ of\ correct\ predictions}{Total\ predictions\ made}$$

Another metric is *Receiver Operating Characteristic curve (ROC curve)*, which is a plot that is used in a binary classification. The ROC curve represents a model's ability to discriminate between positive and negative classes, where an area of 1.0 means a perfect prediction and 0.5 represents a model that is as good as a random guess.

Confusion Matrix (also known as *error matrix*) is an evaluation metric that presents the accuracy of a model with two or more categories, taking the following form in Table 3:

True positive (TP) means that an instance is predicted as positive and the prediction is true (i.e., in the example from Section 2.2, a post related to *program* is predicted as *program*). Similarly, true negative (TN) means that an instance is predicted negative and the prediction is true (a post not related to *program* is not predicted as *program*). False positive (FP, also known as Type 1 Error) indicates that an instance is predicted positive, but it is negative (a post is related to *hardware*, but it is predicted as *program*). False negative (FN, also known as Type 2 Error)

Table 3. Different combinations of predicted and actual values

		Actual Values	
		Positive	Negative
Predicted Values	Positive	True Positive (TP)	False Positive (FP)
	Negative	False Negative (FN)	True Negative (TN)

indicates that an instance is predicted negative, but it is positive (a post related to *program*, but it is predicted as *hardware*).

Precision, *recall* and *F-measure* are widely used metrics in performance evaluation. Precision (also called "positive predictive value") is the "fraction of relevant instances among the retrieved instances" (Alvarez, 2002). It usually refers to the accuracy of the result and is defined as:

$$Precision = \frac{TP}{TP + FP}$$

Recall (also known as "sensitivity") is the "fraction of relevant instances that have been retrieved over the total amount of relevant instances" (Alvarez, 2002). It usually refers to the completeness of the prediction result and it is defined as:

$$Recall = \frac{TP}{TP + FN}$$

Combining the measurements of Precision and Recall, we can obtain a metric that evaluates the correctness and completeness at the same time: F-measure. It is defined as:

$$F - measure = \frac{2 \times Precision \times Recall}{Precision + Recall}$$

2.5 Empirical Classification

In this section, we present our post classification from empirical mining on the LabVIEW discussion forum. We first introduce web scraping – a technique used in our experiment to obtain the text data from the forum. Following this, we discuss how supervised machine learning techniques are applied to find post distribution among predefined categories. A result is given based on our approach in the end of this section.

2.5.1 Data Source and Pre-Processing

Background: Web Scraping

Web scraping is the process of automatically mining data to collect information from a rendered web page. There are several techniques for web scraping, ranging from manual examination to fully automated approaches. The most naive approach for web scraping is human copy-and-paste. However, this approach requires much human effort when the dataset is large. The most popular approach for web scraping is based on parsing text represented as HTML (Hypertext Markup Language, a standard language for creating web pages and web applications). In this section, we focus our discussion on HTML parsing.

In general, web scraping based on HTML parsing for an online discussion forum consists of three main parts:

- ***Data Acquisition.*** This step builds a connection between a client and a website. It uses an HTML request library or a headless browser (a web browser without a graphical user interface). A popular method for data acquisition is to use the Node.js request-promise module (Simpson, 2015). There are several tools supporting this method, such as Puppeteer (De Lara, Wallach, & Zwaenepoel, 2001). By sending a request to the URL, the method receives a promise that specifies the format of the returned object. A client will receive the raw HTML format from the web page if the connection is built successfully.
- ***Source Inspection.*** This step finds the exact pattern/tag that a client is looking for in the code. Most current web browsers support the function of inspecting the source code of a web page. An HTML ***selector*** is often used to locate the target element and extract HTML and text within the selected element.
- ***Data Parsing.*** The last step is to parse the HTML by calling handler methods when start tags, end tags, text, comments, and other markup elements are encountered. Clients can customize the output to export and save the results to different file formats, such as a simple text file, Excel file, or CSV file.

Dataset

Our dataset was collected from the official LabVIEW discussion forum. With our web scraping approach mentioned above, we implemented a JavaScript web crawler to automatically retrieve all the user posts from the LabVIEW discussion forum.

We collected 184,203 posts from May 18th, 1999 to February 15th, 2019. Among these posts, we removed: 1) Posts that are not written in English: 4,116 posts in total; 2). Meaningless posts (such as empty posts, posts with characters only, etc.): 2,592 posts in total. After filtering, 177,495 posts were remained as our dataset.

We first preprocessed text data in the posts through stemming and lemmatization (find the root of a word, such as converting 'playing' to 'play', 'books' to 'book'), and removed stop words (common words such as 'the,' 'an,' 'a'). Then, we represented each post with a numeric vector based on TF-IDF.

2.5.2 Machine Training

We manually labelled 1,800 posts randomly chosen from the dataset. Based on our exploration of the dataset, we labelled each post belonging to one of the four categories: program, hardware, tools and support, and others. The "program" category includes any posts related to program problems, such as program design/debugging, graph processing, coding/language, function/control, program performance etc. For example:

" ... Does LabVIEW 7 have an easy way allow the user at runtime to change the default values of controls? ... "

" ... Hello. I am new in the LabView, and I have to do a task. When I will get lowercase it has to be display as an uppercase and uppercase to lowercase ... Any ideas how to fix it?"

Any question related to hardware issues is classified into the "hardware" category, such as hardware driver, computer hardware, controller, chassis, sensor and any external hardware supported/developed by National Instruments. A complete hardware list can be found at the National Instruments official website. Examples of hardware related posts are:

"... Does anybody have experience booting LabVIEW RT disklessly over the internet using PXE on a PXI Embedded slot 1 controller...?"

"... Hello has somebody developed a LabView driver for the Diamond-MM-16 board. If yes, I'm interested ..."

We label a post as "tools and support" if the question is asked about LabVIEW itself (such as version, license and installation) or any existing external tools/ architectures/libraries supported by LabVIEW. For example:

" *... How can I download all NI software and packages that our academic license covers? I know that the license covers many tools, and I wish to download and install them all ...*"

" *... I want to know if there is any easy way that I can update LabVIEW 11.0 to 16.0. Do I have to uninstall the old one and download the new one? ...*"

Any posts that do not belong to the above categories will be classified as "others." For example:

"Is it the word "vi" pronounced like "vee" or "v-i" (each letter separately). All opinions welcomed."

"Happy New Year to all the LabVIEW users."

2.5.3 Evaluation Results

In our work, 10-fold cross validation is used to evaluate the classification performance. Our evaluation metrics are *Precision* and *Recall* and *F-measure*. The performance of applying Multinomial Naive Bayes, SMO (a fast implementation of SVM) (Bach, Lanckriet, & Jordan, 2004) and Random Forest on our training set is shown in Table 4.

2.5.4 Prediction

From Table 4, we can see Multinomial Naive Bayes (minTermFreq = 1) has the best performance (marked in red in Table 2). So we chose this model as our prediction model. Applying Multinomial Naive Bayes (minTermFreq = 1) to predict all the

Table 4. Evaluation results. MinTermFreq-N means only keep words that appeared at least N times in all documents. Pre = Precision, Rec = Recall

	MinTermFreq-1	MinTermFreq-2	MinTermFreq-3	MinTermFreq-5
Multinomial Navie Bayes	Pre:0.766 Rec:0.753 F-1:0.758	Pre:0.753 Rec:0.728 F-1:0.740	Pre:0.761 Rec:0.733 F-1:0.745	Pre:0.761 Rec:0.733 F-1:0.745
SMO	Pre:0.701 Rec:0.726 F-1:0.711	Pre:0.709 Rec:0.727 F-1:0.715	Pre:0.704 Rec:0.719 F-1:0.710	Pre:0.702 Rec:0.714 F-1:0.707
Random Forest	Pre:0.704 Rec:0.721 F-1:0.648	Pre:0.699 Rec:0.714 F-1:0.641	Pre:0.701 Rec:0.724 F-1:0.656	Pre:0.701 Rec:0.724 F-1:0.656

posts in our dataset, we obtained a post distribution shown in Figure 5. We can see that posts related to "program" have the largest portion (120,085 posts are related to program out of 177,495 posts). There are 28,636 posts that are predicted as "tools and support," which is a little more than posts predicted as "hardware" (27,541 posts). 1,233 posts are predicted as "others."

The prediction result shows that most LabVIEW discussion forum users are interested in the topic of *program*. Therefore, it would be beneficial in our analysis to understand what subtopics are discussed most among *program* related posts. However, with a wide range of topics, it is difficult to suggest predefined subcategories. To this end, we applied unsupervised machine learning techniques to delve into subtopic clustering among different "program" categories.

3. TOPIC MODELING

Applying unsupervised ML techniques to find topics in the text is referred to as "topic modeling" or "topic clustering." The task of topic modeling is to find groups/ clusters of similar topics in the dataset. The similarity is computed through a similarity function. The term "unsupervised" indicates this process is done automatically without any human seeding or initiation of the process. The cluster can be in different levels of granularities, such as sentences, phrases and words. Conventional unsupervised

Figure 5. Post distribution prediction for LabVIEW discussion forum

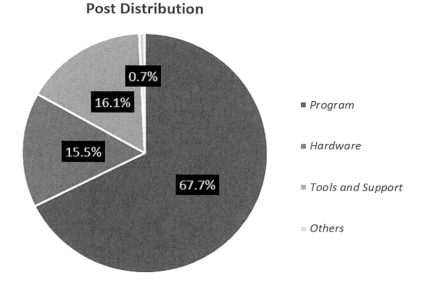

Post Distribution

ML techniques for topic clustering include k-means clustering (Hartigan & Wong, 1979), hierarchical clustering (Johnson, 1976), and Latent Dirichlet Allocation (LDA) (Blei, Ng, & Jordan, 2003). A comparison of these approaches is summarized by Steinbach (Karypis, Kumar, & Steinbach, 2000). Unsupervised machine learning for topic modeling mainly consists of four steps:

Step 1: Data Pre-processing
Step 2: Feature Extraction
Step 3: Unsupervised Clustering
Step 4: Results Interpretation

The approaches used in Step 1 and Step 2 are similar to supervised machine learning techniques for text classification. Therefore, in this section, we mainly discuss the techniques used in Step 3. The empirical example from LabVIEW online discussion forum is introduced in the end of this section to show how unsupervised clustering is adopted in practice.

3.1 Unsupervised Machine Learning Algorithms

3.1.1 K-Means Clustering

K-means clustering (Hartigan & Wong, 1979) is a popular technique for cluster analysis in data mining based on vector quantization. It helps to identify similar groups of data (Xiong, Hua, Lv, & Li, 2016). K-means clustering partitions n observations into K clusters in which each observation belongs to the cluster with the nearest mean. The basic steps of K-Means clustering include:

1. Initialize K centroids randomly (also known as the K seeds);
2. Convert data to vector and compute the distance between observation data and each centroid, and assign this observation to the closest centroid;
3. Recompute the centroid based on the data assigned to the respective cluster;
4. Repeat step 2 and step 3 until stopping criteria are reached. Stopping criteria include
    a. Centroids do not change location;
    b. No data change its cluster;
    c. Reach the iteration time defined manually.

Clustering is sensitive to the distance measure. Distance measure is used to provide a relationship between each element in the dataset. The most simple distance measure is called *Manhattan Distance*. This measure simply calculates the sum of the horizontal and vertical distances between two points p and q. For example, in a 2D space, Manhattan Distance is defined as:

$$d(p,q) = |q_x - p_x| + |q_y - p_y|$$

In K-means clustering, pairwise *Euclidean distance* is applied implicitly. In mathematics, Euclidean distance represents the length of the line segment connecting two points. In a 2-dimension space, it is defined as:

$$d(p,q) = d(q,p) = \sqrt{(p_1 - q_1)^2 + (p_2 - q_2)^2}$$

One of the advantages of Euclidean distance is that the distance between any two objects is not affected by the addition of new objects to the analysis.

Another way to measure the distance is to apply *cosine distance*. In K-means clustering, using cosine distance rather than Euclidean distance is referred to as *Spherical K-means clustering*. Cosine distance is defined as:

$$d(\vec{A}, \vec{B}) = 1 - \frac{\vec{A} \cdot \vec{B}}{\vec{A}\vec{B}}$$

In this equation, $\vec{A} \cdot \vec{B}$ is the dot product of vector A and vector B and $\vec{A}\vec{B}$ is the multiplication of the norm of vector A and vector B. $\dfrac{\vec{A} \cdot \vec{B}}{\vec{A}\vec{B}}$ is also known as *cosine similarity*.

Each distance calculation approach has its own advantages and disadvantages. In the context of text mining, Li and Han (Li & Han, 2003) conducted an empirical evaluation on different distance measuring metrics on three text datasets (20 Newsgroups, containing 20 categories with 11,293 training examples and 7,528 testing examples; Reuters 52c, containing 52 categories with 6,532 documents for training, and 2,568 documents for test; and Sector, containing 104 categories with 6,412 training samples and 3,207 test samples). Their results suggest that cosine distance has the best performance on average.

The algorithm configuration of K-Means cluster mainly includes: 1) a distance function to compare the similarity between different instances (we introduced this parameter in the above discussion; 2) max iterations to define the iteration time for the algorithm running; and 3) number of clusters (i.e., the value of K).

3.1.2 Hierarchical Clustering

Hierarchical clustering (Johnson, 1976) (also known as hierarchical cluster analysis, HCA) is an alternative approach to K-means clustering for identifying groups in the dataset. It is a method of cluster analysis in data mining to build a hierarchy of clusters. Hierarchical clustering is the hierarchical decomposition of the data based on group similarities. The result of clustering resembles a tree structure, called a *dendrogram*. Unlike k-means clustering, hierarchical clustering does not need to specify the number of clusters.

Based on the manner of how a dendrogram is constructed, HCA can be divided into two types: agglomerative HCA and divisive HCA.

1. **Agglomerative HCA**: In agglomerative HCA, the dendrogram is built in a bottom-up manner. At first, each text data is considered as a single cluster. At each step, the similarity between each cluster is calculated (the similarity calculation approach is the same as the techniques for K-means cluster we discussed earlier in this section). The two clusters that are most similar are combined into a new larger cluster. This process iterates until all the clusters are combined into one final cluster.
2. **Divisive HCA**: In divisive HCA, the dendrogram is built from top to bottom. Initially, all the text data is treated as one single cluster. At each step of iteration, the most heterogeneous cluster is divided into two. This process iterates until all objects are in their own cluster.

Figure 6 shows the process of building a dendrogram in an agglomerative and divisive manner. In this example, we can see that from the agglomerative perspective over the first three iterations, plotting and graph (marked as blue in Figure 6), coding and language (marked as orange in Figure 6), chassis and compactRIO (marked as gray in Figure 6) are grouped as one cluster. Then, the blue cluster and the orange cluster are merged into a larger cluster (marked as green in Figure 6) at the fourth iteration. At the fifth and sixth iteration, program cluster and green cluster, hardware and gray cluster merged to a bigger cluster respectively. In the last iteration, all of the clusters are combined into just one cluster (marked as black in Figure 6). The clustering process stops because all of the clusters are merged into one cluster. The divisive HCA is executed in the same manner, but from top to bottom.

The parameters used in hierarchical clustering are similar to configurations in K-means clustering. In particular, hierarchical clustering also needs a provided distance function. However, in order to calculate the similarity between two clusters, another parameter is needed. This parameter is called the link type. Usually, there are three kinds of link types: nearest neighbor, complete linkage and group average.

Figure 6. An example showing the process of hierarchy clustering

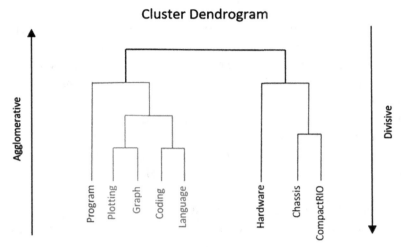

Nearest neighbor connects two clusters based on the nearest points in two different clusters and complete linkage does the opposite: choose the furthest points in two clusters to combine into one cluster. The group average calculates the distance of all the points among different clusters and computes the average value. The cluster link is based on this average value.

3.1.3 Latent Dirichlet Allocation

Latent Dirichlet Allocation (LDA) (Blei et al., 2003) is a statistical topic modeling approach that is widely used in NLP. It automatically discovers topics in the documents. The topic inference for LDA is built upon Dirichlet-multinomial distribution (Ronning, 1989), a family of discrete multivariate probability distributions from finite non-negative integers. The number of clusters needs to be specified manually in LDA at the beginning of the process. There are two principles in LDA:

- Each document contains multiple topics.
- Each topic contains multiple words.

For example, given three documents (e.g., posts from the LabVIEW discussion forum):

Post 1: "LabVIEW program is hard to debug."
Post 2: "CompactRIO cannot connect to LabVIEW."

Post 3: "Share your example program with others in the NI community."

Suppose we want to find two topics among these posts. Applying LDA to thee three posts, it may produce a result like:
Building topic for documents:

Post 1: 100% belongs to Topic A;
Post 2: 100% belongs to Topic B;
Post 3: 80% belongs to Topic A, 20% belongs to Topic B.

Building words for topics:

For Topic A: 95% program, 70% debug, 30% share ...
For Topic B: 90% CompactRIO, 60% connect ...

At this point, LDA cannot specify what is Topic A and what is Topic B. The result of LDA needs human (usually domain expert) interpretation. Based on our domain knowledge, Topic A could be interpreted as *program* and Topic B could be interpreted as *hardware*.

Compared with k-means clustering and hierarchical clustering, LDA has many advantages. First, it is a probabilistic model that can be interpreted easily by humans. Second, since LDA does not involve similarity comparison between different data objects, which sometimes can be extremely expensive to compute, it saves calculation space and time. LDA has revolutionized the field as a popular technique for topic modeling since it was first introduced in 2002.

The parameters LDA need are more complicated than K-means and hierarchical clustering. The most important parameters include:

- The number of topics K: the number of requested latent topics to be extracted from the training corpus. It is similar to the number of clusters in K-Means clustering.
- Prior estimator α: the average frequency that each topic within a given document occurs.
- Topic-word estimator β: a collection of k topics where each topic is given a probability distribution over the vocabulary used in a document corpus.

In general, higher alpha values mean documents contain more similar topic contents. The same is true for beta – a higher beta value means a topic contains more similar topic words. In our experiment, we chose 3 as the value of K. We implemented our algorithm based on an LDA Python library – Gensim (Khosrovian, Pfahl &

Garousi, 2008). In Gensim, the value of and α are β are tailored to the structure of a dataset. This is known as "asymmetric prior."

3.2 Empirical Example of Topic Modeling

In this section, we discuss topic clustering using our case study from the LabVIEW discussion forum. Section 2.4 in this chapter introduced our post classifications based on the LabVIEW discussion forum and the results suggested that forum participants are more interested in *program* related questions. Based on this observation, we want to look deeper into program related posts. Because the posts in the forum spanned a very wide range of topics, it is difficult to suggest predefined subcategories. To this end, we applied unsupervised machine learning techniques to identify several important sub-topics. Because the LDA algorithm is a powerful tool for discovering and exploiting hidden topics (Liu, Tang, Dong, Yao, & Zhou, 2016), we applied LDA for topic clustering on our discussion forum.

The first step for LDA is to choose a clustering number. In our experiment, we examined three different clusters: 3, 5 and 10. Experimental results suggest that when using 5 and 10 clusters, there are many overlapping concepts across each cluster. Therefore, we chose 3 topic clusters in the following empirical discussion.

3.2.1 Dataset

As mentioned in Section 2.4, there are 120,085 posts (out of 177,495) that are related to the topic of *program*. Among the 120,085 posts that were predicted as *program* related, we chose posts with prediction probability equals to 1, which means the prediction model is very confident about the selected posts are related to *program* category. After filtering according to this confidence level, 92,655 posts remained.

3.2.2 Clustering Results

We developed a Python program for LDA based on pyLDAvis (Sievert & Shirley, 2014), a library for helping users interpret the results in a topic model that has been fit to a corpus of text data. We applied LDA topic clustering on the dataset with 3 clusters. The result for one iteration is as follows:

```
(1, '0.014×"control" + 0.014×"array" + 0.009×"button"
+ 0.009×"event" + 0.008×"panel" + 0.008×"problem" +
0.007×"change" + 0.007×"try" + 0.007×"front" + 0.007×"value"')
(2, '0.008×"try" + 0.008×"array" + 0.008×"write" +
0.008×"example" + 0.007×"problem" + 0.007×"error"
```

```
+ 0.007×"signal" + 0.007×"graph" + 0.006×"input" +
0.006×"sample"')
(3, '0.014×"graph" + 0.009×"problem" + 0.008×"control"
+ 0.007×"try" + 0.007×"display" + 0.007×"output" +
0.007×"waveform" + 0.006×"array" + 0.006×"input" +
0.005×"could"')
```

Because LDA is a probabilistic model, when running multiple times, we may get different results. We applied LDA to the same dataset five times. In order to find uniqueness in each cluster, we eliminated repeated words across different clusters. Table 5 shows the frequency of unique terms after 5 times LDA running. From Table 3, we can interpret the three clusters as: program change, file operation and graph processing (this interpretation also requires domain knowledge of the dataset).

The combination of supervised and unsupervised machine learning techniques revealed several interesting insights. For example, the results tell us that most forum posters are concerned about program related questions compared with other categories. Additionally, in the program related posts, many posts focused on program change, file operation and graph processing.

Our experiment reveals several interesting research implications. First, from the results we obtained in Section 2.3, the "change" always appears in the largest cluster. Motivated by this, we are particularly interested in understanding posts containing the keyword 'change,' in which many of the posts implied an intention of "refactoring," as used in software engineering. By examining posts belonging to the first cluster, we found many posts that discussed the effects of bad smells for LabVIEW system models. Some posts contain bad smells that are common in source code that also appear in LabVIEW. For example,

Table 5. Unique Term frequency in three clusters after 3 iterations. Cluster 1 represents the largest topic distribution, cluster 3 represents the smallest distribution.

Unique Term Frequency	5	4	3	2	1
Unique terms in Cluster 1		change	event, button	graph, panel, event	example, control, display, front
Unique terms in Cluster 2			output, value, function	write, number, file	attach, example
Unique terms in Cluster 3		graph	waveform, sample	point, display	create, value, however, input, signal, control, output, could

"... A lot of duplicated code. Most of it is the same except selected cluster element changes..."

-We are currently investigating the summarization of bad smells in LabVIEW system models from an end user's perspective. Second, LabVIEW users expressed concern about the best way to design software that eliminates redundancies and can be maintained for a long period. For example, the user post

" "...we have a big LV-project with some conditional disabled or with a switch unused VI's. But LabVIEW still tries to load them when building an application (even when they are not used). Something like ignore unused/missing VI's during built?..."

suggests that errors were made during the design that eventually led to some unreached model elements during the execution. We are also working on design analysis of LabVIEW system models, but all of these topics are outside of the scope of the context of this paper and are focused more on the example domain

4. FUTURE TRENDS

A recent trend has emerged towards applying deep learning methods to address the challenges of text classification and topic modeling. In this section, we first introduce deep learning in text classification and then we move to the future trends in applying deep learning to topic modeling.

4.1 Deep Learning in Text Classification

Convolutional Neural Networks (CNNs) (LeCun, Bottou, Bengio, & Haffner, 1998) and Recurrent Neural Networks (RNNs) (Rumelhart, Hinton, & Williams, 1986) are the two most popular approaches for text classification based on deep learning. Compared with traditional machine learning algorithms, deep learning techniques reduce the need for feature extraction and have shown better performance (Joulin, et al., 2016).

Research into Convolutional Neural Networks (CNNs) is inspired from how animal visual cortex works for seeing objects. CNNs have shown impressive results in several areas, such as image recognition (Girshick, 2015) and text classification (Conneau, et al. 2017). Given a corpus of documents, CNN first vectorizes all the documents. The input for CNN-based text classification is a matrix. The width of the matrix (d) is the word embedding (a technique that is capable of capturing context of a word in a document and relation with other words. Word2Vec is one of the most popular methods to learn word embedding dimension). The height of a matrix is the number of words in the document. After receiving the input matrix, CNN performs a set of continuous operations named convolution and pooling.

A Recurrent Neural Network (RNN) is a sequence of artificial neural network blocks linked to each other, thus generating a directed graph. This connection allows RNNs to exhibit temporal dynamic behavior. RNN is based on Rumelhart's work (Rumelhart et al., 1986). It is widely used in connected handwriting recognition and speech recognition through the power of processing sequences of input (Graves, Mohamed, & Hinton, 2013). Some researchers have applied RNN to NLP applications (Lai et al., 2015) (Kowsari et al., 2017). There are several classification architectures built upon RNN, such as Zhou's work (Zhou et al., 2015) and Cho's work (Cho et al., 2014). Zhou's work is based on Long Short-Term Memory (LSTM) (Hochreiter & Schmidhuber, 1997) and Cho's work is based on Gated Recurrent Units (GRUs), a variation to LSTM. Compared with LSTM, GRU modifies the structure of the network unit.

Another technique based on deep learning for text classification is Hierarchical Attention Network (HAN) (Yang et al., 2016). This approach contains a hierarchical structure that mirrors the hierarchical structure in documents. It also incorporates mechanisms that enable this approach to recognize the importance of content at two levels: word level and sentence level.

There is not a fixed answer to the question of which approach is better to solve text classification problems. Yin (Yin et al., 2017) conducted an empirical study to compare the performance of three deep learning based approaches: CNN, GRU and LSTM on 7 datasets. The result shows that given different dataset, different approaches exhibited varied performance. Although applying deep learning techniques to solve text classification problems is a future trend, these techniques usually require a large amount of data and are computationally expensive (Chen and Lin, 2014). However, many investigations have shown that deep learning algorithms outperform traditional machine learning algorithms (Zhang, Zhao, & LeCun, 2015) (Majumder et al., 2017) (Hassan & Mahmood, 2018). Utilizing deep learning techniques for text classification remains an open research topic.

4.2 Deep Learning in Topic Modeling

Xu (Xu et al., 2015) proposed a topic modeling approach called STCC (Short Text Clustering via Convolutional neural networks), a clustering technique that considers a single constraint on learned features through a self-taught learning framework without using any external tags/labels. By applying their proposed work to two datasets, the authors compared their results with the best baselines and found that their approach achieved several improvements. Based on this, Xu (Xu et al., 2017) extended their original work and proposed a flexible Self-Taught Convolutional neural network framework for Short Text Clustering (dubbed STC2). It could incorporate more useful semantic features and learn non-biased deep text representation in an unsupervised manner.

Wang (Wang, Mi & Ittycheriah, 2016) proposed a semi-supervised methodology to combine the representation learning process and K-Means clustering to achieve short text clustering via deep representation learning. In their approach, texts are presented as distributed vectors with neural networks. Some labeled data are also adopted to specify the intention of clustering.

Compared with applying deep learning techniques to text classification, topic modeling approaches based on deep learning has not been widely investigated. We believe applying deep learning techniques in topic modeling will be a future trend in the area of text summarization.

5. FUTURE WORK AND CONCLUSION

This chapter introduced two key techniques related to text summarization in the context of understanding online discussion forums - supervised machine learning techniques for text classification and unsupervised machine learning techniques for topic modeling. As a supporting technique, web scraping - an approach to automatically download text from forum posts, is also addressed in this chapter. We also discussed two text classification techniques based on deep learning: Convolutional Neural Networks (CNNs) and Recurrent Neural Networks (RNNs).

Currently, we are working on a full examination of the LabVIEW discussion forum through the application of supervised and unsupervised machine learning techniques. To improve the model performance, we are examining more posts to enlarge training dataset. To validate our results, we are planning to conduct an empirical analysis among LabVIEW experts. The empirical analysis will be done through a survey asking the participants 1): to what extent do the participants agree with our classification strategy used in supervised machine learning technique; 2) to what extent do the participants agree with the post distribution obtained from end-users.

We believe the results will offer insights into future research directions, thus leading to advanced capabilities that improve the effectiveness of LabVIEW end-users who develop systems models for their domain-specific work. Moreover, our proposed technique is generalizable to other modeling forums. We are also working on the examination of another popular systems modeling discussion forum – Simulink. By cross comparisons between LabVIEW and Simulink, our work will come up with new needs and visions for the future development of systems modeling tools. At an even more generalized level, we believe that our work can be applied to many discussion forums that capture domain expertise that is spread across a broad range of user posts.

REFERENCES

Abbasi, A., France, S., Zhang, Z., & Chen, H. (2010). Selecting attributes for sentiment classification using feature relation networks. *IEEE Transactions on Knowledge and Data Engineering*, *23*(3), 447–462. doi:10.1109/TKDE.2010.110

Akcaoglu, M., & Lee, E. (2016). Increasing social presence in online learning through small group discussions. *The International Review of Research in Open and Distributed Learning*, *17*(3), 1–17. doi:10.19173/irrodl.v17i3.2293

Altınel, B., & Ganiz, M. C. (2018). Semantic text classification: A survey of past and recent advances. *Information Processing & Management*, *54*(6), 1129–1153. doi:10.1016/j.ipm.2018.08.001

Alvarez, S. A. (2002). *An exact analytical relation among recall, precision, and classification accuracy in information retrieval*. Boston College. Technical Report BCCS-02-01.

Bach, F. R., Lanckriet, G. R., & Jordan, M. I. (2004, July). Multiple kernel learning, conic duality, and the SMO algorithm. In *Proceedings of the twenty-first international conference on Machine learning* (p. 6). Banff, Canada: ACM. 10.1145/1015330.1015424

Bayes, T. (1763). LII. An essay towards solving a problem in the doctrine of chances. By the late Rev. Mr. Bayes, FRS communicated by Mr. Price, in a letter to John Canton, AMFR S. *Philosophical Transactions of the Royal Society of London*, (53): 370–418.

Blake, R. (2015). *A Test Cell for Mission-Critical Aerospace Gearbox Testing*. Retrieved from https://www.gsystems.com/case-study-bell-helicopter

Blei, D. M., Ng, A. Y., & Jordan, M. I. (2003). Latent dirichlet allocation. *Journal of Machine Learning Research*, *3*(Jan), 993–1022.

Cambria, E. (2016). Affective computing and sentiment analysis. *IEEE Intelligent Systems*, *31*(2), 102–107. doi:10.1109/MIS.2016.31

Chen, X. W., & Lin, X. T. (2014). Big data deep learning: Challenges and perspectives. *IEEE Access: Practical Innovations, Open Solutions*, *2*, 514–525. doi:10.1109/ACCESS.2014.2325029

Cho, K., van Merrienboer, B., Gulcehre, C., Bahdanau, D., Bougares, F., Schwenk, H., & Bengio, Y. (2014). Learning Phrase Representations using RNN Encoder–Decoder for Statistical Machine Translation. In *Proceedings of the 2014 Conference on Empirical Methods in Natural Language Processing (EMNLP)* (pp. 1724-1734). Doha, Qatar: Association for Computational Linguistics. 10.3115/v1/D14-1179

Conneau, A., Schwenk, H., Barrault, L., & Lecun, Y. (2017). Very deep convolutional networks for text classification. In *Proceedings of the 15th Conference of the European Chapter of the Association for Computational Linguistics* (pp. 1107-1116). Valencia, Spain. Association for Computational Linguistics. 10.18653/v1/E17-1104

De Lara, E., Wallach, D. S., & Zwaenepoel, W. (2001). Puppeteer: Component-based adaptation for mobile Computing. In *USENIX Symposium on Internet Technologies and Systems* (pp. 159 - 170). San Francisco, CA: USENIX Association.

Deerwester, S., Dumais, S. T., Furnas, G. W., Landauer, T. K., & Harshman, R. (1990). Indexing by latent semantic analysis. *Journal of the American Society for Information Science, 41*(6), 391–407. doi:10.1002/(SICI)1097-4571(199009)41:6<391::AID-ASI1>3.0.CO;2-9

Deshpande, M. (2018). *Classification with Support Vector Machines*. Retrieved from https://pythonmachinelearning.pro/classification-with-support-vector-machines/

Duda, R. O., Hart, P. E., & Stork, D. G. (2012). *Pattern classification*. John Wiley & Sons.

Ertugrul, N. (2000). Towards virtual laboratories: A survey of LabVIEW-based teaching/learning tools and future trends. *International Journal of Engineering Education, 16*(3), 171–180.

Ertugrul, N. (2002). *LabVIEW for electric circuits, machines, drives, and laboratories*. Prentice Hall PTR.

Falcon, J. (2017). Facilitating Modeling and Simulation of Complex Systems through Interoperable Software. In *International Conference on Model Driven Engineering Languages and Systems*. Austin, TX: ACM.

Girshick, R. (2015). Fast r-cnn. In *Proceedings of the IEEE international conference on computer vision* (pp. 1440-1448). San Diego, CA: IEEE.

Graves, A., Mohamed, A. R., & Hinton, G. (2013, May). Speech recognition with deep recurrent neural networks. In *2013 IEEE international conference on acoustics, speech and signal processing* (pp. 6645-6649). Vancouver, Canada: IEEE.

Hartigan, J. A., & Wong, M. A. (1979). Algorithm AS 136: A k-means clustering algorithm. *Journal of the Royal Statistical Society. Series C, Applied Statistics*, *28*(1), 100–108.

Hassan, A., & Mahmood, A. (2018). Convolutional recurrent deep learning model for sentence classification. *IEEE Access: Practical Innovations, Open Solutions*, *6*, 13949–13957. doi:10.1109/ACCESS.2018.2814818

Hochreiter, S., & Schmidhuber, J. (1997). Long short-term memory. *Neural Computation*, *9*(8), 1735–1780. doi:10.1162/neco.1997.9.8.1735 PMID:9377276

Joachims, T. (2006, August). Training linear SVMs in linear time. In *Proceedings of the 12th ACM international conference on Knowledge discovery and data mining* (pp. 217-226). Philadelphia, PA: ACM.

Johnson, S. C. (1967). Hierarchical clustering schemes. *Psychometrika*, *32*(3), 241–254. doi:10.1007/BF02289588 PMID:5234703

Jorczak, R. (2014). Differences in classroom versus online exam performance due to asynchronous discussion. *Online Learning Journal*, *18*(2), 1–9.

Joulin, A., Grave, E., Bojanowski, P., & Mikolov, T. (2017). Bag of tricks for efficient text classification. In *Proceedings of the 15th Conference of the European Chapter of the Association for Computational Linguistics* (pp. 3-7), Valencia, Spain: ACM. 10.18653/v1/E17-2068

Karypis, M. S. G., Kumar, V., & Steinbach, M. (2000, August). A comparison of document clustering techniques. In *TextMining Workshop at KDD 2000*. Boston, MA: ACM.

Khosrovian, K., Pfahl, D., & Garousi, V. (2008). GENSIM 2.0: a customizable process simulation model for software process evaluation. In *International Conference on Software Process* (pp. 294-306). Springer, Berlin, Heidelberg.

Kohavi, R. (1995, August). A study of cross-validation and bootstrap for accuracy estimation and model selection. *International Joint Conference on Artificial Intelligence (IJCAI)*, *14*(2), 1137-1145.

Kowsari, K., Brown, D. E., Heidarysafa, M., Meimandi, K. J., Gerber, M. S., & Barnes, L. E. (2017, December). Hdltex: Hierarchical deep learning for text classification. In *2017 16th IEEE International Conference on Machine Learning and Applications (ICMLA)* (pp. 364-371). Cancun, Mexico: IEEE.

Kumar, S., Gao, X., Welch, I., & Mansoori, M. (2016, March). A machine learning based web spam filtering approach. In *2016 IEEE 30th International Conference on Advanced Information Networking and Applications (AINA)* (pp. 973-980). Crans-Montana, Switzerland: IEEE. 10.1109/AINA.2016.177

Lai, S., Xu, L., Liu, K., & Zhao, J. (2015, February). Recurrent convolutional neural networks for text classification. In *Twenty-ninth AAAI conference on artificial intelligence* (pp. 2267-2273). Austin, TX. ACM.

LeCun, Y., Bottou, L., Bengio, Y., & Haffner, P. (1998). Gradient-based learning applied to document recognition. *Proceedings of the IEEE, 86*(11), 2278–2324. doi:10.1109/5.726791

Li, B., & Han, L. (2013, October). Distance weighted cosine similarity measure for text classification. In *International Conference on Intelligent Data Engineering and Automated Learning* (pp. 611-618). Hefei, China: Springer. 10.1007/978-3-642-41278-3_74

Lilleberg, J., Zhu, Y., & Zhang, Y. (2015, July). Support vector machines and word2vec for text classification with semantic features. In *2015 IEEE 14th International Conference on Cognitive Informatics & Cognitive Computing (ICCI* CC)* (pp. 136-140). Beijing, China: IEEE. 10.1109/ICCI-CC.2015.7259377

Liu, L., Tang, L., Dong, W., Yao, S., & Zhou, W. (2016). An overview of topic modeling and its current applications in bioinformatics. *SpringerPlus, 5*(1), 1608. doi:10.118640064-016-3252-8 PMID:27652181

Luhn, H. P. (1957). A statistical approach to mechanized encoding and searching of literary information. *IBM Journal of Research and Development, 1*(4), 309–317. doi:10.1147/rd.14.0309

Majumder, N., Poria, S., Gelbukh, A., & Cambria, E. (2017). Deep learning-based document modeling for personality detection from text. *IEEE Intelligent Systems, 32*(2), 74–79. doi:10.1109/MIS.2017.23

Manning, C. D., Raghavan, P., & Schütze, H. (2008). Scoring, term weighting and the vector space model. *Introduction to Information Retrieval, 100*, 2-4.

MathWorks. (2019). *Simulink Introduction*. Retrieved from https://www.mathworks.com/products/simulink.html

Miltsakaki, E., & Troutt, A. (2008, June). Real-time web text classification and analysis of reading difficulty. In *Proceedings of the third workshop on innovative use of NLP for building educational applications* (pp. 89-97). Columbus, OH: Association for Computational Linguistics. 10.3115/1631836.1631847

Morita, T. (2018). *Advancing Subaru Hybrid Vehicle Testing Through Hardware-in-the-Loop Simulation*. Retrieved from http://sine.ni.com/cs/app/doc/p/id/cs-15982#

National Instruments. (2019). *LabVIEW Introduction*. Retrieved from http://www.ni.com/en-us/shop/labview/labview-details.html

Nenkova, A., & McKeown, K. (2012). A survey of text summarization techniques. In *Mining text data* (pp. 43–76). Boston, MA: Springer. doi:10.1007/978-1-4614-3223-4_3

Pendry, L. F., & Salvatore, J. (2015). Individual and social benefits of online discussion forums. *Computers in Human Behavior*, *50*, 211–220. doi:10.1016/j.chb.2015.03.067

Razon, A., & Barnden, J. (2015). A New Approach to Automated Text Readability Classification based on Concept Indexing with Integrated Part-of-Speech n-gram Features. In *Proceedings of the International Conference Recent Advances in Natural Language Processing* (pp. 521-528). Academic Press.

Ronning, G. (1989). Maximum likelihood estimation of Dirichlet distributions. *Journal of Statistical Computation and Simulation*, *32*(4), 215–221. doi:10.1080/00949658908811178

Rumelhart, D. E., Hinton, G. E., & Williams, R. J. (1988). Learning representations by back-propagating errors. *Cognitive Modeling, 5*(3), 1.

Salton, G., & Yang, C. S. (1973). On the specification of term values in automatic indexing. *The Journal of Documentation*, *29*(4), 351–372. doi:10.1108/eb026562

Sievert, C., & Shirley, K. (2014). LDAvis: A method for visualizing and interpreting topics. In *Proceedings of the workshop on interactive language learning, visualization, and interfaces* (pp. 63-70). Baltimore, MD: Association for Computational Linguistics. 10.3115/v1/W14-3110

Simpson, K. (2015). *You Don't Know JS: Async & Performance*. O'Reilly Media, Inc.

Sparks Jones, K. (1972). A statistical interpretation of term specificity and its application in retrieval. *The Journal of Documentation*, *28*(1), 11–21. doi:10.1108/eb026526

Suganya, S., & Gomathi, C. (2013). Syntax and semantics based efficient text classification framework. *International Journal of Computers and Applications*, *65*(15).

Xiong, C., Hua, Z., Lv, K., & Li, X. (2016, November). An Improved K-means text clustering algorithm By Optimizing initial cluster centers. In *2016 7th International Conference on Cloud Computing and Big Data (CCBD)* (pp. 265-268). Macau, China: IEEE.

Xu, J., Peng, W., Guanhua, T., Bo, X., Jun, Z., Fangyuan, W., & Hongwei, H. (2015). Short text clustering via convolutional neural networks. In *13th Annual Conference of the North American Chapter of the Association for Computational Linguistics: Human Language Technologies* (pp. 62 - 69). Denver, CO: Association for Computational Linguistics. 10.3115/v1/W15-1509

Xu, J., Xu, B., Wang, P., Zheng, S., Tian, G., Zhao, J., & Xu, B. (2017). Self-taught convolutional neural networks for short text clustering. *Neural Networks*, *88*, 22–31. doi:10.1016/j.neunet.2016.12.008 PMID:28157556

Yang, Z., Yang, D., Dyer, C., He, X., Smola, A., & Hovy, E. (2016). Hierarchical attention networks for document classification. In *Proceedings of the 2016 Conference of the North American Chapter of the Association for Computational Linguistics: Human Language Technologies* (pp. 1480-1489). San Diego, CA: Association for Computational Linguistics.

Yin, W., Kann, K., Yu, M., & Schütze, H. (in press). *Comparative study of CNN and RNN for natural language processing*. Clinical Orthopaedics and Related Research. Retrieved from https://arxiv.org/abs/1702.01923

Zhang, X., Zhao, J., & LeCun, Y. (2015). Character-level convolutional networks for text classification. In *Advances in neural information processing systems* (pp. 649–657). Montreal, Canada: Neural Information Processing Systems.

Zhang, Y., Jin, R., & Zhou, Z. H. (2010). Understanding bag-of-words model: A statistical framework. *International Journal of Machine Learning and Cybernetics*, *1*(1-4), 43–52. doi:10.100713042-010-0001-0

Zhou, P., Qi, Z., Zheng, S., Xu, J., Bao, H., & Xu, B. (2016, December). Text Classification Improved by Integrating Bidirectional LSTM with Two-dimensional Max Pooling. In *Proceedings of COLING 2016, the 26th International Conference on Computational Linguistics: Technical Papers* (pp. 3485-3495). Osaka, Japan: The COLING 2016 Organizing Committee.

Chapter 7
Summarization in the Financial and Regulatory Domain

Jochen L. Leidner
ⓘD https://orcid.org/0000-0002-1219-4696
Refinitiv Labs, UK & University of Sheffield, UK

ABSTRACT

This chapter presents an introduction to automatic summarization techniques with special consideration of the financial and regulatory domains. It aims to provide an entry point to the field for readers interested in natural language processing (NLP) who are experts in the finance and/or regulatory domain, or to NLP researchers who would like to learn more about financial and regulatory applications. After introducing some core summarization concepts and the two domains are considered, some key methods and systems are described. Evaluation and quality concerns are also summarized. To conclude, some pointers for future reading are provided.

INTRODUCTION

Inderjeet Mani defined the goal of *automatic summarization* (also "summarisation" in British English) as *"to take an information source, extract content from it, and present the most important content to the user in a condensed form and in a manner sensitive to the user's or application's need"* (Mani, 2001). Therefore, the business value of it lies in its potential for enhancing the productivity of human information consumption (Modaresi *et al.*, 2017): the output of the task of summarizing an input text document comprising English prose is a shorter new document or shorter version of the original document that conveys most of the most important information

DOI: 10.4018/978-1-5225-9373-7.ch007

Figure 1. Single-document summarization (left) versus multi-document summarization (right).

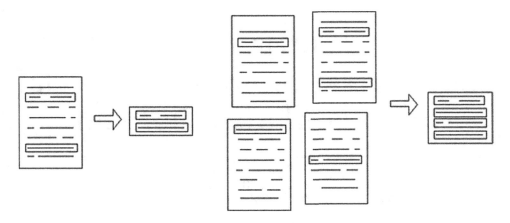

contained in the original document, yet takes less time to read than the original full document.

Traditionally, we can distinguish between *single document summarization*, which takes as input a single document (*source document*) that needs to be summarized, and *multi-document summarization*, which takes as input a set of documents covering the same topic or topic area (Figure 1). In both cases, a single document, the summary (*target document*) is to be created. We can further distinguish between *extractive summarization*, which computes summaries by selecting text spans (phrases, sentences, passages) from the original document or documents, and *abstractive summarization*, which extracts pieces of information in a pre-processing step, and then constructs a synthetic new document, which is a summary that communicates said extracted facts, or it may even introduce new language not found in the source document(s) (Figure 2, right). Mathematically speaking, extractive summarization can be seen as a sequence of projections. Extractive summarization have the advantage of circumventing the problem of how to generate grammatical sentences as it merely selects from existing sentences; it has the disadvantages that a sequence of selected sentences may not make for smooth reading, as it is hard to combine them so as to maintain cohesion (broadly, to be linked together well at the micro-level) and coherence (roughly, to form a meaningful and logical text at the macro-level). The history of automatic summarization goes back to the German researcher Hans Peter Luhn, who worked on automatic summarization at IBM, where he created the method for extractive single-document summarization now named after him (Luhn, 1958).[1]

We can also distinguish between various kinds of methods. *Heuristic methods* like the Luhn method (outlined below) typically use a human-conceived scoring

Figure 2. Extractive (left) versus abstractive (right) Summarization

function to select relevant text spans that ought to be included in the summary, while *machine learning methods* derive evidence that leads to the rejection or acceptance for inclusion from data. This can be done in one of two ways: in *supervised learning*, the most relevant sentences or phrases have been marked up in a set of documents, and an induction algorithm learns which properties of the input text are statistically correlated with high relevance during training time. During runtime, it can then classify pieces of text as relevant or not relevant, or rank (order) pieces of text from most to least relevant. In *unsupervised learning*, clustering algorithms group documents or text fragments using similarity measures. Pieces similar to others are important if repeated, and at the same time redundancy in the output summary is to be avoided.

The remainder of this chapter is structured as follows: the next section explains the particular properties of the financial and regulatory domains; the following section surveys quality criteria that mark good summaries; the next section outlines some common ways to evaluate summarization methods quantitatively. The next section describes some key methods from automatic summarization in general, and the section after describes some implemented summarization systems, in particular those relevant to financial, risk and regulatory, and the final section concludes with some reflections, suggestions for future work and pointers for further reading.

Table 1. Some commercially available summarization systems for English

Provider	Summarization Product	Year
Microsoft Corporation	Word for Windows AutoSummarize	1997
General Electric Corporation	N/A	1999
SRA Inc.	DimSum	1999
Xerox Corporation	InXight	2000
DBI Technologies	Extractor	2000
IBM Corporation	Intelligent Miner for Text	2000
Agolo	N/A	2017

THE FINANCIAL AND REGULATORY DOMAINS

Finance and Summarization

Financial markets are trading exchanges where capital owners (*e.g.* investment banks, asset managers representing wealthy private individuals or families, pension funds or university endowments) meet capital seekers (companies) to trade for mutual financial gain. A multitude of financial instruments (company shares, currencies, exchange traded funds, gold futures, real estate swaps *etc.*) belonging to a range of asset classes are bought and sold, deals of others are monitored, and deals are hedged using options, futures and other derivatives to reduce risk exposure of parties.

Financial instruments are the vehicles or tools that permit participation in a trade: for example, a Microsoft company share (MSFT.N company equity share instrument) formalizes in-part ownership of the Redmond-based company, and also permits profit participation through its annual dividend payments. Companies are organizational units that represent legal persons that conduct business, a useful abstraction, and "real" people are running companies, as executives, employees or board members. People also run other companies as competitors, partners and customers, and stakeholders are interested in their formal and relationship connections as well as other information that may help forecast or explain market moves (*e.g.* CEO changes, mergers and acquisitions *etc.*).

This leads us to the question of what kind of documents the financial domain is dealing with, and what exactly the summarization needs in finance might be? Since the goal is value creation by trading, summarization of opportunities seen by others (past trade deals and rumors of current negotiations) are relevant as reported in news, social media, and by special analysts in analyst reports and brokerage reports. Top deals of the week (*i.e.*, by time), by sector or by geography are worthy of summarization and so are executive scandals and litigation. Abstractive summarization may weave in elements of synthetic language generated from data by natural language generation (NLG) methods, such as price moves. Figure 3 shows excerpts from some sample documents from the financial domain, including an Initial Public Offering (IPO) prospectus[2], a financial news story[3], a financial analyst report[4], and a financial earnings call transcript.[5]

Regulatory and Summarization

Governments delegate some of their powers to regulatory bodies in order to make a realm (e.g.~financial markets) more effective, to steer it away from undesired behavior, whilst ensuring agility, avoiding micro-management, and to ease the burden on courts in case of disagreements between actors. The hope is that the market

Figure 3. (Excerpts from) Sample Financial Documents: (a) Initial Public Offering Prospectus (top left); (b) Financial News Story (top right); (c) Analyst Report (bottom left); and (d) Earnings Call Transcript (bottom right).

bpost SA/NV

Centre Monnaie-Muntcentrum, 1000 Brussels, Belgium

Offering of up to 47,000,000 Ordinary Shares, which may be increased by up to 9,000,000 Ordinary Shares

Listing of all Shares on Euronext Brussels

This is an initial public offering (the "Offering") of ordinary shares without nominal value (the "Shares") of bpost SA/NV (the "Company"), a limited liability company under public law organized under the laws of Belgium. All of the shares offered (the "Offer Shares") are being offered by CVC Funds through Post Invest Europe S.à r.l. (the "Selling Shareholder"). The Selling Shareholder will receive all of the net proceeds of the Offering. The Offering consists of (i) an initial public offering to retail and institutional investors in Belgium (the "Belgian Offering"); (ii) a public offering without listing in Japan (the "Japanese Public Offering"); (iii) a private placement in the United States to persons who are reasonably believed to be "qualified institutional buyers" or "QIBs" (as defined in Rule 144A ("Rule 144A") under the U.S. Securities Act of 1933, as amended (the "U.S. Securities Act")), in reliance on Rule 144A; and (iv) private placements to institutional investors in the rest of the world. The Offering outside the United States will be made in compliance with Regulation S ("Regulation S") under the U.S. Securities Act.

The Selling Shareholder is initially offering up to 47,000,000 Offer Shares in the Offering. In the case of oversubscription, the Selling Shareholder may decide to increase the number of Offer Shares by up to 9,000,000 Offer Shares (the "Increase Option"), in accordance with Article 10 of the Royal Decree of May 17, 2007 on primary market practices. If the Increase Option is exercised in full, the Selling Shareholder will offer a total of 56,000,000 Offer Shares.

And now, I'll turn the call over to Larry. Larry.

H. Lawrence Culp, Jr. - General Electric Co.

Todd, thanks. Good morning, everyone, and thank you for joining us. We have a lot to share with you, so let's get to it. During the third quarter, we saw positive results in most segments with outstanding performance in our Aviation (01:36-02:19)

Now, I know there's been renewed speculation on our future strategic direction. The strategy was announced on June 26 to create a more focused portfolio that sets up our businesses to win and strengthening our balance sheet is today the right plan going forward.

Consistent with this strategy, we are announcing two actions this morning. First, GE plans to reduce its quarterly dividend from $0.12 to $0.01 per share beginning with the board's next dividend declaration which is expected to occur in December 2018. This change will allow GE to retain about $3.9 billion of cash per year compared to the prior payout level. Going forward, we will target a dividend payout ratio in line with peers over time.

Second, we will take a materially different approach to running our Power business. The past 30 days I've spent a lot of time with Russell Stokes and his team it has become clear to us that we need to simplify the business structure. Therefore today we are announcing our intent to reorganize Power into two units, both of which will report directly to me. The first is a unified Gas lifecycle business combining our product and services group gas power systems and power services with the second constituting the portfolio of Steam, Grid, Nuclear, and Power Conversion.

ASTANA (Reuters) - Kazakhstan expects the participants in a pact to curb global oil output to stabilize prices in the first quarter of 2019 and make a joint statement next month "in order to support the market", Energy Minister Kanat Bozumbayev said on Wednesday.

SPONSORED

The Organization of the Petroleum Exporting Countries (OPEC), led by Saudi Arabia, along with non-OPEC members such as Russia, agreed this month to begin curbing production in January to reduce a supply glut that has pressured benchmark crude prices to their lowest in more than a year.

- Unvested equity awards partially or fully accelerate upon the CEO's termination, characteristic of 89% of companies in the home market. Accelerated equity vesting allows executives to realize pay opportunities without necessarily having earned them through strong performance.
- The company has not disclosed specific, quantifiable performance target objectives for the CEO, essential for investors to assess the rigor of incentive programs.
- The company pays long-term incentives to executives without requiring the company to perform above the median of its peer group. Incentive plans that pay for mediocre performance undermine the linkage between pay and performance.
- The CEO's total summary pay for the last reported period was more than three times the median pay for the company's other named executive officers. Such disparity in pay raises concerns regarding the company's succession planning process and the distribution of responsibilities among the executive management team.

players, stakeholders in the economical system, are mostly able to self-organize their dealings. If a systemic issue arises, the regulatory bodies send out calls for input in a consultation period, and after consolidating evidence received regulations are codified. Once a rule book is accepted for implementation, the regulatory body applies it and reprimands market players that break the rules, potentially awarding fines. An example for a regulatory body is the Securities and Exchange Commission of the U.S., which was installed by the *Securities and Exchange Act* (1934) to create more fairness and transparency for investors by forcing public companies to disclose many of their performance parameters publicly using a standard process that grants everybody access to this information at the same time. Again, we must ask what kind of documents the regulatory domain is dealing with, and what exactly the summarization needs in the regulatory realm might be? The goals of governments are oversight and good governance, whereas the goals of companies are to reach compliance and then to stay compliant in the light of forever-changing regulations and entirely new regulations. Relevant laws and regulatory documents are long and complex, they often use very specialized terminology drawn from the legal, financial, administrative or governance domains. There are opportunities for summarization systems that help explain what regulatory documents are about in essence, what one needs to do exactly to comply (how to comply?), and identifying who (which kinds of organizations) need to be in the scope affected by the regulation in the first place (what do I need to comply with?). The regulatory domain is also similar to the legal domain in that there is value in tracking the entire life cycle of regulations from establishing existing issues in society that may require regulations to the creation of new regulations (and associated lobbying), and finally the withdrawal of existing but no longer needed (or deemed ineffective) regulations. Even political considerations impact the world of regulations substantially (e.g. favoring more versus less government regulation based on different economic doctrines associated with political parties, or focusing on different values, which may affect which areas are more scrutinized). All these areas call for extensive tool support to provide decision makers with better actionable intelligence.

Figure 4(a) shows an extract from the MIFID II regulations (*Markets in Financial Instruments (MiFID II) - Directive 2014/65/EU*), which aim to ensure fairer, safer and more efficient markets and facilitate greater transparency for market participants by prescribing new reporting requirements, reduce risk for certain kinds of trading, improve transparency, among other goals.[6] Figure 4(b) shows a piece of an SEC Form 10-K[7] for IBM for the year, which ended on December 31, 2017.[8] Item 1 of this form describes the company's business, and the extracted section discloses some information about IBM's R&D budget and intellectual property situation. From these two examples, it should become clear that the language used in the regulatory domain is more legal-oriented and abstract than *e.g.* the language used in news stories; it also shares with the legal domain its heavy use of terms of art, many of which are explicitly introduced in each document.

With this brief introduction to the financial and regulatory domains, we can now turn to what makes a good summary.

Figure 4. Sample Regulatory Documents: (a) Excerpt from MIFID II Regulations (left); (b) Part from a SEC Form 10-K Filing (right).

Article 9
Management body

1. Competent authorities granting the authorisation in accordance with Article 5 shall ensure that investment firms and their management bodies comply with Article 88 and Article 91 of Directive 2013/36/EU.

ESMA and EBA shall adopt, jointly, guidelines on the elements listed in Article 91(12) of Directive 2013/36/EU.

2. When granting the authorisation in accordance with Article 5, competent authorities may authorise members of the management body to hold one additional non-executive directorship than allowed in accordance with Article 91(3) of Directive 2013/36/EU. Competent authorities shall regularly inform ESMA of such authorisations.

EBA and ESMA shall coordinate the collection of information provided for under the first subparagraph of this paragraph and under Article 91(6) of Directive 2013/36/EU in relation to investment firms.

3. Member States shall ensure that the management body of an investment firm defines, oversees and is accountable for the implementation of the governance arrangements that ensure effective and prudent management of the investment firm including the segregation of duties in the investment firm and the prevention of conflicts of interest, and in a manner that promotes the integrity of the market and the interest of clients.

Without prejudice to the requirements established in Article 88(1) of Directive 2013/36/EU, those arrangements shall also ensure that the management body define, approve and oversee:

(a) the organisation of the firm for the provision of investment services and activities and ancillary services, including the skills, knowledge and expertise required by personnel, the resources, the procedures and the arrangements for the provision of services and activities, taking into account the nature, scale and complexity of its business and all the requirements the firm has to comply with;

(b) a policy as to services, activities, products and operations offered or provided, in accordance with the risk tolerance of the firm and the characteristics and needs of the clients of the firm to whom they will be offered or provided, including carrying out appropriate stress testing, where appropriate;

Research, Development and Intellectual Property

IBM's research and development (R&D) operations differentiate the company from its competitors. IBM annually invests 7 to 8 percent of total revenue for R&D, focusing on high-growth, high-value opportunities. IBM Research works with clients and the company's business units through global labs on near-term and mid-term innovations. It delivers many new technologies to IBM's portfolio every year and helps clients address their most difficult challenges. IBM Research scientists are conducting pioneering work in artificial intelligence, quantum computing, blockchain, security, cloud, nanotechnology, silicon and post-silicon computing architectures and more—applying these technologies across industries including healthcare, IoT, education and financial services.

In 2017, for the 25th consecutive year, IBM was awarded more U.S. patents than any other company. IBM's 9,043 patents awarded in 2017 represent a diverse range of inventions in artificial intelligence, cloud, cybersecurity and other strategic growth areas for the company.

Properties and Quality Dimensions of Summaries

Several properties can be listed that distinguish summarization methods and the summaries that they generate, and many of these factors determine the quality of a summary. *Relevance*, the core quality dimension, is the degree of representativeness of the original content; in other words, does the summary represent the most important and relevant information of the original document? Among experts, there is consensus that in general, what is relevant or not vastly depends on the task of the human user that uses the summary, and cannot be defined or measured irrespective of the ask.[9]

Given this, it is very surprising how little attention actual summarization methods discussed in the research literature pay to elicit requirements, detail these requirements in writing and develop methods that are informed by these task-specific requirements. A likely cause for that is the lack of easy access to crucial stakeholders (*e.g.* finance and regulatory professionals, in the context of this paper) of summarization researchers in academia. *Redundancy*, the absence of repetition, is a mandatory property of any good summary. The presence of redundant information (together with irrelevant information) means the space real estate (in terms of number of characters or pages) of the target document comprising the summary is not put to good use. A document is more easily summarizable than another if the former is more redundant than the latter. *Readability* pertains to how complex the language is that a document's author used in the summary. The ability of a human to comprehend the target summary is arguably important, and in the case of extractive summarization depends very strongly on the readability of the source document. *Grammaticality* is the linguistic quality of the output summary, taken as a piece of prose. It is very important for achieving user acceptance (the ultimate criterion for a project's success) to produce readable and grammatical summaries. Furthermore, we can also identify a number of qualities of the various summarization *methods*, in order to compare them better:

- "language agnostic" versus "language dependent": all things being equal, a method that does not depend on language-specific rules algorithms or data is superior to a method that works for all languages without customization;
- "heuristic" versus "trainable": some methods for summarization depend on heuristics like similarity metrics between sentences, and these may work better for some text types than others. In contrast, other methods are trainable, which permits us to develop a model that is known to work well for documents similar to a chosen sample. Trainable methods (based on machine learning) require training data, and often ground truth (human) summaries, which is expensive and time-intensive, whereas heuristic methods are less flexible but low cost;

- "slow" versus "fast": some methods require less computational processing than other methods. All other things being equal, a simpler and less computationally expensive method is to be preferred to other methods;
- "batch" versus "incremental" (streaming): some methods for summarizing a set of documents are designed to read and process the input in total before output summaries can be generated. For certain situations, it is desirable to use methods that can compose summaries incrementally, based on incrementally available (streaming) data, *e.g.* a real-time news-wire feed;
- "cross-domain robust" versus "domain-specific": some methods work well on certain domains and may be limited in utility to these, whereas other methods may work reasonably across a range of methods while not showing stellar results on any particular domains--depending on the application (what do we know about the range of input text types?) a generalist method or a domain-specific method could be advantageous;
- "domain knowledge-informed" versus "not domain knowledge-informed": some methods can (or even must) leverage formalized domain knowledge, whereas other summarization methods are domain-agnostic. The latter usually perform robustly across domains whereas the former usually can excel in domains where formalized domain knowledge is available;
- "coherent" versus "incoherent": when comparing two summaries, one can "make more sense" with regards to its logical structure. For example, a well-structured document that is coherent puts forward an argument by sequentially listing a couple of premises, perhaps each followed by a statement of support so the reader can accept the premises, followed by a conclusion. In contrast, an incoherent summary jumps between various lines of thoughts and ramblings and the reader finds it hard to follow;
- "cohesive" versus "incohesive": a document can be woven together to form a cohesive fabric, in which sentences are smoothly linked together; in contrast, in an incohesive summary facts may be listed side by side without guidance about why they are presented in a particular order or which function they serve. Crude extractive summarization methods may lead to poor examples of cohesion: for example, the first sentence of a summary should not start with a discourse connective like ``Therefore,''; and finally,
- "deep (linguistic) processing based" versus "shallow processing based": documents can be seen as sequences of characters or as complex linguistic signs. Different summarization methods vary with respect to the depth of linguistic processing deployed to do its job. Some methods exploit syntactic parse trees and discourse markers whereas others use only "shallow" (word-level and phrasal-level) linguistic pre-processing such as part of speech

tagging (POS tagging) or chunking (tagging of non-recursive (base) noun or verb phrases).

The different dimensions across which quality can be measured must ideally inform the evaluation metrics chosen. In the next section, we will look at a range of methods that have been proposed and are being used for the automatic evaluation of automatic summarization methods.

EVALUATION

Component-Based Evaluation

Any two different methods, or variants of the same methods, can be compared quantitatively in order to establish which method produces better-quality summaries. Ideally, we would like to conduct automated evaluations that do not require repeat attention of human raters (also called annotators, evaluators or judges). A number of methods have been proposed.

Component-based evaluations requires reference summaries, which in the past were not easily available. Recently, Grusky *et al.* (2018) have collected Newsroom, a dataset of 1.3 million news stories with human-written summaries from 38 publishers covering the time span of 1998-2017, contained in the Internet Archive.

Automatic Evaluation With ROUGE

Recall-Oriented Understudy for Gisting Evaluation (ROUGE), a set of metrics and a software package used for evaluating automatic summarization and machine translation software Lin (2004), has become one of the de-facto standard metrics for assessing the quality of a summarization automatically. ROUGE requires a collection of documents and associated gold-standard summaries (reference summaries, ground truth summaries). There can be more than one reference summary per document, written by different human subjects to capture the potential diversity of how a "right" solution may look like. Then ROUGE-n essentially measures recall (how many of the reference summary word token n-grams were captured by the summarization system's generated output?). For multiple gold summaries we obtain multiple recall numbers and can choose the maximum value

$$\sum_{S \in \text{ReferenceSummaries}} \sum_{\text{gram\_n} \in S} \text{count}(\text{gram}_{\text{match}}(\text{gram\_n})) \,/\, \sum_{S \in \text{ReferenceSummaries}} \sum_{\text{gram\_n} \in S} \text{count}(\text{gram\_n}),$$

where n is the length (number of sequential tokens) of the n-gram *"n-gram"*, and *count(gram_n)* is the maximum number of n-grams co-occurring in a system generated candidate summary and a set of reference summaries *ReferenceSummaries*. Five common variants of ROUGE have been proposed: ROUGE-n is based on the overlap of n-grams between the system and reference summary; ROUGE-*1* is based on the overlap of unigrams between the system and reference summary; ROUGE-*2* refers to the overlap of bi-grams (pairs of subsequent word tokens) between the system and reference summaries; ROUGE-*L* is based on longest common subsequence-based statistics. Longest common subsequence problem takes into account sentence level structure similarity naturally and identifies longest co-occurring in sequence n-grams automatically; ROUGE-*W*: weighted LCS-based statistics that favors consecutive longest common sub-sequences; ROUGE-*S* is based on skip-bigram based co-occurrence statistics. A skip-bigram is any cpair of words in their sentence order; and ROUGE-*SU* is based on skip-bigram plus unigram-based co-occurrence statistics.

The Pyramid Method

The Pyramid method (Nenkova and Passonneau, 2004; Nenkova, Passonneau and McKeown, 2007) was developed to account for the observation that no single best human model summary exists; rather, salient facts that should appear in a good summary are distributed over pools of multiple human model summaries. Salient facts, called "Summary Content Units" (SCUs) or "nuggets" comprise alternate realizations of the same meaning, with different weights that reflect how broadly distribute an SCU is across a pool of model summaries. Intuitively, a good short summary should contain all and only top-weighted SCUs, and a good longer summary should contain higher-weighted SCUs before using lower-weighted SCU levels because these might be less relevant as they are found in fewer model summaries.

Multi-Dimensional Human Grading

A sample of N (*e.g.* $N=100$) test documents (*e.g.* news stories) are drawn. For each, we show the original article, a human-prepare ground truth summary as well as summaries generated by different models side by side to each human evaluator. The human evaluator does not know which summaries come from which model or which one is the ground truth. Two ordinal scores, often from 1 to 5 (Likert scale), are then assigned to each summary, one grade for relevance, *i.e.* how well the summary captures the important parts of the story, and one grade for readability, *i.e.* how well-written the summary is perceived to be. Results are typically averaged across all documents and evaluating subjects. Even where regular automatic evaluation is used, occasional human grading is recommended. Other dimensions relevant to the purpose of summary generation can be assessed in the same way, and where needed they can be combined, with appropriate weights, into a single aggregate metric for progress tracking (is quality improving quality over time?) or scrutinized individually for diagnostic purposes – *i.e.,* which dimension caused a drop or lack of improvement in overall quality?

Task-Based Evaluation

Another way to evaluate automatic summarization processes and systems is to apply a summarization method and then compare the performance of a downstream application on the original document from which a summary was created and the summary. A poorer-performing summarization method can be expected to lead to a stronger drop in performance of the downstream system in a task (*e.g.* automatic question answering).

A task-based evaluation can also be conducted using human raters: for example, a list of questions can be given to three or five human raters,[10] who are tasked with finding the answer to the questions in the summaries, the *experimental* group, versus in the documents, the *control* group. The distinction between task-based and component-based summarization is orthogonal from the distinction between human and automatic evaluation. Having discussed the evaluation setup to scrutinize produced summaries, we can now proceed to look at some summarization methods and systems that use them.

METHODS

Heuristic Sentence Selection Methods

Luhn (1958)'s paper pioneered extractive single-document summarization for the English language with his system that uses heuristic scoring of sentences based on sentence length, content word frequency and their density within a sliding window (using both stemming as a recall-enhancing device and stop-words). Because the approach is agnostic with respect to linguistic resources, it can easily be applied to many other languages without requiring customization beyond providing a list of stop-words that are to be ignored. Das (2014: 37-40) lists the source code of a simple heuristic summarizer in the programming language R, and demonstrates its application to a financial news story. The idea is to sort the original story's sentences by degree of word overlap with other sentences (using Jaccard distance, a metric of pairwise item overlap) so that the most dissimilar story ranks top.

Filippova *et al.* (2009) propose a method for financial summarization that uses a variant of TFIDF weighting in the relevance weighting for sentences where the inverse document frequency is conditioned specifically on company relevant documents, which penalizes words common to company information (such as words like "company", "CEO" but also more specifically "apple", "computer", "iPad" for Apple Inc., for instance). Unlike most other previous work, they assume the (professional) user is already familiar with the company profile (*e.g.*, a financial investment analyst whose job it is to study one particular oil company on a daily does not need to be told the name of its CEO). Their objective is to provide actionable information for near-term trading of the company (inference from news to stock price movement within a day). They also introduce a novel query expansion method based on the company's name.

Generally, in financial document summarization it matters what changes pertain to specific companies, currencies, commodities and their associated financial instruments, so the underlying theme is predicting change and responding timely to change. In the regulatory domain, user are likewise interested in change, but change happens more slowly and gradually. In contrast with the financial domain, the change can potentially be influenced (lobbying) with respect to direction and magnitude, and the underlying questions are what to comply with and how to comply, i.e.~what actions ought to be undertaken to be considered to be in compliance by regulatory bodies. Contrary to summarization for consumers (or any layperson in a domain), familiarity with the underlying instrument can and should be assumed, so only novel information is relevant.

Statistical Methods

Kupiec, Pederson and Chen (1995) present a statistical method for supervised machine learning based summarization using a multinomial Bayes classification model. They use 5 features: a sentence-length cut-off (is the sentence longer than 5 tokens?), a fixed phrasal lexicon feature with 26 entries (does the sentence contain phrases like "in conclusion", "this letter" *etc.*?), a positional feature (where is the sentence under consideration located within the present paragraph?), a binary feature that indicates whether a sentence contains the most ``thematic words'' (defined as frequent content words) among all sentences in the document, and an upper-case feature (a binary feature that assesses whether the present sentence has the most capitalized words that are not measurement units). The authors report that for an evaluated sample of science/engineering summaries, generated extractive summaries with 25% of the length of the original input document, their method selected 84% of sentences also picked by professionals.

Knight and Marcu (2000) apply Shannon's noisy channel model to "translate" source documents *s* into their shorter summaries *t*: given that large collections of text/abstract pairs are available online, both representations are parsed syntactically, and the resulting trees are used to calculate probability estimates for a source model *P(s)*, a channel model *P(t|s)* and a decoder to find the string *s* that maximizes *P(s|t)* (which means maximizing *P(s) · P(t|s)*).

Algebraic Methods (Distributional Semantics)

Policy Analysis. While policies are not regulations, they also fall in the area of compliance, and they often use the same normative language: policies implement regulations by ensuring compliant behavior if adhered to. Stamey and Rossi (2009) present the *HERMES* system for the automatic analysis of privacy policies, and apply it to 50 e-commerce Web sites. They attempt to group policy clauses into a predefined group of six separate section types, apply Latent Semantic Analysis (LSA) to achieve "topical separation". The HERMES system's primary aim appears to be the extraction of potentially ambiguous terms rather than a complete analysis into the six categories, and the system does not go beyond vectorial representations of words.

Information Extraction Based Methods

Leidner *et al.* propose a set of methods for computer-supported risk analysis based on information extraction (Leidner and Schilder, 2010; Leidner, 2015; Nugent and Leidner, 2016; Leidner and Nugent, 2018). Risk identification from document collections including earning reports and news is framed as a combination of weakly supervised learning of a risk taxonomy (Leidner and Schilder, 2010) and relation extraction of company-risk mentions (Nugent and Leidner, 2016): first, an offline step mines a taxonomy of risk types from the Web by extracting risk-indicative language from search engine result page (SERP) snippets and arranging it in a hierarchy in order to obtain a data-driven set of risk types and their inter-relationships, which can be re-executed to keep it "fresh" in the light of new risk types that can emerge and lead to new terminology (*e.g.* "climate change", "DDOS risk", "Brexit"). Secondly named entity tagger extracts company names, mentions of the induced taxonomy terms are looked up and a supervised relationship learner links risks to companies and disambiguates true risks (*"Microsoft received a fine, said Bill Gates."* → { Finanical Risk > Regulatory Enforcement }) from candidate risks that do not constitute actual risks (*"'I feel fine', said Bill Gates at Microsoft."* → { }). The relation extractor outputs risk mention triples of the form ‹*Company; IsExposedTo; RiskType*› and associated confidence scores. On a sample of unseen

Reuters News, their method achieved F1=82.4%, and it method can be used to populate some of the quadrants of automatic SWOT analysis type diagrams (Table 2) with specific data.

Discourse-Based Methods

Marcu (1997) presents a first method for exploiting the hierarchical nature of rhetorical relations among clauses of a document to be summarized. Applying a Rhetorical Structure Theory (RST) parser yields binary trees of a document's clauses, some of which *paratactic* (same-level), others *hypotactic* (subordinate-level), and the latter can be dropped in the summarization process as they convey only peripheral information.

Graph-Based Methods

TextRank (Mihalcea and Tarau, 2004; Barrios *et al.*, 2016) is a popular and competitive graph-based heuristic extractive summarization method. A graph representing the document to be summarized is constructed as follows. If S is the set of $|S|$ sentences, create an $|N|^2$ matrix of sentence similarity scores using any suitable similarity metric (both cosine similarity over TFIDF word vectors and BM25 have been found to work well in practice as similarity functions, typically applied only over nouns and verbs extracted using part-of-speech tagging or keywords extracted using standard keyword extraction methods like PMI). This matrix can be viewed as a graph $G=(V; E)$. Let every sentence $s\epsilon S$ be a node $v\epsilon V$ in said graph, and let each node v in the graph have a node weight v_n (representing the number of visits and initially set to 0). Construct an edge $e\epsilon E$ between the nodes representing the k most similar sentences. Convert similarity scores so they look like probabilities, and conduct a random walk, choosing a random node and, with probability β, select a next node based on the edge's probability, or with probability $1-\beta$, choose to "beam" the random walker, *i.e.* let him or her jump to another random node (for instance with $\beta=0.85$):

$$score(v_i) = (1 - \beta) + \beta \sum\nolimits_{k\epsilon In(vi)} score(v_j) / |Out(v_j)|,$$

Table 2. SWOT analysis

Strengths	Weaknesses
positive, internal	*negative, intern*
Opportunities	**Threats**
positive, external	*negative, external*

where $In(v_x)$ is the set of vertices pointing to v_x (incoming), and $Out(v_x)$ is the set of vertices that v_x points to (outgoing). During these traversals, increase the visit count v_n associated with each node by *1*. Then sort the nodes in the graph (representing sentences) by the number of times they got visited, and select the top-ranking ℓ sentences (*e.g.* $\ell=10$) to make up the desired extractive summary (output in the order the sentences have in the original text). Filippova *et al.* (2009) also use a form of query-dependent PageRank for sentence ranking, in addition to the term weighting already mentioned above.

Neural Methods

Automatic Neural Networks (ANNs), in particular Multi-Layer Perceptrons ("deep learning") like Recurrent Neural Networks (RNNs) can be used for document summarization.[11] The problem is typically framed as sequence-to-sequence re-writing task, where the output sequence is shorter than the input sequence. Filippova *et al.* (2015) describe the use of a *Long-Short Term Memory (LSTM)* neural network model (Hochreiter and Schmidhuber, 1997) for extractive summarization: their model learns how to generate summaries by removing tokens from the input sequence without any kind of linguistic feature extraction.

Singh *et al.* (2018) also use an LSTM for extractive summarization; specifically, they use an across-sentence boundary LSTM-based language model for unsupervised, query-focused, *extractive* multi-document summarization, and they find a bi-directional version of this outperforms other approaches significantly on an event summarization task. Nallapati, Zhai and Zhou (2017) descibe *SummaRuNNer*, an RNN-based sequence model for extractive summarization of documents. Their model permits the visualization of the relative contribution of abstract features such as information content, salience and novelty to the overall outcome. Their method can be trained on document-summary pairs without requiring sentence-level labels annotating for extractive relevance. Nallapati *et al.* (2016) present a neural sequence-to-sequence model for abstractive summarization based on a feature-rich-encoder: they use an embedding vector each for POS, NER tags and discretized TF and IDF values, which are concatenated together with word embeddings as input to the encoder. Paulus, Xiong and Socher (2017) propose a model that combines supervised word prediction based on an attentional encoder-decoder mechanism with reinforcement learning.

Rush, Chopra and Weston (2015) present a first neural attention model for *abstractive* sentence summarization. However, standard attentional sequence-to-sequence neural models have two undesirable properties: 1. they introduce inaccuracies (caused by their ability to introduce "new" text in a summary that was not part of the original document to be summarized) and 2. the often contain redundant information, because there is no global control over what has been generated already. See, Liu and Manning (2017) introduce pointer generator models to address the former issue: at each decoding step (token position) a probabilistic choice is made between either generating a word (abstractive) or copying a word from the source text (extractive); in a way, their (overall abstractive) model is a hybrid. They additionally use coverage to keep track of what has already been said, addressing the latter issue.

Methods Applied to Financial Documents, Regulations and Policies

Regulations and policies are normative documents, *i.e.* they comprise sets of rules regards mandated behavior and their application conditions. For example, the EU General Data Protection Regulation (GDPR)[12] protects all EU citizens from privacy and data breaches by regulating the behaviors of companies that deal with any personal information of EU citizens. Table 3 shows an extractive summary of the GDPR regulation document (54,876 words). As we can see, the summary is useful, but it also has limitations:

- There are important sentences missing that a human summary by a professional would include;
- the first and the last sentence are redundant, so the last sentence could really be dropped;
- the text has limited cohesion: due to the purely extractive nature of the method, sentences are not sufficiently linked together compared to human-written prose; and
- there are enumeration artifacts ("(4)", "(6)") that do not make any sense when included in a summary since they are taken out of context.

The topic of summarization of regulations for a professional audience is has not received a lot of attention: for example, Bholat *et al.* (2015), a recent study surveying the utility of text mining methods for central banks, does not mention automatic summarization in a glossary of relevant terminology. However, there is some consumer-facing work on automatic privacy policy analysis and summarization that may be considered relevant. Ammar *et al.* (2012) analyze a corpus of Web privacy policies with respect to the presence or absence of concepts, for example whether a membership's termination by a user is mentioned therein. The connection of this and other information extraction work with the topic of summarization is shown by work of Kelly *et al.* (2009), who propose a "nutrition label" for privacy, in other words a concise, standardized summary display of a user's rights and obligations shown on Websites. Such standardization is useful for consumer-facing education

Table 3. Automatic summary of the EU GDPR privacy regulation (6 sentences; Luhn's (1958) method)

Natural persons increasingly make personal information available publicly and globally.
Natural persons should have control of their own personal data.
Legal and practical certainty for natural persons, economic operators and public authorities should be enhanced.
(4) The processing of personal data should be designed to serve mankind.
(6) Rapid technological developments and globalisation have brought new challenges for the protection of personal data.
The exchange of personal data between public and private actors, including natural persons, associations and undertakings across the Union has increased.

regarding the implementation of regulations and policies; however summarization of the actual regulations across all possible policies, more general mechanisms will be needed. We already mentioned the Hermes system above (Stamey & Rossi, 2009), an approach that analyzes e-commerce privacy policies, with the aim to find unclear and ambiguous language use such as hedging; they use Latent Semantic Analysis (LSA) to cluster vague words. Liu, Sadeh and Smith (2014) used Hidden Markov Models (HMMs) to align passages of multiple privacy policies so that the issues they address can be better compared. Xiao *et al.* (2012) describe *Text2Policy*, an approach to extract the rules regarding access control of people or processes to resources as contained in Access Control Policies (ACPs) and formulated in natural language, here English, using shallow parsing and a domain dictionary.

Many of the issues addressed in these works also apply to summarization for professionals of regulations. Constantino (1997) recognized the value of information extraction in the context of real-time news summarization:

"[A] real-time information extraction system could also be used by other financial operators to process and summarize incoming real-time news from on-line services – i.e. Dow-Jones or Bloomberg." Constantino (1997: 135)

Beyond summarization policies and regulations in mere natural language goes a proposal by Michael, Ong and Rowe (2019); they attempt to translate policies from English to a formal language, logical forms in Prolog notation. Such a representation can serve multiple goals, including consistency checks, matching of policy scopes against situation scopes, but it can also be used for generating abstractive summaries from logical forms.

Other Relevant Methods

In this chapter, the focus is on surveying summarization where the input is text in prose form. In the financial domain, it is often a requirement to summarize numeric time series. What may be called "Time Series Summarization" from a business point of view, would more likely be dealt with as "Natural Language Generation" (NLG) from structured numeric data sets in the field of natural language processing. For example, Ahmad, Taskaya-Temizel and Ahmad (2004) use wavelet analysis to identify regularities such as seasonality effects, correlations and other patterns in time series, which can then be summarized by generating prose to explain the observed regularities.

The regulatory domain is somewhat similar to the legal domain, and whereas there are few studies focusing specifically on summarizing regulations, there are several approaches to legal summarization.

The *SALOMON* system aims to improve access to Belgian criminal cases based on a text grammar (Moens and Uyttendaele, 1997), and follow-on work has since identified and partially addressed challenges in the areas of concept learning and argument recognition (Moens, 2007). Galgani, Compton and Hoffmann (2012) describe a hybrid summarization method for Australian legal cases; in their approach, instead of a pre-annotated legal corpus, human experts craft rules, which then get extended with exceptions where needed in an iterative work-flow informed by observed errors. A set of 16 features are extracted, which can be used by human experts to describe the location of "catchphrases" that indicate relevant content. While the authors report that with just 23 rules they were able to obtain a higher precision (P=87.4%) than with other automatic methods tried, the approach appears to be potentially prone to overfitting since humans cannot maintain comprehensive and objective error statistics in their mental model while reviewing system output for errors. (Hachey and Grover, 2005; Hachey and Grover, 2005; Hachey and Grover, 2006) describe an extractive summarization method that applies supervised machine learning to the creation of summaries from a corpus of House of Lords Judgments (HOLJ), based on standard linguistic features and rhetorical role classification in particular. Note, however, that regulations are more similar to statutes, but the above mentioned and many other legal summarization approaches have been tested mostly on cases.

Table 4 shows some of the pros and cons of the various families of methods that have been covered in this survey; note that it is of course difficult to generalize about whole groups of methods (for each criterion, there may be exceptions to the rule); nevertheless, the synopsis presents the author's assessment based on typical representatives of each group.

Table 4. Synopsis of summarization methods and some of their properties

Method Family	Degree of Language Independence	Cross-Domain Robustness	Requires Human Training Data?
Heuristic Based	☐☐☐☐	☐☐☐☐☐	no
Statistics Based	☐	☐	yes
Information Extraction Based	-	☐	often yes
Graph Based	☐☐☐☐	☐☐☐☐☐	no
Discourse Based	-	-	sometimes no
Neural Network Based	☐	☐	yes

Further Reading

Maybury and Mani (2001) is a detailed and accessible tutorial on automatic summarization. The monograph Mani (2001) covers an introduction in the state of the art of summarization until its publication, including the process of human summarization. He also discusses multi-media summarization, creating summaries using components other than text. TorresMoreno (2014) is an excellent and more recent textbook overview over the various methods of document summarization until just before the advent of neural methods. Nenkova and McKeown (2011) also survey traditional methods for automatic summarization; they also include natural language generation for abstractive summarization and discuss domain adaptation in the medical and general scientific domains, email and Web text types and speech medium. Neither of these standard texts contain any treatment of the specifics of the financial or regulatory domain.

Systems News Summarization

News are an important ingredient for financial market, since news drive the prices of financial instruments. Naturally, many companies that sell financial information, such as Reuters News (from Thomson Reuters or Refinitiv) or Bloomberg, sell news as well. Columbia *Newsblaster* (McKeown *et al.*, 2002) aggregate and summarizes news found on the Web: it crawls news from the Web, extracts news articles, clusters them into groups, summarizes them, classifies them by topic, and generates a Web page for human consumption and exploration. A multilingual version has been developed that uses automatic machine translation (Evants, Klavans and McKeown, 2004).

The *FastSum* system is am extractive multi-document summarization system for news based on supervised learning (Schilder and Kondadadi, 2008). It exploits the observation that the first sentence of any news story in most cases is a good summary of the story as a whole; sentences are included in the summary if they are similar in nature to first sentences that the system was trained on. *Financial Summarization* Lam and Ho (2001) describe their *FNDS* system (short for *"Financial News Digest System"*), which aims to facilitate analysis of English news in the finance domain. The system conducts shallow syntactic analysis and named entity extraction steps before populating a relational database based on a set of hand-written information extraction templates. A database question answering system permits a user to query the extracted facts in English (e.g. *"How much did Samsung earn in 2001?"*), which gets translated into SQL.

Wu and Liu (2003) present a financial summarization system that is guided by a human-constructed ontology, which is used to maintain frequency counts at multiple levels of generality: at each term encounter, the ontology node corresponding to the term and all its more general parents' counts get incremented by one; thus, a set of (sub-)topic signature are created, which are then used to score paragraphs. Colmenares *et al.* (2015) describe a method for the generation of headlines, an important part of automatic summarization of news.

Regulation Summarization

To date, there appears to be a lack of published work on regulatory summarization. Conrad *et al.* (2009) present a modification of the FastSum system for the query-based summarization of legal/regulatory blogs; this is a useful capability to stay informed about professionals' discussions of emerging legal and regulatory topics such as draft bills or proposed regulations. The informal language of blogs is of course far removed from the stylized technical language of regulations, but professional blogs are at least likely to use similar terms of art. In the regulatory space, Cleland-Huang *et al.* (2010) are concerned with traceability, the property of linking a system's requirements all the way from rationales over regulatory codes to exhibited behaviors. While not technically an example of summarization, this work is relevant as it pertains to the realm of connecting regulation with regulated reality.

Mobile Summarization

Financial professionals and business executives desire to be able to access market and regulatory information also when they are on the move. Buyukkokten, Garcia-Molina and Paepcke (2001) describe *Power Browser*, a Luhn-based summarizer of Web content for early personal digital assistants; its authors apply a crude form of weight learning. Yang and Wang (2003) and Otterbacher, Radev and Kareem (2006) describe news summarizers for early smart phones supporting the now-obsolete Wireless Access Protocol WAP. More recently, *Reuters TV* is a mobile application

Figure 5. Reuters TV: Video Summary of a Day
(Photo by the Author; © Copyright 2019, Thomson Reuters. Used with permission).

(available for Apple iPhone and iPad devices) and Website[13] that provides flexible video summaries of daily news: the user communicates a desired time frame (*e.g.* 5 or 15 minutes) and the system summarizes the news of the day in video form, taking exactly the desired time by composing video clips of varying duration.

Open-Source Research Systems

MEAD (Radev *et al.*, 2004) is a collection of freely available, open-source summarization method implementations with a unified driver program suitable for research into automatic summarization; it includes many popular methods for use as baselines for comparison. For example, MEAD was one of the systems used in a large-scale comparative evaluation of summarization methods (Radev *et al.*,

2004). When evaluating one's summarizer specialized in the financial, regulatory or other domains, it is recommended to run a generic summarizer like MEAD as a baseline for comparison to establish meaningful quality reference points with the state of the art.

SUMMARY, CONCLUSION, AND OUTLOOK

In this chapter, the state of the art in automatic document summarization was reviewed, with particular consideration of the domains of finance and regulations. We have looked at key methods and some systems after discussing quality criteria and prominent quantitative evaluation methods.

A couple of observations are due: Automatic summarization can best be done when the system designers know about the purpose that the resulting summaries serve: who are its users and what questions are they trying to answer? This stands in stark contrast with marketing pitches by technology vendors and even position statements by scientists of summarization as a general purpose technology; at the time of writing (2019), not one-size-fits-all method is available. Many systems exist that operate on news, which reflects both the fact that news reports are an important and generic category, but also the availability of data to scientists specializing on summarization (academics may not have access to commercial proprietary analyst reports) or the lack of domain expertise to cope with other domains (regulatory rules are easily available online but may be hard to comprehend for scholars with a more technical background not part of an interdisciplinary research team). Finally, there is a clear need for benchmark collections in the domains of finance and regulations to provide researchers with new shared tasks, perhaps similar to what the Reuters corpus RCV1 has achieved in the task of text classification.

An overall assessment has to be that not a lot of summarization work has been, conducted in the financial and regulatory domains, with the exception of financial news and policy analysis. This is perhaps due to the lack of access to domain expertise and use cases among summarization researchers. While it is often argued that summarization is required in order to save time or to increase productivity, in practice the \emph{human consumption} of automatic summaries *also* takes time, and as long as quality of automatic summaries remains poor, human double-checking is still required, at least for critical tasks.

For future work, we propose empirical demonstrations of the time-saving abilities of automatic summarization, which is broadly claimed yet remains often an unsupported conjecture that has motivated much of summarization research. More research on human interfaces is also required: current summarizers treat the summary as a static piece of text that gets output, rather than as a visual element part of an interactive Graphical User Interface that the user can interact with. For example, in the spirit of explainability (→ *explainable information retrieval*), interlinking extracted sentences with their source location so the context from which they were extracted can easily be inspected, would be a welcome standard feature. Overall, the research work on financial and regulatory documents has just begun, so we propose a collection of use cases backed up by user stories with personae and associated document collections and use case specific requirements capture. *For summarization to become more useful to professional audiences, the summarization task must be analyzed within its work-flow context, taking into account the role of its consuming user and his or her task environment.*

In the future, it will be explored how neural methods can be made more transparent (why is a sentence contained in the present summary?), and methods will be explored that can make do with smaller training data. Finally, methods that make use of domain knowledge for reasoning should be devised, ideally based on applying weakly supervised machine

learning for the induction of human-understandable representations that can then be leveraged to support neural models.

For further reading, the reader interested in progress of the state of the art in summarization methods may be referred to regular NLP conferences like ACL (including EACL and NAACL), EMNLP, COLING, *SEM, SEMEVAL, RANLP or CICling. In particular, NIST's TAC (*Text Analysis Conference*), a recurring workshop held in Gaithersburg, MD,

USA, is relevant to the summarization community. To the best of the author's knowledge there is no dedicated forum for summarization specifically targeting finance, but general financial technology trade fairs ("FinTech") may cover it. In the regular space, both the *International Conference on AI in Law* (ICAIL) and JURIX, an annual conference organized since 1988 by the JURIX Foundation, publish material relevant to regulatory technology ("RegTech"), including summarization.

REFERENCES

Ahmad, S., Taskaya-Temizel, T., & Ahmad, K. (2004). Summarizing time series: Learning patterns in 'volatile' series. In Z. R. Yang, H. Yin, & R. M. Everson (Eds.), *Intelligent Data Engineering and Automated Learning (IDEAL 2004)* (pp. 523–532). Berlin, Germany: Springer. doi:10.1007/978-3-540-28651-6_77

Barrios, F., López, F., Argerich, L., & Wachenchauzer, R. (2016). Variations of the similarity function of textrank for automated summarization. Academic Press.

Buyukkokten, O., Garcia-Molina, H., & Paepcke, A. (2001). Seeing the whole in parts: Text summarization for Web browsing on handheld devices. In: *Proceedings of the 10th International Conference on World Wide Web (WWW 2001)*. New York, NY: ACM. 10.1145/371920.372178

Cleland-Huang, J., Czauderna, A., Gibiec, M., & Emenecker, J. (2010). A machine learning approach for tracing regulatory codes to product specific requirements. In: *Proceedings of the 32Nd ACM/IEEE International Conference on Software Engineering*. ACM. 10.1145/1806799.1806825

Colmenares, C. A., Litvak, M., Mantrach, A., & Silvestri, F. (2015). HEADS: Headline generation as sequence prediction using an abstract feature-rich space. In: *Proceedings of the 2015 Conference of the North American Chapter of the Association for Computational Linguistics: Human Language Technologies (NAACL-HLT 2015)*. Association for Computational Linguistics. 10.3115/v1/N15-1014

Conrad, J. G., Leidner, J. L., Schilder, F., & Kondadadi, R. (2009). Query-based opinion summarization for legal blog entries. In *The 12th International Conference on Artificial Intelligence and Law, Proceedings of the Conference*. ACM. 10.1145/1568234.1568253

Constantino, M. (1997). *Financial information extraction using pre-defined and user-definable templates in the Lolita system* (Ph.D. thesis). Durham University, Durham, UK.

Das, S. R. (2014). Text and Context: Language Analytics in Finance. Boston, MA: Now.

Evans, D. K., Klavans, J. L., & McKeown, K. R. (2004). Columbia Newsblaster: Multilingual news summarization on the Web. In D. M. Susan Dumais, & S. Roukos (Eds.), *Proc. HLT-NAACL 2004: Demonstration Papers*. Association for Computational Linguistics. 10.3115/1614025.1614026

Filippova, K., Alfonseca, E., Colmenares, C. A., Kaiser, L., & Vinyals, O. (2015). Sentence compression by deletion with LSTMs. In *Proceedings of the 2015 Conference on Empirical Methods in Natural Language Processing (EMNLP 2015)*. Association for Computational Linguistics. 10.18653/v1/D15-1042

Filippova, K., Surdeanu, M., Ciaramita, M., & Zaragoza, H. (2009). Company-oriented extractive summarization of financial news. In *Proceedings of the 12th Conference of the European Chapter of the ACL (EACL 2009)*. Association for Computational Linguistics.

Galgani, F., Compton, P., & Hoffmann, A. (2012). Combining different summarization techniques for legal text. In *Proceedings of the Workshop on Innovative Hybrid Approaches to the Processing of Textual Data*. Association for Computational Linguistics.

Goldberg, Y. (2017). Neural Network Methods for Natural Language Processing. In *Synthesis Lectures on Human Language Technologies* **10**. San Francisco: Morgan Claypool. doi:10.2200/S00762ED1V01Y201703HLT037

Grusky, M., Naaman, M., & Artzi, Y. (2018). Newsroom: A Dataset of 1.3 Million Summaries with Diverse Extractive Strategies. In *Proceedings of the 2018 Conference of the North American Chapter of the Association for Computational Linguistics: Human Language Technologies*. Association for Computational Linguistics. 10.18653/v1/N18-1065

Hachey & Grover. (2005a). *Automatic legal text summarisation: Experiments with summary structuring*. Academic Press.

Hachey, B., & Grover, C. (2005b). Sentence extraction for legal text summarisation. *Proceedings of the Nineteenth International Joint Conference on Artificial Intelligence (IJCAI 2005)*, 1686-1687.

Hachey, B., & Grover, C. (2006). Extractive summarisation of legal texts. *Artificial Intelligence and Law*, *14*(4), 305–345. doi:10.100710506-007-9039-z

Hochreiter, S., & Schmidhuber, J. (1997). Long short-term memory. *Neural Computation*, *9*(8), 1735–1780. doi:10.1162/neco.1997.9.8.1735 PMID:9377276

Knight, K., & Marcu, D. (2000). Statistics-Based Summarization – Step One: Sentence Compression. In *Proceedings of the Seventeenth National Conference on Artificial Intelligence and Twelfth Conference on Innovative Applications of Artificial Intelligence*, (pp. 703-710). AAAI Press.

Kupiec, J., Pedersen, J., & Chen, F. (1995). A trainable document summarizer. In *Proceedings of the 18th Annual International ACM SIGIR Conference on Research and Development in Information Retrieval (SIGIR 1995)*. ACM.

Lam, W., & Ho, K. S. (2001). FIDS: An intelligent financial web news articles digest system. *IEEE Transactions on Systems, Man, and Cybernetics. Part A, Systems and Humans*, *31*(6), 753–762. doi:10.1109/3468.983433

Leidner, J. L. (2015). *Computer-supported risk identification*. Technical report. https://arxiv.org/abs/1510.08285 (cited 2019-07-17).

Leidner, J. L., & Nugent, T. (2018). Cognitive inhibitors for threat assessment and automated risk management. *Proceedings of the 53rd ESReDA Seminar: European Safety, Reliability & Data Association/European Commission*, 285-291.

Leidner, J. L., & Schilder, F. (2010). Hunting for the black swan: Risk mining from text. *Proceedings of the ACL: Demonstrations (ACL 2010)*.

Lin, C.-Y. (2004). ROUGE: A package for automatic evaluation of summaries. In M.-F. Moens & S. Szpakowicz (Eds.), *Text Summarization Branches Out: Proceedings of the ACL-04 Workshop*. Association for Computational Linguistics.

Luhn, H. P. (1958). The automatic creation of literature abstracts. *IBM Journal of Research and Development*, 2(2), 159–165. doi:10.1147/rd.22.0159

Mani, I. (2001). *Automatic Summarization*. Amsterdam, The Netherlands: John Bejamins. doi:10.1075/nlp.3

Marcu, D. (1997). The rhetorical parsing of natural language texts. In *The Proceedings of the 35th Annual Meeting of the Association for Computational Linguistics (ACL/EACL)*. Association for Computational Linguistics.

Maybury, M. T., & Mani, I. (2001). Automatic summarization. In *European Conference on Computational Linguistics (EACL 2001)*. ACL. Tutorial Notes.

McKeown, K. R., Barzilay, R., Evans, D., Hatzivassiloglou, V., Klavans, J. L., Nenkova, A., ... Sigelman, S. (2002). Tracking and summarizing news on a daily basis with Columbia's Newsblaster. In *Proceedings of the Second International Conference on Human Language Technology Research (HLT 2002)*. Morgan Kaufmann. 10.3115/1289189.1289212

Mihalcea, R., & Tarau, P. (2004). TextRank: Bringing order into text. In *Proceedings of the 2004 Conference on Empirical Methods in Natural Language Processing (EMNLP 2004)*. ACL.

Modaresi, P., Gross, P., Sefidrodi, S., Eckhof, M., & Conrad, S. (2017). On (commercial) benefits of automatic text summarization systems in the news domain: A case of media monitoring and media response analysis. Academic Press.

Moens, M.-F. (2007). Summarizing court decisions. *Information Processing & Management*, 43(6), 1748–1764. doi:10.1016/j.ipm.2007.01.005

Moens, M.-F., & Uyttendaele, C. (1997). Automatic structuring and categorization as a first step in summarizing legal cases. *Information Processing & Management*, 33(6), 727–737. doi:10.1016/S0306-4573(97)00035-6

Nallapati, R., Zhai, F., & Zhou, B. (2017). SummaRuNNer: A recurrent neural network based sequence model for extractive summarization of documents. *AAAI Conference on Artificial Intelligence.*

Nallapati, R., Zhou, B., dos Santos, C., Gulcehre, C., & Xiang, B. (2016). Abstractive text summarization using sequence-to-sequence RNNs and beyond. In *Proceedings of the 20th SIGNLL Conference on Computational Natural Language Learning (CoNLL 2016).* Association for Computational Linguistics. 10.18653/v1/K16-1028

Nenkova & McKeown. (2011). *Automatic Summarization.* Delft, The Netherlands: Now.

Nenkova, Passonneau, & McKeown. (2007). The Pyramid method: Incorporating human content selection variation in summarization evaluation. *ACM Trans. Speech Lang. Process., 4*(2), Article 4.

Nenkova, A., & Passonneau, R. (2004). Evaluating content selection in summarization: The Pyramid method. In *Proceedings of the Human Language Technology Conference of the North American Chapter of the Association for Computational Linguistics (HLT-NAACL 2004).* ACL.

Nugent & Leidner. (2016). *Risk mining: Company-risk identification from unstructured sources.* In 2016 IEEE 16th International Conference on Data Mining Workshops (ICDMW), 12-15 December, 2016, Barcelona, Spain, pp. 1308–1311..

Otterbacher, Radev, & Kareem. (2006). *News to go: Hierarchical text summarization for mobile devices.* In Proceedings of the 29th Annual International ACM SIGIR Conference on Research and Development in Information Retrieval, SIGIR 2006, New York, NY, USA, pp. 589–596. ACM.

Paulus, Xiong, & Socher. (n.d.). *A deep reinforced model for abstractive summarization.* Academic Press.

Radev, D., Allison, T., Blair-Goldensohn, S., Blitzer, J., Çelebi, A., Dimitrov, S., . . . Zhang, Z. (2004). MEAD – a platform for multidocument multilingual text summarization. In *Proceedings of the Fourth International Conference on Language Resources and Evaluation (LREC 2004).* European Language Resources Association (ELRA).

Radev, D. R., Teufel, S., Saggion, H., Lam, W., Blitzer, J., Qi, H., ... Drabek, E. (2003). Evaluation challenges in large-scale document summarization. In *Proceedings of the 41st Annual Meeting of the Association for Computational Linguistics (ACL 2003).* Association for Computational Linguistics.

Rush, Chopra, & Weston. (2015). A neural attention model for abstractive sentence summarization. I: *Proceedings of the 2015 Conference on Empirical Methods in Natural Language Processing (EMNLP 2015)*. Association for Computational Linguistics. 10.18653/v1/D15-1044

Schilder, F., & Kondadadi, R. (2008). FastSum: Fast and accurate query-based multi-document summarization. In *Proceedings of ACL-08: Human Language Technology*. Association for Computational Linguistics. 10.3115/1557690.1557748

Schilder, F., Kondadadi, R., Leidner, J. L., & Conrad, J. G. (2008). Thomson Reuters at TAC 2008: Aggressive filtering with FastSum for update and opinion summarization In *Proceedings of the First Text Analysis Conference (TAC 2008)*. NIST.

See, A., Liu, P. J., & Manning, C. D. (2017). Get to the point: Summarization with pointer-generator networks. In *Proceedings of the 55th Annual Meeting of the Association for Computational Linguistics (ACL 2017)*. Association for Computational Linguistics. 10.18653/v1/P17-1099

Singh, M., Mishra, A., Oualil, Y., Berberich, K., & Klakow, D. (2018). Long-span language models for query-focused unsupervised extractive text summarization. In G. Pasi, B. Piwowarski, L. Azzopardi, & A. Hanbury (Eds.), *Advances in Information Retrieval – Proceedings of the 40th European Conference on IR Research (ECIR 2018)*. Springer. 10.1007/978-3-319-76941-7_59

Torres-Moreno, J.-M. (2014). *Automatic Text Summarization*. Hoboken, NJ: Wiley.

Wu, C., & Liu, C. (2003). Ontology-based text summarization for business news articles. In N. C. Debnath (Ed.), *Proceedings of the 18th International Conference Computers and Their Applications (ISCA 2003)*. ISCA.

Yang, C. C., & Wang, F. L. (2003). Fractal summarization for mobile devices to access large documents on the Web. In *Proceedings of the 12th International Conference on World Wide Web (WWW 2003)*. ACM. 10.1145/775152.775183

ENDNOTES

[1]   H. P. Luhn also invented a popular method for checksum generation to avoid data entry errors for social security numbers and other important numeric identifiers, incidentally also often called "Luhn algorithm".

[2]   bpost SA/NV IPO Prospectus, https://corporate.bpost.be/~/media/Files/B/Bpost/documents/prospectus-bpost-en.pdf (cited 2018-12-26)

3   Reuters (2018), Kazakhstan: OPEC, non-OPEC nations must stabilize oil prices in first-quarter, https://uk.reuters.com/article/us-kazakhstan-opec/kazakhstan-opec-non-opec-nations-must-stabilize-oil-prices-in-first-quarter-idUSKCN1OP0GJ (cited 2018-12-26)

4   McRitchie, James (2016), MMM -- 3M Co: Proxy Score 53, https://www.corpgov.net/2016/05/mmm-3m-co-proxy-score-53/ (cited 2018-12-26)

5   NASDAQ (2018) (eds.) General Electric Corporation, 3rd Quarter 2018 Earnings Call Transcript, https://www.nasdaq.com/aspx/call-transcript.aspx?StoryId=4215813&Title=general-electric-ge-q3-2018-results-earnings-call-transcript (cited 2018-12-26)

6   MIFID II, https://www.esma.europa.eu/policy-rules/mifid-ii-and-mifir (cited 2018-12-25)

7   Form 10-K, Annual Report Pursuant To Section 13 or 15(d) of the Securities Exchange
      Act of 1934 -- General Instructions, https://www.sec.gov/files/form10-k.pdf (cited 2018-12-24)

8   FORM 10-K Annual Report, International Business Machines Corporation, https://www.sec.gov/Archives/edgar/data/51143/000104746918001117/a2233835z10-k.htm (cited 2018-12-24)

9   Karen Spärck Jones, *personal comm.* (2002); Donna Harman, *personal comm.* (2016)

10   an odd number of raters is recommended to avoid having to break ties

11   An introduction to neural networks is beyond the scope of this chapter, but the interested reader may consult Goldberg (2017) for an excellent introduction to the aspects relevant to NLP.

12   https://ec.europa.eu/commission/priorities/justice-and-fundamental-rights/data-protection/2018-reform-eu-data-protection-rules_en (cited 2019-02-01)

13   https://reuters.tv (cited 2018-12-28)

Chapter 8
Opinion Mining and Product Review Summarization in E-Commerce

Enakshi Jana
Pondicherry University, India

V. Uma
 https://orcid.org/0000-0002-7257-7920
Pondicherry University, India

ABSTRACT

With the immense increase of the number of users of the internet and simultaneously the massive expansion of the e-commerce platform, millions of products are sold online. To improve user experience and satisfaction, online shopping platform enables every user to give their reviews for each and every product that they buy online. Reviews are long and contain only a few sentences which are related to a particular feature of that product. It becomes very difficult for the user to understand other customer views about different features of the product. So, we need accurate opinion-based review summarization which will help both customers and product manufacture to understand and focus on a particular aspect of the product. In this chapter, the authors discuss the abstractive document summarization method to summarize e-commerce product reviews. This chapter has an in-depth explanation about different types of document summarization and how that can be applied to e-commerce product reviews.

DOI: 10.4018/978-1-5225-9373-7.ch008

INTRODUCTION

With the current trends of internet user, e-commerce platforms are getting more popular and user started buying product starting from clothes to foods from online e-commerce platform. Some retail behemoth like amazon.com Walmart shipped over 100 million products during 24 to 36-hour in the USA in 2018 (Sharma, 2018). This trend is in everywhere across the world. So before order a product from online, user always try to get an insight about the product from the past reviews and as well as manufacturer also try to improve their product quality based on the customer reviews.

When users are buying product more from online, reviews are also increasing in large scale size. Among the products few popular products have thousands of reviews. Among thousands of reviews, few reviews are long and some are saying about the particular feature of that product. From these kind of reviews for a customer its really very hard to take the decision for that product. To get an insight view of any product, the customer needs to read almost all the reviews. Even Manufacturers also need to keep the trace for every reviews for any particular feature of the product. So, to get an unbiased feature wise insight of any particular product there is need of product review summarization.

Automatic document summarization is a process that takes a set of documents and generates the most important content as a summary in a manner sensitive to the central concept of the source documents. In this chapter, we discuss document summarization as a method to summarize e-commerce product reviews of a particular feature of a product. There are two types of summarization. Extractive summarization generates the summary by constructing sentences from the source document whereas the abstractive summarization tries to generate summary sentences by its own which may not be directly present in the source document.

Generating abstractive summarization is more challenging as compared to extractive summarization. There are different methods for generating extractive and abstractive summarization. In this chapter, we discuss abstractive summarization of the product reviews using deep neural network model. This chapter also discusses word embeddings that are used to represent words in vector space and represent each sentence in a review in the word's semantics space. Word embedding is a process of learning the vector space representation of words or phrases. Word embedding can be generated using a global matrix factorization method or shallow context windows-based method. These details will be discussed in detail.

Section 1 and section 2 start with a discussion on aspect and opinion identification and extraction from product reviews. Here we explain different methods used for opinion identification and extraction. Dependency parsing is explained in the context of identifying all nn modifier and amod modifier. Section 3 explains document summarization types, methods used for summarization and different evaluation metrics for summarization. Regarding review summarization, attention-based bidirectional long short-term memory (LSTM) will be discussed in detail. We end this chapter with the evaluation method of summarization.

SECTION 1

The Demand for Opinion Detection, Extraction, and Opinion-Wise Review Summarization

To get an insight view of any product, the customer needs to read almost all the reviews. Even Manufacturers also need to keep the trace for every review for any particular feature of the product. So, to get an unbiased feature wise insight of any particular product there is need of product review summarization.

E-commerce product review summarization is not as simple as news article summarization. In any e-commerce platform sometimes users analyse the product feature wise. For example- user wants to buy smart phone, in that situation user would like to analyse the reviews based on the features like battery life, internal memory and camera quality . To satisfy this kind of user requirement, reviews are grouped together aspect wise for a particular product then need to accurate sentiment classification and aspect wise review summarization.

Opinion in the Product Review

Following is a sample example review for a mobile phone.

*"The **mobile** which I purchased has bright **display**, the quality of the **camera** is awesome. One of the best price phone in that range."*

In the above review ***mobile, display***, and ***camera*** are the aspects and the opinion related to those aspects are ***best price, bright, awesome***. In the review mobile and phone are synonymous and the opinion ***best price*** specified in the context of phone.

What Might Be Involved? An Example

In this chapter, we discuss e-commerce product review summarization opinion wise. Following are the complete steps involved-

1.   Aspect extraction
2.   Opinion extraction for each aspect

3.   Grouping of sentences aspect wise
4.   Sentiment classification of each sentence of an aspect
5.   Summarization of all the sentences of a particular aspect for a particular sentiment polarity.

Consider following a sample set of reviews for mobile phone

*Review 1: ""The **mobile** which I purchased has **very bright display**, the quality of the **camera** is **awesome**. One of the **best price phone** in that range. But the **battery** is **draining quickly**."*

*Review 2: "Excellent Phone for its price range. Excellent looks, **beautiful display**, **great battery** life. Super **smooth performance**, **perfect camera** for its price range, nice software experience. Overall **Super cool phone**. Highly Recommend."*

Following are the work involved in the above set of reviews-

1.   Aspect extraction. In aspect extraction phase we extract (*display, camera, mobile, battery, performance*) from the above set of reviews. The details of the extraction method we describe in subsequent sections.
2.   Opinion extraction for each aspect. In opinion extraction phase we extract (*very bright, awesome, best price, great, beautiful, perfect, smooth, super cool, draining quickly*) from the above set of reviews.
3.   Grouping of sentences aspect wise. In this phase, we group all the sentences for a particular aspect. For this, we use NLTK sentence tokenizer. Following is the grouping of sentences for each aspect.
     a.   Display
          i.   *The **mobile** which I purchased has **very bright display**.*
          ii.   *Excellent Phone for its price range. Excellent looks, beautiful **display**, great battery life.*
     b.   Camera
          i.   *the quality of the **camera** is **awesome**.*
          ii.   *Super smooth performance, perfect **camera** for its price range, nice software experience.*
     c.   Mobile
          i.   *The **mobile** which I purchased has **very bright display**.*
          ii.   *One of the **best price phone** in that range.*
     d.   Battery
          i.   *The **battery** is draining quickly.*
          ii.   *Excellent looks, beautiful display, great **battery** life.*

e. Performance

    i. *Super smooth **performance**, perfect camera for its price range, nice software experience.*

4. Sentiment classification of each sentence of an aspect. In this phase, we classify each sentence as positive/negative for each aspect.

a. Display

    i. *The **mobile** which I purchased has **very bright display**.* – **Positive**

    ii. *Excellent Phone for its price range. Excellent looks, beautiful **display**, great battery life.* - **Positive**

b. Camera

    i. *the quality of the **camera** is **awesome**.* – **Positive**

    ii. *Super smooth performance, perfect **camera** for its price range, nice software experience.* - **Positive**

c. Mobile

    i. *The **mobile** which I purchased has **very bright display**.* – **Positive**

    ii. *One of the **best price phone** in that range.* - **Positive**

d. Battery

    i. *The **battery** is draining quickly.* – **Negative**

    ii. *Excellent looks, beautiful display, great **battery** life.* - **Positive**

e. Performance

    i. *Super smooth **performance**, perfect camera for its price range, nice software experience.* - **Positive**

5. Summarization of all the sentences of a particular aspect for a particular sentiment polarity. In this phase, we summarize all the review sentence for each aspect. The details of summarization we describe in subsequent section.

SECTION 2

This section focuses on the process of aspect and opinion extraction. In product reviews, the aspect is a key characteristic of the product about which a customer expresses their view and the opinion is the modifier of the aspect.

Aspect and Opinion Identification

For product review summarization, aspect and opinion identification is a pre-requisite which can improve the process of summarization and formulation of the different method of summarization. There are different approaches for the extraction and identification of aspect and opinion. Simple NLP feature combined with basic heuristics can provide better performance for the same. NLP feature may include

Parts of Speech or POS tag, typed of untyped parse structure of dependencies of tokens of reviews. For basic heuristics simple frequency based count of aspect and opinion with threshold can be used for this purpose.

Parsing

Parsing is a method of resolving the structural ambiguity in a natural language piece of text in a formal way. The method of parsing of English language sentences has an early history from the 1980s. *Noam Chomsky* used context-free grammar to formulate the structure of the English language (Chomsky, 1986). There are two types of parsing normally used in NLP. Dependency parsing mainly focuses on establishing a relationship between words in a natural language sentence. Whereas Phrase structure parsing focuses on identifying different phrases and their recursive structure and relationship. We use dependency parsing for aspect identification in product reviews. The general structure of an (opinion and noun) pair appears in a review as an adjective (opinion) modifying the noun (aspect).

Dependency Parsing

Dependency parsing mainly focuses on analyzing the grammatical structure in a given sentence and try to establish a relationship between the headword and the modifier word which modify the headword.

Figure 1 shows a dependency parsing for a sample review sentence. The label over the arrows shows the exact nature of the dependency relationship. The arrow from the word "*display*" to word "*awesome*" indicates "*display*" is a headword and the word "*awesome*" modifying display with "amod" (adjective modifier) relationship. There are different types of relationship can appear in an English sentence. Following are a few types of nature of the dependency relationship.

- **Dependent**

Figure 1. Dependency parsing of a sample review

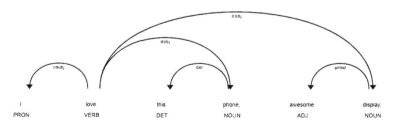

- ◦ **Aux**: The link between a content verb and an auxiliary verb, e.g. '*I have used the mobile*' – aux (used, have).
- ◦ **Conj**: Link between two (content) words connected by a conjunction, e.g. 'Bill is big and honest' – conj (big, honest).
- ◦ **CC**: The link between a content word and a conjunction, e.g. 'Bill is big and honest' – cc (big, and).
- ◦ **Subj**: The link between a verb and its subject, e.g. 'Clinton defeated Dole' – subj (defeated, Clinton).
- ◦ **Nsubj**: The link between a verb and an NP subject, e.g. 'Clinton defeated Dole' - nsubj(defeated, Clinton).
- ◦ **Obj**: The link between a verb and one of its objects, e.g. 'she gave me a raise' - obj(gave, me), obj (gave, raise).
- ◦ **Dobj**: The link between a verb and one of its accusative objects, e.g. 'she gave me a raise' – dobj (gave, raise).
- ◦ **Iobj**: The link between a verb and its dative object, e.g. 'she gave me a raise' - iobj(gave, me) bought' – ref (book, which).

- **Modifier**
  - ◦ **Amod:** Link from a noun to an adjective modifier, e.g. 'Sam eats red meat' - amod(meat, red).
  - ◦ **Infmod**: Link from a noun to a verb of a VPto post modifier, e.g. 'points to establish are ...' – infmod (points, establish).
  - ◦ **Num**: Link from a noun to a number premodifier, e.g. 'three sheep' – num (sheep, three).
  - ◦ **Number**: Link from one part of a number phrase or currency unit to a number, e.g. '$ 3 billion' - number ($, billion).
  - ◦ **Advmod**: Link from a word to an adverb, e.g. 'genetically modified' - advmod(modified, genetically), 'less often' - advmod(often, less).
  - ◦ **Neg**: Link from a predictive word to a negative word, e.g. 'Bill is not a scientist' - neg (scientist, not), 'Bill doesn't drive'.
  - ◦ **Possessive**: Link from a noun to its genitive suffix, e.g. 'John's book' - possessive (John,'s).
  - ◦ **Det**: Link from a noun to its determiner, e.g. 'the man' - det(man,the), 'which man' - det(man, which).
  - ◦ **Quantmod**: Link between a quantifier and a modifier, e.g. 'about 200 people' - quantmod(200, about).

Typed

In Figure 1 the labels are the example for typed dependency parsing. Typed dependency parsing finds the relationship between words and also finds the nature of the relationship.

Untyped

The Untyped dependency parsing only finds the headword and modifying words without the nature of the relationship. The untyped relationship is easy to parse as compared to Typed dependency parsing.

Shift-Reduce Parsing

Shift-Reduce parser is the most commonly used method for dependency parsing. It uses the shift-reduce context-free grammars to parse the dependency. Given a sentence, predict each token from left-to-right. It uses a queue to hold all the unobserved token and a stack of all observed token. It reads one token from the queue at a time and move the token to the stack but before moving to the stack it tries to find the relationship of the selected token with the top of the stack using different features. At a particular time, the parser has three choices.

1. Move to selected token to the top of the stack
2. Make the top of the stack as headword and the selected token as a modifier (**shift left**)
3. Make the selected token as headword and top of the stack as a modifier (**shift right**).

To choose one of the above options it uses any classifier. The shift-reduce dependency method is fast and liner but has slightly less accurate. Stanford NLP dependency parser is an example of shift-reduce dependency parser. Figure 2 shows an example of shift-reduce based dependency parsing. The parser selects one word at a time and performs one of the three operations described above.

Spanning Tree

Spanning tree can also be used for dependency parsing. It calculates full tree at once. Because of its tree building cost, most of the recent library for dependency parsing uses shift-reduced based dependency parsing. Spanning tree-based dependency parsing has slightly better accuracy than shift-reduce parsing. MSTParser and Eda (Japanese) are the examples of spanning tree-based dependency parsing.

Figure 2. Shift-Reduce Parsing

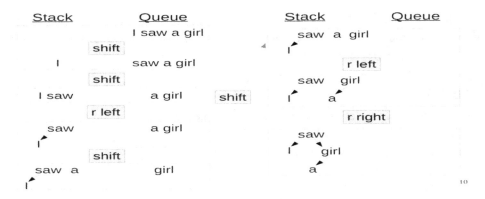

Phrase Structure

Phrase structure tries to identify the phases and the recursive structure between phrases. Figure 3 is an example of phase structure in an English sentence *"the big dog chased the cat"*. In the sentence, the phrase structure identifies the noun phrase (NP) as *"the big dog"* and the verb phrase (VP) as *"Chased the cat"*. Although recursive in a sentence is important to solve different NLP related problems but in aspect and opinion identification from the review, we use only dependency parsing.

Feature for Aspect and Opinion Extraction

The aspect and opinion extraction can be processed as a classification problem. We need to tokenize the whole review and tag/classify each token as an aspect, opinion

Figure 3. Phrase Structure Parsing

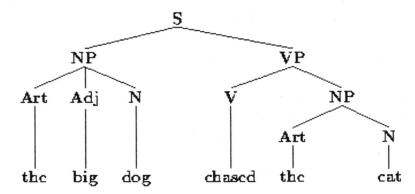

Figure 4. Parts of Speech tagging of a sample review

The	best	phone	with	bright	display.
DET	ADJ	NOUN	ADP	ADJ	NOUN

or others. This is a supervised problem and we need enough training data to train the model. But empirical it is shown that unsupervised combination of NLP feature and simple heuristic frequency count based method performs better for aspect and opinion extraction (Wu, Zhang, Huang & Wu, 2009). NLP parts of speech tagging and dependency parsing can be used to identify the aspects and opinion.

POS Tagging

In Figure 4 we display the parts of speech tag of a simple review for a mobile. In the review both the *phone* and *display* is tagged with noun. But only *display* is an aspect not the *phone*. So we can say aspect is always a noun but not all the noun is always an aspect. In the review the token *bright,* which is tagged ad adjective is the opinion modifying the noun *display*. So, for aspect and opinion extraction we need to correctly detect the *(noun, adjective)* pair from the reviews and there should be some heuristics to filter out only those noun which is as aspect.

Amod (Adjective Modifier) Modifier

Dependency parsing is very important to unambiguously determining the association between aspect and opinion. Figure 5 show the dependency parsing of a sample reviews. In the review the noun *display* is modified by the adjective *bright*. This relationship is called the amod or adjective modifier relationship in the typed

Figure 5. amod modifier in the dependency parsing

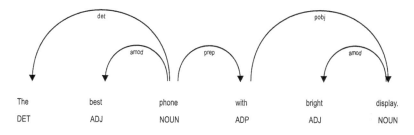

dependency parsing described in Section 2.1.1. So the amod relationship is an indicator of the association of *(aspect and opinion)* pair in the review.

Heuristics-Based Approach: On Aspect Frequency

Dependency parsing is a way of identifying the *(noun, adjective)* pair described in section 2.1.1. But all the *(noun, adjective)* pair or all nouns are not an aspect. So we need some short of heuristics on the corpus to conclude a *(noun, adjective)* pair as a true *(aspect, opinion)* pair. If the frequency of a particular noun in the corpus is too high then that noun may not be an aspect. For example the *brand name* in the reviews of a particular product may appear multiple times but normally *brand name* is not an aspect. So we need some threshold on the frequency of an noun to declare the noun as an aspect. If the frequency of the *(noun, adjective)* greater than some predefined thresholds we can conclude that as a true pair else the pair is an invalid pair.

Opinion and Aspect Beyond Unigram (Phases)

In the previous section we describe unigram opinion related to an aspect. But the opinion and aspect may be beyond the boundary of a single token. Sometimes aspect and opinion appears as bigrams or trigrams. For example in Figure 6 the opinion *(extremely bright)* related to the aspect *display* is bigram. In this chapter we only describe unigram and bigram opinion.

In Figure 6 *bright* is the amod modifier to the noun *display. Extremely* is another modifier which modify the adjective *bright* with advmod relationship (adverb modifier). So, there is a indirect or transitive relationship from *(display, bright)* to *(bright, extremely)*. As *'bright'* is modified by *'extremely'*, we can conclude *'extremely bright'* as a bi-gram opinion of the aspect *display*.

Figure 6. Identify bigram opinion related to an aspect

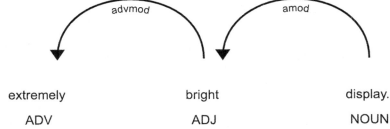

Topic-Oriented Aspect

Sometimes the aspect of a review is indirect and is not specified as any combination of the tokens in the reviews. This type of aspect can be formularized as the topic of the reviews and need to use topic model for extracting the predefined aspect. For this type of reviews, the number of aspects should be fixed before applying the topic model. Consider the following review. In the review, there is no token as *"Installation"* but we can use the topic model to tag the following piece of review as topic *"Installation"* from given set of reviews. Here topic "Installation" is an aspect.

Review: "I purchased the washing machine on Christmas. The technician came the very next day and set up the washing machine. I am fully satisfied with the quick response from the technician for setting up the appliance"

SECTION 3

Summarization

Text summarization is a process of generating a gist of a given set of content while preserving the inherent information of the content in the gist. Summarization has a wide range of application in the different domain. Summarization can be used in news for summarizing an article, in medical for summarizing patient history, in e-commerce for summarizing product reviews, in travel for summarizing reviews of hotels, destination, and places. Summarization can also be used for generating abstracts from scientific articles, creating a snippet for web pages. There is a lot of other application of summarization in the different domains. In this chapter, we discuss summarization in more details for e-commerce product reviews.

Summarization is one of the most difficult tasks in natural language processing. It poses different challenges. The most difficult task is that the generated summary should be complete and correct. While preserving the correctness and completeness the generated summary should be coherent and proper coreference should be maintained.

Types of Summarization

The method of text summarization can be divided broadly into two categories. We can categorize the summarization method based on the size of the documents and the type of the generated content.

Single-Document Summarization

When summarization is generated from a given single piece of text or documents we can call it as single document summarization. Single document summarization can be used for generating the summary of patient history in medical where the patient history is represented as a single document.

Multi-Document Summarization

When summarization is generated from a given set of documents, we can call it as multi-document summarization. Multi-document summarization can be used in the news where a set of news articles are used as input to the summarization method.

Generating single document summarization are easy as compared to multi-document summarization. In multi-document summarization, we have to deal with multiple documents which pose its own challenges. The generated summary should be the central concept of all the documents. While generating a summary by taking sentences from different documents, there should be a measure of similarity between sentences so that redundancy can be removed from the summary by not selecting a sentence which is very similar to the already selected summary sentences. In multiple document summarization while ordering sentences in summary from different documents, need special care about coherence between sentences and proper coreference in summary. Whereas in single document summarization we preserve the order of sentences within the original document in summary.

Extractive Summarization

Extractive summarization is the simplex kind of summarization method in which summary is generated by a combination of phrases and sentences from the original documents.

Abstractive Summarization

In abstractive summarization, the summary text is generated using different words or phrases which may not be lexically present in the original document.

An abstractive summary is one of the most difficult tasks in natural language processing and is an active area of research in the NLP research community. In this chapter, we discuss both abstractive and extractive summarization for e-commerce product reviews.

Approaches

Following are the different approaches of summarization. We divide the different summarization method broadly into 1) Surface level approach 2) corpus-based approach 3) coherence-based approach 4) Rhetoric-Based Approach 5) graph-based approach. We discuss each of the approaches in details.

Surface Level Approaches

It is one of the earliest approach of text summarization. It is mainly used to detect which part of a text is important. To find the sentence relevance it uses Term Frequencies. The idea behind it for a particular topic, when the document is developed, the same words are repeated multiple times. So, term relevance is proportional to its in-document frequency. The summary are generated using term-frequency which is used to score the sentences for summary. A particular sentence is selected based on the presence of some cue or indicator words and the term frequency of individual words.

Corpus-Based Approaches

It is similar like for a particular field document share common term in that field, that does not carry any hidden information. The relevance of a term in a document is inversely proportional to the number of documents in the corpus containing the term. The term frequency indicated the importance of the term within the document. But when we have set of document we need to calculate the inverse term frequency which penalizes the term frequency. This is called the TF-IDF score of each term for a particular documents. To rank the sentences for summary generation we can generate the score of the sentence as sum of all the term score (TF-IDF).

An alternate idea to measure term relevance using WordNet. Example occurrence of the car is counted when the car is found as well as for - '*brake*', '*accelerator*', '*door*' etc.

Cohesion-Based Approaches

Extractive method may fail to find the relations between concepts in a text. Text cohesion establishes the relation between expressions which determine the text connectivity. There are few summarization approaches which is used to find cohesive properties of the text. In a method, Lexical Chains uses the WordNet database to determine cohesive relations (synonymy, antonymy, hypernymy, and homonymy) between terms. Chains are made by related terms. Their scores are determined based on the number and type of relations in the chain. In sentences where strongest chain is there, selected for the summary.

Rhetoric-Based Approaches

Rhetorical Structure Theory provides an idea about the text organization. It finds the count of rhetorical relations that tie together text units. All relations are connected together to form the nucleus. Finally, a tree-like structure is defined and for the summary, the text units have to be extracted. Based on the rhetorical participation in a tree, sentences are penalized (Ono, Sumita & Miike, 1994). The total score of sentences is calculated by the sum of weights from the root of the tree to the sentence. Every parent node identifies its nuclear children. If we recursive down the tree, children are connected to the parent level. Finally, the score of a unit is calculated.

Graph-Based Approaches

Graph-based algorithms like HITS (Kleinberg & M, 1999) or Google's page rank (Brin, & Page, 1998), which are mainly used to find Citation Analysis, Social Network Analysis, Link Structure Analysis of the web etc. In a graph-based ranking algorithm, the importance of a vertex is recursively calculated from the entire graph. Graph-based Ranking algorithm is used for the text ranking in Natural Language Processing. The graph is created by adding a vertex for each sentence in a text and edges for the interconnection between the sentences. Using the ranking algorithm on a graph the score is calculated. Then sentences are sorted in a reverse order of their score. Now top-ranked sentences give the summary.

Beyond Sentence Extraction

All the previous approach we discuss are called the extractive summarization where the summary is generated by a combination of phrases from the given original text. But there is another method of summarization called abstractive where the summarization is generated with new phrases which may not be identically present in the original documents. The abstractive generation of the summary is one of the most difficult tasks in natural language processing and natural language generation task. We can find a huge gap between the abstracts written by human experts and summaries produced by current automatic summarizes. The reason behind this extraction is when a system cannot identify important topics of the document. When extracted sentences are very much different from the original document, the result may be incorrect. Later Non-sentence-extractive summarization method developed, where full sentences from the text do not produce. Instead of this it compresses the sentences or regenerates new sentences from scratch.

Six editing operations are there in human abstracting.

1. Sentence reduction
2. Sentence combination

3. Synthetic transformation
4. Lexical paraphrasing
5. Generalization and specialization
6. Reordering

Opinion-Wise Abstractive Review Summarization

In this section, we discuss about the abstractive review summarization using the novel deep learning method. We use word embeddings to represent each word in higher dimension space. This subsection starts with word embeddings and different method of word embeddings. We discuss different types of RNN and how RNN can be used for abstractive review summarization.

Word Embeddings

Word embeddings are a dense vector representation of a word that allows word with syntactic or semantic meaning has similar vector representation. Word embeddings is a densely distributed representation of a word which is generated from the corpus statistics. Word embedding is perhaps the reason for the impressive performance of recent deep learning-based architecture on complex natural language processing task. The learned embeddings can capture the semantics meaning like vector(king) - vector(man) + vector(woman) = vector(queen). Figure 7 shows the semantics meaning and relationship between different words in the learned vector space.

There is a different way of representing a word as a distributed vector. We can divide the word embeddings as matrix factorization method and shallow context windows-based method.

Figure 7. Word embeddings and their semantic relationship

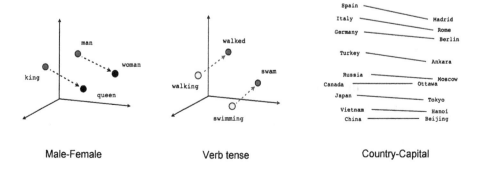

Male-Female   Verb tense   Country-Capital

Matrix Factorization Method

In matrix factorization method the global word-word co-occurrence statistics are collected in a large sparse matrix and using dimension reduction the dense word representation is created in lower dimension space. This method has the drawback of adding new words into space as the matrix size is fixed at the beginning and need to redo the whole process from the start.

Shallow Context Window Based Method

In shallow context windows-based method instead of creating a large sparse matrix, a sliding window of small context are considered and rolled over the whole corpus to create the training example and the word embeddings are created by training a single hidden layer neural network. There are two different shallow contexts window-based methods (1) skip gram and (2) continuous bag of words.

Skip Gram (SG)

In skip gram model a single hidden layer neural network is trained to predict the context word given the center word (Mikolov, Le & Sutskever, 2013). Consider the following example reviews -

Review: "I love the camera selfie mode"

In skip gram model the training example are while considering windows size= 2: (I, love), (I, the), (love, I), (love, the), (love, camera), (the, love), (the, I), (the, camera), (the, selfie), (camera, the), (camera, love), (camera, selfie), (camera, mode), (selfie, the), (selfie, camera), (selfie, mode), (mode, camera), (mode, selfie).

Continuous Bag of Word (CBW)

The Continuous Bag of Word (CBW) model try to predict the center word given the context words (Mikolov, Le & Sutskever, 2013) . The input to the model can be $wi-2$, $wi-1$, $wi+1$, $wi+2$ i.e. preceding and following the word of the current word and output of the neural network will be wi (current word). It means "predicting a current word given its context". Hence, input to the CBOW is several input word vectors and output will be a single word vector.

CBOW works well for more frequent words and it does not work well for rare words because it maximizes the probability of the current word using its context. For example, given a sentence like "Yesterday the food was really ___". The probability of predicting words like "good", "nice" will be more than rarely occurring words like "fantabulous". Because common words occur more frequently in the training examples as compared to the rare words. CBOW is several times faster to train than skip gram model.

Global Vector (Glove)

It leverages the benefits of global corpus statistics while building the model on only the non-zero elements of the word-word co-occurrence matrix instead of training on the full sparse matrix and not using shallow small context around a particular word. The global corpus statics is maintained in the model.

Document Vector (doc2vec)

Like word embeddings, any piece of text (sentence, paragraph, documents) can be represented as a dense vector representation which is called as doc2vec.

Recurrent Neural Network (RNN)

In feedforward neural network, we assume that inputs and outputs are independent of each other but that's not always the case. For example, in the case of sentence formation the next words depend on the previous context/words. Hence there is a need to store the previous information or words to predict future words. RNN makes use of sequential information present in the data.

Recurrent neural networks (RNN) is a class of artificial neural networks which is used for sequential data like text, audio, time series data. There are three different types of recurrent neural network 1) Vanilla RNN 2) Long short-term memory (LSTM) and Gated Recurrent Unit (GRU). Figure 8 is a block diagram of a unidirectional RNN for any sequence learning problem.

The main drawback of RNN is the long-term dependency. If the sequence size is very long, it's very difficult to store all the previous information in case of RNN which causes the vanishing grading problem. Vanishing gradient problem may also

Figure 8. An example of recurrent neural network

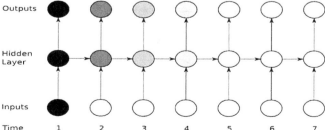

233

occur because of the choice of the activation function. RNN can avoid the vanishing gradient problem with the use of LSTM.

Long Short-Term Memory (LSTM)

LSTM is a type of recurrent neural network which can store more contextual information than simple recurrent neural network. The major difference between Simple RNN and LSTM lies in the architecture of each neuron. LSTM has a cell structure. Within each cell, it has three types of gate. Output gate maintains how much information needs to pass to output. Input gate controls the information inflow to the cell and forgets gate control the information stored within a cell. With the combination of all the gates, it can maintain how much information needs to store and how much information need to pass to the next layer. Because of this gated structure LSTM does not need to store long-term dependency. Figure 9 is the block structure of a single cell of a LSTM model.

Bi-Directional Long Short-Term Memory (Bi-LSTM)

Like bi-RNN LSTM can also have the bidirectional model. In bi-directional LSTM information can flow both ways to capture the proper relationship in both directions. Figure 10 is a block diagram of a simple bi-directional LSTM model.

Abstractive Review Summarization

With the availability of a large number of review and the gold ideal summary we can formulate the abstractive review summarization method as a machine translation problem (MT) were given a sentence from a source language need to translate it to another sentence from the target language. For review summarization both the source and target language are same. Bi-Directional LSTM with attention mechanism is the best suited method for this problem. During training, in the encoder of LSTM, we

Figure 9. Block diagram of LSTM Cell

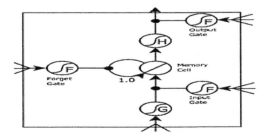

Figure 10. Block diagram of bi-directional LSTM

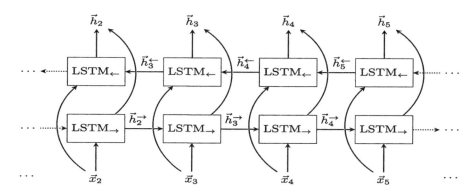

produce the original review as input and the system generated summary as output to the decoder.

Evaluation Measures

Summarization evaluation is one of the difficult tasks as the evaluation need to assess by human annotator which introduces biases to individuals, and it is very difficult to get an ideal gold standard for summarization task. The summarization evaluation taxonomy can be divided into the intrinsic and extrinsic evaluation.

Intrinsic Measure

Intrinsic evaluation measures the quality of linguistic feature of the summary. The intrinsic measure can be divided into text quality evaluation and content evaluation.

Text Quality Evaluation

Text quality evaluation most of the time assessed by human annotators. They select a particular value from a predefined scale for each summary. The same summary is evaluated by multiple human annotators. The final evaluation measure determined by average or voting of all the annotator. Following are the different aspect of linguistic quality measure -

Grammatically

The summary should be grammatically correct. It should not contain any punctuation or word error.

Figure 11. Precision

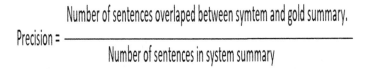

Non-Redundancy

The generated summary should be correct and complete and should not contain redundant information.

Referential Clarity

The noun and pronoun in the generated summary should properly. If a pronoun is there in the summary, it should contain proper referenced noun.

Structure and Coherence

The generated summary should be coherent and properly structured. The cause and effect sentence should be properly structured in the generated summary.

This evaluation cannot be done automatically. So, the human annotator needs to assign each sentence with a particular from a predefined scale (for example 1: Very good, 2: Good, 3: Average 4: bad, 5: Very bad).

Content Evaluation

Content evaluation is an intrinsic measure which can be evaluated automatically with the presence of an ideal gold summary. Content evaluation is divided into co-selection and content-based evaluation.

Co-Selection

The co-selection measure is evaluated by Precision, Recall, and F-Score.

Precision (P)

The Precision is measured by the number of sentences overlap between system generated summary and gold summary divided by the number of sentences in the systems summary.

Figure 11 is the formula for precision.

Recall (R)

The recall is measured by the number of sentences overlap between system generated summary and gold summary divided by the number of sentences in the gold summary. Figure 12 is the formula for recall.

F-Score

F-Score is a composite measure of Precision and Recall. F-Score is actually measured as the harmonic mean of Precision and Recall. Figure 13 is the formula for F-Score.

Relative Utility

The inherent problem in Precision and Recall based evaluation is that they cannot capture the relativity between sentences. For example, for a summary evaluation let system 1 generates sentences [A, B] and system 2 generates sentences [A, C]. If the ideal summary contains sentences [A, B, D] then system 1 will get more score as compared to system 2. But what if sentence B and C are semantically equivalent? In an ideal summary, the choice of sentence B or C depends on the individual bias of human annotator. The equivalent relationship between sentence B and C cannot be captured in Precision and Recall. To resolve the above problem the relative utility of evaluation was proposed (Radev, Jing & Budzikowska, 2000). In this method, instead of 0/1 0 - absence, 1 – presence) score of occurrence of a sentence in the generated summary, a utility of each of the sentence in the summary is assigned by human annotator. So in the above example both the sentence (B and C) will get similar utility values while judging by human annotator.

Figure 12. Recall

$$Precision = \frac{Number\ of\ sentences\ overlaped\ between\ symtem\ and\ gold\ summary.}{Number\ of\ sentences\ in\ gold\ summary}$$

Figure 13. F-Score

$$F\text{-}Score = \frac{2.\ P.\ R}{P + R}$$

Content-Based

Co-selection measures the count for the same sentence occurrence. When two sentences carry the same meaning though they are written differently, Content-Based Measures ignore those sentences.

Example

S1: The visit of the President of India to China
S2: The India president visited China

In the above sentence co-selection measures cannot be performed, but content-based measures can give result.

Cosine Similarity

It's a basic content-based similarity measure. Figure 14 is the formula for cosine similarity.
While x and y are the representations of system summary and reference document on Vector Space Model.
Example:

D1: I got IR into IR text
D2: You got IR matrices into matrices

a= (1,1,2,1,1,0,0)

Figure 14. Cosine Similarity

$$ s(\mathbf{x}, \mathbf{y}) = \frac{\mathbf{x} \cdot \mathbf{y}}{\|\mathbf{x}\| \|\mathbf{y}\|} = \frac{\sum_{i=0}^{n-1} x_i y_i}{\sqrt{\sum_{i=0}^{n-1} (x_i)^2} \times \sqrt{\sum_{i=0}^{n-1} (y_i)^2}} $$

Table 1. The count of each token in docs

Words	D1	D2
I	1	0
got	1	1
IR	2	1
into	1	1
text	1	0
you	0	1
metrices	0	2

b= (0,1,1,1,0,1,2)

$dp_{aa} = 1.1+1.1+2.2+1.1+1.1+0.0+0.0 = 8$

$dp_{bb} = 0.0+1.1+1.1+1.1+0.0+1.1+2.2 = 8$

$dp_{ab} = 1.0+1.1+2.1+1.1+1.0+0.1+0.2 = 4$

Length Information:

$L_{pa} = \sqrt{dp_{aa}} = \sqrt{8} = 2\sqrt{2}$

$L_{pb} = \sqrt{dp_{bb}} = \sqrt{8} = 2\sqrt{2}$

$L_{pa} \cdot L_{pb} = 2\sqrt{2} \cdot 2\sqrt{2} = 2\sqrt{2}$

Length Information:

Figure 15. Cosine Similarity

$$\cos(\theta) = \frac{A \cdot B}{\|A\|\|B\|}$$

$$LP_{a} = \sqrt{dP_{aa}} = \sqrt{8} = 2\sqrt{2}$$

$$LP_{b} = \sqrt{dP_{bb}} = \sqrt{8} = 2\sqrt{2}$$

$$LP_{ab} = LP_{a} \cdot LP_{b} = 2\sqrt{2} \cdot 2\sqrt{2} = 8$$

$$Cos\theta = \frac{DPab}{LPab} = 4/8 = 1/2$$

$\theta = 60 < 90 \sim$ acute angle

$Cos\theta = 1 \sim$ identical direction means same document

$Cos\theta = 0 \sim$ orthogonal

$>45 \sim$ more similar

$<45 \sim$ less similar

Unit Overlap

Unit overlap is another type of similarity measure.

$$\text{Overlap(x,y)} = \frac{\lor x \cap y \lor}{\lor x \lor + \lor y \lor - \lor x \cap y \lor}$$

where x, y are the representation of the set of words or lemmas, ‖x‖ determines the size of set x.

Longest Common Subsequence

Longest common subsequence is another content-based measure.

$$\text{LCS(x,y)} = \frac{Length\left(x\right) + Length\left(y\right) + edit\left(x, y\right)}{2}$$

where x, y is the representation of the sequence of words or lemmas. LCS(x,y) determines the length of the longest common subsequence between x and y. Length x gives the length of the string x.

ROUGE-N

Recall oriented Understanding of gisting Evaluation (ROUGE) is a measure of n-gram based co-occurrence statistics (Lin & Hovy, 2003). ROUGE-N measures the n-gram recall between system summary and ideal gold summary. For example, consider for a review the system generated summary is *"The camera is awesome. The flash is perfectly working for me."* and ideal gold summary is *"The camera is awesome with perfectly working flash, Like the selfie mode"*. If we calculate ROUGE-2, then the bigrams in system summary are *[(the, camera), (camera, is), (is, awesome), (the, flash), (flash, is), (is, perfectly), (perfectly, working), (working, for), (for, me)]* and bigrams in ideal gold summary are *[(the, camera), (camera, is), (is, awesome), (awesome, with), (with, perfectly), (perfectly, working), (working, flash), (flash, like), (like, the), (the, selfie), (selfie, mode)]*. The overlapped bigram count between two set of bigrams is 4. The bigram count in ideal gold summary is 11. So the ROUGH-2 score for this summary is 4/11.

ROUGE-L

ROUGE-L is one of the variants of ROUGE evaluation which measures a ROUGE score based on longest common subsequence.

ROUGE-SU4

ROUGE-SU4 is another variant of ROUGE measure. The SU means "Skip Unigram". So ROUGE-SU4 is similar to ROUGE-2 which is a bigram measure which can skip 4 unigrams while choosing subsequent bigram.

LSA Based Measure

Latent Semantic Analysis (LSA), which mainly covered the important topics out of a document. When in a given corpus abstract is not mentioned, then LSA based measure can give the best result.

Pyramids

This method is a novel method for semi-automatic evaluation (Nenkova & Passonneau 2005). It identifies the summarization contained unit SCUs in a document. Then SCU annotations identify similar sentences. After SCU annotation pyramids will be formed based on their greater weights. The lower in the pyramid appears the lower weight. In this way, the existing pyramid compares between the peer summary and Manual summary.

Extrinsic Measure (Task-Based)

Task-based methods does not analyse the sentence is in the summary. It tries to measure prospect if using summaries for a particular given task. There are various approaches under task-based summarisation.

Document Categorization

Document categorization can correctly categorize the documents based on certain information. For this task, a Corpus of documents is needed. Categorization is performed by manually or by a machine classifier. We can compare the summarization system with the manual categorization task. There are two evaluation matrices for categorization, Precision, and Recall. Precision is a measure of relevant topics assigned to a document divided by the total retrieved documents. The recall is a measure of the topic wise relevant retrieved divided by total relevant documents.

Information Retrieval

Information Retrieval (IR) is another way to measure for task-based evaluation of a summary quality. When moving from full documents to its summaries, relevance correlation gives us the output of measures for assessing the relative decrease in retrieval performance. Summaries give the result as main points of a document. IR machine index is built on it so that it produces good results. If summaries give a good result for full documents, then can be expected that ranking will be similar. There are several methods for similarity measure of the rankings, like Relevance Correlation, Linear Correlation, etc. where Search Engine produces the relevant score.

Question Answering

With the task of question answering, evaluation is performed on summarization. In this system, some comprehension exercises are given to few sets of peoples. The exercises are multiple choice, the single answer is selected from a set of answers of a particular question. Here we measure, how many questions are correctly answered under different conditions.

CONCLUSION

In this chapter, we discuss the method of aspect identification from e-commerce product review. We also discuss the different method of summarization and how deep learning can be used for abstractive summarization. We model the abstractive review summarization as a machine translation task using bidirectional LSTM with attention mechanism. We end the chapter with the discussion of the different summarization evaluation method.

REFERENCES

Brin, S., & Page, L. (1998). The Anatomy of a Large-Scale Hypertextual Web Search Engine. Computer Networks and ISDN Systems.

Chomsky, N. (1986). *Knowledge of Language: Its Nature, Origin and Use*. Westport, CT: Praeger.

Kleinberg, J. M. (1999). Authoritative Sources in a Hyper-Linked Environment. Journal of the ACM, 604–632.

Lin, C., & Hovy, E. (2003). Automatic Evaluation of Summaries Using n-Gram Co- Occurrence Statistics. *Proceedings of HLT-NAACL*. 10.3115/1073445.1073465

Mikolov, T., Le, Q. V., & Sutskever, I. (2013). Exploiting Similarities among Languages for Machine Translation. *Computer Science*, 1–10.

Nenkova, A., & Passonneau, R. (2005). Evaluating Content Selection in Summarization*: The Pyramid Method. In Document Understanding Conference*, Vancouver, Canada.

Ono, K., Sumita, K., & Miike, S. (1994). Abstract Generation Based on Rhetorical Structure Extraction. *Proceedings of the International Conference on Computational Linguistics*, 344-348. 10.3115/991886.991946

Radev, D., Jing, H., & Budzikowska, M. (2000). Centroid-Based Summarization of Multiple Documents. *ANLP/NAACL Workshop on Automatic Summarization*.

Sharma, V. (2018). *Speakers, TVs, Kleenex in Demand on Amazon Prime Day*. Retrieved 17 Dec, 2018, from https://www.reuters.com/article/us-amazon-com-primeday/speakers-tvs-kleenex-in-demand-on-amazon-prime-day-idUSKBN1K81S4?il=0.

Wu, Y., Zhang, Q., Huang, X., & Wu, L. (2009). Phrase Dependency Parsing for Opinion Mining. *Conference on Empirical Methods in Natural Language Processing*, 1533-1541.

Chapter 9
Scaling and Semantically– Enriching Language– Agnostic Summarization

George Giannakopoulos
ⓘ https://orcid.org/0000-0003-2459-589X
NCSR Demokritos, Greece & SciFY PNPC, Greece

George Kiomourtzis
SciFY PNPC, Greece & NCSR Demokritos, Greece

Nikiforos Pittaras
NCSR Demokritos, Greece & National and Kapodistrian University of Athens, Greece

Vangelis Karkaletsis
NCSR Demokritos, Greece

ABSTRACT

This chapter describes the evolution of a real, multi-document, multilingual news summarization methodology and application, named NewSum, the research problems behind it, as well as the steps taken to solve these problems. The system uses the representation of n-gram graphs to perform sentence selection and redundancy removal towards summary generation. In addition, it tackles problems related to topic and subtopic detection (via clustering), demonstrates multi-lingual applicability, and—through recent advances—scalability to big data. Furthermore, recent developments over the algorithm allow it to utilize semantic information to better identify and outline events, so as to offer an overall improvement over the base approach.

DOI: 10.4018/978-1-5225-9373-7.ch009

INTRODUCTION

Automatic summarization has been under research since the late 50's (Luhn, 1958) and has tackled a variety of interesting real-world problems. The problems faced range from news summarization (Barzilay & McKeown, 2005; Huang, Wan, & Xiao, 2013; Kabadjov, Atkinson, Steinberger, Steinberger, & Goot, 2010; D. Radev, Otterbacher, Winkel, & Blair-Goldensohn, 2005; Wu & Liu, 2003) to scientific summarization (Baralis & Fiori, 2010; Teufel & Moens, 2002; Yeloglu, Milios, & Zincir-Heywood, 2011) and meeting summarization (Erol, Lee, Hull, Center, & Menlo Park, 2003; Niekrasz, Purver, Dowding, & Peters, 2005). More recently, document summarization has moved on to specific genres and domains, such as (micro-)review summarization (Nguyen, Lauw & Tsaparas, 2015; Gerani, Carenini & Ng, 2019) and financial summarization (Isonuma et al, 2017).

The significant increase in the rate of content creation due to the Internet and its social media aspect, moved automatic summarization research to a multi-document requirement, taking into account the redundancy of information across sources (Afantenos, Doura, Kapellou, & Karkaletsis, 2004; Barzilay & McKeown, 2005; J. M Conroy, Schlesinger, & Stewart, 2005; Erkan & Radev, 2004; Farzindar & Lapalme, 2003). Recently, the fact that the content generated by people around the world is clearly multilingual, has urged research to revisiting summarization under a multilingual prism (Evans, Klavans, & McKeown, 2004; Giannakopoulos et al., 2011; Saggion, 2006; Turchi, Steinberger, Kabadjov, & Steinberger, 2010; Wan, Jia, Huang, & Xiao, 2011).

However, this volume of summarization research does not appear to have reached a wider audience, possibly based on the evaluated performance of automatic systems, which consistently perform worse than humans (John M Conroy & Dang, 2008; Hoa Trang Dang & Owczarzak, 2009; Giannakopoulos et al., 2011). We should note at this point, however, that even summary evaluation itself is a challenging scientific topic (Lloret, Aker & Plaza, 2018).

In this chapter, we show how a novel, multilingual multi-document news summarization method, without the need for training, can be used as an everyday tool. We show how we designed and implemented an automatic summarization solution, named NewSum, which summarizes news from a variety of sources, using language-agnostic methods. We describe the requirements studied during the design and implementation of NewSum, how these requirements were met and how people evaluated the outcome of the effort.

Our main contributions in this chapter are, thus, as follows:

- We briefly study the requirements of a real-world summarization application, named NewSum. We describe task-aware specifications based on user and application context limitations (e.g. device, communication), source limitations and legal limitations.

- We describe a generic, language-agnostic method for extractive summarization, taking into account redundancy constraints. The method needs no training and minimizes the effort of crossing language boundaries, since it functions at the character level.
- We describe an open architecture for responsive summarization on a mobile setting.
- We provide an evaluation of the system based on non-expert evaluations, to represent market applicability of the system.

In the following section we provide some background on automatic summarization to sketch the related summarization research.

BACKGROUND

In this section, we briefly discuss summarization methods and systems that have been available as either research efforts, but also as real applications. We refer to the projects that aim at summarization and sketch the current state-of-the-art of the summarization sub-domains of salience detection and redundancy removal.

Summarization has been defined as a reductive transformation of a given set of texts, usually described as a three-step process: selection of salient portions of text, aggregation of the information for various selected portions, (optionally) abstraction of this information and, finally, presentation of the final summary text (S. Jones, 1999; I. M. Mani & Bloedorn, 1999). The summarization research community addresses major problems that arise during the summarization process.

- How can one group texts into topics, given a big set of texts of varying topics?
- How can one detect and select salient information to be included in the summary (ideally without training)?
- How can one avoid redundant or repeated information in the output summary, especially when multiple documents are used as input to the summarization process?
- Can one develop methods that will function independently from the language of documents? To what degree can this independence be achieved?

Up to date, many summarization systems have been developed, presented and evaluated, especially within such endeavors as the Document Understanding Conferences (DUC) and Text Analysis Conferences (TAC)[1].

The summarization community has moved from single-text (single-document) to multi-text (multi-document) input and has also reached such domains as opinion summarization and "trend" summarization, as in the case of NTCIR[2].

Different evaluations performed in recent years have proved that the multi-summarization task is highly complex and demanding, and that automatic summarizers have a long way to go to perform equally well to humans (Dang & Owczarzak, 2008; Dang, 2005, 2006).

A study on how well a system can perform summarization (Genest, Lapalme, Yousfi-Monod, & Montréal, 2009) compared two basic methods of summarization: the extractive and the abstractive. In extractive summarization the summarizer forms a summary by selecting sentences from the original texts. In the abstractive approach, which is how humans tend to summarize, the summarizer creates a (mental) abstraction of the information and then composes a new text based on this abstraction. The study showed that extractive summarization has an upper limit of performance. This upper limit in the study was the performance of humans (considered the best summarizers), who applied extractive summarization through simple sentence selection and reordering. Abstractive summarization seems to be able to perform better than the extractive process.

In the domain of news summarization, there exist efforts that provided publicly available, proof-of-concept systems. Such systems are the NewsInEssence system (D. Radev et al., 2005), the Columbia NewsBlaster (Evans et al., 2004) and the multilingual NewsGist (Kabadjov et al., 2010). A number of commercial efforts for products and services related to summarization are currently available. We briefly overview these efforts in the following paragraphs.

Related Summarization Systems and Software

Summly (summly.com) is a single-document summarizer, applied on web pages and has just recently been embedded into the Yahoo! mobile application. Wavii (wavii.com) is an application offering a social media view of news integration, by generating a stream of summarized news. It is multi-document, but applied on a single language (English). It was recently bought by Google and is currently unavailable. Another effort is that of iResearch Reporter (iresearch-reporter.com), which is an English-only summarization solution, provided via a web interface. It is search-based, meaning that it summarizes the results of searches in a structured report. Similarly, JistWeb and JistDesktop (jastatechnologies.com) are a set of web and desktop based tools that summarize search results into a single document. Ultimate Research Assistant (urast.com) is a search-based, multi-document, multilingual summarizer. It incorporates no redundancy removal and provides both web-based access and also via a programmatic Application Programming Interface (API).

TLDR Reader (tldrstuff.com) is a mobile application that provides single document summaries on articles and pages. It only works on English texts. TLDR can be also used via an (API). ReadBorg (readborg.com), based on the TextTeaser summarizer, provides single document summaries of news in English. The summarization service is provided as a website and also via a web service API.

Other efforts and products related to NewSum include EMMNewsExplorer (emm.newsexplorer.eu) which is a web-based news aggregator applied on many languages, which however provides no summary – similarly to a variety lots of aggregators like Google News (news.google.com), Fark (fark.com) and others.

What none of the above solutions provide is a multilingual, multi-document, news clustering and summarizing infrastructure and front-end software, offering an effective glimpse of news, made to suit mobile user needs.

In the next paragraphs we overview research works on the summarization subtasks of salience (or importance) detection and redundancy removal, to support the novelty of our n-gram graph based proposed methods.

Sentence and Information Salience

To determine salience of information, researchers have used *positional and structural* properties of the judged sentences with respect to the source texts. These properties can be the sentence position (e.g., number of sentence from the beginning of the text, or from the beginning of the current paragraph) in a document, or the fact that a sentence is part of the title or of the abstract of a document (Edmundson, 1969; D. R. Radev, Jing, Stys, & Tam, 2004). Also, the *relation* of sentences with respect to a user-specific query or to a specified topic (J. M Conroy et al., 2005; Park, Lee, Ahn, Hong, & Chun, 2006; Varadarajan & Hristidis, 2006) are features providing evidence towards importance of information. Cohesion (proper name anaphora, reiteration, synonymy, and hypernymy) and coherence - based on Rhetorical Structure Theory (Mann & Thompson, 1987) - relations between sentences were used in (I. Mani, Bloedorn, & Gates, 1998) to define salience. The idea was that of a graph, where each sentence is a vertex. Vertices in this graph are connected by edges when there is a cohesion or coherence relation between them (e.g. common anaphora). The salience of a sentence, given this graph, is computed as the result of an operation dependent on the graph representation (e.g. spreading activation starting from important nodes). Before studying the graph-based methods any further, we first overview other common approaches to salience detection in summarization.

Oftentimes, following the *bag-of-words* assumption, a sentence is represented as a word-feature vector, as in (Torralbo, Alfonseca, Guirao, & Moreno-Sandoval, 2005). In such cases, the sequence of the represented words is ignored. The vector dimensions represent word frequency or the Term Frequency - Inverse Document

Frequency (TF-IDF) value of a given word in the source texts. In other cases, further analysis is performed, aiming to reduce dimensionality and produce vectors in a *latent topic space* (Flores, Gillard, Ferret, & Chandelar, 2008; Steinberger & Jezek, 2004). Vector representations can be exploited for measuring the semantic similarity between information chunks, by using measures such as the cosine distance or Euclidean distance between vectors.

When the feature vectors for the chunks have been created, clustering of vectors can be performed for identifying clusters corresponding to specific topics. A cluster can then be represented by a single vector, for example the centroid of the corresponding cluster's vectors (Radev, Jing, & Budzikowska, 2000). Chunks closest to these representative vectors are considered to be the most salient. We must point out that for the aforementioned vector-based approaches one needs to perform preprocessing to avoid pitfalls due to stop-words and inflection of words that create feature spaces of very high dimension.

However, the utility of the preprocessing step, which usually involves stemming and stop-word removal, is an issue of dispute (Ledeneva, 2008; Leite, Rino, Pardo, & Nunes, 2007).

More recent approaches use *machine learning techniques* and sets of different features to determine whether a source text chunk (sentence) should be considered salient and included in the output summary. In that case the feature vector calculated for every sentence may include information like sentence length, sentence absolute position in the text, sentence position within its corresponding paragraph, number of verbs and so forth - e.g. see Teufel & Moens (2002).

It has been shown that for specific tasks, such as the news summarization task of DUC, simple *positional features* for the determination of summary sentences can be very promising for summarization systems (Dang, 2005). However, in other domains or genres these features are not adequate. The example of short stories falls into this type of case, where a completely different approach is needed to perform the summarization (Kazantseva & Szpakowicz, 2010): the specific summary type described may be expected to describe the setting without giving away the details or surprises of the plot. In (Jatowt & Ishizuka, 2006), we find an approach where time-aware summaries take into account the frequency of terms over time in different versions of web pages to determine salience.

The notion of Bayesian expected risk (or loss) is applied in the summarization domain by Kumar, Pingali, & Varma (2009), where the selection of sentences is viewed as a decision process. In this process the selection of each sentence is considered a risky decision and the system has to select the sentences that minimize the risk.

The CLASSY system (J. M Conroy, Schlesinger, & O'Leary, 2007; J. M. Conroy, Schlesinger, & O'Leary, 2009) extracts frequently occurring ("signature") terms from source texts, as well as terms from the user query. Using these terms, the system estimates an "oracle score" for sentences, which relates the terms contained within the candidate sentences to an estimated "ideal" distribution based on term appearance in the query, the signature terms and the topic document cluster. Different optimization methods (e.g. Integer Linear Programming) can then be used to determine the best set of sentences for a given length of summary, given sentence weights based on their "oracle score".

Focusing on the graph-related literature on multi-document summarization, we visit a number of works that build on graph structures to build summaries. In (Varadarajan & Hristidis, 2006) the authors create a graph, where the nodes represent text chunks and edges indicate relation between the chunks. In that work, the maximum spanning tree of the document graph that contains all the keywords is considered an optimal summary. More recently, the G-FLOW method (Christensen, Mausam, & Etzioni, 2013) builds on estimated discourse relations to build Approximate Discourse Graphs (ADGs). The summarizing process then uses the graph to select one from various candidate extractive summaries, maximizing coherence. The candidate summaries are also graded via a regression model of salience (based on ROUGE scores of training corpora) and a redundancy detector (based on information extraction). The result is a summarizer that searches through possible ordered lists of sentences - by applying a stochastic hill-climbing algorithm - to find a summary that contains maximally salient, non-redundant sentences that form a maximally coherent text.

In multi-document summarization, different iterative ranking algorithms like PageRank (Brin & Page, 1998) and HITS (Kleinberg, 1999) over graph representations of texts have been used to determine the salient terms over a set of source texts (Mihalcea, 2005). Salience has also been determined based on the fact that documents can be represented as "small world" topology graphs (Matsuo, Ohsawa, & Ishizuka, 2001). In these graphs important terms appear highly linked to other terms. Finding the salient terms, one can determine the containing sentences' salience and create the final summary.

In another approach (Hendrickx & Bosma, 2008), content units (sentences) are assigned a normalized value (0 to 1) based on a set of graphs representing different aspects of the content unit. These aspects include: query-relevance; cosine similarity of sentences within the same document (termed *relatedness*); cross-document relatedness, which is considered an aspect of redundancy; redundancy with respect to prior texts; and coreference based on the number of coreferences between different content units. All the above aspects and their corresponding graphs are combined into one model that assigns the final value of salience using an iterative process. The process spreads importance over nodes based on the "probabilistic centrality" method that takes into account the direction of edges to either augment or penalize the salience of nodes, based on their neighbors' salience.

In a related study of graph methods for multi-document summarization (Ribaldo, Akabane, Rino, & Pardo, 2012), we see that cross-document structure (via the Cross-document Structure Theory) can be embedded into a sentence-by-sentence similarity graph to enrich available information. Then, node traits such as node grade, clustering coefficient are used to select the most salient sentences across all source texts.

In a work by Cai and Li (2012), the authors use a mutual reinforcement principle to determine salient sentences in a query-driven summarization task. The idea is that "a sentence should be ranked higher if it is contained in the theme cluster which is more relevant to the given query while a theme cluster should be ranked higher if it contains many sentences which are more relevant to the given query". To apply this intuition on importance propagation, the authors form a two-layered graph. One layer of the graph contains vertices mapped to topic clusters; the other layer contains vertices mapped to sentences. Edges are drawn between vertices weighted by the cosine similarity of the corresponding vector space representations of the vertex items. Two reinforcement-based methods - Reinforcement After Relevance Propagation (RARP) and Reinforcement During Relevance Propagation (RDRP) – are proposed to determine the importance of sentences in the graph.In the MUSE multi-document summarizer system (Litvak & Last, 2012) a set of features related to graphs are used as input features to a genetic algorithm. The algorithm, exploiting a training document set, creates a weighting scheme that allows ranking sentences based on the graph (and several other types of) features. The graph in MUSE shows positional proximity between words (Litvak, Last, & Friedman, 2010): nodes are words and edges are drawn between words that are found to be consecutive in the original text. The system is extended to the MUSEEC system (Litvak, Dlikman and Last, 2015), which employs a genetic algorithm that learns linear combination of multiple linguistic, statistical and semantic sentence features to rank sentences in a language-independent manner towards extractive salience-based selection.

Several, rather recent, approaches heavily rely on vector space models for word or sentence representations, ranging from term-weight vectors to dense, distributed representation schemes. The NTNU architecture (Hung, Shih and Chen, 2015) ranks sentences by cosine score comparisons of TF-IDF, CBOW or paragraph vector embeddings (Mikolov et al., 2014). Similar approaches mine term inter-similarity by exploiting distributional and co-occurrence information to arrive at similar semantic content (Tanev and Balahur, 2015). Statistical sentence and word-level features are used in LIA-RAG (Pontes, Torres-Moreno and Linhares, 2015), with a sentence-wise graph clustering approach grouping similar sentences together via the Jenshen-Shannon divergence measure. In another approach (Vicente, Alcon and Llorent, 2015), the authors employ semantic information infusion via semantic graphs (e.g. Wordnet (Miller, 1995)) and named entity extraction, followed by a post-processing of resulting semantic vectors with PCA. The work of Balikas and Amini (Balikas and Amini, 2015) examine a variety of sentence embeddings learned by deep neural networks, in conjunction with an examination of serial and pooling-based sentence selection strategies, comparing vectors via the cosine similarity.

Furthermore, the Sheffield-Trento system (Aker et al., 2015) implements source linking by computing a quotation score that quantifies the degree of inter-reference, using term vectors along with detected named entity information. Subsequently, instances are compared with a multitude of similarity measures to extract related pairs. Word and character n-gram features are employed in the work of (Krejzl et al., 2015), where LDA-based topic modelling is used to produce topic distributions of input source texts. In the work of Xu et al. (Xu et al., 2017), the authors use an attentive encoder-decoder architecture (Chopra et al., 2016), employing doc2vec embeddings (Le and Mikolov, 2014) for the encoder, pre-trained on the Gigaword corpus and fed to an LSTM decoder (Hochreiter and Schmidhuber, 1997). The authors train each component separately and examine a variety of ways of passing the embeddings to the decoder, reporting sub-par performance of the decoupled model when applied on out-of-domain data. Rossiello, Basile and Semerano (Rossiello, Basile and Semerano, 2017) aggregate word embeddings to a sentence vector, scoring the latter with respect to their similarity to the document centroid. A subset of the most similar sentences are retained, while simultaneously considering redundancy between adjacently-ranked sentences.

Moreover, Vanetik and Litvak (Vanetik and Litvak, 2017) apply a compression scheme where sentence itemsets are replaced with an encoding, following a minimum description length (MDL) principle. Sentence ranking is subsequently applied to generate summary according to a desired length.

Li, Mao and Chen (Li, Mao and Chen, 2017) tackle content linking by employing word embeddings, using their inner product and Wordnet (Miller et al., 1997) for sentence similarity extraction. Additionally, they use LDA-based approaches (Chen et al., 2014) for sentiment mining and argument labelling. The work of Lloret et al. (Lloret et al., 2017) tackle multi-domain summarization from social media and online reviews, using manual polarity annotations, term frequency and noun phrase length for sentence ranking. Summaries are formed based on target length and sentiment constraints, as well as the candidate cosine similarity score to each polarity group.

Other works adopt a topic-based analysis, implemented by various approaches available in the topic modelling literature. The AllSummarizer system (Aries, Zegour and Hidouci, 2015) forms clusters using the cosine similarity on vectors composed of variety of lexical and sentence-level statistical features, while the ExB model (Thomas et al., 2015) extracts topic-central sentences by iterative applications of TextRank (Mihalcea and Tarau, 2004) on a sentence graph, built by various sentence vector bag approaches (BoW, TF-IDF) and similarity measures (Jaccard, cosine, and a semantic similarity extraction system). Additionally, the CIST system (Wan et al., 2015) use LDA-based modelling (Blei et al., 2003) to construct topics, with the approach additionally utilized towards extracting representation useful for sentiment annotation of the source texts. Another system (Vicente, Alcon and Llorent, 2015) examines a "topic-focused" approach via PCA projection, where a single salient sentence - with respect to the highest weight on the principal component axis the source sentence feature vectors are projected to - is retained, arguing that such topic-salient sentences will correspond to the transformation eigenvectors, however with limited success.

Alongside the above studies on main summarization pipelines, there have been advances in instrumental summarization sub-tasks. Regarding splitting and tokenization, an evaluation from Conroy and Davis (Conroy and Davis, 2015) reports the Porter stemmer-based FASST-E underperforming against the Rosseta and NLTK splitters on multi-document summarization; they additionally highlight the value of hierarchical sentence interleaving, an approach that uses the structure of the document rather than statistical features, for large document summarization. In addition, the utilization of sentiment, i.e. the expressed polarity in the text as a feature in the downstream task of summarization has been widely used. In the work of Tanev and Balahur, (Tanev and Balahur, 2015), unigram and bigram counts, sentiment lexicons and domain-specific resources are employed in conjunction with SVM classifiers towards online forum sentiment extraction. Others use LDA-based approaches (Wan et al., 2015) to arrive at dense representations for sentiment classification, while the approach in (Aker et al., 2015) employs a feature selection step prior to a support vector regression scorer. The study of Krejzl et al. (Krejzl et al., 2015) use maximum entropy classification on a variety of n-gram-based features.

Finally, on the summary evaluation subtask, Ellouze, Jaoua and Belguith (Ellouze, Jaoua and Belguith, 2017) build a summary evaluation system that employs multiple summary evaluation scores, lexical and syntactic features, concatenated to vectors to represent summaries. The latter are fed into a feature selection post-processing step, the result of which is used to score summaries via a variety of ensemble learning models.

In light of the existing body of related studies, within this work we tackle the problems of salience detection in extractive multi-document summarization using a unified, language independent and generic framework based on n-gram graphs.

The contributed methods offer a basic, language-neutral, easily adaptable set of tools. The basic idea behind this framework is that neighborhood and relative position of characters, words and sentences in documents offer more information than that of the `bag-of-words' approach. Furthermore, the methods go deeper than the word level of analysis into the sub-word (character n-gram) level, which offers further flexibility and independence from language and acts as a uniform representation for sentences, documents and document sets.

As opposed to related works, we do not use centrality traits of the n-gram graph nodes or other graph properties to determine salience. We do not use training or search to rank our sentences. We do not apply propagation of some kind to determine importance. Salience in our system is determined via a set of similarity operators that are applied between topic- and sentence-representative n-gram graphs. The representative graphs are generated via a custom graph merging operator applied on sets of sentence n-gram graphs.

The work presented in this book heavily builds upon conclusions and lessons from previous technical reports (e.g. (Giannakopoulos, Vouros, & Karkaletsis, 2010)). However, the summarization method described herein has significantly different analysis and steps e.g., for subtopic detection, as well as a different overall approach on segmentation (no sub-sentential chunking), essentially constituting a completely novel method of summarization.

Redundancy Detection

A problem that is somewhat complementary to salience selection is that of *redundancy detection*. Redundancy indicates the unwanted repetition of information in a summary. Research on redundancy has given birth to the Marginal Relevance measure (Carbonell & Goldstein, 1998) and the Maximal Marginal Relevance (MMR) selection criterion. The basic idea behind MMR is that "good" summary sentences (or documents) are sentences (or documents) that are relevant to a topic without repeating information already in the summary. The MMR measure is a generic linear combination of any two principal functions that can measure relevance and redundancy.

Another approach to the redundancy problem is that of the Cross-Sentence Informational Subsumption (CSIS) (Radev et al., 2000), where one judges whether the information offered by a sentence is contained in another sentence already in the summary. The "informationally subsumed" sentence can then be omitted from the summary. The main difference between the two approaches is the fact that CSIS is a binary decision on information subsumption, whereas the MMR criterion offers a graded indication of utility and non-redundancy.

Other approaches, overviewed in (Allan, Wade, & Bolivar, 2003), use statistical characteristics of the judged sentences with respect to sentences already included in the summary to avoid repetition. Such methods are the NewWord and Cosine Distance methods (Larkey, Allan, Connell, Bolivar, & Wade, 2003) that use variations of the bag-of-words based vector model to detect similarity between all pairs of candidate and summary sentences. Other, language model-based methods create a language model of the summary sentences, either as a whole or independently, and compare the language model of the candidate sentence to the summary sentences model (Zhang, Callan, & Minka, 2002). The candidate sentence model with the minimum KL-divergence from the summary sentences' language model is supposed to be the most redundant.

The CLASSY system (Conroy et al., 2009) represents documents in a term vector space and enforces non-redundancy through the following process: Given a pre-existing set of sentences A corresponding to a sentence-term matrix M_A, and a currently judged set of sentences B corresponding to a matrix M_B, B is judged using the term sub-space that is orthogonal to the eigenvalues of the space defined by A; this means that only terms that are not already considered important in A will be taken into account as valuable content.

The G-FLOW method (Christensen, Mausam, & Etzioni, 2013) uses a triple representation to represent sentences and to determine redundancy across sentences.

In this work, we have used and a statistical, graph-based model of sentences by exploiting character n-grams. The strategy, similarly to CSIS, compares all the candidate sentences and determines the redundant ones. We use no deep analysis and we function in a language-independent manner, by using the sub-word (character-based) representation of n-gram graphs. The redundant sentences are removed from the list of candidate sentences before generating the summary.

In the following sections, we provide the study and details related to our proposed method: we overview the requirements of a real world news summarization system; we discuss the research problems behind some of the requirements and how a novel method of summarization and an open architecture were devised to provide a solution. We then provide an evaluation of our approach based on user studies and we conclude the paper.

NewSum: NEWS SUMMARIZATION IN THE REAL WORLD

Real-World Requirements

We saw that, in the summarization domain, a variety of problems arise when attempting to provide human-level summaries. NewSum was our effort to provide a task-specific - or "full-purpose" as Sparck-Jones put it (K. S. Jones, 2007) - implementation of a summarization system with one specific goal: allow humans to get a maximum coverage picture of everyday news in a limited time, avoiding redundancy. The implied process for the generation of summaries in such a system, as was indicated in the introduction, is as follows. First, we gather articles from various news sources, which we then group. The grouping is based on the real events they refer to. We determine the most important aspects of an event. Then we try to detect and extract the most representative sentences covering these aspects to form a summary, while avoiding redundancy of information.

We identified several user requirements plausible related to a news summarization application. First, the summary should be provided with minimal delay (ideally in real-time). Second, all the implementation details should be hidden behind a friendly and effective interface. Third, the system should be multilingual to maximize the impact of the application.

We decided that another important aspect of our system would be a feature allowing the user to provide feedback on the summaries. This would support error detection and analysis, as well as an estimation of how users (who are usually non-experts in linguistics) perceive the performance of the system.

One thing we should stress here is that we decided to follow a strategy which would be penalized in most summarization research tracks (e.g., TAC, DUC): our summaries would not be cohesive, fluent summaries; they would be a set of points. The promise of the system, essentially based on a corresponding specification, is to provide the main points of an event and the user is made aware of this promise. We selected this approach because we assumed that a user expecting a cohesive, fluent, short text summary will be disappointed if he sees an extractive summary (i.e., a collection of extracted sentences). We remind the reader that the assumption is completely in line with the task-specific requirements we have set: extractive summaries may well be suited for a daily news update.

Another aspect of the user requirements is related to the provenance of information. When an application consumes and broadcasts content, the application publisher should be aware of the legal problems that may arise: an application cannot claim ownership of the content it uses from external sources. Especially in our case, where the system draws from copyrighted material we wanted to:

- make "fair use" of the provided material.
- point to our source, to allow the user to check the full text and verify the validity of the summary.
- provide a list of all the sources used for an event, even if the sentences used in the summary are only from a subset. This implies that there are cases where different sources have significant overlap of information, and the text from one subsumes the text from the other. This is very common in the world of news.
- allow the user to select a subset of sources for the summaries (based on his preferences).

Given the above discussion, more requirements were added to the original set. Summaries were to be provided as sets of sentences/points. In each such point we should refer to the original source, while also keeping links to all the sources that were used to describe the event. Finally, we should allow the user to select a subset of the available sources to suit one's need.

We said that the aim of NewSum was not clearly a research aim, but the processing we needed to perform demanded the support of a variety of research domains to build a usable system. In the following section we show how different research domains map to the individual steps of the processing NewSum performs.

From n-Gram Graphs to Markov Clustering

We have claimed that the steps for analyzing content into summaries are four: gather articles from various news sources; group articles into news events; determine the most important aspects of an event; determine the most representative sentences covering these aspects; avoid redundancy of information in the summary. The only step that does not require a research effort is the gathering step (which we will describe in the next section). The other steps are mapped to corresponding research domains as follows: the grouping of articles and the detection of important aspects is mapped to text clustering; the selection of important sentences is mapped to salience detection in the summarization domain; the avoidance of repetition of information is mapped to redundancy removal.

We note that NewSum is multilingual, i.e. language-agnostic, which sets an important requirement on the applicable research methods. Previous research (Giannakopoulos & Karkaletsis, 2009; Giannakopoulos & Palpanas, 2009; Giannakopoulos et al., 2010) has shown that the n-gram graph text representation is a powerful tool that allows representing texts and combining them, comparing them regardless of underlying language. N-gram graphs have, notably, given birth to state-of-the-art summary evaluation methods (Giannakopoulos & Karkaletsis, 2013; Giannakopoulos et al., 2008). In the following paragraphs we review the basics of n-gram graphs and see how they were combined with Markov Clustering (MCL) (Dongen, 2000) to achieve text clustering. We also describe how they were an indispensable part of the summarization pipeline, providing - together with the n-gram graph framework algorithms and operators - a generic tool for summarization subtasks.

n-gram Graphs: The Basics

An n-gram graph is a graph representing how n-grams are found to be neighbors, within a distance of each other, in a given text. An n-gram is a, possibly ordered, set of words or characters, containing n elements. The n-gram graph is a graph $G = <V, E, L, W>$, where V is the set of vertices, E is the set of edges, L is a function assigning a label to each vertex and to each edge and W is a function assigning a weight to every edge. The graph has n-grams labeling its vertices v ∈ V. The edges e ∈ E connecting the n-grams indicate proximity of the corresponding vertex n-grams. Our chosen labeling function L assigns to each edge e =< v_1, v_2 > the concatenation of the labels of its corresponding vertices' labels in a predefined order: e.g., L(e) = L(v_1) + SEP + L(v_2), where SEP is a special separator character and the operator + is, in this context, the operator of string concatenation. For directed graphs the order is essentially the order of the edge direction. In undirected graphs the order can be the lexicographic order of the vertices' labels.

It is important to note that in n-gram graphs each vertex is unique. To ensure that no duplicate vertices exist, we also require that the labeling function is a one-to-one function. The weight of the edges can indicate a variety of traits: distance between the two neighboring n-grams in the original text, or the number of co-occurrences within a given window (we note that the meaning of distance and window size changes by whether we use character or word n-grams). In our implementation we apply as weight of an edge, the frequency of co-occurrence of the n-grams of its constituent vertices in the original text.

A Function Assigning a Weight w(e) to Every Edge

We repeat that the edges E are assigned weights of $c_{i,j}$ where $c_{i,j}$ is the number of times a given pair S_i, S_j of n-grams happen to be neighbors in a string within some distance D_{win} of each other. The distance d of two n-grams S_i, which starts at position i, and S_j, which starts at position j, is $d = |i - j|$. The selection of a distance value allows different levels of fuzziness in our representation. We note that more in depth analysis of different types of n-gram graphs can be found in the corresponding original paper on n-gram graphs (Giannakopoulos et al., 2008).

Here, we will briefly illustrate the process of mapping a string to a *character n-gram graph*, which is a language-agnostic version of n-gram graphs.

Given a string, e.g. "abcdef", 2 steps are needed to form an n-gram graph (cf. Figure 1):

- First we extract all (overlapping) unique n-grams, e.g. 2-grams and form one node per n-gram. In our example this would be: "ab", "bc", "cd", "de", "ef".
- Second, we connect with edges all the n-grams that are found to be neighbors. Two n-grams are considered neighbors, when they are found to be within D characters of each other in the original string. In the example of the figure, "ab" is a neighbor of "bc" for D=3, but "ab" is not a neighbor of "ef".

Figure 1. From string to n-gram graph.

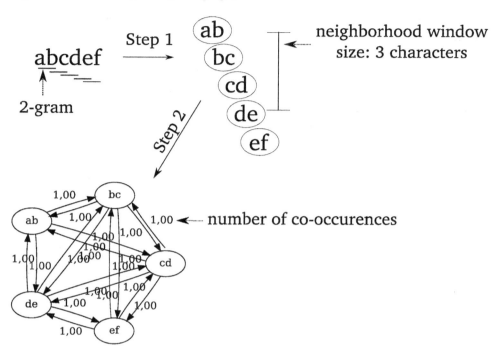

Once we have drawn the edges, we assign weights to them. The weight of an edge indicates the number of times the two node n-grams were found to be neighbors in the original string (thus, the weight is a positive integer number). In our string all n-grams are found to be neighbors only once. Due to the fact that in this work we look for neighbors in both directions (left and right) the resulting graph has two edges per pair of neighboring n-grams and is essentially equivalent to an undirected graph.

Given this process, we can represent everything from a single sentence to a whole text as an n-gram graph. We note that no preprocessing (stemming, lemmatization, punctuation removal or stop-word removal) is performed on the string.

A second way to use the n-gram graphs is to use *token (e.g., word) n-grams*. In this case some preprocessing is implied, even if only to split the text into tokens. The mapping process is the same, with the difference that distances are measured in tokens instead of characters.

Given a set of n-gram graphs, we can perform several operators (Giannakopoulos, 2009). The *conjunction operator* is a binary operator which keeps the common part (edge set) between two graphs A and B. For a common edge (i.e, an edge that appears in A and in B, regardless of its weight) with weights w_A and w_B in the corresponding graphs, the weight in the resulting graph is the average of w_A and w_B. The *update*

259

operator allows merging a set of graphs into a representative (or class) graph. The merged graph contains all the edges of the source graphs, and common edges in the source graphs result in a single edge with averaged weight in the resulting graph (Giannakopoulos & Karkaletsis, 2011).

On the other hand, several similarity functions have been used to compare n-gram graphs (Giannakopoulos et al., 2008). In this work, we use the *Size Similarity* (SS), *Value Similarity* (VS) and the *Normalized Value Similarity* (NVS) functions.

The SS function is simply the ratio of the edge counts of two graphs. Thus, given two graphs G_1 and G_2, with corresponding edge counts of $|G_1|$ and $|G_2|$, then $SS(G_1, G_2) = \min(|G_1|, |G_2|)/\max(|G_1|, |G_2|)$.

We note that to form the ratio we always use the minimum count as the nominator and the maximum count as the denominator. The SS function is trivial, in that it pays no attention to the contents of the graphs, but only to their relative size (edge count).

The VS function compares two graphs based on their common edges and also takes into account their edge weights and relative graph sizes. In VS (G_1, G_2), each edge *e* that is common between G_1, G_2 and has a weight of w_1, w_2 in the corresponding graphs, contributes a value of $VR(e) = \min(w_1, w_2) / \max(w_1, w_2)$ to the similarity. If SR is the sum of all the VR values for all the common edges between G_1, G_2, then $VS = SR / \max(|G_1|, |G_2|)$.

The NVS Function Is Calculated as NVS = VS / SS

NVS ignores the relative graph sizes, but takes into account common edges and edge weights. We note that all three similarity functions reported here return values between 0.0 (no similarity) and 1.0 (maximum similarity).

In the case where each string is represented with two different n-gram graphs, e.g. a 2-gram graph and a 3-gram graph, one can calculate the *Overall Similarity* (OS) between two strings S_1 and S_2, taking into account both levels of analysis. We first calculate the similarities between the graphs with equal n values (2-gram graph of S_1 and 2-gram graph of S_2; then, 3-gram graph of S_1 and 3-gram graph of S_2), which gives e.g. V_2 and V_3. Then, we calculate OS as the weighted average of the similarities: $OS = (2xV_2 + 3xV_3)/(2+3)$. Once again, the similarity values output from OS are between 0.0 and 1.0, assigning higher importance to higher n-grams (the weighting factor).

In the following paragraphs we describe how the above representation and operators – termed the *n-gram graph framework* - can be applied to face the different research problems NewSum needs to face.

Event Detection as Text Clustering

In NewSum we have used two sets of hand-picked sources: one for Greek and one for English news. Each source provided news via an RSS feed, which encodes article information in a semi-structured manner. Each feed was assigned a category label by its publisher. Given this set of sources providing news feeds, we needed to group news items per news category into events. We need to perform this grouping, because a summary makes more sense per event than over irrelevant documents.

The topic clustering needs to be a very responsive process, thus we used a mechanism similar to blocking for entity resolution - e.g. see (Elmagarmid, Ipeirotis, & Verykios, 2006). The idea is that we use a very quick, similarity-based process to perform the clustering into events, however in our case we have a bias to cluster precision than recall. In other words, we do not mind that much if the cluster misses a single text, but we do mind if the cluster contains an irrelevant text. This is related to the fact that an irrelevant text in a news cluster causes problems in all the following steps, while the missing text may simply be found in a separate cluster (possibly alone) and thus no significant loss is conceded.

The document clustering has several steps, as follows. First, we pre-process the text (including the title) to keep only *Capitalized* words and numbers that appear. This step attempts to perform a very simplistic and high-speed named entity recognizer equivalent, with the addition of a number recognizer. This heuristic implies that the named entities and the numbers are the main identifying information a news item. The output of the process is a series of tokens which are either capitalized words or numbers. For example, given the title "U.S. tells North Korea new missile launch would be huge mistake", the resulting series would be <"U.S.", "North", "Korea">.

We then use word n-gram graphs to represent the series (n takes values in {1,2} and D=3). This representation implies that the way entities and numbers are found to co-occur in the above series is important and not simply the series themselves. This approach also helps with noise from the previous step, since the co-occurrence of entities is important and, thus, noise may be isolated (it does not repeatedly co-occur with other entities).

Based on the word n-gram graphs, we compare all possible pairs of texts. We use a heuristic rule to connect two texts as referring to the same event: the NVS should be above 0.20 while the SS should be above 0.10. This heuristic (converging to these values through trial and error experiments), is based on the assumptions that we need the texts to be overlapping over a certain degree (NVS threshold), but we also need them to be comparable in size (SS threshold). The success over previously unseen instances given the above values was a cluster precision of over 95% with a cluster recall of about 65%. We note that cluster precision indicates the percentage of texts that were correctly positioned within a cluster (based on the cluster topic). Cluster recall indicates the percentage of the texts that belong to a topic which indeed were assigned to the cluster topic. What this achieved is that we were very strict in our selection of the texts for a given topic: no irrelevant texts should enter. If they did, then the summary would make no sense. The second part of the heuristic related to the size similarity (SS) was inserted to avoid problems of very short texts that appeared to have significant overlaps with almost any other text (due to commonly used words). The result of this step was that texts talking about the same event are connected to each other via a "talk about the same event" relation.

The final step is based on the assumption of transitivity of the relation "talk about the same event". Thus, if A and B "talk about the same event" and B and C "talk about the same event", then A and C "talk about the same event". This assumption completes the clustering process, by forming groups of texts, where all texts within a group talk about a single event.

Given the clusters of texts, we now need to detect topics and subtopics that form the essence of each event. In the next paragraphs we focus on this detection process.

Subtopic Detection and Representation

In NewSum we consider that an event has several aspects, or subtopics. This approach builds on existing related efforts, exploiting (sub-)topic detection for summarization like (Angheluta, De Busser, & Moens, 2002).

In our approach, we start by segmenting the text into sentences. In order to remain maximally language independent we use a statistical sentence splitter (SentenceDetectorME class of the Apache OpenNLP java package[3]) to perform the splitting. Our splitter is trained per language and creates a maximum entropy classifier which can determine split-points in a given sentence. We have trained the splitter on both English and Greek texts to support both languages.

We continue by comparing all pairs of sentences, based on their character n-gram representation. We use character 3-grams and a neighborhood distance of 3 to represent the sentences. These values have been shown to perform well in a variety of settings (Giannakopoulos & Karkaletsis, 2011; Giannakopoulos et al., 2008). The output of this step is a similarity matrix between sentences, based on the NVS between the n-gram graphs of the sentence pairs.

We then apply Markov Clustering - MCL (Dongen, 2000) - on the similarity matrix. The result of this process is a set of hard clusters (i.e., no sentence can belong to two clusters at the same time) which we consider as representing different subtopics of an event. Essentially, what we claim is that sentences that are similar to each other in terms of their character n-gram graphs, may talk about the same subtopic. This claim is in agreement with the distributional similarity hypothesis: texts that have a similar distribution of n-grams are likely to speak about the same topic. Since the n-gram graphs represent the co-occurrence statistics of the n-grams in a text and the similarity functions measure the similarity these statistics, our claim is indeed in agreement. MCL is an unsupervised way to determine automatically – and efficiently – a good number of subtopics, based on the similarities among sentences. This provides an advantage over methods like k-means, which would need an explicit number of topics (k) to work. Furthermore, MCL is very quick to converge, which offers an advantage to several well-known statistical methods for clustering, such as LDA (Blei, Ng, & Jordan, 2003).

Given the subtopics, described as sets of sentences that cover the same subtopics, we now need to extract the essence of each subtopic. In the n-gram graph framework, we consider that the essence of a set of graphs is the maximum common sub-graph of all the set. Thus, to extract the essence of a subtopic, we use the conjunction operator over all pairs of n-gram graphs within a subtopic sentence cluster. In other words, if a subtopic T_i consists of sentences $\{S_1, S_2, ..., S_n\}$ represented by the corresponding character n-gram graphs $\{G_1, G_2, ..., G_n\}$, and x is the conjunction operator, then the essence E_i of T_i is:

$$E_i = G_1 \times G_2 \times ... \times G_n$$

For a whole event, the subtopic detection and essence extraction process results in a set of n-gram graphs, each of which represents the essence of a subtopic. In order to provide the essence of the whole event, we simply need to combine these essences into one representative graph. To this end we use the update operator over all the essences of the subtopics. The resulting merged graph E_O is the overall representative graph of the event.

Measuring Salience and Avoiding Redundancy

We presume that a sentence is salient if it is similar to the essence of an event. Going back to the n-gram graph framework, the value similarity (VS) is the type of similarity that takes into account whether a given n-gram graph is maximally similar to another, also using the relative size. In other words, VS is the best choice when we want to take into account the overlap between two graphs (vs. the maximum *possible* overlap based on the graph sizes, which is reflected by NVS).

In order to provide a salience based ordering of sentences, we compare (the graph of) each sentence from the source documents of an event cluster to (the graph of) the essence of the event. Ordering the sentences based on their similarity to the essence, we have a salience-based list of candidates for our final summary.

Naively, we could start creating the summary by simply running through the candidate sentences in descending order of similarity to the essence. However, several sentences might talk about the same thing, especially since we are in a multi-document setting. To avoid this problem and tackle redundancy, we perform an a priori filtering of redundant sentences based on the candidate list.

The algorithm starts with the most salient sentence S_1. It compares it to all the following candidate sentences S_i, i>1, by terms of NVS on their character n-gram graphs. If the similarity is above a given threshold (heuristically chosen value in our current setting: 0.3), it means that the later candidate repeats the information of the first candidate and is removed from the candidate list. We iteratively repeat the filtering process for each sentence S_j, j>1, until we reach the end of the candidate list and have removed all redundant sentences.

The result of this process is a set of sentences, which maximally cover the essence of a topic, without repeating information. This set of sentences is, for NewSum, the optimal subset of sentences from the original documents that can form an extractive summary.

To exploit the results of this process, we created the NewSum application, which provides the infrastructure, the interface and the feedback mechanisms that allow using and evaluating our summarization system in a real-life setting. In the next paragraphs, we present novel modifications of the n-gram graph architecture of NewSum, followed by elaboration of its application details in following paragraphs.

Incorporating Entity Information in n-gram Graphs

In the preceding sections, the n-gram graph model is constructed by considering lexical information in the text (i.e. token n-grams and their co-occurrence counts). Other types of information (e.g. higher level concepts, word relations and interdependences, etc.) are expected to be inferred from n-gram distributional information in the text and learned from scratch from the training data. A straight-forward improvement to this procedure is the direct incorporation of pre-existing human knowledge in the representation, towards aiding the NLP system to handle the task at hand, rather than expecting it to generate everything from scratch. Such human knowledge can be accessed in a structured form via semantic resources such as semantic graphs, entity databases and various such sources if high-level data. The node-based architecture of the n-gram graph model provides a straightforward extension mechanism towards considering such semantic information units, both in a semantic-only setting as well as a multimodal scenario where both lexical and semantic information is leveraged in the model. Such an approach is examined in two text clustering settings (Tsekouras et al., 2017; Pittaras et al., 2018) and includes a two-fold information extraction process. Firstly, TF-IDF filtering retains only the most important terms in the input text, handling tokens with low-information content such as stopwords and other overly prevalent words in the dataset with a variety of strategies (e.g. replacing with a placeholder token or entirely discarding them). Secondly, named entity information is extracted from the text and inserted as semantic metadata objects in the n-gram graph. This results in an n-gram graph with both highly informative terms and named entities, merging lexical and semantic information in a single representation. An experimental evaluation on multilingual article classification (i.e. articles on a fixed topic in multiple languages) from Wikipedia (MultiLing 2015 dataset) as well as news domain data (the 20 Newsgroups dataset) indicates the utility and usefulness of the augmented approach. Specifically, the entity-based modelling improves regular TF-IDF vector space features in terms of F1 score, with the performance improvement being most pronounced in documents rich with named entities that can lead to overlaps. On the other hand, sparse information content does not introduce consistent improvements over clustering results. This finding carries over in the multilingual articles case, where named entity extraction appears to be highly translation invariant, leading to shared entities across multilingual versions of the same text. Finally, the TF-IDF filtering radically reduces the time complexity of the n-gram graph modelling procedure.

Additionally, the entity augmentation approach is applied in document clustering formulated as a record linkage problem (Pittaras et al., 2018). There, n-gram graphs provide competitively results to TF-IDF-based representations, and, although the contribution of text versus entity-based information seem to be dependent on the dataset, the n-gram graph approach that leverages both appears to outperform the corresponding text-only or entity-only n-gram graph baselines. This study is also examined in the following section that deals with scalability of the n-gram graph pipeline.

Scaling n-gram Graph-Based Analysis

In this section we examine an extension of the n-gram graph comparison pipeline towards achieving better scalability. The extension is applied in two scenarios. First, we look into scalable n-gram graph construction and similarity extraction in supervised text classification. Secondly, we examine improving the pipeline's performance in the context of document clustering, applied in the unsupervised text event detection and record linkage tasks.

ARGOT (**A**pache spa**R**k based text minin**G** t**O**olki**T**) is a distributed implementation for n-gram graph operations (Kontopoulos, Giannakopoulos and Varlamis, 2017). It employs Apache SPARK, a cluster computing framework for large-scale data processing (Zaharia, 2016). SPARK is a popular and powerful parallelization tool for distributed data processing where operations can be shared in parallel between multiple machines towards improved runtime performance. It has been used for stream-based text processing and text classification (Li, 2015; Capdevila

2016; Semberecki, 2016). In ARGOT, the authors scale the graph creation process with a mechanism by which graph edges mapping to same vertices are constrained to the same SPARK partition (processing node), thereby improving merging and calculation efficiency of downstream graph operations. The classification process entails building a "class graph", i.e. an n-gram graph composed of content from training documents for each class label, using instance and class graph similarity scores as feature vectors for learning classifiers. To this end, a graph similarity extraction procedure is implemented by broadcasting the (small) n-gram graph representation of each instance to all partitions, followed by a filtering process to only retain overlapping graph edges, and collect them to the master node for computation of the similarity score. The authors perform a classification and runtime performance analysis on the RCV2 multilingual news dataset, where 10-run average timings are displayed on Figures 4 and 5, representing experiments on a single-node commodity machine and distributed cluster, respectively. On the first setting (Figure 2, top), a large scalability capacity is observed, with the algorithm introducing an approximately 50% speedup from 8 to 48 SPARK partitions -- especially on classes with many samples (with respect to samples, class 2 > class 4 > class 1 > class 3). The run on the computer cluster (Figure 2, bottom) showcases some performance penalties on larger partition numbers with communication overheads countering gains from distributed processing.

In order to illustrate the relationship between scalability and the number of instances per class, two subsets of the dataset were created, each comprising 10,000 documents in total, from two and four classes respectively (9,000 training instances and 1,000 testing instances in each subset). The same experiments were performed (10 times per setting and averaging results), this time using 2 to 24 partitions on the single node setup. Figure 3 shows the average merging time per class per experiment, illustrating that merging time depends on the number of the documents in a topic. As illustrated in the average feature extraction time per experiment, having less documents per topic and the same number of total training instances results in longer extraction times. The difference lies in the number of graph comparisons, which are greater in the last case. From this, we can infer that the feature extraction time depends on the number of topics; better scalability of the algorithm can be deduced, as the number of documents (and thus the size of the graphs) increases.

Finally, a comparison of the method to the current multi-threaded implementation (JINSECT toolkit[4]) is performed. Figure 4 shows the average graph merging times in the aforementioned subsets correspondingly, as well as the comparison of the ARGOT average feature extraction time to JINSECT. It is evident that ARGOT is faster in graph merging but slower in feature extraction. However, JINSECT fails on the full dataset due to lack of memory scalability, which is not a problem for

Figure 2. Average time elapsed versus the number of SPARK partitions, for experiments run on a single-node machine (top) and a computer cluster (bottom). Columns indicate graph merging (left), feature extraction (middle) and graph comparison (right). Lower is better.

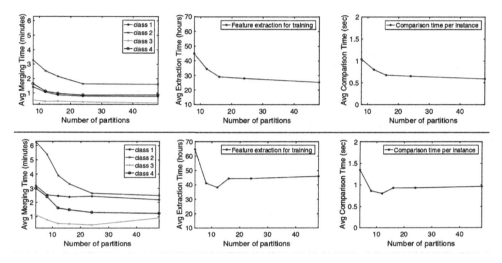

Figure 3. Average time elapsed for merging 2 topics (left), merging 4 topics (middle) and feature extraction

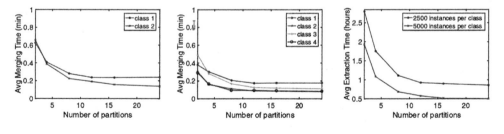

Figure 4. ARGOT vs the multi-threaded JINSECT implementation

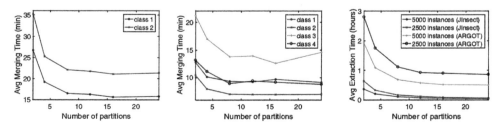

ARGOT. As expected, ARGOT yields the same results as JINSECT in terms of classification performance.

Regarding n-gram graphs in document clustering, we first examine unsupervised event detection in text (Hogenboom, 2011). Here, clustering looks for useful structural patterns in the space of the input (i.e. documents mapped to n-gram graph models) and partitions data in meaningful groups (Barlow, 1989). As a result, event detection corresponds to the formation of clusters based on document comparison via appropriate similarity metrics, after some necessary representation transformations.

This event detection process is studied as a component of the Security challenge of the "Big Data Europe" (BDE) project (Auer et al., 2017), and is further refined with the Geosensor system (Argyriou et al., 2018; Pittaras et al., 2019). The component's task is to form events from news and social media source streams in two steps, from data collection to periodic event formation, enrichment and update. Given the very large volumes of data -- harvested for multiple RSS feeds and twitter accounts – the scalability of the event clustering component is critical. An investigation of the time complexity of the procedure identified the document similarity extraction as an important bottleneck of the event detection task. To this end, an implementation of the relevant pipeline was developed in apache SPARK.

The event extraction process follows the NewSum summarization algorithm and is based on news documents acquired from the RSS source feeds. First, all unique news item pairs are generated in order to facilitate comparisons of each article with the other. After n-gram graph mapping, pairs of graphs are compared with the Normalized Value Similarity operator, with pairs mapped to a similarity exceeding a pre-defined threshold (fine-tuned for the task) are marked as related and retained, while the rest are discarded. The second phase consists of grouping related pairs into clusters, filtered with a support threshold of 2 (i.e. singleton-pair groups are discarded). Subsequently, formed event clusters are enriched with social media items via a similarity-based n-gram graph classification. In addition, news and social media items are augmented with location names, geographical geometry coordinates, named-entities and photographs, extracted from the text, metadata and location names mined from each text. As a result, each formed event consists of a variety of information: news items, social media posts portraying public opinion, location names with geometries and photographs and named entities (e.g. key players that are related to the event). This enhances the utility of formed events towards decision making as well as automated downstream tasks. Figure 5 illustrates the event detection workflow.

One important identified bottleneck of this workflow is the discovery of similar article pairs, where all unique tuples need to be generated from the input article list and compared via the similarity extraction – an operation introducing quadratic complexity with respect to the input list size. We parallelize this procedure with

Figure 5. The BDE event detection process

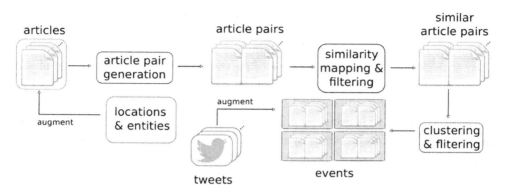

apache SPARK by transforming the input articles into SPARK resilient data structures (RDDs), a collection of fault-tolerant, immutable data objects distributed across the cluster with each partition processed in parallel by its host machine. RDD processing is done by transformations like map, filter and reduce operations, which transform, filter and aggregate the data respectively (Zaharia, 2016).

We generate all article pairs by applying a Cartesian product operation on the RDD, followed by thresholding steps that first discard trivial pairs (e.g. singleton identity pairs of the form (x, x), x being an input article) and second, keep only one

Figure 6. The distributed similarity mapping process of the event detection workflow. Green indicates similarity, while red dissimilarity. The color intensity/saturation indicates grades of (dis)similarity.

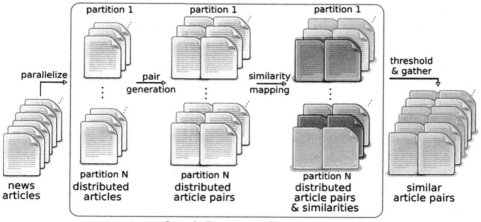

instance out of the two permutations of the same article tuple. This results in $n(n-1)/2$ combinations for n input articles. Article pairs are subsequently converted into pairs of word n-gram graphs which are reduced to a similarity score using the NVS operator. After similarity threshold filtering, relevant article pairs are retrieved to the host machine and forwarded to the rest of the event detection pipeline. A graphical illustration of the process is presented in Figure 6.

An evaluation of the distributed event detection implementation was performed, using the Reuters-21578 text categorization dataset, a collection of 21578 documents that appeared on the Reuters newswire in 1987. We used Cassandra 2.2.4 (Lakshman, 2010) with Docker 1.6.2 (Merkel, 2014) for the storage backend and the SPARK 2.11 java API. The experiments ran on Ubuntu 14.04 on an 8-core 2.6 GHz processor with 24 GB of RAM. Regarding the experimental setting, the number of input articles n was varied from 32 to 10000, doubling the input at each step. This resulted in a size of article pairs ranging from 496 to approximately 50 million. SPARK partition sizes were set to p=2, 4, 8 and 16. A non-distributed multi-threaded run on a single multi-core machine was also performed as the baseline, using all available CPUs. We ran 5 experiments on each (input size, partition size) configuration and the baseline, measuring the elapsed time in seconds for the similarity mapping operation, from the article acquisition from Cassandra up to and including the computation and filtering of the similar pairs. As we are only interested in measuring the time performance of each scenario, we do not evaluate the comparison results themselves.

Experimental results in terms of elapsed seconds per run are depicted in a logarithmic scale in Figure 7. A number of observations can be made. Firstly, the non-linear nature of the problem is apparent, with execution time increasing in an exponential fashion as the number of articles increases. Secondly, the introduction of SPARK is surprisingly detrimental to performance, for an input size less than 4096. This indicates that distributing the similarity extraction process with SPARK for small workloads does not introduce performance benefits; on the contrary, it appears to result in larger extraction times. This deterioration could occur as a result of the SPARK overhead cost being comparable to the distributed execution speedup for smaller article sets, given the computational performance of the n-gram graph algorithm as well as the limited document size in the Reuters-21578 dataset. On the other hand, at an input size of 8192 documents the introduction of distributed execution clearly benefits the running time of the task, with every distributed configuration outperforming the baseline and the partition size of $p = 4$ exhibiting the best performance, i.e. a relative 45.78% increase over the multi- threaded baseline. For 10000 input articles, the SPARK version remains the best performer, with the 8-partition configuration performing best albeit with diminishing gains, resulting in a 23.28% relative performance increase over the parallel run. Moreover, among the distributed execution runs, a partition size of 2 always yields the worst

Figure 7. Runtime performance results on the Reuters dataset in a logarithmic scale. Lower is better.

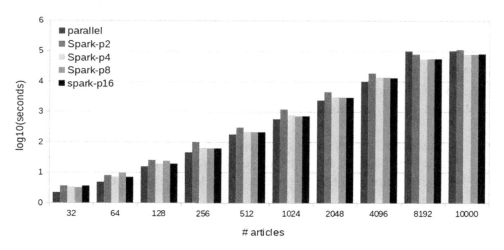

performance compared to other partition settings, for every input size. No clear conclusion can be drawn, on the other hand, for the best performing partition size. In addition, partition sizes of 4, 8 and 16 demonstrate similar performance, for an input size larger than 128 articles. This suggests that the similarity mapping task can benefit from distributed execution for large workloads, with gains however severely diminishing as the number of partitions / workers is increased past a certain point (4, in our case).

Given these observations, we observe that performance boosts are attainable in the n-gram graph similarity extraction pipeline using SPARK-based computation distribution. However, considerable fine-tuning is necessary in order to make sure that the workload, input document size and composition are appropriate to attain such speedups. Future work could examine additional domains (i.e. domains other than news articles), workload sizes or additional parallelization frameworks in order to further establish, extend or revise the above findings.

An additional document clustering scaling scenario examined is expressed as a record linkage problem. We use JedAI (Papadakis et al., 2017), a domain-independent entity resolution toolkit that employs a multitude of representation methods and blocking techniques towards efficient record linkage solutions. In the study of Pittaras et al. (Pittaras et al., 2018), n-gram graphs and a multitude of vector-based representations are employed on text as well as entity-based data, along with a variety of similarity measures for comparing name-value instances towards generation of clusters representing a common category. This setting corresponds to record linkage, in the sense that name-value instances (documents) are aligned to a single real-world entity (clusters). In an experimental evaluation on the 20 Newsgroups and Multiling 2015 datasets, it is observed that JedAI achieves considerable runtime performance improvements (around 63%), with a trade-off of around 5% of F-measure performance, by introducing data blocking, comparison refinement and pruning schemes of the underlying entity similarity graph. This approach provides another avenue towards accelerating the n-gram graph pipeline, this time by adopting a lossy – but efficient – method of reducing the pool of pairwise comparisons.

What all the above experiments indicate is that:

- Summarization based on n-gram graphs can be scaled effectively.
- The scaling strategy is not trivial to determine, since a number of factors (text size, number of texts, genre, etc.) may lead to different data distribution approaches.
- Scaling can also be achieved by applying blocking and other appropriate complexity reduction techniques.
- In a variety of the summarization subtasks, scaling does not appear to strongly affect the effectiveness of the method with respect to the summarization outcome.

NewSum: The Architecture and the Application

We now focus on the NewSum application itself, which integrates the majority of all conducted research into one, free, open-source application, while taking into account real-world requirements. In the NewSum application the main entities are the news article, the news source, the news category, the news feed, the news summary and the news event (or topic). A *news article* is a time and date annotated piece of news, providing a title and the article body. The annotation is implied in the RSS feed (cf. *news feed* below) that provides the article. The *news source* is essentially a news site providing a variety of articles via RSS feeds. The *news category* is a label describing the broad domain of a news article or a news source. Examples of such categories are: world news, local news, politics, science, etc. In most cases a news source is pre-assigned a category by its editor. NewSum uses this information to create its own news categories. The *news feed* is a specific type of web resource (RSS feed), identified by a URL, which provides articles for a specific news category in a semi-structured manner. The *news summary* is a list of sentences (bullets) related to an event. Each sentence is annotated with its originating news feed. If different source texts contain the same sentence, then either of the sources may appear as the origin of the sentence. The *news event (or news topic)* is an abstraction of a real-world event. It is described by a set of news articles referring to the event, a title (derived from the most recent news article) and a date. The date of the news event is the date of the latest news article contained in the news event. News aggregators often perform clustering of news articles to form news topic article sets.

Having described the main entities in the NewSum application, we overview the architecture of the NewSum system built by the analysis server, the web service and the clients.

The *NewSum analysis server* is the processing backbone of the NewSum architecture. At the server we gather and analyze all the articles from a set of predefined news sources, ending up with the processed summaries. The server periodically queries the news sources for new articles. It performs all the analysis required to order the sentences based on salience but it does not remove redundancy at this point. This last step is kept for the moment when a client requests a summary, because clients can choose their news sources and, thus, redundancy can only be determined after a client requests a summary for a given event for a given subset of the data sources.

In order for client software to use the NewSum analysis server output, we provide a web service endpoint (via the Open Source Edition of the Glassfish Server[5]) which simply serves the analyzed, summarized information: t*he NewSum web service*. The endpoint provides the Application Programming Interface (API) for interoperating with the server, getting the detected news topics and the summaries. The web service provides all the required methods to:

- Read the news categories the server covers.
- Get the possible sources that a user can select.
- Read the events (or topics) available at the server, using specific sources.
- Get the summary of a given event, using specific sources.

The NewSum web service makes sure that all the details of the analysis are hidden from client applications and that information is provided at a per-request basis. This latter strategy is meant to minimize network load and latency and allows more flexibility to the client and lower overhead to the server. Furthermore, the fact that the web service is independent of the analysis server allows better workload management and minimizes the impact of one subsystem to the other. Finally, it fulfills the requirements related to speed and responsiveness, since all the data that are sent are a priori available (provided as the output of the execution cycles of the analysis server).

To provide a friendly user interface, independent from the underlying infrastructure, we have created different *NewSum clients* corresponding to different settings. The main client is the Android client, which can be used on portable and mobile devices. In collaboration with the NewSum community, we are also implementing web-based versions of NewSum, as well as a variety of widgets aimed at desktop and virtual desktop settings (e.g., Windows widgets, KDE widget, iGoogle widget). The clients are built upon client libraries that facilitate developers in their application building effort and boost the reusability of the system.

In Figure 8 we provide two snapshots of the current version of the NewSum Android application. In the first part we show the basic category interface, illustrating topics pertaining to the selected category, as well as buttons for switching categories and accessing settings and help options. In the second part we show how NewSum renders summaries as lists of sentences, also providing the referring link back to the source document on the Web. The reader should also note the rating button that provides simple-to-use evaluation (1 to 5 stars) for the summary viewed, as well as an option to share the summary through social media.

An early version of NewSum[6] is available as anopen source project, building upon the well-established JInsect framework of n-gram graphs (Giannakopoulos, 2010), which is also an open source, free project. It is an effort completed by SciFY[7], with the research support of the SKEL Lab of NCSR "Demokritos". The Android

Figure 8. NewSum snapshots: (a) Left, the main screen with the topics list for the current category (b) On the right, the summary screen, where sentence snippets and summary sources are accessible

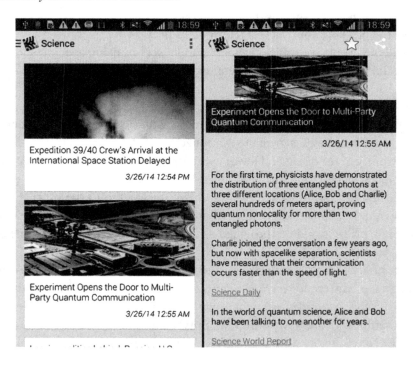

application, as well as some web-based preview variations, are available via the SciFY website.

Concerning the performance and computational requirements of the summarization method over real data, we note the following: for a total of 110 sources (news feeds) over 18 categories the running time of the whole summarization pipeline (gather, cluster, extract summary) at a server with 8 CPU cores (Intel Xeon at 2.2 GHz) and 12GB of system memory is less than 2 minutes. The implementation is fully parallelizable, scaling with more CPUs.

Both the application and the research behind NewSum make more sense if enough people find its results usable. To determine whether such summarization software makes sense, we conducted evaluations on two main aspects: one on the application usability and one on the summary quality, using the feedback mechanics of the software itself. We elaborate on these evaluations in the next paragraphs.

Evaluation of Summaries

NewSum had two main questions that needed an answer:

- What do people think about the summaries provided?
- Does the use of NewSum (or a similar application) facilitate reading news, by providing global information from various sources?

We conducted three independent studies to answer these questions. Two studies (one preliminary and one more advanced) were meant to answer the summary quality question. The third was meant to answer the question of whether NewSum serves its purpose.

The first user study related to summary quality was conducted during an "open beta" phase of the application. The "open beta" took place between January 2013 and March 2013. During this phase 18 volunteer beta testers were asked to use the program and provide feedback on the summaries they read. The grades were assigned using a 5-star scale: the 1-star rating was mapped to a value of "unacceptable", while the 5-star rating was mapped to a value of "excellent". The feedback we gathered contained 119 different summary ratings. The distribution of grades over all the summaries, from all the users is illustrated in Figure 9. No information was kept related to who sent the rating and thus user bias cannot be determined in this preliminary dataset. The per language performance - 88 instances for Greek and 31 for English - is similar to the overall distribution of grades, with the Greek average rating having a value of 3.89 (and standard deviation of 1) and the English average a value of 3.55 (with a standard deviation of 1). A Kolmogorov-Smirnoff test (preferred over t-test due to the abnormality of the distributions) showed that we

Figure 9. Preliminary "Open Beta" summary grades (119 ratings: 31 for English, 88 for Greek)

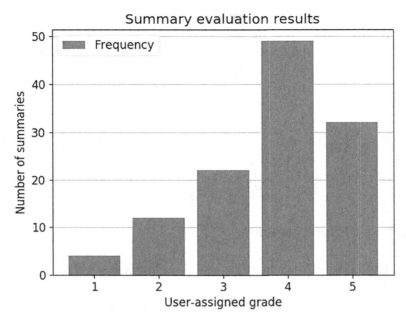

cannot reject that the two distributions (Greek and English grades) are derived from the same distribution. In other words, the two distributions appear very similar. In the rating, grade 1 was meant to indicate "useless or nonsensical summary", grade 3 was mapped to "Acceptable" and grade 5 to "Excellent". What is very interesting is that the percentage of summaries with a grade of 3 or higher is almost 87% of the total summaries. This showed that, even though there is space for improvement, most of the times the summary is at least usable (or much better). Moreover, 2 out of 3 summaries were graded with 4 or 5 ("very good" or "excellent" grades).

In the second study, which started within the CICLing 2013 conference, a newer version of the NewSum application, as well as a website were used to conduct a second experiment. This time an anonymized, persistent user ID was assigned to each participating user. We meant to measure the individual bias of users towards higher or lower grades. Figure 10 illustrates the distribution of grades over all languages and users.

An ANOVA test indicated that the user is indeed a statistically significant factor related to the summary grades assigned (F-value: 4.162, p-value: $<10^{-6}$). The language was similarly highly statistically significant, and this was also shown by the average performances: for Greek the average was 4.14 (with a standard deviation of 1.07), while for English the average was 3.73 (with a standard deviation of 1.34). This

Figure 10. User-aware evaluation summary grades (720 ratings: 267 for English, 453 for Greek)

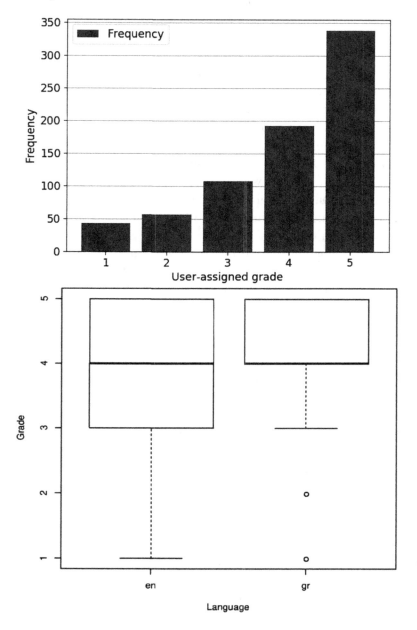

showed that fine-tuning may make sense on individual languages. In both languages the average performance was good, with more than 90% of the summaries having an acceptable (or better) grade for Greek and more than 80% for English. We stress that Greek and English news do not appear simultaneously in the interface (a program option changes the language used in the application). Of course, we could not test where the users originated from and thus part of the bias may relate to the fluency of the users related to one of the languages.

As a result of the deliberately open experiment setting, users varied heavily as related to their contribution: 58 users contributed ratings, with an average contribution of about 12 ratings each, but the median was between 6 and 7 comments, while a single user provided almost 120 ratings. We tried to remove the user with the 120 ratings, in case he dominated the ratings, but there was slight change in the mean evaluation numbers (-0.01 in the Greek case and -0.15 in the English case).

We also checked via ANOVA whether the source of the data (mobile application or web site) was important for the grading and we found out that it was not statistically significant for the evaluation. Thus, the interface did *not* cause a bias related to the perceived quality of a summary.

Overall, our evaluation showed that the *users think highly of the summaries NewSum creates in both Greek and English*. We should however note that applying the same evaluation at large scale with more information per user, would significantly help detect and remove biases from specific user backgrounds and groups. We are also planning to allow richer feedback in the next versions, to be able to perform better error analysis and also allow our system to learn from user feedback via machine learning.

To answer the question of whether a summarization application facilitates news reading, we performed a small scale user experience experiment, limited to 18 Greek and 7 English beta testers. These testers, who were recruited via an open call, were provided a questionnaire that measured different aspects of user experience. The question we will discuss here was expressed as "The use of NewSum allowed me to get informed of the latest news more globally and thoroughly than before". The answer allowed a 5-scale response from "I totally disagree" to "I totally agree". 11 out of 18 (61%) Greek users and 4 out of 7 (58%) English users have an answer of 4 or 5 to this question. Only 1 user per language thought that NewSum did not really help (2, in the 5-scaled response). The mean grade for Greek was 4 with a standard error of 0.24; for English the mean was 3.86 with a standard error of 0.46. Thus, these preliminary results indicate that users tend to believe that NewSum can improve their news reading, fulfilling its purpose.

FUTURE RESEARCH DIRECTIONS

What is obvious from our research so far is that summarization can be a useful tool. It appears that optimizing existing algorithms to different needs is the way to engineer generic research tools into usable applications, with a societal and commercial impact. Projects like the NOMAD project[8], harvesting information from a variety of sources and aiming to provide actionable updates to decision makers, are examples of the value summarization can bring into this exploding user content generation era.

Summarization is essential due to the increase of content. The applicability of summarization will lie in its ability to gather possible millions of sources (texts or other types of data) and combine them into coherent summaries. Such an approach implies research efforts towards a variety of domains as follows.

- Language-independent summarization: How can we provide summarization infrastructures over languages that have not been tackled so far, but have millions of speakers and writers (e.g., Chinese, Hindi)?
- Sentiment and argument summarization: Summarizing news has been the focus of numerous research efforts. However, there are many more types of information that would benefit from summarization. Summarizing sentiment and arguments can be of critical importance in domains like policy modeling and business intelligence, since it can provide actionable feedback for decision support. But how can we achieve the summarization in such complex domains, and indeed provide summaries that make sense and can be used as social evidence?
- Summarization as a scientific tool: How can we summarize research in an effective way, to support such domains as bio-informatics, where the production of papers and studies is difficult for researchers to cope with?
- Holistic summarization: How can we combine different types of content (unstructured, semi-structured, fully-structured) into fused summaries of information? Such summaries could provide invaluable feedback for decision support, without the need to skim through completely different types of data to get updated on facts and numbers. Ongoing efforts in the MultiLing community try to focus on such difficult settings, for example the financial narrative summarization task[9].

Several ongoing efforts have been fueling the research in these domains and much more is to be seen in the foreseeable future. What we would like to add to this set of research efforts is:

- an effort that would focus on the generalization ability of existing summarization systems and results to new domains and languages.
- an effort that would allow to measure the extrinsic value of summarization systems from the stakeholders: the users.

NewSum is, for, us a milestone towards these two dimensions of summarization system research.

CONCLUSION

In this chapter we presented a multilingual, multi-document summarization method, implemented within a real-world setting. We discussed user and system requirements related to a news summarization application. We showed how existing research, mostly based on n-gram graphs, can support and implement a summarization system that covers different languages – namely Greek and English. We overviewed an effective system, called NewSum, which provides a full infrastructure and user endpoints for the exploitation of summarization on texts provided by real news providers. We described how user studies indicate that summarization is a feasible and useful way to facilitate users in everyday news search. We also described two studies indicating the performance of the presented system, from the viewpoint of (non-linguist) users, i.e. the market setting. We then highlighted how NewSum moved to a larger scale, through the study of alternative scaling strategies, with promising results.

We learnt many lessons throughout our effort. First, summarization is useful and can help people, starting today. Second, there exist ways to be language-agnostic in one's methods of summarization. The n-gram graph framework is an effective method to begin with, offering an efficient way to analyze, represent and act upon texts for summarization purposes. Third, we learnt that open, per task evaluations can help judge the usefulness of an approach on a real setting. Integrating response mechanisms in applications and using user feedback may be a good way to perform such an evaluation. Fourth, our open source effort showed that openness allows combining and improving systems, reusing expertise and promoting common experience on a subject. NewSum was built on open source principles, using open source software and will be provided as an open source application itself. Finally, open architectures allow combining different components of summarization under a unified interface. This leads to an implied proposal: why not use summarization applications as a means to evaluate underlying summarization methods?

As future work, we plan to apply the proposed methods on corpora of multi-document, cross-/multi-lingual summarization (e.g. from the MultiLing workshops) to test the cross-language applicability. We also plan to incorporate weights for different sources to support different levels of confidence for different sources.

Summarization is an indispensable tool for the information overload era. Researchers should also heed popular needs related to summarization and provide the tools and infrastructures to quantify these needs and accordingly evaluate existing systems. This is the main way to large-scale adoption of summarization and to the full exploration of its potential.

ACKNOWLEDGMENT

The research leading to these results has received funding from the OntoSum project (www.ontosum.org). The method is being exploited for argument summarization within the NOMAD FP7 EU project (www.nomad-project.eu), which has partially funded related extensions of the NewSum summarization technology. Parts of the presented research have also been supported from the BigDataEurope project (funded by grant from the European Union'sHorizon 2020 research Europe flag and innovation program for - GA no. 644564) as well as the Stavros Niarchos Foundation Industrial Scholarhips program (https://www.snf.org/).

REFERENCES

Afantenos, S. D., Doura, I., Kapellou, E., & Karkaletsis, V. (2004). Exploiting Cross-Document Relations for Multi-Document Evolving Summarization. Lecture Notes in Artificial Intelligence (Subseries of Lecture Notes in Computer Science), 3025, 410–419.

Aker, A., Celli, F., Funk, A., Kurtic, E., Hepple, M., & Gaizauskas, R. (2016). *Sheffield-Trento System for Sentiment and Argument Structure Enhanced Comment-to-Article Linking in the Online News Domain*. Academic Press.

Allan, J., Wade, C., & Bolivar, A. (2003). Retrieval and novelty detection at the sentence level. In *Proceedings of the 26th annual international ACM SIGIR conference on Research and development in information retrieval* (pp. 314–321). ACM. 10.1145/860435.860493

Angheluta, R., De Busser, R., & Moens, M.-F. (2002). The use of topic segmentation for automatic summarization. In *Proceedings of the ACL-2002 Workshop on Automatic Summarization*. Retrieved from https://www.law.kuleuven.be/icri/publications/51DUC2002.pdf

Aries, A., Zegour, D. E., & Hidouci, K. W. (2015). AllSummarizer system at MultiLing 2015: Multilingual single and multi-document summarization. In *Proceedings of the 16th Annual Meeting of the Special Interest Group on Discourse and Dialogue* (pp. 237-244). Academic Press. 10.18653/v1/W15-4634

Auer, S., Scerri, S., Versteden, A., Pauwels, E., Charalambidis, A., Konstantopoulos, S., ... Ikonomopoulos, A. (2017, June). The BigDataEurope platform–supporting the variety dimension of big data. In *International Conference on Web Engineering* (pp. 41-59). Springer. 10.1007/978-3-319-60131-1_3

Baralis, E., & Fiori, A. (2010). Summarizing biological literature with BioSumm. In *Proceedings of the 19th ACM international conference on Information and knowledge management* (pp. 1961–1962). Retrieved from http://dl.acm.org/citation.cfm?id=1871785

Barzilay, R., & McKeown, K. R. (2005). Sentence Fusion for Multidocument News Summarization. *Computational Linguistics*, *31*(3), 297–327. doi:10.1162/089120105774321091

Blei, D. M., Ng, A. Y., & Jordan, M. I. (2003). Latent dirichlet allocation. *Journal of Machine Learning Research*, *3*, 993–1022.

Brin, S., & Page, L. (1998). The anatomy of a large-scale hypertextual Web search engine. *Computer networks and ISDN systems, 30*(1-7), 107–117.

Cai, X., & Li, W. (2012). Mutually Reinforced Manifold-Ranking Based Relevance Propagation Model for Query-Focused Multi-Document Summarization. *IEEE Transactions on Audio, Speech, and Language Processing*, *20*(5), 1597–1607. doi:10.1109/TASL.2012.2186291

Carbonell, J., & Goldstein, J. (1998). Use of MMR, Diversity-Based Reranking for Reordering Documents and Producing Summaries, The. In *Proceedings of the 21st Annual International ACM SIGIR Conference on Research and Development in Information Retrieval* (pp. 335–336). ACM. 10.1145/290941.291025

Christensen, J., Mausam, S. S., & Etzioni, O. (2013). Towards Coherent Multi-Document Summarization. In *Proceedings of NAACL-HLT* (pp. 1163–1173). Retrieved from http://www.aclweb.org/anthology/N/N13/N13-1136.pdf

Conroy, J. M., Schlesinger, J. D., & O'Leary, D. P. (2007). CLASSY 2007 at DUC 2007. *Proceedings of Document Understanding Conference (DUC) Workshop 2006*.

Conroy, J. M., Schlesinger, J. D., & O'Leary, D. P. (2009). CLASSY 2009: Summarization and Metrics. *Proceedings of the Text Analysis Conference (TAC) 2009*.

Conroy, J. M., Schlesinger, J. D., & Stewart, J. G. (2005). CLASSY Query-Based Multi-Document Summarization. *Proceedings of the Document Understanding Conf. Wksp. 2005 (DUC 2005) at the Human Language Technology Conf./Conf. on Empirical Methods in Natural Language Processing (HLT/EMNLP 2005)*.

Conroy, J. M., & Dang, H. T. (2008). Mind the Gap: Dangers of Divorcing Evaluations of Summary Content from Linguistic Quality. In *Proceedings of the 22nd International Conference on Computational Linguistics (Coling 2008)* (pp. 145–152). Manchester, UK: Coling 2008 Organizing Committee. Retrieved from http://www.aclweb.org/anthology/C08-1019

Dang, H. T. (2005). Overview of DUC 2005. *Proceedings of the Document Understanding Conf. Wksp. 2005 (DUC 2005) at the Human Language Technology Conf./Conf. on Empirical Methods in Natural Language Processing (HLT/EMNLP 2005)*.

Dang, H. T. (2006). Overview of DUC 2006. *Proceedings of HLT-NAACL 2006*.

Dang, H. T., & Owczarzak, K. (2008). Overview of the TAC 2008 Update Summarization Task. In *TAC 2008 Workshop - Notebook papers and results* (pp. 10–23). Retrieved from http://www.nist.gov/tac

Dang, H. T., & Owczarzak, K. (2009, November 16). *Overview of the TAC 2009 Summarization Track*. Presented at the TAC 2009, NIST. Retrieved from http://www.nist.gov/tac/publications/2009/presentations/TAC2009_Summ_overview.pdf

Dongen, S. (2000). Performance criteria for graph clustering and Markov cluster experiments. Amsterdam, The Netherlands: CWI (Centre for Mathematics and Computer Science).

Edmundson, H. P. (1969). New Methods in Automatic Extracting. *Journal of the Association for Computing Machinery, 16*(2), 264–285. doi:10.1145/321510.321519

Ellouze, S., Jaoua, M., & Belguith, L. H. (2017, April). Machine learning approach to evaluate multilingual summaries. In *Proceedings of the MultiLing 2017 workshop on summarization and summary evaluation across source types and genres* (pp. 47-54). Academic Press. 10.18653/v1/W17-1007

Elmagarmid, A., Ipeirotis, P. G., & Verykios, V. (2006). Duplicate Record Detection: A Survey. *SSRN eLibrary*. Retrieved from http://papers.ssrn.com/sol3/papers.cfm?abstract_id=1281334

Erkan, G., & Radev, D. R. (2004). Lexpagerank: Prestige in Multi-Document Text Summarization. In *Proceedings of EMNLP* (pp. 365–371). Academic Press.

Erol, B., Lee, D. S., Hull, J., Center, R. C., & Menlo Park, C. A. (2003). Multimodal summarization of meeting recordings. In *Multimedia and Expo, 2003. ICME'03. Proceedings. 2003 International Conference on* (Vol. 3). Academic Press.

Evans, D. K., Klavans, J. L., & McKeown, K. R. (2004). Columbia newsblaster: multilingual news summarization on the Web. In Demonstration Papers at HLT-NAACL 2004 (pp. 1–4). Academic Press. doi:10.3115/1614025.1614026

Farzindar, A., & Lapalme, G. (2003). Using Background Information for Multi-Document Summarization and Summaries in Response to a Question. *Proceedings of DUC03: NAACL 2003 Workshop in Automatic Text Summarization.*

Flores, J. G., Gillard, L., Ferret, O., & de Chandelar, G. (2008). Bag of senses versus bag of words: comparing semantic and lexical approaches on sentence extraction. In *TAC 2008 Workshop - Notebook papers and results* (pp. 158–167). Retrieved from http://www.nist.gov/tac

Genest, P. E., Lapalme, G., Yousfi-Monod, M., & Montréal, Q. (2009). HEXTAC: the Creation of a Manual Extractive Run. TAC2009 Notebook, Gaithersburg, MD.

Gerani, S., Carenini, G., & Ng, R. T. (2019). Modeling content and structure for abstractive review summarization. *Computer Speech & Language, 53*, 302–331. doi:10.1016/j.csl.2016.06.005

Giannakopoulos, G. (2009). *Automatic Summarization from Multiple Documents.* University of the Aegean. Retrieved from http://www.iit.demokritos.gr/~ggianna/thesis.pdf

Giannakopoulos, G. (2010). *JInsect: The n-gram graph framework implementation.* Retrieved from http://sourceforge.net/projects/jinsect/

Giannakopoulos, G., El-Haj, M., Favre, B., Litvak, M., Steinberger, J., & Varma, V. (2011). TAC2011 MultiLing Pilot Overview. In *TAC 2011 Workshop.* Presented at the TAC 2011, Gaithersburg, MD.

Giannakopoulos, G., & Karkaletsis, V. (2009). N-gram graphs: Representing documents and document sets in summary system evaluation. In *Proceedings of Text Analysis Conference TAC2009.* Presented at the Text Analysis Conference (TAC2009).

Giannakopoulos, G., & Karkaletsis, V. (2011). AutoSummENG and MeMoG in Evaluating Guided Summaries. In *TAC 2011 Workshop.* Presented at the TAC 2011, Gaithersburg, MD.

Giannakopoulos, G., & Karkaletsis, V. (2013). *Together we stand NPowER-ed.* Presented at the CICLing 2013, Karlovasi, Samos, Greece.

Giannakopoulos, G., Karkaletsis, V., Vouros, G., & Stamatopoulos, P. (2008). Summarization system evaluation revisited: N-gram graphs. *ACM Trans. Speech Lang. Process.*, *5*(3), 1–39. doi:10.1145/1410358.1410359

Giannakopoulos, G., & Palpanas, T. (2009). Adaptivity in Entity Subscription Services. In *Proceedings of ADAPTIVE2009.* Presented at the ADAPTIVE2009, Athens, Greece.

Giannakopoulos, G., Vouros, G., & Karkaletsis, V. (2010). MUDOS-NG: Multi-document Summaries Using N-gram Graphs (Tech Report). *1012.2042.* Retrieved from http://arxiv.org/abs/1012.2042

Hendrickx, I., & Bosma, W. (2008). Using correference links and sentence compression in graph-based summarization. In *TAC 2008 Workshop - Notebook papers and results* (pp. 429–435). Retrieved from http://www.nist.gov/tac

Huang, X., Wan, X., & Xiao, J. (2013). Comparative news summarization using concept-based optimization. *Knowledge and Information Systems*, 1–26.

Isonuma, M., Fujino, T., Mori, J., Matsuo, Y., & Sakata, I. (2017, September). Extractive summarization using multi-task learning with document classification. *Proceedings of the 2017 Conference on Empirical Methods in Natural Language Processing*, 2101-2110. 10.18653/v1/D17-1223

Jatowt, A., & Ishizuka, M. (2006). Temporal multi-page summarization. *Web Intelligence and Agent Systems*, *4*(2), 163–180.

Jones, K. S. (2007). Automatic summarising: The state of the art. *Information Processing & Management*, *43*(6), 1449–1481. doi:10.1016/j.ipm.2007.03.009

Jones, S. (1999). Automatic Summarizing: Factors and Directions. In Advances in Automatic Text Summarization (pp. 1–12). Academic Press.

Kabadjov, M., Atkinson, M., Steinberger, J., Steinberger, R., & van der Goot, E. (2010). NewsGist: A Multilingual Statistical News Summarizer. In J. L. Balcázar, F. Bonchi, A. Gionis, & M. Sebag (Eds.), *Machine Learning and Knowledge Discovery in Databases* (pp. 591–594). Springer Berlin Heidelberg. doi:10.1007/978-3-642-15939-8_40

Kazantseva, A., & Szpakowicz, S. (2010). Summarizing Short Stories. *Computational Linguistics*, *36*(1), 71–109. doi:10.1162/coli.2010.36.1.36102

Kleinberg, J. M. (1999). Authoritative sources in a hyperlinked environment. *Journal of the Association for Computing Machinery, 46*(5), 604–632. doi:10.1145/324133.324140

Kontopoulos, I., Giannakopoulos, G., & Varlamis, I. (2017, September). Distributing N-Gram Graphs for Classification. In *European Conference on Advances in Databases and Information Systems* (pp. 3-11). Springer.

Krejzl, P., Steinberger, J., Hercig, T., & Brychcín, T. (2016). *UWB Participation in the Multiling's OnForumS Task*. Academic Press.

Kumar, C., Pingali, P., & Varma, V. (2009). Estimating Risk of Picking a Sentence for Document Summarization. In *Proceedings of the 10th International Conference on Computational Linguistics and Intelligent Text Processing* (pp. 571–581). Academic Press. 10.1007/978-3-642-00382-0_46

Lakshman, A., & Malik, P. (2010). Cassandra: A decentralized structured storage system. *Operating Systems Review, 44*(2), 35–40. doi:10.1145/1773912.1773922

Larkey, L. S., Allan, J., Connell, M. E., Bolivar, A., & Wade, C. (2003). UMass at TREC 2002: Cross Language and Novelty Tracks. In TREC 2002 Proceedings (pp. 721–732). National Institute of Standards & Technology.

Ledeneva, Y. (2008). Effect of Preprocessing on Extractive Summarization with Maximal Frequent Sequences. In Proceedings of MICAI 2008 (pp. 123–132). Academic Press. doi:10.1007/978-3-540-88636-5_11

Leite, D. S., Rino, L. H. M., Pardo, T. A. S., & Nunes, M. das G. V. (2007). Extractive Automatic Summarization: Does more Linguistic Knowledge Make a Difference? In *Proceedings of the Second Workshop on TextGraphs: Graph-Based Algorithms for Natural Language Processing* (pp. 17–24). Rochester, NY: Association for Computational Linguistics. Retrieved from http://www.aclweb.org/anthology/W/W07/W07-0203

Li, L., Mao, L., & Chen, M. (2017, April). Word Embedding and Topic Modeling Enhanced Multiple Features for Content Linking and Argument/Sentiment Labeling in Online Forums. In *Proceedings of the MultiLing 2017 Workshop on Summarization and Summary Evaluation Across Source Types and Genres* (pp. 32-36). Academic Press. 10.18653/v1/W17-1005

Litvak, M., & Last, M. (2012). Cross-lingual training of summarization systems using annotated corpora in a foreign language. *Information Retrieval*, 1–28.

Litvak, M., Last, M., & Friedman, M. (2010). A new approach to improving multilingual summarization using a genetic algorithm. In *Proceedings of the 48th Annual Meeting of the Association for Computational Linguistics* (pp. 927–936). Academic Press. Retrieved from http://dl.acm.org/citation.cfm?id=1858776

Litvak, M., & Vanetik, N. (2017, April). Query-based summarization using MDL principle. In *Proceedings of the multiling 2017 workshop on summarization and summary evaluation across source types and genres* (pp. 22-31). Academic Press. 10.18653/v1/W17-1004

Lloret, E., Boldrini, E., Martinez-Barco, P., & Palomar, M. (2017, April). Ultra-Concise Multi-genre Summarisation of Web2. 0: towards Intelligent Content Generation. In *Proceedings of the MultiLing 2017 Workshop on Summarization and Summary Evaluation Across Source Types and Genres* (pp. 37-46). Academic Press. 10.18653/v1/W17-1006

Lloret, E., Plaza, L., & Aker, A. (2018). The challenging task of summary evaluation: An overview. *Language Resources and Evaluation*, *52*(1), 101–148. doi:10.100710579-017-9399-2

Luhn, H. P. (1958). Automatic Creation of Literature Abstracts, The. *IBM Journal of Research and Development*, *2*(2), 159–165. doi:10.1147/rd.22.0159

Mani, I., Bloedorn, E., & Gates, B. (1998). Using cohesion and coherence models for text summarization. In *Intelligent Text Summarization Symposium* (pp. 69–76). Academic Press.

Mani, I. M., & Bloedorn, E. M. (1999). Summarizing Similarities and Differences Among Related Documents. *Information Retrieval*, *1*(1), 35–67. doi:10.1023/A:1009930203452

Mann, W. C., & Thompson, S. A. (1987). *Rhetorical Structure Theory: A Theory of Text Organization*. University of Southern California, Information Sciences Institute.

Matsuo, Y., Ohsawa, Y., & Ishizuka, M. (2001). A Document as a Small World. In Proceedings the 5th World Multi-Conference on Systemics, Cybenetics and Infomatics (SCI2001) (Vol. 8, pp. 410–414). Academic Press. doi:10.1007/3-540-45548-5_60

Merkel, D. (2014). Docker: lightweight linux containers for consistent development and deployment. *Linux Journal, 2014*(239), 2.

Mihalcea, R. (2005). Multi-Document Summarization with Iterative Graph-Based Algorithms. *Proceedings of the First International Conference on Intelligent Analysis Methods and Tools (IA 2005)*.

Nguyen, T. S., Lauw, H. W., & Tsaparas, P. (2015, February). Review synthesis for micro-review summarization. In *Proceedings of the eighth ACM international conference on web search and data mining* (pp. 169-178). ACM. 10.1145/2684822.2685321

Niekrasz, J., Purver, M., Dowding, J., & Peters, S. (2005). Ontology-Based Discourse Understanding for a Persistent Meeting Assistant. *Proceedings of the AAAI Spring Symposium Persistent Assistants: Living and Working with AI.*

Papadakis, G., Tsekouras, L., Thanos, E., Giannakopoulos, G., Palpanas, T., & Koubarakis, M. (2017, May). Jedai: The force behind entity resolution. In *European Semantic Web Conference* (pp. 161-166). Springer.

Park, S., Lee, J. H., Ahn, C. M., Hong, J. S., & Chun, S. J. (2006). Query Based Summarization Using Non-Negative Matrix Factorization. *Proceeding of KES*, 84–89. 10.1007/11893011_11

Pittaras, N., Papadakis, G., Stamoulis, G., Argyriou, G., Taniskidou, E. K., Thanos, E., ... Koubarakis, M. (2019, April). GeoSensor: semantifying change and event detection over big data. In *Proceedings of the 34th ACM/SIGAPP Symposium on Applied Computing* (pp. 2259-2266). ACM. 10.1145/3297280.3297504

Pontes, E. L., Torres-Moreno, J. M., & Linhares, A. C. (2016). *LIA-RAG: a system based on graphs and divergence of probabilities applied to Speech-To-Text Summarization.* arXiv preprint arXiv:1601.07124

Radev, D., Otterbacher, J., Winkel, A., & Blair-Goldensohn, S. (2005). NewsInEssence: Summarizing Online News Topics. *Communications of the ACM, 48*(10), 95–98. doi:10.1145/1089107.1089111

Radev, D. R., Jing, H., & Budzikowska, M. (2000). Centroid-Based Summarization of Multiple Documents: Sentence Extraction, Utility-Based Evaluation, and User Studies. *ANLP/NAACL Workshop on Summarization.*

Radev, D. R., Jing, H., Stys, M., & Tam, D. (2004). Centroid-based summarization of multiple documents. *Information Processing & Management, 40*(6), 919–938. doi:10.1016/j.ipm.2003.10.006

Ribaldo, R., Akabane, A. T., Rino, L. H. M., & Pardo, T. A. S. (2012). Graph-based methods for multi-document summarization: exploring relationship maps, complex networks and discourse information. In *Computational Processing of the Portuguese Language* (pp. 260–271). Springer. doi:10.1007/978-3-642-28885-2_30

Rossiello, G., Basile, P., & Semeraro, G. (2017, April). Centroid-based text summarization through compositionality of word embeddings. In *Proceedings of the MultiLing 2017 Workshop on Summarization and Summary Evaluation Across Source Types and Genres* (pp. 12-21). Academic Press. 10.18653/v1/W17-1003

Rossiello, G., Basile, P., & Semeraro, G. (2017, April). Centroid-based text summarization through compositionality of word embeddings. In *Proceedings of the MultiLing 2017 Workshop on Summarization and Summary Evaluation Across Source Types and Genres* (pp. 12-21). Academic Press. 10.18653/v1/W17-1003

Saggion, H. (2006). Multilingual Multidocument Summarization Tools and Evaluation. *Proceedings, LREC 2006.*

Steinberger, J., & Jezek, K. (2004). Using latent semantic analysis in text summarization and summary evaluation. In *Proc. ISIM '04* (pp. 93–100). Academic Press.

Tanev, H., & Balahur, A. (2016). Tackling the OnForumS Challenge. *Museec: A multilingual text summarization tool. Proceedings of ACL-2016 System Demonstrations,* 73-78.

Teufel, S., & Moens, M. (2002). Summarizing Scientific Articles: Experiments with Relevance and Rhetorical Status. *Computational Linguistics, 28*(4), 409–445. doi:10.1162/089120102762671936

Thomas, S., Beutenmüller, C., de la Puente, X., Remus, R., & Bordag, S. (2015). Exb text summarizer. In *Proceedings of the 16th Annual Meeting of the Special Interest Group on Discourse and Dialogue* (pp. 260-269). Academic Press. 10.18653/v1/W15-4637

Torralbo, R., Alfonseca, E., Guirao, J. M., & Moreno-Sandoval, A. (2005). Description of the UAM System at DUC-2005. *Proceedings of the Document Understanding Conf. Wksp. 2005 (DUC 2005) at the Human Language Technology Conf./Conf. on Empirical Methods in Natural Language Processing (HLT/EMNLP 2005).*

Tsekouras, L., Varlamis, I., & Giannakopoulos, G. (2017, September). *A Graph-based Text Similarity Measure That Employs Named Entity Information.* RANLP. doi:10.26615/978-954-452-049-6_098

Turchi, M., Steinberger, J., Kabadjov, M., & Steinberger, R. (2010). Using parallel corpora for multilingual (multi-document) summarisation evaluation. *Multilingual and Multimodal Information Access Evaluation,* 52–63.

Varadarajan, R., & Hristidis, V. (2006). A System for Query-Specific Document Summarization. *Proceedings of the 15th ACM International Conference on Information and Knowledge Management*, 622–631.

Vicente, M., Alcón, O., & Lloret, E. (2015). The University of Alicante at MultiLing 2015: approach, results and further insights. In *Proceedings of the 16th Annual Meeting of the Special Interest Group on Discourse and Dialogue* (pp. 250-259). Academic Press. 10.18653/v1/W15-4636

Wan, X., Jia, H., Huang, S., & Xiao, J. (2011). Summarizing the differences in multilingual news. In *Proceedings of the 34th international ACM SIGIR conference on Research and development in Information* (pp. 735–744). Academic Press.

Wan, S., Li, L., Huang, T., Gao, Z., Mao, L., & Huang, F. (2015). *CIST System Report for SIGdial MultiLing 2015*. Academic Press.

Wu, C. W., & Liu, C. L. (2003). Ontology-Based Text Summarization for Business News Articles. *Proceedings of the ISCA 18th International Conference on Computers and Their Applications*, 389–392.

Xu, Y., Lau, J. H., Baldwin, T., & Cohn, T. (2017, April). Decoupling encoder and decoder networks for abstractive document summarization. In *Proceedings of the MultiLing 2017 Workshop on Summarization and Summary Evaluation Across Source Types and Genres* (pp. 7-11). Academic Press. 10.18653/v1/W17-1002

Yeloglu, O., Milios, E., & Zincir-Heywood, N. (2011). Multi-document summarization of scientific corpora. In *Proceedings of the 2011 ACM Symposium on Applied Computing* (pp. 252–258). Academic Press. 10.1145/1982185.1982243

Zaharia, M., Xin, R. S., Wendell, P., Das, T., Armbrust, M., Dave, A., ... Ghodsi, A. (2016). Apache spark: A unified engine for big data processing. *Communications of the ACM, 59*(11), 56–65. doi:10.1145/2934664

Zhang, Y., Callan, J., & Minka, T. (2002). Novelty and redundancy detection in adaptive filtering. In *Proceedings of the 25th annual international ACM SIGIR conference on Research and development in information retrieval* (pp. 81–88). Academic Press. 10.1145/564376.564393

ADDITIONAL READING

Angheluta, R., De Busser, R., & Moens, M.-F. (2002). The use of topic segmentation for automatic summarization. In *Proceedings of the ACL-2002 Workshop on Automatic Summarization*. Retrieved from https://www.law.kuleuven.be/icri/publications/51DUC2002.pdf

Das, D., & Martins, A. F. (2007). A survey on automatic text summarization. *Literature Survey for the Language and Statistics II course at CMU*.

Fattah, M. A., & Ren, F. (2009). GA, MR, FFNN, PNN and GMM based models for automatic text summarization. *Computer Speech & Language*, *23*(1), 126–144. doi:10.1016/j.csl.2008.04.002

Filippova, K., Surdeanu, M., Ciaramita, M., & Zaragoza, H. (2009). Company-oriented extractive summarization of financial news. In *Proceedings of the 12th Conference of the European Chapter of the Association for Computational Linguistics* (pp. 246–254). 10.3115/1609067.1609094

Huang, X., Wan, X., & Xiao, J. (2013). Comparative news summarization using concept-based optimization. *Knowledge and Information Systems*, 1–26.

Kumar, N., Srinathan, K., & Varma, V. (2012). Using graph based mapping of co-occurring words and closeness centrality score for summarization evaluation. *Computational Linguistics and Intelligent Text Processing*, 353–365.

Lerman, K., & McDonald, R. (2009). Contrastive summarization: an experiment with consumer reviews. In *Proceedings of Human Language Technologies: The 2009 Annual Conference of the North American Chapter of the Association for Computational Linguistics, Companion Volume: Short Papers* (pp. 113–116). 10.3115/1620853.1620886

Owczarzak, K., Conroy, J. M., Dang, H. T., & Nenkova, A. (2012). An Assessment of the Accuracy of Automatic Evaluation in Summarization. *NAACL-HLT*, *2012*, 1.

Pitler, E., Louis, A., & Nenkova, A. (2010). Automatic evaluation of linguistic quality in multi-document summarization. In *Proceedings of the 48th Annual Meeting of the Association for Computational Linguistics* (pp. 544–554). Retrieved from http://dl.acm.org/citation.cfm?id=1858737

Radev, D. R., Hovy, E., & McKeown, K. (2002). Introduction to the special issue on summarization. *Computational Linguistics*, *28*(4), 399–408. doi:10.1162/089120102762671927

Wang, D., Zhu, S., Li, T., & Gong, Y. (2013). Comparative Document Summarization via Discriminative Sentence Selection. *ACM Transactions on Knowledge Discovery from Data*, *7*(1), 2. doi:10.1145/2435209.2435211

KEY TERMS AND DEFINITIONS

Mobile Application: A software application which runs on a mobile platform (e.g., Android).

Multi-Document Summarization: The process of applying summarization to a set of documents to create one representative summary for the whole set.

Multilingual Summarization: The process of applying a summarization algorithm on texts of different languages (possibly not simultaneously).

N-Gram Graph: A text representation representing how n-grams co-occur within a given text.

N-Gram Graph Framework: The set of algorithms applicable on the n-gram graph representation, together with the representation itself, usable as an analysis method and toolkit.

Summary: A reductive transformation of a text, keeping as much information as possible.

Summary Evaluation: The process of evaluating a summary.

ENDNOTES

[1] See http://duc.nist.gov/ and http://www.nist.gov/tac/ for more information on DUC and TAC.

[2] See http://research.nii.ac.jp/ntcir/ for more information on NTCIR.

[3] See http://opennlp.apache.org/ for more information on the Apache OpenNLP library.

[4] Cf. https://github.com/ggianna/JInsect

[5] See http://glassfish.java.net/ for more information on the Glassfish server.

[6] See http://www.scify.gr/site/en/our-projects for more information on the NewSum project.

[7] See http://www.scify.org for more information on SciFY.

[8] See http://www.nomad-project.eu for more information on the NOMAD project.

[9] See e.g. http://multiling.iit.demokritos.gr/pages/view/1648/task-financial-narrative-summarization.

Compilation of References

Abbasi, A., France, S., Zhang, Z., & Chen, H. (2010). Selecting attributes for sentiment classification using feature relation networks. *IEEE Transactions on Knowledge and Data Engineering*, *23*(3), 447–462. doi:10.1109/TKDE.2010.110

Abstract. (1828). In *Merriam Webster*. Retrieved from http://www.merriam-webster.com/dictionary/abstract

Abstract. (1989). In *Oxford Dictionaries* Retrieved from http://www.oxforddictionaries.com/definition/english/abstract

Abstract. (1995). In *Cambridge Dictionary*. Retrieved from http://dictionary.cambridge.org/dictionary/english/abstract

Afantenos, S. D., Doura, I., Kapellou, E., & Karkaletsis, V. (2004). Exploiting Cross-Document Relations for Multi-Document Evolving Summarization. Lecture Notes in Artificial Intelligence (Subseries of Lecture Notes in Computer Science), 3025, 410–419.

Agrawal, R., Imieliński, T., & Swami, A. (1993). Mining association rules between sets of items in large databases. *SIGMOD Record*, *22*(2), 207–216. doi:10.1145/170036.170072

Ahmad, S., Taskaya-Temizel, T., & Ahmad, K. (2004). Summarizing time series: Learning patterns in 'volatile' series. In Z. R. Yang, H. Yin, & R. M. Everson (Eds.), *Intelligent Data Engineering and Automated Learning (IDEAL 2004)* (pp. 523–532). Berlin, Germany: Springer. doi:10.1007/978-3-540-28651-6_77

Akcaoglu, M., & Lee, E. (2016). Increasing social presence in online learning through small group discussions. *The International Review of Research in Open and Distributed Learning*, *17*(3), 1–17. doi:10.19173/irrodl.v17i3.2293

Aker, A., Celli, F., Funk, A., Kurtic, E., Hepple, M., & Gaizauskas, R. (2016). *Sheffield-Trento System for Sentiment and Argument Structure Enhanced Comment-to-Article Linking in the Online News Domain*. Academic Press.

Alaa El-Dine, A. H. F., & El-zahraa El-taher. (2012). Automatic Summarization of Arabic post. *The first International Conference for Faculty of Computers and Information*.

Al-Dhelaan, M. (2015). StarSum: A Simple Star Graph for Multi-document Summarization. In *Proceedings of the 38th International ACM SIGIR Conference on Research and Development in Information Retrieval.* ACM.

Alguliyev, R. M., Aliguliyev, R. M., Isazade, N. R., Abdi, A., & Idris, N. (2018). COSUM: Text summarization based on clustering and optimization. *Expert Systems: International Journal of Knowledge Engineering and Neural Networks.*

Aliguliyev, R. M. (2010). Clustering Techniques and Discrete Particle Swarm Optimization Algorithm for Multi-Document Summarization. *Computational Intelligence, 26*(4), 420–448. doi:10.1111/j.1467-8640.2010.00365.x

Allan, J., Wade, C., & Bolivar, A. (2003). Retrieval and novelty detection at the sentence level. In *Proceedings of the 26th annual international ACM SIGIR conference on Research and development in information retrieval* (pp. 314–321). ACM. 10.1145/860435.860493

Al-Saleh, A. B., & Menai, M. E. B. (2016). Automatic Arabic text summarization: A survey. *Artificial Intelligence Review, 45*(2), 203–234. doi:10.100710462-015-9442-x

Altınel, B., & Ganiz, M. C. (2018). Semantic text classification: A survey of past and recent advances. *Information Processing & Management, 54*(6), 1129–1153. doi:10.1016/j.ipm.2018.08.001

Alvarez, S. A. (2002). *An exact analytical relation among recall, precision, and classification accuracy in information retrieval.* Boston College. Technical Report BCCS-02-01.

Angheluta, R., De Busser, R., & Moens, M.-F. (2002). The use of topic segmentation for automatic summarization. In *Proceedings of the ACL-2002 Workshop on Automatic Summarization.* Retrieved from https://www.law.kuleuven.be/icri/publications/51DUC2002.pdf

Aries, A., Zegour, D. E., & Hidouci, K. W. (2015). AllSummarizer system at MultiLing 2015: Multilingual single and multi-document summarization. In *Proceedings of the 16th Annual Meeting of the Special Interest Group on Discourse and Dialogue* (pp. 237-244). Academic Press. 10.18653/v1/W15-4634

Asgari, H., Masoumi, B., & Sheijani, O. S. (2014, February). Automatic text summarization based on multi-agent particle swarm optimization. In *Intelligent Systems (ICIS), 2014 Iranian Conference on* (pp. 1-5). IEEE. 10.1109/IranianCIS.2014.6802592

Aslam, J. A., Ekstrand-Abueg, M., Pavlu, V., Diaz, F., & Sakai, T. (2013, November). TREC 2013 Temporal Summarization. TREC.

Auer, S., Scerri, S., Versteden, A., Pauwels, E., Charalambidis, A., Konstantopoulos, S., ... Ikonomopoulos, A. (2017, June). The BigDataEurope platform–supporting the variety dimension of big data. In *International Conference on Web Engineering* (pp. 41-59). Springer. 10.1007/978-3-319-60131-1_3

Automatic summarization. (2019, June 19). Retrieved from https://en.wikipedia.org/wiki/Automatic_summarization

Azmi, A., & Al-Thanyyan, S. (2009). *Ikhtasir—A user selected compression ratio Arabic text summarization system.* Paper presented at the Natural Language Processing and Knowledge Engineering, 2009. NLP-KE 2009. International Conference on.

Azmi, A. M., & Altmami, N. I. (2018). An abstractive Arabic text summarizer with user controlled granularity. *Information Processing & Management, 54*(6), 903–921. doi:10.1016/j.ipm.2018.06.002

Babar, S. (2013). *Text Summarization: An Overview.* Retrieved from https://www.researchgate.net/publication/257947528_Text_SummarizationAn_Overview

Bach, F. R., Lanckriet, G. R., & Jordan, M. I. (2004, July). Multiple kernel learning, conic duality, and the SMO algorithm. In *Proceedings of the twenty-first international conference on Machine learning* (p. 6). Banff, Canada: ACM. 10.1145/1015330.1015424

Bahdanau, D., Cho, K., & Bengio, Y. (2014). *Neural Machine Translation by Jointly Learning to Align and Translate.* CoRR, abs/1409.0473

Banarescu, L., Bonial, C., Cai, S., Georgescu, M., Griffitt, K., Hermjakob, U., . . . Schneider, N. (2013). *Abstract Meaning Representation for Sembanking.* Academic Press.

Banerjee, S., & Lavie, A. (2005). METEOR: An automatic metric for MT evaluation with improved correlation with human judgments. *Proceedings of the acl workshop on intrinsic and extrinsic evaluation measures for machine translation and/or summarization.*

Banerjee, S., Mitra, P., & Sugiyama, K. (2015). Generating abstractive summaries from meeting transcripts. *Proceedings of the 2015 ACM Symposium on Document Engineering.* 10.1145/2682571.2797061

Baralis, E., & Fiori, A. (2010). Summarizing biological literature with BioSumm. In *Proceedings of the 19th ACM international conference on Information and knowledge management* (pp. 1961–1962). Retrieved from http://dl.acm.org/citation.cfm?id=1871785

Baralis, E., & Cagliero, L. (2018). Highlighter: Automatic Highlighting of Electronic Learning Documents. *IEEE Transactions on Emerging Topics in Computing, 6*(1), 7–19. doi:10.1109/TETC.2017.2681655

Baralis, E., Cagliero, L., Fiori, A., & Garza, P. (2015). Mwi-sum: A multilingual summarizer based on frequent weighted itemsets. *ACM Transactions on Information Systems, 34*(1), 5. doi:10.1145/2809786

Baralis, E., Cagliero, L., Jabeen, S., & Fiori, A. (2012). *Multi-document summarization exploiting frequent itemsets.* SAC. doi:10.1145/2245276.2245427

Baralis, E., Cagliero, L., Jabeen, S., Fiori, A., & Shah, S. (2013). Multi-document summarization based on the Yago ontology. *Expert Systems with Applications, 40*(17), 6976–6984. doi:10.1016/j.eswa.2013.06.047

Baralis, E., Cagliero, L., Mahoto, N., & Fiori, A. (2013). GRAPHSUM: Discovering correlations among multiple terms for graph-based summarization. *Information Sciences*, *249*, 96–109. doi:10.1016/j.ins.2013.06.046

Barrios, F., López, F., Argerich, L., & Wachenchauzer, R. (2016). Variations of the similarity function of textrank for automated summarization. Academic Press.

Barzilay, R., & McKeown, K. R. (2005). Sentence Fusion for Multidocument News Summarization. *Computational Linguistics*, *31*(3), 297–327. doi:10.1162/089120105774321091

Bayes, T. (1763). LII. An essay towards solving a problem in the doctrine of chances. By the late Rev. Mr. Bayes, FRS communicated by Mr. Price, in a letter to John Canton, AMFR S. *Philosophical Transactions of the Royal Society of London*, (53): 370–418.

Bazghandi, M., Tabrizi, G. T., Jahan, M. V., & Mashahd, I. (2012). Extractive Summarization Of Farsi Documents Based On PSO Clustering. *jiA, 1*, 1.]

Belal, M., Gaber, J., El-Sayed, H., & Almojel, A. (2006). Swarm Intelligence. In Handbook of Bioinspired Algorithms and Applications. Chapman & Hall.

Bengfort, B. (2013, April 17). *An Introduction to Named Entity Recognition in Natural Language Processing - Part 1*. Retrieved from http://www.datacommunitydc.org/blog/2013/04/a-survey-of-stochastic-and-gazetteer-based-approaches-for-named-entity-recognition

Bengio, Y., Ducharme, R., Vincent, P., & Janvin, C. (2003). A neural probabilistic language model. *Journal of Machine Learning Research*, *3*, 1137–1155.

Beni, G., & Wang, J. (1993). Swarm intelligence in cellular robotic systems. In *Robots and Biological Systems: Towards a New Bionics?* (pp. 703–712). Springer Berlin Heidelberg. doi:10.1007/978-3-642-58069-7_38

Bhandari, N., Chowdri, R., Singh, H., & Qureshi, S. R. (2017). Resolving Ambiguities in Named Entity Recognition Using Machine Learning. *Next Generation Computing and Information Systems (ICNGCIS) 2017 International Conference on*, 159-163.

Binwahlan, M. S., Salim, N., & Suanmali, L. (2009d). *Fuzzy Swarm Based Text Summarization 1.*] Academic Press.

Binwahlan, M. S. N., & Suanmali, L. (2009a). Swarm based features selection for text summarization. *International Journal of Computer Science and Network Security IJCSNS.*, *9*(1), 175–179.

Binwahlan, M. S. N., & Suanmali, L. (2009c). Swarm Diversity Based Text Summarization. In *Neural Information Processing* (pp. 216–225). Springer. doi:10.1007/978-3-642-10684-2_24

Binwahlan, M. S., Salim, N., & Suanmali, L. (2009). Swarm Based Text Summarization. *Proceedings of the 2009 International Association of Computer Science and Information Technology-Spring Conference*. 10.1109/IACSIT-SC.2009.61

Blair, D. C. (1990). *Language and Representation in Information Retrieval.* New York: Elsevier North-Holland, Inc.

Blake, R. (2015). *A Test Cell for Mission-Critical Aerospace Gearbox Testing.* Retrieved from https://www.gsystems.com/case-study-bell-helicopter

Blei, D. M., Ng, A. Y., & Jordan, M. I. (2003). Latent dirichlet allocation. *Journal of Machine Learning Research, 3*(Jan), 993–1022.

Boudin, F., Huet, S., & Torres-Moreno, J. M. (2011). A graph-based approach to cross-language multi-document summarization. *Polibits, 43,* 113–118. doi:10.17562/PB-43-16

Brin, S., & Page, L. (1998). The anatomy of a large-scale hypertextual Web search engine. *Computer networks and ISDN systems, 30*(1-7), 107–117.

Brin, S., & Page, L. (1998). The Anatomy of a Large-Scale Hypertextual Web Search Engine. Computer Networks and ISDN Systems.

Brin, S., & Page, L. (1998) The Anatomy of a Large-Scale Hypertextual Web Search Engine. In *Seventh International World-Wide Web Conference (WWW 1998),* Brisbane, Australia. 10.1016/S0169-7552(98)00110-X

Buyukkokten, O., Garcia-Molina, H., & Paepcke, A. (2001). Seeing the whole in parts: Text summarization for Web browsing on handheld devices. In: *Proceedings of the 10th International Conference on World Wide Web (WWW 2001).* New York, NY: ACM. 10.1145/371920.372178

Cabrera-Diego, L. A., Torres-Moreno, J. M., & Durette, B. (2016, June). Evaluating Multiple Summaries without Human Models: A First Experiment with a Trivergent Model. In *International Conference on Applications of Natural Language to Information Systems* (pp. 91-101). Springer International Publishing. 10.1007/978-3-319-41754-7_8

Cagliero, L., Farinetti, L., & Baralis, E. (2019). Recommending Personalized Summaries of Teaching Materials. *IEEE Access: Practical Innovations, Open Solutions, 7,* 22729–22739. doi:10.1109/ACCESS.2019.2899655

Cagliero, L., Garza, P., & Baralis, E. (2019). ELSA: A Multilingual Document Summarization Algorithm Based on Frequent Itemsets and Latent Semantic Analysis. *ACM Transactions on Information Systems, 37*(2), 21. doi:10.1145/3298987

Cai, X., & Li, W. (2012). Mutually Reinforced Manifold-Ranking Based Relevance Propagation Model for Query-Focused Multi-Document Summarization. *IEEE Transactions on Audio, Speech, and Language Processing, 20*(5), 1597–1607. doi:10.1109/TASL.2012.2186291

Cambria, E. (2016). Affective computing and sentiment analysis. *IEEE Intelligent Systems, 31*(2), 102–107. doi:10.1109/MIS.2016.31

Cambria, E., & White, B. (2014). Jumping nlp curves: *A review of natural language processing research review article. Comput Intell Mag I EEE, 9*(2), 48–57. doi:10.1109/MCI.2014.2307227

Carbonell, J., & Goldstein, J. (1998, August). The use of MMR, diversity-based reranking for reordering documents and producing summaries. In *Proceedings of the 21st annual international ACM SIGIR conference on Research and development in information retrieval* (pp. 335-336). ACM. 10.1145/290941.291025

Chakraborti, S., & Dey, S. (2015, October). Product news summarization for competitor intelligence using topic identification and artificial bee colony optimization. In *Proceedings of the 2015 Conference on research in adaptive and convergent systems* (pp. 1-6). ACM. 10.1145/2811411.2811465

Chali, Y., & Hasan, S. A. (2012). Query focused multi-document summarization: Automatic data annotations and supervised learning approaches. *Natural Language Engineering*, *18*(1), 109–145. doi:10.1017/S1351324911000167

Chang, C.-T., Huang, C.-C., & Hsu, J. Y.-j. (2018). *A Hybrid Word-Character Model for Abstractive Summarization*. CoRR, abs/1802.09968

Chen, Q., Zhu, X., Ling, Z., Wei, S., & Jiang, H. (2016). Distraction-based neural networks for modeling documents. *Proceedings of the Twenty-Fifth International Joint Conference on Artificial Intelligence*.

Chen, X. W., & Lin, X. T. (2014). Big data deep learning: Challenges and perspectives. *IEEE Access: Practical Innovations, Open Solutions*, *2*, 514–525. doi:10.1109/ACCESS.2014.2325029

Cho, K., van Merrienboer, B., Gulcehre, C., Bahdanau, D., Bougares, F., Schwenk, H., & Bengio, Y. (2014). Learning Phrase Representations using RNN Encoder–Decoder for Statistical Machine Translation. In *Proceedings of the 2014 Conference on Empirical Methods in Natural Language Processing (EMNLP)* (pp. 1724-1734). Doha, Qatar: Association for Computational Linguistics. 10.3115/v1/D14-1179

Chomsky, N. (1986). *Knowledge of Language: Its Nature, Origin and Use*. Westport, CT: Praeger.

Chopra, S., Auli, M., & Rush, A. M. (2016). Abstractive sentence summarization with attentive recurrent neural networks. *Proceedings of NAACL-HLT*. 10.18653/v1/N16-1012

Christensen, J. M. (2015). *Towards large scale summarization* (Doctoral dissertation). University of Washington.

Christensen, J., Mausam, S. S., & Etzioni, O. (2013). Towards Coherent Multi-Document Summarization. In *Proceedings of NAACL-HLT* (pp. 1163–1173). Retrieved from http://www.aclweb.org/anthology/N/N13/N13-1136.pdf

Cleland-Huang, J., Czauderna, A., Gibiec, M., & Emenecker, J. (2010). A machine learning approach for tracing regulatory codes to product specific requirements. In: *Proceedings of the 32Nd ACM/IEEE International Conference on Software Engineering*. ACM. 10.1145/1806799.1806825

Cohn, T., & Lapata, M. (2008). Sentence compression beyond word deletion. *Proceedings of the 22nd International Conference on Computational Linguistics*.

Colmenares, C. A., Litvak, M., Mantrach, A., & Silvestri, F. (2015). HEADS: Headline generation as sequence prediction using an abstract feature-rich space. In: *Proceedings of the 2015 Conference of the North American Chapter of the Association for Computational Linguistics: Human Language Technologies (NAACL-HLT 2015).* Association for Computational Linguistics. 10.3115/v1/N15-1014

Colorni, A., Dorigo, M., & Maniezzo, V. (1992, September). An Investigation of some Properties of an Ant Algorithm. In PPSN (Vol. 92, pp. 509-520). Academic Press.

Complete guide to build your own Named Entity Recognizer with Python. (2018, April 29). Retrieved from https://nlpforhackers.io/named-entity-extraction/

Conneau, A., Schwenk, H., Barrault, L., & Lecun, Y. (2017). Very deep convolutional networks for text classification. In *Proceedings of the 15th Conference of the European Chapter of the Association for Computational Linguistics* (pp. 1107-1116). Valencia, Spain. Association for Computational Linguistics. 10.18653/v1/E17-1104

Conrad, J. G., Leidner, J. L., Schilder, F., & Kondadadi, R. (2009). Query-based opinion summarization for legal blog entries. In *The 12th International Conference on Artificial Intelligence and Law, Proceedings of the Conference.* ACM. 10.1145/1568234.1568253

Conroy, J. M., & Dang, H. T. (2008). Mind the Gap: Dangers of Divorcing Evaluations of Summary Content from Linguistic Quality. In *Proceedings of the 22nd International Conference on Computational Linguistics (Coling 2008)* (pp. 145–152). Manchester, UK: Coling 2008 Organizing Committee. Retrieved from http://www.aclweb.org/anthology/C08-1019

Conroy, J. M., Schlesinger, J. D., Goldstein, J., & O'leary, D. P. (2004). Left-brain/right-brain multi-document summarization. *Proceedings of the Document Understanding Conference.*

Conroy, J. M., Schlesinger, J. D., & O'Leary, D. P. (2006). *Topic-Focused Multi-Document Summarization Using an Approximate Oracle Score.* ACL. doi:10.3115/1273073.1273093

Conroy, J. M., Schlesinger, J. D., & O'Leary, D. P. (2007). CLASSY 2007 at DUC 2007. *Proceedings of Document Understanding Conference (DUC) Workshop 2006.*

Conroy, J. M., Schlesinger, J. D., & O'Leary, D. P. (2009). CLASSY 2009: Summarization and Metrics. *Proceedings of the Text Analysis Conference (TAC) 2009.*

Conroy, J. M., Schlesinger, J. D., & Stewart, J. G. (2005). CLASSY Query-Based Multi-Document Summarization. *Proceedings of the Document Understanding Conf. Wksp. 2005 (DUC 2005) at the Human Language Technology Conf./Conf. on Empirical Methods in Natural Language Processing (HLT/EMNLP 2005).*

Constantino, M. (1997). *Financial information extraction using pre-defined and user-definable templates in the Lolita system* (Ph.D. thesis). Durham University, Durham, UK.

Dang, H. T. (2005, October). Overview of DUC 2005. In *Proceedings of the document understanding conference (Vol. 2005,* pp. 1-12). Academic Press.

Dang, H. T., & Owczarzak, K. (2008). Overview of the TAC 2008 Update Summarization Task. In *TAC 2008 Workshop - Notebook papers and results* (pp. 10–23). Retrieved from http://www.nist.gov/tac

Dang, H. T., & Owczarzak, K. (2009, November 16). *Overview of the TAC 2009 Summarization Track*. Presented at the TAC 2009, NIST. Retrieved from http://www.nist.gov/tac/publications/2009/presentations/TAC2009_Summ_overview.pdf

Dang, H. T. (2005). Overview of DUC 2005. *Proceedings of the Document Understanding Conf. Wksp. 2005 (DUC 2005) at the Human Language Technology Conf./Conf. on Empirical Methods in Natural Language Processing (HLT/EMNLP 2005)*.

Dang, H. T. (2006). Overview of DUC 2006. *Proceedings of HLT-NAACL 2006*.

Das, D., & Martins, A. F. (2007). A survey on automatic text summarization. *Literature Survey for the Language and Statistics II course at CMU, 4*, 192-195.

Das, S. R. (2014). Text and Context: Language Analytics in Finance. Boston, MA: Now.

Das, I., & Dennis, J. E. (1998). Normal-boundary intersection: A new method for generating the Pareto surface in nonlinear multicriteria optimization problems. *SIAM Journal on Optimization, 8*(3), 631–657. doi:10.1137/S1052623496307510

De Lara, E., Wallach, D. S., & Zwaenepoel, W. (2001). Puppeteer: Component-based adaptation for mobile Computing. In *USENIX Symposium on Internet Technologies and Systems* (pp. 159 - 170). San Francisco, CA: USENIX Association.

Deerwester, S., Dumais, S. T., Furnas, G. W., Landauer, T. K., & Harshman, R. (1990). Indexing by latent semantic analysis. *Journal of the American Society for Information Science, 41*(6), 391–407. doi:10.1002/(SICI)1097-4571(199009)41:6<391::AID-ASI1>3.0.CO;2-9

Demir, S., Carberry, S., & McCoy, K. F. (2010). A discourse-aware graph-based content-selection framework. *Proceedings of the 6th International Natural Language Generation Conference*.

Deshpande, M. (2018). *Classification with Support Vector Machines*. Retrieved from https://pythonmachinelearning.pro/classification-with-support-vector-machines/

DistrictDataLabs. (2017, December 27). *Named Entity Recognition and Classification for Entity Extraction*. Retrieved from https://medium.com/district-data-labs/named-entity-recognition-and-classification-for-entity-extraction-6f23342aa7c5

Doddington, G., Mitchell, A., Przybocki, M., Ramshaw, L., Strassel, S., & Weischedel, R. (2004). The Automatic Content Extraction (ACE) program-tasks, data, and evaluation. *Proceedings of LREC. 2*.

Dongen, S. (2000). Performance criteria for graph clustering and Markov cluster experiments. Amsterdam, The Netherlands: CWI (Centre for Mathematics and Computer Science).

Donis-Díaz, C. A., Rafael, B., & Janusz, K. (2014). Using ant colony optimisation and genetic algorithms for the linguistic summarization of creep data. In Intelligent Systems. Springer International Publishing.

Dorigo, M., Maniezzo, V., & Colorni, A. (1991). *The ant system: An autocatalytic optimizing process.* Academic Press.

Dragoni, M. (2015, April). Exploiting multilinguality for creating mappings between thesauri. In *Proceedings of the 30th Annual ACM Symposium on Applied Computing* (pp. 382-387). ACM. 10.1145/2695664.2695768

Duda, R. O., Hart, P. E., & Stork, D. G. (2012). *Pattern classification.* John Wiley & Sons.

Eberhart, R., & Kennedy, J. (1995, October). A new optimizer using particle swarm theory. In Micro Machine and Human Science. In *Proceedings of the Sixth International Symposium on* (pp. 39-43). IEEE.

Edmundson, H. P. (1969). New methods in automatic extracting. *Journal of the Association for Computing Machinery, 16*(2), 264–285. doi:10.1145/321510.321519

Eiji, A., Miura, Y. T. M., Tomoko, O., Hiroshi, M., & Kazuhiko, O. (2009). TEXT2TABLE: Medical Text Summarization System Based on Named Entity Recognition and Modality Identification. *Proceedings of the BioNLP 2009 Workshop, 2009, Association for Computational Linguistics,* 185-192.

El-Fishawy, N., Hamouda, A., Attiya, G. M., & Atef, M. (2014). Arabic summarization in twitter social network. *Ain Shams Engineering Journal, 5*(2), 411–420. doi:10.1016/j.asej.2013.11.002

Elhadad, M., Miranda-Jiménez, S., Steinberger, J., & Giannakopoulos, G. (2013). Multi-document multilingual summarization corpus preparation, part 2: Czech, hebrew and spanish. In *Proceedings of the MultiLing 2013 Workshop on Multilingual Multi-document Summarization* (pp. 13-19). Academic Press.

El-Haj, M., Kruschwitz, U., & Fox, C. (2011, December). Exploring clustering for multi-document Arabic summarisation. In *Asia Information Retrieval Symposium* (pp. 550-561). Springer Berlin Heidelberg.

El-Haj, M., Kruschwitz, U., & Fox, C. *Using Mechanical Turk to Create a Corpus of Arabic Summaries.* Paper presented at the Editors & Workshop Chairs.

Ellouze, S., Jaoua, M., & Belguith, L. H. (2017, April). Machine learning approach to evaluate multilingual summaries. In *Proceedings of the MultiLing 2017 workshop on summarization and summary evaluation across source types and genres* (pp. 47-54). Academic Press. 10.18653/v1/W17-1007

Elmagarmid, A., Ipeirotis, P. G., & Verykios, V. (2006). Duplicate Record Detection: A Survey. *SSRN eLibrary.* Retrieved from http://papers.ssrn.com/sol3/papers.cfm?abstract_id=1281334

Embar, V. R., Deshpande, S. R., Vaishnavi, A., Jain, V., & Kallimani, J. S. (2013). *sArAmsha-A Kannada abstractive summarizer.* Paper presented at the Advances in Computing, Communications and Informatics (ICACCI), 2013 International Conference on.

Entity extraction: How does it work? (2016, July 7). Retrieved from https://www.expertsystem. com/entity-extraction-work/

Erkan, G., & Radev, D. R. (2004). Lexpagerank: Prestige in Multi-Document Text Summarization. In *Proceedings of EMNLP* (pp. 365–371). Academic Press.

Erkan, G., & Radev, D. R. (2004). Lexrank: Graph-based lexical centrality as salience in text summarization. *Journal of Artificial Intelligence Research, 22*, 457–479. doi:10.1613/jair.1523

Erol, B., Lee, D. S., Hull, J., Center, R. C., & Menlo Park, C. A. (2003). Multimodal summarization of meeting recordings. In *Multimedia and Expo, 2003. ICME'03. Proceedings. 2003 International Conference on* (Vol. 3). Academic Press.

Ertugrul, N. (2000). Towards virtual laboratories: A survey of LabVIEW-based teaching/learning tools and future trends. *International Journal of Engineering Education, 16*(3), 171–180.

Ertugrul, N. (2002). *LabVIEW for electric circuits, machines, drives, and laboratories.* Prentice Hall PTR.

Evans, D. K., Klavans, J. L., & McKeown, K. (2004). *Columbia Newsblaster: Multilingual News Summarization on the Web.* HLT-NAACL. doi:10.3115/1614025.1614026

Falcon, J. (2017). Facilitating Modeling and Simulation of Complex Systems through Interoperable Software. In *International Conference on Model Driven Engineering Languages and Systems.* Austin, TX: ACM.

Fang, C., Mu, D., Deng, Z., & Wu, Z. (2017). Word-sentence co-ranking for automatic extractive text summarization. *Expert Systems with Applications, 72*, 189–195. doi:10.1016/j.eswa.2016.12.021

Farzindar, A., & Lapalme, G. (2003). Using Background Information for Multi-Document Summarization and Summaries in Response to a Question. *Proceedings of DUC03: NAACL 2003 Workshop in Automatic Text Summarization.*

Fattah, M. A., & Ren, F. (2009). GA, MR, FFNN, PNN and GMM based models for automatic text summarization. *Computer Speech & Language, 23*(1), 126–144. doi:10.1016/j.csl.2008.04.002

Filatova, E., & Hatzivassiloglou, V. (2004). A formal model for information selection in multi-sentence text extraction. *Proceedings of the 20th international conference on Computational Linguistics*, 397. 10.3115/1220355.1220412

Filippova, K., Alfonseca, E., Colmenares, C. A., Kaiser, L., & Vinyals, O. (2015). Sentence compression by deletion with LSTMs. In *Proceedings of the 2015 Conference on Empirical Methods in Natural Language Processing (EMNLP 2015).* Association for Computational Linguistics. 10.18653/v1/D15-1042

Filippova, K., Surdeanu, M., Ciaramita, M., & Zaragoza, H. (2009). Company-oriented extractive summarization of financial news. In *Proceedings of the 12th Conference of the European Chapter of the ACL (EACL 2009)*. Association for Computational Linguistics.

Flores, J. G., Gillard, L., Ferret, O., & de Chandelar, G. (2008). Bag of senses versus bag of words: comparing semantic and lexical approaches on sentence extraction. In *TAC 2008 Workshop - Notebook papers and results* (pp. 158–167). Retrieved from http://www.nist.gov/tac

Fowler, D. S. (2018, Feb 20). *How Many Websites Are There In The World?* Retrieved from https://tekeye.uk/computing/how-many-websites-are-there

Franco-Salvador, M., Rosso, P., & Montes-y-Gómez, M. (2016). A systematic study of knowledge graph analysis for cross-language plagiarism detection. *Information Processing & Management*, *52*(4), 550–570. doi:10.1016/j.ipm.2015.12.004

Fu, B., Brennan, R., & O'sullivan, D. (2010). Cross-Lingual Ontology Mapping and Its Use on the Multilingual Semantic Web. *MSW*, *571*, 13–20.

Galgani, F., Compton, P., & Hoffmann, A. (2012). Combining different summarization techniques for legal text. In *Proceedings of the Workshop on Innovative Hybrid Approaches to the Processing of Textual Data*. Association for Computational Linguistics.

Gambhir, M., & Gupta, V. (2016). Recent automatic text summarization techniques: A survey. *Artificial Intelligence Review*, 1–66.

Ganesan, K., Zhai, C., & Han, J. (2010). Opinosis: a graph-based approach to abstractive summarization of highly redundant opinions. *Proceedings of the 23rd international conference on computational linguistics*.

Gao, S., Chen, X., Li, P., Ren, Z., Bing, L., Zhao, D., & Yan, R. (2018). *Abstractive Text Summarization by Incorporating Reader Comments*. arXiv preprint arXiv:1812.05407.

Genest, P. E., Lapalme, G., Yousfi-Monod, M., & Montréal, Q. (2009). HEXTAC: the Creation of a Manual Extractive Run. TAC2009 Notebook, Gaithersburg, MD.

Gerani, S., Carenini, G., & Ng, R. T. (2019). Modeling content and structure for abstractive review summarization. *Computer Speech & Language*, *53*, 302–331. doi:10.1016/j.csl.2016.06.005

Giannakopoulos, G. (2009). *Automatic Summarization from Multiple Documents*. University of the Aegean. Retrieved from http://www.iit.demokritos.gr/~ggianna/thesis.pdf

Giannakopoulos, G. (2010). *JInsect: The n-gram graph framework implementation*. Retrieved from http://sourceforge.net/projects/jinsect/

Giannakopoulos, G., & Karkaletsis, V. (2009). N-gram graphs: Representing documents and document sets in summary system evaluation. In *Proceedings of Text Analysis Conference TAC2009*. Presented at the Text Analysis Conference (TAC2009).

Giannakopoulos, G., & Karkaletsis, V. (2011). AutoSummENG and MeMoG in Evaluating Guided Summaries. In *TAC 2011 Workshop*. Presented at the TAC 2011, Gaithersburg, MD.

Giannakopoulos, G., & Karkaletsis, V. (2013). *Together we stand NPowER-ed*. Presented at the CICLing 2013, Karlovasi, Samos, Greece.

Giannakopoulos, G., & Palpanas, T. (2009). Adaptivity in Entity Subscription Services. In *Proceedings of ADAPTIVE2009*. Presented at the ADAPTIVE2009, Athens, Greece.

Giannakopoulos, G., El-Haj, M., Favre, B., Litvak, M., Steinberger, J., & Varma, V. (2011). *TAC 2011 MultiLing pilot overview*. Academic Press.

Giannakopoulos, G., El-Haj, M., Favre, B., Litvak, M., Steinberger, J., & Varma, V. (2011). TAC2011 MultiLing Pilot Overview. In *TAC 2011 Workshop*. Presented at the TAC 2011, Gaithersburg, MD.

Giannakopoulos, G., Vouros, G., & Karkaletsis, V. (2010). MUDOS-NG: Multi-document Summaries Using N-gram Graphs (Tech Report). *1012.2042*. Retrieved from http://arxiv.org/abs/1012.2042

Giannakopoulos, G., Karkaletsis, V., Vouros, G., & Stamatopoulos, P. (2008). Summarization system evaluation revisited: N-gram graphs. *ACM Trans. Speech Lang. Process.*, *5*(3), 1–39. doi:10.1145/1410358.1410359

Gillick, D., Favre, B., & Hakkani-Tür, D. Z. (2008). *The ICSI Summarization System at TAC 2008*. TAC.

Girshick, R. (2015). Fast r-cnn. In *Proceedings of the IEEE international conference on computer vision* (pp. 1440-1448). San Diego, CA: IEEE.

Goldberg, Y. (2017). Neural Network Methods for Natural Language Processing. In *Synthesis Lectures on Human Language Technologies* **10**. San Francisco: Morgan Claypool. doi:10.2200/S00762ED1V01Y201703HLT037

Goldstein, J., Mittal, V., Carbonell, J., & Kantrowitz, M. (2000). Multi-Document Summarization By Sentence Extraction. *Proceedings of the ANLP/NAACL Workshop on Automatic Summarization*, 40-48.

Gong, Y., & Liu, X. (2001). *Generic Text Summarization Using Relevance Measure and Latent Semantic Analysis*. SIGIR. doi:10.1145/383952.383955

Goutte, C., & Gaussier, E. (2005). A Probabilistic Interpretation of Precision, Recall and *F*-Score, with Implication for Evaluation. In D. E. Losada & J. M. Fernández-Luna (Eds.), Lecture Notes in Computer Science: Vol. 3408. *Advances in Information Retrieval. ECIR 2005*. Berlin: Springer. doi:10.1007/978-3-540-31865-1_25

Graff, D., Kong, J., Chen, K., & Maeda, K. (2003). English gigaword. Linguistic Data Consortium, 4(1), 34.

Graves, A., Mohamed, A. R., & Hinton, G. (2013, May). Speech recognition with deep recurrent neural networks. In *2013 IEEE international conference on acoustics, speech and signal processing* (pp. 6645-6649). Vancouver, Canada: IEEE.

Greenbacker, C. F. (2011). Towards a framework for abstractive summarization of multimodal documents. *Proceedings of the ACL 2011 Student Session.*

Grishman, R., & Sundheim, B. (1996, August). Message Understanding Conference-6: A Brief History. In COLING (Vol. 96, pp. 466-471). Academic Press.

Grusky, M., Naaman, M., & Artzi, Y. (2018). Newsroom: A Dataset of 1.3 Million Summaries with Diverse Extractive Strategies. In *Proceedings of the 2018 Conference of the North American Chapter of the Association for Computational Linguistics: Human Language Technologies.* Association for Computational Linguistics. 10.18653/v1/N18-1065

Gupta, S., & Gupta, S. K. (2018). Abstractive Summarization: An Overview of the State of the Art. *Expert Systems with Applications, 121,* 49–65. doi:10.1016/j.eswa.2018.12.011

Güran, A., Güler Bayazit, N., & Gürbüz, M. Z. (2013). Efficient feature integration with Wikipedia-based semantic feature extraction for Turkish text summarization. *Turkish Journal of Electrical Engineering and Computer Sciences, 21*(5), 1411–1425. doi:10.3906/elk-1201-15

Gutjahr, W. J. (2000). A graph-based ant system and its convergence. *Future Generation Computer Systems, 16*(8), 873–888. doi:10.1016/S0167-739X(00)00044-3

Hachey & Grover. (2005a). *Automatic legal text summarisation: Experiments with summary structuring.* Academic Press.

Hachey, B., & Grover, C. (2005b). Sentence extraction for legal text summarisation. *Proceedings of the Nineteenth International Joint Conference on Artificial Intelligence (IJCAI 2005),* 1686-1687.

Hachey, B., & Grover, C. (2006). Extractive summarisation of legal texts. *Artificial Intelligence and Law, 14*(4), 305–345. doi:10.100710506-007-9039-z

Haghighi, A., & Vanderwende, L. (2009, May). Exploring content models for multi-document summarization. In *Proceedings of Human Language Technologies: The 2009 Annual Conference of the North American Chapter of the Association for Computational Linguistics* (pp. 362-370). Association for Computational Linguistics. 10.3115/1620754.1620807

Hahn, U., & Mani, I. (2000). The Challenges of Automatic Summarization. *Computer, 33*(11), 29–36. doi:10.1109/2.881692

Harabagiu, S., & Lacatusu, F. (2005, August). Topic themes for multi-document summarization. In *Proceedings of the 28th annual international ACM SIGIR conference on Research and development in information retrieval* (pp. 202-209). ACM.

Harrag, F., Hamdi-Cherif, A., & Salman Al-Salman, A. (2010). Comparative study of topic segmentation algorithms based on lexical cohesion: Experimental results on Arabic language. *Arabian Journal for Science and Engineering, 35*(2), 183.

Hartigan, J. A., & Wong, M. A. (1979). Algorithm AS 136: A k-means clustering algorithm. *Journal of the Royal Statistical Society. Series C, Applied Statistics, 28*(1), 100–108.

Hassan. O. F. (2015). *Text summarization using ant colony optimization algorithm* (Doctoral dissertation). Sudan University of Science and Technology.]

Hassan, A., & Mahmood, A. (2018). Convolutional recurrent deep learning model for sentence classification. *IEEE Access: Practical Innovations, Open Solutions, 6*, 13949–13957. doi:10.1109/ACCESS.2018.2814818

Hassel, M. (2003). Exploitation of Named Entities in Automatic Text Summarization for Swedish. *Proceedings of NODALIDA'03 – 14th Nordic Conferenceon Computational Linguistics.*

Hassel, M. (2004). Evaluation of Automatic Text Summarization, A practical implementation. *Licentiate Thesis Stockholm,* 59-67.

Hendrickx, I., & Bosma, W. (2008). Using correference links and sentence compression in graph-based summarization. In *TAC 2008 Workshop - Notebook papers and results* (pp. 429–435). Retrieved from http://www.nist.gov/tac

Hochreiter, S., & Schmidhuber, J. (1997). Long short-term memory. *Neural Computation, 9*(8), 1735–1780. doi:10.1162/neco.1997.9.8.1735 PMID:9377276

Huang, X., Wan, X., & Xiao, J. (2013). Comparative news summarization using concept-based optimization. *Knowledge and Information Systems,* 1–26.

Ismail, S. S., Aref, M., & Moawad, I. (2013). *Rich semantic graph: A new semantic text representation approach for arabic language.* Paper presented at the 17th WSEAS European Computing Conference (ECC'13).

Ismail, S., Moawd, I., & Aref, M. (2013). Arabic text representation using rich semantic graph: A case study. *Proceedings of the 4th European conference of computer science (ECCS'13).*

Isonuma, M., Fujino, T., Mori, J., Matsuo, Y., & Sakata, I. (2017, September). Extractive summarization using multi-task learning with document classification. *Proceedings of the 2017 Conference on Empirical Methods in Natural Language Processing,* 2101-2110. 10.18653/v1/D17-1223

Jagadish, S. (2016, January). Statistical and analytical study of guided abstractive text summarization. *Research Communications. Current Science, 110*(1), 10.

Jatowt, A., & Ishizuka, M. (2006). Temporal multi-page summarization. *Web Intelligence and Agent Systems, 4*(2), 163–180.

Jean, S., Cho, K., Memisevic, R., & Bengio, Y. (2014). *On Using Very Large Target Vocabulary for Neural Machine Translation.* CoRR, abs/1412.2007

Jhalani & Meena. (2017). An Abstractive Approach For Text Summarization. *International Journal of Advanced Computational Engineering and Networking, 5*(1), 5-10.

Jhaveri, N., Gupta, M., & Varma, V. (2018). A Workbench for Rapid Generation of Cross-Lingual Summaries. *Proceedings of the Eleventh International Conference on Language Resources and Evaluation (LREC-2018).*

Jhaveri, N., Gupta, M., & Varma, V. (2019, January). clstk: The Cross-Lingual Summarization Tool-Kit. In *Proceedings of the Twelfth ACM International Conference on Web Search and Data Mining* (pp. 766-769). ACM. 10.1145/3289600.3290614

Jiang, R., & Banchs, E. (2016). Evaluating and Combining Name Entity Recognition Systems. Academic Press. doi:10.18653/v1/W16-2703

Joachims, T. (2006, August). Training linear SVMs in linear time. In *Proceedings of the 12th ACM international conference on Knowledge discovery and data mining* (pp. 217-226). Philadelphia, PA: ACM.

Johnson, S. C. (1967). Hierarchical clustering schemes. *Psychometrika, 32*(3), 241–254. doi:10.1007/BF02289588 PMID:5234703

Jones, K. S. (1999). Automatic summarizing: factors and directions. *Advances in Automatic Text Summarization*, 1-12.

Jones, S. (1999). Automatic Summarizing: Factors and Directions. In Advances in Automatic Text Summarization (pp. 1–12). Academic Press.

Jones, K. S. (2007). Automatic summarising: The state of the art. *Information Processing & Management, 43*(6), 1449–1481. doi:10.1016/j.ipm.2007.03.009

Jorczak, R. (2014). Differences in classroom versus online exam performance due to asynchronous discussion. *Online Learning Journal, 18*(2), 1–9.

Josef & Karel. (2009). Evaluation Measures For Text Summarization. Computing and Informatics, 28, 1001–1026.

Joulin, A., Grave, E., Bojanowski, P., & Mikolov, T. (2017). Bag of tricks for efficient text classification. In *Proceedings of the 15th Conference of the European Chapter of the Association for Computational Linguistics* (pp. 3-7), Valencia, Spain: ACM. 10.18653/v1/E17-2068

Kabadjov, M., Atkinson, M., Steinberger, J., Steinberger, R., & van der Goot, E. (2010). NewsGist: A Multilingual Statistical News Summarizer. In J. L. Balcázar, F. Bonchi, A. Gionis, & M. Sebag (Eds.), *Machine Learning and Knowledge Discovery in Databases* (pp. 591–594). Springer Berlin Heidelberg. doi:10.1007/978-3-642-15939-8_40

Kabeer, R., & Idicula, S. M. (2014). *Text summarization for Malayalam documents—An experience.* Paper presented at the Data Science & Engineering (ICDSE), 2014 International Conference on.

Kallimani, J. S., Srinivasa, K., & Eswara Reddy, B. (2011). *Information extraction by an abstractive text summarization for an Indian regional language.* Paper presented at the Natural Language Processing and Knowledge Engineering (NLP-KE), 2011 7th International Conference on. 10.1109/NLPKE.2011.6138217

Kamath & Wagh. (2017). Named Entity Recognition Approaches and Challenges. *International Journal of Advanced Research in Computer and Communication Engineering, 6*(2).

Karaboga, D. (2005). *An idea based on honey bee swarm for numerical optimization* (Vol. 200). Technical report-tr06, Erciyes University, Engineering Faculty, Computer Engineering Department.

Karypis, M. S. G., Kumar, V., & Steinbach, M. (2000, August). A comparison of document clustering techniques. In *TextMining Workshop at KDD 2000*. Boston, MA: ACM.

Kazantseva, A., & Szpakowicz, S. (2010). Summarizing Short Stories. *Computational Linguistics, 36*(1), 71–109. doi:10.1162/coli.2010.36.1.36102

Kennedy, J., & Eberhart, R. (1995). Synthetic structure of industrial plastics (Book style with paper title and editor). In *Proceeding of the 1995IEEE International Conference on Neural Networks* (pp. 1942-1948). IEEE. 10.1109/ICNN.1995.488968

Khabiri, E., Caverlee, J., & Hsu, C. F. (2011, July). Summarizing User-Contributed Comments. ICWSM.

Khan, A., Salim, N., & Kumar, Y. J. (2015). A framework for multi-document abstractive summarization based on semantic role labelling. *Applied Soft Computing, 30*, 737–747. doi:10.1016/j.asoc.2015.01.070

Khosrovian, K., Pfahl, D., & Garousi, V. (2008). GENSIM 2.0: a customizable process simulation model for software process evaluation. In *International Conference on Software Process* (pp. 294-306). Springer, Berlin, Heidelberg.

Kleinbauer, T., & Murray, G. (2012). Summarization. In A. Popescu-Belis, H. Bourlard, J. Carletta, & S. Renals (Eds.), *Multimodal Signal Processing: Human Interactions in Meetings* (pp. 170–192). Cambridge, UK: Cambridge University Press. doi:10.1017/CBO9781139136310.010

Kleinberg, J. M. (1999). Authoritative Sources in a Hyper-Linked Environment. Journal of the ACM, 604–632.

Kleinberg, J. M. (1999). Authoritative sources in a hyperlinked environment. *Journal of the Association for Computing Machinery, 46*(5), 604–632. doi:10.1145/324133.324140

Knight, K., & Marcu, D. (2000). Statistics-Based Summarization – Step One: Sentence Compression. In *Proceedings of the Seventeenth National Conference on Artificial Intelligence and Twelfth Conference on Innovative Applications of Artificial Intelligence*, (pp. 703-710). AAAI Press.

Kohavi, R. (1995, August). A study of cross-validation and bootstrap for accuracy estimation and model selection. *International Joint Conference on Artificial Intelligence (IJCAI), 14*(2), 1137-1145.

Kontopoulos, I., Giannakopoulos, G., & Varlamis, I. (2017, September). Distributing N-Gram Graphs for Classification. In *European Conference on Advances in Databases and Information Systems* (pp. 3-11). Springer.

Korabu, K., & Ingale, M. S. V. (2013). Semantic Summarization Of Web Documents. *International Journal of Computer Science & Communication Networks*, *3*(3), 173.

Kowsari, K., Brown, D. E., Heidarysafa, M., Meimandi, K. J., Gerber, M. S., & Barnes, L. E. (2017, December). Hdltex: Hierarchical deep learning for text classification. In *2017 16th IEEE International Conference on Machine Learning and Applications (ICMLA)* (pp. 364-371). Cancun, Mexico: IEEE.

Krejzl, P., Steinberger, J., Hercig, T., & Brychcín, T. (2016). *UWB Participation in the Multiling's OnForumS Task*. Academic Press.

Kripke, S. (1982). *Naming and Necessity*. Boston: Harvard University Press.

Kullback, S., & Leibler, R. A. (1951). On information and sufficiency. *Annals of Mathematical Statistics*, *22*(1), 79–86. doi:10.1214/aoms/1177729694

Kumar, C., Pingali, P., & Varma, V. (2009). Estimating Risk of Picking a Sentence for Document Summarization. In *Proceedings of the 10th International Conference on Computational Linguistics and Intelligent Text Processing* (pp. 571–581). Academic Press. 10.1007/978-3-642-00382-0_46

Kumar, S., Gao, X., Welch, I., & Mansoori, M. (2016, March). A machine learning based web spam filtering approach. In *2016 IEEE 30th International Conference on Advanced Information Networking and Applications (AINA)* (pp. 973-980). Crans-Montana, Switzerland: IEEE. 10.1109/AINA.2016.177

Kumar, N., Srinathan, K., & Varma, V. (2013). A knowledge induced graph-theoretical model for extract and abstract single document summarization. In *Computational Linguistics and Intelligent Text Processing* (pp. 408–423). Springer. doi:10.1007/978-3-642-37256-8_34

KumarP. (2013, November 22). *Document Summarization*. Retrieved from https://www.slideshare.net/pratikkumarshanu/document-summarization

Kunder, M. d. (2018, Dec 15). *The size of the World Wide Web (The Internet)*. Retrieved from https://www.worldwidewebsize.com

Kupiec, J., Pedersen, J., & Chen, F. (1995). A trainable document summarizer. In *Proceedings of the 18th Annual International ACM SIGIR Conference on Research and Development in Information Retrieval (SIGIR 1995)*. ACM.

Lai, S., Xu, L., Liu, K., & Zhao, J. (2015, February). Recurrent convolutional neural networks for text classification. In *Twenty-ninth AAAI conference on artificial intelligence* (pp. 2267-2273). Austin, TX. ACM.

Lakshman, A., & Malik, P. (2010). Cassandra: A decentralized structured storage system. *Operating Systems Review*, *44*(2), 35–40. doi:10.1145/1773912.1773922

Lam, W., & Ho, K. S. (2001). FIDS: An intelligent financial web news articles digest system. *IEEE Transactions on Systems, Man, and Cybernetics. Part A, Systems and Humans*, *31*(6), 753–762. doi:10.1109/3468.983433

Larkey, L. S., Allan, J., Connell, M. E., Bolivar, A., & Wade, C. (2003). UMass at TREC 2002: Cross Language and Novelty Tracks. In TREC 2002 Proceedings (pp. 721–732). National Institute of Standards & Technology.

Le, H. T., & Le, T. M. (2013). *An approach to abstractive text summarization.* Paper presented at the Soft Computing and Pattern Recognition (SoCPaR), 2013 International Conference of. 10.1109/SOCPAR.2013.7054161

LeCun, Y., Bottou, L., Bengio, Y., & Haffner, P. (1998). Gradient-based learning applied to document recognition. *Proceedings of the IEEE, 86*(11), 2278–2324. doi:10.1109/5.726791

Ledeneva, Y. (2008). Effect of Preprocessing on Extractive Summarization with Maximal Frequent Sequences. In Proceedings of MICAI 2008 (pp. 123–132). Academic Press. doi:10.1007/978-3-540-88636-5_11

Leidner, J. L. (2015). *Computer-supported risk identification.* Technical report. https://arxiv.org/abs/1510.08285 (cited 2019-07-17).

Leidner, J. L., & Nugent, T. (2018). Cognitive inhibitors for threat assessment and automated risk management. *Proceedings of the 53rd ESReDA Seminar: European Safety, Reliability & Data Association/European Commission, 285-291.*

Leidner, J. L., & Schilder, F. (2010). Hunting for the black swan: Risk mining from text. *Proceedings of the ACL: Demonstrations (ACL 2010).*

Leite, D. S., Rino, L. H. M., Pardo, T. A. S., & Nunes, M. das G. V. (2007). Extractive Automatic Summarization: Does more Linguistic Knowledge Make a Difference? In *Proceedings of the Second Workshop on TextGraphs: Graph-Based Algorithms for Natural Language Processing* (pp. 17–24). Rochester, NY: Association for Computational Linguistics. Retrieved from http://www.aclweb.org/anthology/W/W07/W07-0203

Li, Forascu, El-Haj, & Giannakopoulos. (2013). Multi-document multilingual summarization corpus preparation, Part 1: Arabic, English, Greek, Chinese, Romanian. *MultiLing 2013: Multilingual Multi-document Summarization Proceedings of the Workshop.*

Li, L., Mao, L., & Chen, M. (2017, April). Word Embedding and Topic Modeling Enhanced Multiple Features for Content Linking and Argument/Sentiment Labeling in Online Forums. In *Proceedings of the MultiLing 2017 Workshop on Summarization and Summary Evaluation Across Source Types and Genres* (pp. 32-36). Academic Press. 10.18653/v1/W17-1005

Li, S., & Li, S. (2018, August 17). *Named Entity Recognition with NLTK and SpaCy.* Retrieved from https://towardsdatascience.com/named-entity-recognition-with-nltk-and-spacy-8c4a7d88e7da

Li, B., & Han, L. (2013, October). Distance weighted cosine similarity measure for text classification. In *International Conference on Intelligent Data Engineering and Automated Learning* (pp. 611-618). Hefei, China: Springer. 10.1007/978-3-642-41278-3_74

Li, L., Forascu, C., El-Haj, M., & Giannakopoulos, G. (2013). *Multi-document multilingual summarization corpus preparation, part 1: Arabic, english, greek, chinese, romanian.* Association for Computational Linguistics.

Li, L., Wang, D., Shen, C., & Li, T. (2010). Ontology-enriched multi-document summarization in disaster management. *Proceeding of the 33rd international ACM SIGIR conference on Research and development in information retrieval,* 819-820.

Lilleberg, J., Zhu, Y., & Zhang, Y. (2015, July). Support vector machines and word2vec for text classification with semantic features. In *2015 IEEE 14th International Conference on Cognitive Informatics & Cognitive Computing (ICCI*CC)* (pp. 136-140). Beijing, China: IEEE. 10.1109/ICCI-CC.2015.7259377

Lin, C. Y. (2004, July). Rouge: A package for automatic evaluation of summaries. In *Text summarization branches out: Proceedings of the ACL-04 workshop* (*Vol. 8*). Academic Press.

Lin, C.-Y. (2004). ROUGE: A package for automatic evaluation of summaries. In M.-F. Moens & S. Szpakowicz (Eds.), *Text Summarization Branches Out: Proceedings of the ACL-04 Workshop.* Association for Computational Linguistics.

Lin, C.-Y. (2004). ROUGE: A Package for Automatic Evaluation of Summaries. *Text Summarization Branches Out: Proceedings of the ACL-04 Workshop.*

Lin, C.-Y., & Hovy, E. (2000). *The Automated Acquisition of Topic Signatures for Text Summarization.* Paper presented at the COLING 2000 Volume 1: The 18th International Conference on Computational Linguistics. 10.3115/990820.990892

Lin, H., & Bilmes, J. (2011, June). A class of submodular functions for document summarization. In *Proceedings of the 49th Annual Meeting of the Association for Computational Linguistics: Human Language Technologies-Volume 1* (pp. 510-520). Association for Computational Linguistics.

Lin, C. Y. (2004). *Rouge: A package for automatic evaluation of summaries.* Text Summarization Branches Out.

Lin, C. Y., & Hovy, E. (2001, August). Neats: A multidocument summarizer. *Proceedings of the Document Understanding Workshop.*

Lin, C., & Hovy, E. (2003). Automatic evaluation of summaries using N-gram co-occurrence statistics. *Proceedings of the Conference of the North American Chapter of the Association for Computational Linguistics on Human Language Technology, 1,* 71-78. 10.3115/1073445.1073465

Lin, C.-Y. (2004). ROUGE: A Package for Automatic Evaluation of summaries. *Proceedings of the ACL Workshop: Text Summarization Braches Out.*

Linhares Pontes, E., González-Gallardo, C., Torres-Moreno, J., & Huet, S. (2019). *Cross-lingual speech-to-text summarization.* doi:10.1007/978-3-319-98678-4_39

Li, P., Lam, W., Bing, L., & Wang, Z. (2017). Deep Recurrent Generative Decoder for Abstractive Text Summarization. *Proceedings of the 2017 Conference on Empirical Methods in Natural Language Processing*. 10.18653/v1/D17-1222

Litvak, M., & Last, M. (2013a). Multilingual single-document summarization with muse. In *Proceedings of the MultiLing 2013 Workshop on Multilingual Multi-document Summarization* (pp. 77-81). Academic Press.

Litvak, M., & Vanetik, N. (2013). Mining the gaps: Towards polynomial summarization. In *Proceedings of the Sixth International Joint Conference on Natural Language Processing* (pp. 655-660). Academic Press.

Litvak, M., & Vanetik, N. (2017, April). Query-based summarization using MDL principle. In *Proceedings of the multiling 2017 workshop on summarization and summary evaluation across source types and genres* (pp. 22-31). Academic Press. 10.18653/v1/W17-1004

Litvak, M., Last, M., & Friedman, M. (2010). A new approach to improving multilingual summarization using a genetic algorithm. In *Proceedings of the 48th Annual Meeting of the Association for Computational Linguistics* (pp. 927–936). Academic Press. Retrieved from http://dl.acm.org/citation.cfm?id=1858776

Litvak, M., & Last, M. (2013b). Cross-lingual training of summarization systems using annotated corpora in a foreign language. *Information Retrieval, 16*(5), 629–656. doi:10.100710791-012-9210-3

Litvak, M., Last, M., & Friedman, M. (2010). A new approach to improving multilingual summarization using a genetic algorithm. In *Proceedings of the 48th annual meeting of the association for computational linguistics* (pp. 927-936). Association for Computational Linguistics.

Litvak, M., Vanetik, N., Last, M., & Churkin, E. (2016). Museec: A multilingual text summarization tool. *Proceedings of ACL-2016 System Demonstrations*, 73-78. 10.18653/v1/P16-4013

Liu, F., Flanigan, J., Thomson, S., Sadeh, N., & Smith, N. A. (2015). *Toward abstractive summarization using semantic representations*. Academic Press.

Liu, C. Y., Chen, M. S., & Tseng, C. Y. (2015). Increst: Towards real-time incremental short text summarization on comment streams from social network services. *IEEE Transactions on Knowledge and Data Engineering, 27*(11), 2986–3000. doi:10.1109/TKDE.2015.2405553

Liu, F., & Liu, Y. (2009). From extractive to abstractive meeting summaries: Can it be done by sentence compression? *Proceedings of the ACL-IJCNLP 2009 Conference Short Papers*. 10.3115/1667583.1667664

Liu, L., Tang, L., Dong, W., Yao, S., & Zhou, W. (2016). An overview of topic modeling and its current applications in bioinformatics. *SpringerPlus, 5*(1), 1608. doi:10.118640064-016-3252-8 PMID:27652181

Lloret, E., Boldrini, E., Martinez-Barco, P., & Palomar, M. (2017, April). Ultra-Concise Multi-genre Summarisation of Web2. 0: towards Intelligent Content Generation. In *Proceedings of the MultiLing 2017 Workshop on Summarization and Summary Evaluation Across Source Types and Genres* (pp. 37-46). Academic Press. 10.18653/v1/W17-1006

Lloret, E., & Palomar, M. (2011). Analyzing the use of word graphs for abstractive text summarization. *Proceedings of the First International Conference on Advances in Information Mining and Management.*

Lloret, E., & Palomar, M. (2012). Text summarisation in progress: A literature review. *Artificial Intelligence Review, 37*(1), 1–41. doi:10.100710462-011-9216-z

Lloret, E., Plaza, L., & Aker, A. (2018). The challenging task of summary evaluation: An overview. *Language Resources and Evaluation, 52*(1), 101–148. doi:10.100710579-017-9399-2

Lloret, E., Romá-Ferri, M. T., & Palomar, M. (2013). COMPENDIUM: A text summarization system for generating abstracts of research papers. *Data & Knowledge Engineering, 88*, 164–175. doi:10.1016/j.datak.2013.08.005

Loper, E., & Bird, S. (2002). NLTK: The Natural Language Toolkit. In *Proceedings of the ACL Workshop on Effective Tools and Methodologies for Teaching Natural Language Processing and Computational Linguistics*. Philadelphia: Association for Computational Linguistics. 10.3115/1118108.1118117

Louis, A., & Nenkova, A. (2009, August). Automatically evaluating content selection in summarization without human models. In *Proceedings of the 2009 Conference on Empirical Methods in Natural Language Processing* (pp. 306-314). Association for Computational Linguistics. 10.3115/1699510.1699550

Luhn, H. P. (1957). A statistical approach to mechanized encoding and searching of literary information. *IBM Journal of Research and Development, 1*(4), 309–317. doi:10.1147/rd.14.0309

Luhn, H. P. (1958). The automatic creation of literature abstracts. *IBM Journal of Research and Development, 2*(2), 159–165. doi:10.1147/rd.22.0159

Majumder, N., Poria, S., Gelbukh, A., & Cambria, E. (2017). Deep learning-based document modeling for personality detection from text. *IEEE Intelligent Systems, 32*(2), 74–79. doi:10.1109/MIS.2017.23

Mampaey, M., Tatti, N., & Vreeken, J. (2011). Tell me what I need to know: succinctly summarizing data with itemsets. *Proceedings of the 17th ACM SIGKDD Conference on Knowledge Discovery and Data Mining.*

Mani, I., Bloedorn, E., & Gates, B. (1998). Using cohesion and coherence models for text summarization. In *Intelligent Text Summarization Symposium* (pp. 69–76). Academic Press.

Mani, I. (2001). *Automatic summarization* (Vol. 3). John Benjamins Publishing. doi:10.1075/nlp.3

Mani, I. M., & Bloedorn, E. M. (1999). Summarizing Similarities and Differences Among Related Documents. *Information Retrieval*, *1*(1), 35–67. doi:10.1023/A:1009930203452

Manning, C. D., Raghavan, P., & Schütze, H. (2008). Scoring, term weighting and the vector space model. *Introduction to Information Retrieval, 100*, 2-4.

Mann, W. C., & Thompson, S. A. (1987). *Rhetorical Structure Theory: A Theory of Text Organization*. University of Southern California, Information Sciences Institute.

Marcu, D. (1997). The rhetorical parsing of natural language texts. In *The Proceedings of the 35th Annual Meeting of the Association for Computational Linguistics (ACL/EACL)*. Association for Computational Linguistics.

MathWorks. (2019). *Simulink Introduction*. Retrieved from https://www.mathworks.com/products/simulink.html

Matsuo, Y., Ohsawa, Y., & Ishizuka, M. (2001). A Document as a Small World. In Proceedings the 5th World Multi-Conference on Systemics, Cybenetics and Infomatics (SCI2001) (Vol. 8, pp. 410–414). Academic Press. doi:10.1007/3-540-45548-5_60

Maybury, M. T., & Mani, I. (2001). Automatic summarization. In *European Conference on Computational Linguistics (EACL 2001)*. ACL. Tutorial Notes.

McCrae, J. P., Arcan, M., & Buitelaar, P. (2017). *Linking knowledge graphs across languages with semantic*. Academic Press.

McDonald, D. D. (2000). Issues in the representation of real texts: the design of KRISP. *Natural language processing and knowledge representation*, 77-110.

McDonald, D. D. (1992). An efficient chart-based algorithm for partial-parsing of unrestricted texts. *Proceedings of the third conference on Applied natural language processing*. 10.3115/974499.974534

McDonald, D. D., & Greenbacker, C. F. (2010). 'If you've heard it, you can say it': towards an account of expressibility. *Proceedings of the 6th International Natural Language Generation Conference*.

McKeown, K. R., Barzilay, R., Evans, D., Hatzivassiloglou, V., Klavans, J. L., Nenkova, A., ... Sigelman, S. (2002). Tracking and summarizing news on a daily basis with Columbia's Newsblaster. In *Proceedings of the Second International Conference on Human Language Technology Research (HLT 2002)*. Morgan Kaufmann. 10.3115/1289189.1289212

Mehdad, Y., Carenini, G., & Ng, R. T. (2014). Abstractive summarization of spoken and written conversations based on phrasal queries. *Proceedings of the 52nd Annual Meeting of the Association for Computational Linguistics*. 10.3115/v1/P14-1115

Mehdad, Y., Carenini, G., Ng, R. T., & Joty, S. (2013). Towards Topic Labeling with Phrase Entailment and Aggregation. *Proceedings of NAACL-HLT*.

Meijer, K., Frasincar, F., & Hogenboom, F. (2014). A semantic approach for extracting domain taxonomies from text. *Decision Support Systems, 62*, 78–93. doi:10.1016/j.dss.2014.03.006

Merkel, D. (2014). Docker: lightweight linux containers for consistent development and deployment. *Linux Journal, 2014*(239), 2.

Mihalcea, R. (2005). Multi-Document Summarization with Iterative Graph-Based Algorithms. *Proceedings of the First International Conference on Intelligent Analysis Methods and Tools (IA 2005).*

Mihalcea, R., & Tarau, P. (2004). TextRank: Bringing order into text. In *Proceedings of the 2004 Conference on Empirical Methods in Natural Language Processing (EMNLP 2004).* ACL.

Mihalcea, R., & Tarau, P. (2004). Textrank: Bringing order into text. *Proceedings of the 2004 conference on empirical methods in natural language processing.*

Mikolov, T., Le, Q. V., & Sutskever, I. (2013). Exploiting Similarities among Languages for Machine Translation. *Computer Science*, 1–10.

Miltsakaki, E., & Troutt, A. (2008, June). Real-time web text classification and analysis of reading difficulty. In *Proceedings of the third workshop on innovative use of NLP for building educational applications* (pp. 89-97). Columbus, OH: Association for Computational Linguistics. 10.3115/1631836.1631847

Minkov, E., Wang, R., & Cohen, W. (2005). Extracting Personal Names from Email: Applying Named Entity Recognition to Informal Text. *Conference: HLT/EMNLP 2005, Human Language Technology Conference and Conference on Empirical Methods in Natural Language Processing, Proceedings of the Conference.*

Mirshojaei, S. H., & Masoomi, B. (2015). Text Summarization Using Cuckoo Search Optimisation Algorithm. *Journal of Computer & Robotics, 8*(2), 19–24.

Moawad, I. F., & Aref, M. (2012). *Semantic graph reduction approach for abstractive Text Summarization.* Paper presented at the Computer Engineering & Systems (ICCES), 2012 Seventh International Conference on. 10.1109/ICCES.2012.6408498

Modaresi, P., Gross, P., Sefidrodi, S., Eckhof, M., & Conrad, S. (2017). On (commercial) benefits of automatic text summarization systems in the news domain: A case of media monitoring and media response analysis. Academic Press.

Moens, M.-F. (2007). Summarizing court decisions. *Information Processing & Management, 43*(6), 1748–1764. doi:10.1016/j.ipm.2007.01.005

Moens, M.-F., & Uyttendaele, C. (1997). Automatic structuring and categorization as a first step in summarizing legal cases. *Information Processing & Management, 33*(6), 727–737. doi:10.1016/S0306-4573(97)00035-6

Molĺa, D., van Zaanen, M., & Smith, D. (2006). Named Entity Recognition for Question Answering. *Proceedings of the 2006 Australasian Language Technology Workshop (ALTW2006),* 51–58.

Morita, T. (2018). *Advancing Subaru Hybrid Vehicle Testing Through Hardware-in-the-Loop Simulation.* Retrieved from http://sine.ni.com/cs/app/doc/p/id/cs-15982#

Mosa, M. A., Anwar, A. S., & Hamouda, A. (2019). A survey of multiple types of text summarization with their satellite contents based on swarm intelligence optimization algorithms. *Knowledge-Based Systems, 163*, 518-532. DOI.org/10.1016/j.knosys.2018.09.008

Mosa, M. A., Hamouda, A., & Marei, M. (2017). Graph coloring and ACO based summarization for social networks. *Expert Systems with Applications, 74*, 115–126. doi:10.1016/j.eswa.2017.01.010

Mosa, M. A., Hamouda, A., & Marei, M. (2017a). Ant colony heuristic for user-contributed comments summarization. *Knowledge-Based Systems, 118*, 105–114. doi:10.1016/j.knosys.2016.11.009

Mosa, M. A., Hamouda, A., & Marei, M. (2017c). *How can Ants Extract the Essence Contents Satellite of Social Networks.* LAP Lambert Academic Publishing.

Multi-document summarization. (2018, February 8). Retrieved from https://en.wikipedia.org/wiki/Multi-document_summarization

Munot & Govilkar. (2014). Comparative Study of Text Summarization Methods. *International Journal of Computer Applications, 102*(12).

Munot, N., & Govilkar, S. S. (2015, February). Conceptual Framework For Abstractive Text Summarization. *International Journal on Natural Language Computing, 4*(1), 39–50. doi:10.5121/ijnlc.2015.4104

Nadeau, D., & Sekine, S. (2007). A Survey of Named Entity Recognition and Classification. *Lingvisticae Investigationes., 30.* doi:10.1075/li.30.1.03nad

Nallapati, R., Zhou, B., Gulcehre, C., & Xiang, B. (2016). *Abstractive Text Summarization Using Sequence-to-Sequence RNNs and Beyond.* arXiv preprint arXiv:1602.06023

Nallapati, R., Zhai, F., & Zhou, B. (2017). SummaRuNNer: A recurrent network based sequence model for extractive summarization of documents. *AAAI Conference on Artificial Intelligence.*

Nallapati, R., Zhou, B., dos Santos, C., Gulcehre, C., & Xiang, B. (2016). Abstractive text summarization using sequence-to-sequence RNNs and beyond. In *Proceedings of the 20th SIGNLL Conference on Computational Natural Language Learning (CoNLL 2016).* Association for Computational Linguistics. 10.18653/v1/K16-1028

Napoles, C., Gormley, M., & Van Durme, B. (2012). Annotated gigaword. *Proceedings of the Joint Workshop on Automatic Knowledge Base Construction and Web-scale Knowledge Extraction.*

National Instruments. (2019). *LabVIEW Introduction.* Retrieved from http://www.ni.com/en-us/shop/labview/labview-details.html

Nazari, N., & Mahdavi, M. (2019). A survey on Automatic Text Summarization. *Journal of Artificial Intelligence and Data Mining, 7*(1), 121–135. doi:10.22044/jadm.2018.6139.1726

Nenkova & McKeown. (2011). *Automatic Summarization*. Delft, The Netherlands: Now.

Nenkova, A. (2006). Summarization evaluation for text and speech: issues and approaches. *INTERSPEECH*.

Nenkova, A., & Vanderwende, L. (2005). *The impact of frequency on summarization*. Microsoft Research. Tech. Rep. MSR-TR-2005, 101.

Nenkova, Passonneau, & McKeown. (2007). The Pyramid method: Incorporating human content selection variation in summarization evaluation. *ACM Trans. Speech Lang. Process., 4*(2), Article 4.

Nenkova, A. (2006). *Understanding the process of multi-document summarization: Content selection, rewriting and evaluation*. Columbia University.

Nenkova, A., & McKeown, K. (2012). A survey of text summarization techniques. In *Mining text data* (pp. 43–76). Boston, MA: Springer. doi:10.1007/978-1-4614-3223-4_3

Nenkova, A., & Passonneau, R. (2004). Evaluating content selection in summarization: The Pyramid method. In *Proceedings of the Human Language Technology Conference of the North American Chapter of the Association for Computational Linguistics (HLT-NAACL 2004)*. ACL.

Nenkova, A., & Passonneau, R. (2005). Evaluating Content Selection in Summarization*: The Pyramid Method. In Document Understanding Conference*, Vancouver, Canada.

Nguyen, T. S., Lauw, H. W., & Tsaparas, P. (2015, February). Review synthesis for micro-review summarization. In *Proceedings of the eighth ACM international conference on web search and data mining* (pp. 169-178). ACM. 10.1145/2684822.2685321

Niekrasz, J., Purver, M., Dowding, J., & Peters, S. (2005). Ontology-Based Discourse Understanding for a Persistent Meeting Assistant. *Proceedings of the AAAI Spring Symposium Persistent Assistants: Living and Working with AI*.

Nikoo, M. D., Faraahi, A., Hashemi, S. M., & Erfani, S. H. (2012). A Method for Text Summarization by Bacterial Foraging Optimisation Algorithm. *IJCSI International Journal of Computer Science Issues, 9*(4), 36–40.

Nilofar, M. S. D. (2018). Graph Based Text Summarization using NER and POS. *International Journal for Scientific Research & Development, 5*(12), 85–87.

Nobata, C., Sekine, S., Isahara, H., & Grishman, R. (2002). Summarization System Integrated with Named Entity Tagging and IE pattern Discovery. *The Third International Conference on Language Resources and Evaluation*.

Nugent & Leidner. (2016). *Risk mining: Company-risk identification from unstructured sources*. In 2016 IEEE 16th International Conference on Data Mining Workshops (ICDMW), 12-15 December, 2016, Barcelona, Spain, pp. 1308–1311..

Ono, K., Sumita, K., & Miike, S. (1994). Abstract Generation Based on Rhetorical Structure Extraction. *Proceedings of the International Conference on Computational Linguistics*, 344-348. 10.3115/991886.991946

Otterbacher, Radev, & Kareem. (2006). *News to go: Hierarchical text summarization for mobile devices.* In Proceedings of the 29th Annual International ACM SIGIR Conference on Research and Development in Information Retrieval, SIGIR 2006, New York, NY, USA, pp. 589–596. ACM.

Ouyang, J., Song, B., & McKeown, K. (2019, June). A Robust Abstractive System for Cross-Lingual Summarization. *Proceedings of the 2019 Conference of the North American Chapter of the Association for Computational Linguistics: Human Language Technologies*, 1, 2025-2031.

Ouyang, Y., Li, W., Li, S., & Lu, Q. (2011). Applying regression models to query-focused multi-document summarization. *Information Processing & Management, 47*(2), 227–237. doi:10.1016/j. ipm.2010.03.005

Over, P., Dang, H., & Harman, D. (2007). DUC in context. *Information Processing & Management, 43*(6), 1506–1520.

Page, L., Brin, S., Motwani, R., & Winograd, T. (1999). *The PageRank citation ranking: bringing order to the Web*. Academic Press.

Page, L., Brin, S., Motwani, R., & Winograd, T. (1999). *The PageRank citation ranking: Bringing order to the web*. Stanford InfoLab.

Paice, D. (1990). Constructing Literature Abstracts by Computer: Techniques and Prospects. *Information Processing & Management, 26*(1), 171–186. doi:10.1016/0306-4573(90)90014-S

Panigrahi, B. K., Shi, Y., & Lim, M. H. (Eds.). (2011). *Handbook of swarm intelligence: concepts, principles and applications* (Vol. 8). Springer Science & Business Media.

Papadakis, G., Tsekouras, L., Thanos, E., Giannakopoulos, G., Palpanas, T., & Koubarakis, M. (2017, May). Jedai: The force behind entity resolution. In *European Semantic Web Conference* (pp. 161-166). Springer.

Park, S., Lee, J. H., Ahn, C. M., Hong, J. S., & Chun, S. J. (2006). Query Based Summarization Using Non-Negative Matrix Factorization. *Proceeding of KES*, 84–89. 10.1007/11893011_11

Patel, A., Siddiqui, T.J., & Tiwary, U.S. (2007). *A language independent approach to multilingual text summarization*. Academic Press.

Patil, S.B., & Bhole, A.T. (2015). *Multi-document English Text Summarization using Latent Semantic Analysis*. Academic Press.

Paulus, R., Xiong, C., & Socher, R. (2017). *A Deep Reinforced Model for Abstractive Summarization.* CoRR, abs/1705.04304

Paulus, Xiong, & Socher. (n.d.). *A deep reinforced model for abstractive summarization.* Academic Press.

Pendry, L. F., & Salvatore, J. (2015). Individual and social benefits of online discussion forums. *Computers in Human Behavior*, *50*, 211–220. doi:10.1016/j.chb.2015.03.067

Pennington, J., Socher, R., & Manning, C. (2014). GloVe: Global Vectors for Word Representation. *Proceedings of the 2014 Conference on Empirical Methods in Natural Language Processing (EMNLP)*, 1532–1543. 10.3115/v1/D14-1162

Peyrard, M., & Eckle-Kohler, J. (2016). *A General Optimization Framework for Multi-Document Summarization Using Genetic Algorithms and Swarm Intelligence*. Retrieved from https://pdfs.semanticscholar.org/f744/715aedba86271000c1f49352e0bfdcaa3204.pdf

Pittaras, N., Papadakis, G., Stamoulis, G., Argyriou, G., Taniskidou, E. K., Thanos, E., ... Koubarakis, M. (2019, April). GeoSensor: semantifying change and event detection over big data. In *Proceedings of the 34th ACM/SIGAPP Symposium on Applied Computing* (pp. 2259-2266). ACM. 10.1145/3297280.3297504

Pontes, E. L., Torres-Moreno, J. M., & Linhares, A. C. (2016). *LIA-RAG: a system based on graphs and divergence of probabilities applied to Speech-To-Text Summarization*. arXiv preprint arXiv:1601.07124

Pontes, E. L., Huet, S., & Torres-Moreno, J. M. (2018, October). A Multilingual Study of Compressive Cross-Language Text Summarization. In *Mexican International Conference on Artificial Intelligence* (pp. 109-118). Springer. 10.1007/978-3-030-04497-8_9

Pontes, E. L., Huet, S., Torres-Moreno, J. M., & Linhares, A. C. (2018, June). Cross-language text summarization using sentence and multi-sentence compression. In *International Conference on Applications of Natural Language to Information Systems* (pp. 467-479). Springer.

Prakasam, A., & Savarimuthu, N. (2016). Metaheuristic algorithms and probabilistic behaviour: A comprehensive analysis of Ant Colony Optimization and its variants. *Artificial Intelligence Review*, *45*(1), 97–130. doi:10.100710462-015-9441-y

Qu, P., Zhang, J., Yao, C., & Zeng, W. (2016). Identifying long tail term from large-scale candidate pairs for big data-oriented patent analysis. *Concurrency and Computation*, *28*(15), 4194–4208. doi:10.1002/cpe.3792

Radev, D., Allison, T., Blair-Goldensohn, S., Blitzer, J., Çelebi, A., Dimitrov, S., . . . Zhang, Z. (2004). MEAD – a platform for multidocument multilingual text summarization. In *Proceedings of the Fourth International Conference on Language Resources and Evaluation (LREC 2004)*. European Language Resources Association (ELRA).

Radev, D. R., Jing, H., & Budzikowska, M. (2000). Centroid-Based Summarization of Multiple Documents: Sentence Extraction, Utility-Based Evaluation, and User Studies. *ANLP/NAACL Workshop on Summarization*.

Radev, D. R., Jing, H., Stys, M., & Tam, D. (2004). Centroid-based summarization of multiple documents. *Information Processing & Management*, *40*(6), 919–938. doi:10.1016/j.ipm.2003.10.006

Radev, D. R., Teufel, S., Saggion, H., Lam, W., Blitzer, J., Qi, H., ... Drabek, E. (2003). Evaluation challenges in large-scale document summarization. In *Proceedings of the 41st Annual Meeting of the Association for Computational Linguistics (ACL 2003)*. Association for Computational Linguistics.

Radev, D., Jing, H., & Budzikowska, M. (2000). Centroid-Based Summarization of Multiple Documents. *ANLP/NAACL Workshop on Automatic Summarization.*

Radev, D., Otterbacher, J., Winkel, A., & Blair-Goldensohn, S. (2005). NewsInEssence: Summarizing online news topics. *Communications of the ACM, 48*(10), 95–98. doi:10.1145/1089107.1089111

Radev, D., Teufel, S., Saggion, H., Lam, W., Blitzer, J., Celebi, A., & Liu, D. (2002). *Evaluation of text summarization in a cross-lingual information retrieval framework. Center for Language and Speech Processing, Johns Hopkins University.* Baltimore, MD: Tech. Rep.

Rau, L. F., Jacobs, P. S., & Zernik, U. (1989). Information extraction and text summarization using linguistic knowledge acquisition. *Information Processing & Management, 25*(4), 419–428. doi:10.1016/0306-4573(89)90069-1

Rautray, R., & Balabantaray, R. C. (2017). Cat swarm optimization based evolutionary framework for multi document summarization. *Physica A, 477*, 174–186. doi:10.1016/j.physa.2017.02.056

Razon, A., & Barnden, J. (2015). A New Approach to Automated Text Readability Classification based on Concept Indexing with Integrated Part-of-Speech n-gram Features. In *Proceedings of the International Conference Recent Advances in Natural Language Processing* (pp. 521-528). Academic Press.

Recognition, N. E. (2018, February 6). *Applications and Use Cases.* Retrieved from https://towardsdatascience.com/named-entity-recognition-applications-and-use-cases-acdbf57d595e

Reimer, U., & Hahn, U. (1988). Text condensation as knowledge base abstraction. *Artificial Intelligence Applications, 1988., Proceedings of the Fourth Conference on.*

Rennie, S. J., Marcheret, E., Mroueh, Y., Ross, J., & Goel, V. (2017). *Self-Critical Sequence Training for Image Captioning.* Paper presented at the 2017 IEEE Conference on Computer Vision and Pattern Recognition (CVPR). 10.1109/CVPR.2017.131

Resnik, P., & Smith, N. A. (2006). The web as a parallel corpus. *Computational Linguistics, 29*(3), 349–380. doi:10.1162/089120103322711578

Ribaldo, R., Akabane, A. T., Rino, L. H. M., & Pardo, T. A. S. (2012). Graph-based methods for multi-document summarization: exploring relationship maps, complex networks and discourse information. In *Computational Processing of the Portuguese Language* (pp. 260–271). Springer. doi:10.1007/978-3-642-28885-2_30

Riedhammer, K., Favre, B., & Hakkani-Tür, D. (2010). Long story short- global unsupervised models for keyphrase based meeting summarization. *Speech Communication, 52*(10), 801–815. doi:10.1016/j.specom.2010.06.002

Ronning, G. (1989). Maximum likelihood estimation of Dirichlet distributions. *Journal of Statistical Computation and Simulation, 32*(4), 215–221. doi:10.1080/00949658908811178

Rossiello, G., Basile, P., & Semeraro, G. (2017, April). Centroid-based text summarization through compositionality of word embeddings. In *Proceedings of the MultiLing 2017 Workshop on Summarization and Summary Evaluation Across Source Types and Genres* (pp. 12-21). Academic Press. 10.18653/v1/W17-1003

Rumelhart, D. E., Hinton, G. E., & Williams, R. J. (1988). Learning representations by back-propagating errors. *Cognitive Modeling, 5*(3), 1.

Rush, A. M., Chopra, S., & Weston, J. (2015). *A neural attention model for abstractive sentence summarization.* arXiv preprint arXiv:1509.00685

Rush, Chopra, & Weston. (2015). A neural attention model for abstractive sentence summarization. I: *Proceedings of the 2015 Conference on Empirical Methods in Natural Language Processing (EMNLP 2015).* Association for Computational Linguistics. 10.18653/v1/D15-1044

Saad, S., Moawad, I., & Aref, M. (2011). Ontology-Based Approach for Arabic Text Summarization. *Proceeding of International Conference on Intelligent Computing and Information Systems (ICICIS).*

Saggion, H. (2006). Multilingual Multidocument Summarization Tools and Evaluation. *Proceedings, LREC 2006.*

Saggion, H., Torres-Moreno, J. M., Cunha, I. D., & SanJuan, E. (2010, August). Multilingual summarization evaluation without human models. In *Proceedings of the 23rd International Conference on Computational Linguistics: Posters* (pp. 1059-1067). Association for Computational Linguistics.

Sagheer, D., & Sukkar, F. (2017). A Hybrid Intelligent System for Abstractive Summarization. *International Journal of Computers and Applications, 168*(9).

Salton, G., & Yang, C. S. (1973). On the specification of term values in automatic indexing. *The Journal of Documentation, 29*(4), 351–372. doi:10.1108/eb026562

Sankaran, B., Mi, H., Al-Onaizan, Y., & Ittycheriah, A. (2016). *Temporal Attention Model for Neural Machine Translation.* CoRR, abs/1608.02927

Santhana Megala, S. (2014). Enriching Text Summarization using Fuzzy Logic. *International Journal of Computer Science and Information Technologies, 5*(1), 863–867.

Santra, D., Mondal, A., & Mukherjee, A. (2016). Study of Economic Load Dispatch by Various Hybrid Optimization Techniques. In *Hybrid Soft Computing Approaches* (pp. 37–74). Springer India. doi:10.1007/978-81-322-2544-7_2

Sarkar, K. (2010). Syntactic trimming of extracted sentences for improving extractive multi-document summarization. *Journal of Computers, 2,* 177–184.

Schilder, F., & Kondadadi, R. (2008). FastSum: Fast and accurate query-based multi-document summarization. In *Proceedings of ACL-08: Human Language Technology.* Association for Computational Linguistics. 10.3115/1557690.1557748

Schilder, F., Kondadadi, R., Leidner, J. L., & Conrad, J. G. (2008). Thomson Reuters at TAC 2008: Aggressive filtering with FastSum for update and opinion summarization In *Proceedings of the First Text Analysis Conference (TAC 2008)*. NIST.

See, A., Liu, P. J., & Manning, C. D. (2017). Get To The Point: Summarization with Pointer-Generator Networks. *Proceedings of the 55th Annual Meeting of the Association for Computational Linguistics*. 10.18653/v1/P17-1099

Sharma, V. (2018). *Speakers, TVs, Kleenex in Demand on Amazon Prime Day*. Retrieved 17 Dec, 2018, from https://www.reuters.com/article/us-amazon-com-primeday/speakers-tvs-kleenex-in-demand-on-amazon-prime-day-idUSKBN1K81S4?il=0.

Shen, S. Q., Chen, Y., Yang, C., Liu, Z. Y., & Sun, M. S. (2018). Zero-Shot Cross-Lingual Neural Headline Generation. IEEE/ACM Transactions on Audio. *Speech and Language Processing*, *26*(12), 2319–2327.

Shodhaganga. (2000). *Single and Multi-document Summarization. Optimized Summarization Of Research Papers Using Data Mining Strategies.* SVKM's MPSTME, NMIMS.

Sievert, C., & Shirley, K. (2014). LDAvis: A method for visualizing and interpreting topics. In *Proceedings of the workshop on interactive language learning, visualization, and interfaces* (pp. 63-70). Baltimore, MD: Association for Computational Linguistics. 10.3115/v1/W14-3110

Simpson, K. (2015). *You Don't Know JS: Async & Performance.* O'Reilly Media, Inc.

Singh, M., Mishra, A., Oualil, Y., Berberich, K., & Klakow, D. (2018). Long-span language models for query-focused unsupervised extractive text summarization. In G. Pasi, B. Piwowarski, L. Azzopardi, & A. Hanbury (Eds.), *Advances in Information Retrieval – Proceedings of the 40th European Conference on IR Research (ECIR 2018)*. Springer. 10.1007/978-3-319-76941-7_59

Song, W., Choi, L. C., Park, S. C., & Ding, X. F. (2011). Fuzzy evolutionary optimization modelling and its applications to unsupervised categorization and extractive summarization. *Expert Systems with Applications*, *38*(8), 9112–9121. doi:10.1016/j.eswa.2010.12.102

Sparks Jones, K. (1972). A statistical interpretation of term specificity and its application in retrieval. *The Journal of Documentation*, *28*(1), 11–21. doi:10.1108/eb026526

Sripada, S., Kasturi, V. G., & Parai, G. K. (2010). *Multi-document extraction based Summarization.* Retrieved from https://nlp.stanford.edu/courses/cs224n/2010/reports/

Sripada, S., Kasturi, V., & Parai, G. (n.d.). *Multi-document extraction based Summarization.* CS 224N: Final Project, Stanford University.

Stanoevska-Slabeva, K., Sacco, V., & Giardina, M. (2012). *Content Curation: a new form of gatewatching for social media?* Retrieved from https://pdfs.semanticscholar.org/89e2/06cdb4f3 6ff9b0b69b3244b3be4c883d1f4e.pdf

Steinberger, J., & Jezek, K. (2004). Using latent semantic analysis in text summarization and summary evaluation. In *Proc. ISIM '04* (pp. 93–100). Academic Press.

Steinberger, J., & Jezek, K. (2004). Using latent semantic analysis in text summarization and summary evaluation. *Proc. ISIM, 4*, 93-100.

Steinberger, J., Kabadjov, M. A., Steinberger, R., Tanev, H., Turchi, M., & Zavarella, V. (2011). *JRC's Participation at TAC 2011: Guided and MultiLingual Summarization Tasks.* TAC.

Subramaniam, M., & Dalal, V. (2015). *Test Model for Rich Semantic Graph Representation for Hindi Text using Abstractive Method.* Academic Press.

Suganya, S., & Gomathi, C. (2013). Syntax and semantics based efficient text classification framework. *International Journal of Computers and Applications, 65*(15).

Sui, Z., Chen, Y., & Wei, Z. (2003, October). Automatic recognition of Chinese scientific and technological terms using integrated linguistic knowledge. In *Natural Language Processing and Knowledge Engineering, 2003. Proceedings. 2003 International Conference on* (pp. 444-451). IEEE.

Sulaiman, Abdul Wahid, Sarkawi, & Omar. (2017). Using Stanford NER and Illinois NER to Detect Malay Named Entity Recognition. *International Journal of Computer Theory and Engineering, 9*(2).

Summary. (1828). In *Merriam Webster.* Retrieved from http://www.merriam-webster.com/dictionary/summary

Summary. (1989). In *Oxford Dictionaries* Retrieved from https://en.oxforddictionaries.com/definition/summary

Summary. (1995). In *Cambridge Dictionary.* Retrieved from http://dictionary.cambridge.org/dictionary/english/summary

Takamura, H., & Okumura, M. (2009a). Text summarization model based on maximum coverage problem and its variant. *Proceedings of the 12th Conference of the European Chapter of the Association for Computational Linguistics*, 781-789. 10.3115/1609067.1609154

Takamura, H., & Okumura, M. (2009b). Text summarization model based on the budgeted median problem. *Proceeding of the 18th ACM conference on Information and knowledge management*, 1589-1592. 10.1145/1645953.1646179

Tanev, H., & Balahur, A. (2016). Tackling the OnForumS Challenge. *Museec: A multilingual text summarization tool. Proceedings of ACL-2016 System Demonstrations*, 73-78.

Tang, J., Yao, L., & Chen, D. (2009). Multi-topic-based query-oriented summarization. *SIAM International Conference Data Mining.*

Tan, P. N., Steinbach, M., & Kumar, V. (2006). *Introduction to data mining.* Pearson Addison Wesley Boston.

Tao, Y., Zhou, S., Lam, W., & Guan, J. (2008) Towards more text summarization based on textual association networks. *Proceedings of the 2008 fourth international conference on semantics, knowledge and grid,* 235–240. 10.1109/SKG.2008.17

Teufel, S., & Moens, M. (2002). Summarizing Scientific Articles: Experiments with Relevance and Rhetorical Status. *Computational Linguistics, 28*(4), 409–445. doi:10.1162/089120102762671936

Thomas, S., Beutenmüller, C., de la Puente, X., Remus, R., & Bordag, S. (2015). Exb text summarizer. In *Proceedings of the 16th Annual Meeting of the Special Interest Group on Discourse and Dialogue* (pp. 260-269). Academic Press. 10.18653/v1/W15-4637

Torralbo, R., Alfonseca, E., Guirao, J. M., & Moreno-Sandoval, A. (2005). Description of the UAM System at DUC-2005. *Proceedings of the Document Understanding Conf. Wksp. 2005 (DUC 2005) at the Human Language Technology Conf./Conf. on Empirical Methods in Natural Language Processing (HLT/EMNLP 2005).*

Torres-Moreno, J.-M. (2014). *Automatic Text Summarization.* Hoboken, NJ: Wiley.

Torres-Moreno, J.-M. (2014). *Automatic text summarization.* John Wiley & Sons. doi:10.1002/9781119004752

Tsekouras, L., Varlamis, I., & Giannakopoulos, G. (2017, September). *A Graph-based Text Similarity Measure That Employs Named Entity Information.* RANLP. doi:10.26615/978-954-452-049-6_098

Turchi, M., Steinberger, J., Kabadjov, M., & Steinberger, R. (2010). Using parallel corpora for multilingual (multi-document) summarisation evaluation. *Multilingual and Multimodal Information Access Evaluation,* 52–63.

Turney, P. D. (2002). Learning Algorithms for Keyphrase Extraction. *Information Retrieval, 2*(4), 303–336. arXiv:cs/0212020

Tu, Z., Lu, Z., Liu, Y., Liu, X., & Li, H. (2016). Modeling Coverage for Neural Machine Translation. *Proceedings of the 54th Annual Meeting of the Association for Computational Linguistics.* 10.18653/v1/P16-1008

Van den Bergh, F., & Engelbrecht, A. P. (2002, October). A new locally convergent particle swarm optimiser. In *Systems, Man and Cybernetics, 2002 IEEE International Conference on* (Vol. 3, pp. 6-pp). IEEE. 10.1109/ICSMC.2002.1176018

Varadarajan, R., & Hristidis, V. (2006). A System for Query-Specific Document Summarization. *Proceedings of the 15th ACM International Conference on Information and Knowledge Management,* 622–631.

Veena, G., Gupta, D., Jaganadh, J., & Nithya Sreekumar, S. (2016, December). A Graph Based Conceptual Mining Model for Abstractive Text Summarization. *Indian Journal of Science and Technology, 9*(S1). doi:10.17485/ijst/2016/v9iS1/99876

Vicente, M., Alcón, O., & Lloret, E. (2015). The University of Alicante at MultiLing 2015: approach, results and further insights. In *Proceedings of the 16th Annual Meeting of the Special Interest Group on Discourse and Dialogue* (pp. 250-259). Academic Press. 10.18653/v1/W15-4636

Vinyals, O., Fortunato, M., & Jaitly, N. (2015). Pointer networks. *Proceedings of the 28th International Conference on Neural Information Processing Systems.*

Vogt, P. F., & Miller, M. J. (1998). Development and applications of amino acid-derived chiral acylnitroso hetero Diels-Alder reactions. *Tetrahedron, 54*(8), 1317–1348. doi:10.1016/S0040-4020(97)10072-2

Wan, S., Li, L., Huang, T., Gao, Z., Mao, L., & Huang, F. (2015). *CIST System Report for SIGdial MultiLing 2015.* Academic Press.

Wan, X. (2011, June). Using bilingual information for cross-language document summarization. In *Proceedings of the 49th Annual Meeting of the Association for Computational Linguistics: Human Language Technologies-Volume 1* (pp. 1546-1555). Association for Computational Linguistics.

Wan, X., Jia, H., Huang, S., & Xiao, J. (2011). Summarizing the differences in multilingual news. In *Proceedings of the 34th international ACM SIGIR conference on Research and development in Information* (pp. 735–744). Academic Press.

Wang, D., & Li, T. (2010). Document update summarization using incremental hierarchical clustering. *Proceedings of the 19th ACM international conference on Information and knowledge management,* 279–288. 10.1145/1871437.1871476

Wang, D., Zhu, S., Li, T., Chi, Y., & Gong, Y. (2011). Integrating Document Clustering and Multidocument Summarization. *ACM Transactions on Knowledge Discovery from Data, 5*(3), 14. doi:10.1145/1993077.1993078

Wan, X., Li, H., & Xiao, J. (2010, July). Cross-language document summarization based on machine translation quality prediction. In *Proceedings of the 48th Annual Meeting of the Association for Computational Linguistics* (pp. 917-926). Association for Computational Linguistics.

Wan, X., Luo, F., Sun, X., Huang, S., & Yao, J. G. (2018). Cross-language document summarization via extraction and ranking of multiple summaries. *Knowledge and Information Systems,* 1–19.

Wan, X., & Yang, J. (2006). Improved affinity graph based multi-document summarization. *Proceedings of the Human Language Technology Conference of the NAACL,* 181-184.

Woodsend, K., Feng, Y., & Lapata, M. (2010). Generation with quasi-synchronous grammar. *Proceedings of the 2010 Conference on Empirical Methods in Natural Language Processing.*

Wu, Y., Zhang, Q., Huang, X., & Wu, L. (2009). Phrase Dependency Parsing for Opinion Mining. *Conference on Empirical Methods in Natural Language Processing,* 1533-1541.

Wu, C. W., & Liu, C. L. (2003). Ontology-Based Text Summarization for Business News Articles. *Proceedings of the ISCA 18th International Conference on Computers and Their Applications*, 389–392.

Wu, C., & Liu, C. (2003). Ontology-based text summarization for business news articles. In N. C. Debnath (Ed.), *Proceedings of the 18th International Conference Computers and Their Applications (ISCA 2003)*. ISCA.

Xiong, C., Hua, Z., Lv, K., & Li, X. (2016, November). An Improved K-means text clustering algorithm By Optimizing initial cluster centers. In *2016 7th International Conference on Cloud Computing and Big Data (CCBD)* (pp. 265-268). Macau, China: IEEE.

Xu, Y., Lau, J. H., Baldwin, T., & Cohn, T. (2017, April). Decoupling encoder and decoder networks for abstractive document summarization. In *Proceedings of the MultiLing 2017 Workshop on Summarization and Summary Evaluation Across Source Types and Genres* (pp. 7-11). Academic Press. 10.18653/v1/W17-1002

Xu, J., Peng, W., Guanhua, T., Bo, X., Jun, Z., Fangyuan, W., & Hongwei, H. (2015). Short text clustering via convolutional neural networks. In *13th Annual Conference of the North American Chapter of the Association for Computational Linguistics: Human Language Technologies* (pp. 62 - 69). Denver, CO: Association for Computational Linguistics. 10.3115/v1/W15-1509

Xu, J., Xu, B., Wang, P., Zheng, S., Tian, G., Zhao, J., & Xu, B. (2017). Self-taught convolutional neural networks for short text clustering. *Neural Networks*, *88*, 22–31. doi:10.1016/j.neunet.2016.12.008 PMID:28157556

Yadav, R. K., & Singh, S. (2016). A New Approach to Automated Summarization based on Fuzzy Clustering and Particle Swarm Optimization. *International Journal of Computers and Applications*, *148*(1).

Yang, X-S. (2014). Swarm intelligence based algorithms: A critical analysis. *Evolutionary Intelligence, 7*(1), 17-28.

Yang, C. C., & Wang, F. L. (2003). Fractal summarization for mobile devices to access large documents on the Web. In *Proceedings of the 12th International Conference on World Wide Web (WWW 2003)*. ACM. 10.1145/775152.775183

Yang, Z., Yang, D., Dyer, C., He, X., Smola, A., & Hovy, E. (2016). Hierarchical attention networks for document classification. In *Proceedings of the 2016 Conference of the North American Chapter of the Association for Computational Linguistics: Human Language Technologies* (pp. 1480-1489). San Diego, CA: Association for Computational Linguistics.

Yao, J. G., Wan, X., & Xiao, J. (2015). Phrase-based compressive cross-language summarization. In *Proceedings of the 2015 conference on empirical methods in natural language processing* (pp. 118-127). Academic Press. 10.18653/v1/D15-1012

Yao, Wan, & Xiao. (2017). Recent advances in document summarization. *Knowledge and Information Systems, 53,* 1-40. doi:10.100710115-017-1042-4

Yeloglu, O., Milios, E., & Zincir-Heywood, N. (2011). Multi-document summarization of scientific corpora. In *Proceedings of the 2011 ACM Symposium on Applied Computing* (pp. 252–258). Academic Press. 10.1145/1982185.1982243

Yeniay, Ö. (2014). Comparative study of algorithms for response surface optimization. *Mathematical and Computational Applications, 19*(1), 93–104. doi:10.3390/mca19010093

Yin, W., Kann, K., Yu, M., & Schütze, H. (in press). *Comparative study of CNN and RNN for natural language processing*. Clinical Orthopaedics and Related Research. Retrieved from https://arxiv.org/abs/1702.01923

Zaharia, M., Xin, R. S., Wendell, P., Das, T., Armbrust, M., Dave, A., ... Ghodsi, A. (2016). Apache spark: A unified engine for big data processing. *Communications of the ACM, 59*(11), 56–65. doi:10.1145/2934664

Zelenko, D., Aone, C., & Richardella, A. (2003). Kernel methods for relation extraction. *Journal of Machine Learning Research, 3*(Feb), 1083–1106.

Zeng, W., Yao, C., & Li, H. (2017). The exploration of information extraction and analysis about science and technology policy in China. *The Electronic Library, 35*(4), 709–723. doi:10.1108/EL-10-2016-0235

Zhang, Y., Callan, J., & Minka, T. (2002). Novelty and redundancy detection in adaptive filtering. In *Proceedings of the 25th annual international ACM SIGIR conference on Research and development in information retrieval* (pp. 81–88). Academic Press. 10.1145/564376.564393

Zhang, J., Li, K., & Yao, C. (2018). Event-based Summarization for Scientific Literature in Chinese. *Procedia Computer Science, 129*, 88–92. doi:10.1016/j.procs.2018.03.052

Zhang, J., Sun, Y., & Jara, A. J. (2015). Towards semantically linked multilingual corpus. *International Journal of Information Management, 35*(3), 387–395. doi:10.1016/j.ijinfomgt.2015.01.004

Zhang, J., Sun, Y., & Yao, C. (2017). Semantically linking events for massive scientific literature research. *The Electronic Library, 35*(4), 724–744. doi:10.1108/EL-09-2016-0198

Zhang, J., Yao, C., Sun, Y., & Fang, Z. (2016). Building text-based temporally linked event network for scientific big data analytics. *Personal and Ubiquitous Computing, 20*(5), 743–755. doi:10.100700779-016-0940-x

Zhang, J., Zhou, Y., & Zong, C. (2016). Abstractive cross-language summarization via translation model enhanced predicate argument structure fusing. *IEEE/ACM Transactions on Audio. Speech, and Language Processing, 24*(10), 1842–1853.

Zhang, X., Zhao, J., & LeCun, Y. (2015). Character-level convolutional networks for text classification. In *Advances in neural information processing systems* (pp. 649–657). Montreal, Canada: Neural Information Processing Systems.

Zhang, Y., Jin, R., & Zhou, Z. H. (2010). Understanding bag-of-words model: A statistical framework. *International Journal of Machine Learning and Cybernetics*, *1*(1-4), 43–52. doi:10.100713042-010-0001-0

Zheng, D., Zhao, T., & Yang, J. (2009, March). Research on domain term extraction based on conditional random fields. In *International Conference on Computer Processing of Oriental Languages* (pp. 290-296). Springer. 10.1007/978-3-642-00831-3_27

Zhou, P., Qi, Z., Zheng, S., Xu, J., Bao, H., & Xu, B. (2016, December). Text Classification Improved by Integrating Bidirectional LSTM with Two-dimensional Max Pooling. In *Proceedings of COLING 2016, the 26th International Conference on Computational Linguistics: Technical Papers* (pp. 3485-3495). Osaka, Japan: The COLING 2016 Organizing Committee.

Zitnik, M., Nguyen, F., Wang, B., Leskovec, J., Goldenberg, A., & Hoffman, M. M. (2019). Machine learning for integrating data in biology and medicine: Principles, practice, and opportunities. *Information Fusion*, *50*, 71–91. doi:10.1016/j.inffus.2018.09.012 PMID:30467459

About the Contributors

Alessandro Fiori received the European Ph.D. degree from Politecnico di Torino, Italy. He is project manager at the Candiolo Cancer Institute - FPO IRCCS, Italy, since January 2012. His research interests are in the field of data mining, in particular bioinformatics and text mining. His activity is focused on the development of information systems and analysis frameworks oriented to the management and integration of biological and molecular data. His research activities are also devoted to text summarization and social network analysis.

* * *

Amal Al-Numai received her BSc degree in Computer Science from the Al-Imam Mohammad Ibn Saud Islamic University, and MSc degree in CS from King Saud University, Riyadh. Currently she is a PhD candidate at the Department of Computer Science, King Saud University. Her current research interests include machine learning, Arabic language processing, and data mining.

Mohamed Atef Mosa received his B.Sc., M.Sc., and Ph.D. at computer and system engineering, faculty of engineering, Al-Azhar University, Cairo, Egypt. He is Assistant professor, Institute of Public Administration, Department of Information Technology, Riyadh, Saudi Arabia. He has many publications in Thomson Reuters/ISI journals. Besides, he is a reviewer in some of Thomson Reuters/ISI journals. His research interests include data science, data mining, machine learning, deep learning, reinforcement algorithms, artificial intelligence, swarm intelligence, optimization, natural language processing, and python programming language.

Aqil Azmi received his BSE degree in Elec & Comput Eng. (ECE) from the University of Michigan, Ann Arbor, Michigan, and MSc and PhD degrees in EE and Computer Science respectively from the University of Colorado at Boulder, Colorado. Currently, he is a professor at the Department of Computer Science, King Saud University. He has over 20 publications in high impact factored journals and several book chapters. His research interests include Arabic natural language processing, computational biology, bioinformatics, and using computational analysis of religious texts.

Luca Cagliero has been assistant professor at the Politecnico di Torino since January 2017. His main research interests are the study and application of supervised and unsupervised machine learning techniques to structured and unstructured data.

Paolo Garza received the master's and PhD degrees in computer engineering from the Politecnico di Torino. He has been an assistant professor (with non-tenure track position) at the Dipartimento di Automatica e Informatica, Politecnico di Torino, since December 2010. His current research interests include data mining and database systems. He has worked on the classification of structured and unstructured data, clustering, and itemset mining algorithms.

George Giannakopoulos was born in Athens in 1978. While an undergraduate student, he was also working in the informatics industry for several years, specializing in the domain of Medical Informatics. He graduated from the National and Kapodistrian University of Athens, Department of Informatics and Telecommunications in 2005, having focused my research interests in the domain of AI. Then he joined the Department of Information and Communication Systems Engineering at the University of Aegean, where he completed his PhD on Automatic Summarization. His research was conducted within the Software and Knowledge Engineering Laboratory of NCSR Demokritos, in collaboration with the University of Aegean. From June 2010-June 2011 he was a Research Fellow for the DISI, University of Trento, working for the OKKAM project on `Self-administering Lifecycle Management' of Information. He is currently working as a Research Fellow for the Software and Knowledge Engineering Lab at the Institute of Informatics and Telecommunications of NCSR Demokritos in Athens, Greece. In April 2012 he co-founded (with Vasilis Salapatas) SciFY, which brings Artificial Intelligence applications and systems to the public as open systems (open source, open hardware), for free. He has been teaching classes related to Intelligent Systems (since 2015), Data Mining and Applied Data Mining (since 2017) at MSc Level and supervised more than 30 students over the course of his research. He is a member of the Board of the Hellenic Artificial Intelligence Society and the European Chapter of the ACL (EACL).

Jeff Gray is a Professor in the Department of Computer Science at the University of Alabama. His research interests are software engineering, model-driven engineering, and computer science education. More information about Jeff's work is available at http://gray.cs.ua.edu

Zhe Jiang is an assistant professor in the department of Computer Science at the University of Alabama, Tuscaloosa. He received his Ph.D. in computer science from the University of Minnesota, Twin Cities in 2016, and B.E. in electrical engineering from the the University of Science and Technology of China, Hefei, China, in 2010. His research interests include data mining and knowledge discovery, particularly spatial and spatio-temporal data mining, spatial big data, and their interdisciplinary applications in earth science, transportation, public safety, etc. He is a member of IEEE.

Xin Zhao is a PhD candidate in the Department of Computer Science at University of Alabama. His doctoral research investigates the evaluation of systems models, including the bad smells categorization, model refactoring and metrics analyses of systems models. He obtained his B.E. in the Hebei Normal University, China. Before joining University of Alabama, he was a member of National Engineering Research Center for Multimedia Software, Wuhan University, China.

Enakshi Jana is a master student at Pondicherry University at the department of computer science.

Mahek Kantesaria is currently pursuing M.Tech. from Vellore Institute of Technology, Chennai Campus in Computer Science Engg.

Moreno La Quatra is a PhD student at the Politecnico di Torino. After his graduation in Computer Engineering with a double degree program between Politecnico di Torino and Grenoble INP, he started his PhD in the domain of Multimedia and Text analysis.

Jochen L. Leidner received his M.A. in computational linguistics, English and computer science from FAU Erlangen, his M.Phil. in computer speech, text and Internet technology from the University of Cambridge, and his Ph.D. in informatics from the University of Edinburgh. He has been a Scientist and Director of Research, R&D at several of the Thomson Reuters family of companies (Thomson, West Inc., Thomson Reuters, Reuters Ltd., TRGR, Refinitiv) for over a decade. He is also the Royal Academy of Engineering Visiting Professor of Data Analytics at the University of Sheffield and a Fellow of the Royal Geographical Society. His research focuses on information access by developing and applying methods from natural language processing, machine learning, and information retrieval.

Milad Moradi received his M.Sc. in Computer Engineering at the Department of Electrical and Computer Engineering, Isfahan University of Technology, Iran. He also has been a member of Data and Knowledge Research Laboratory. His research interests include Natural Language Processing, Data Mining, and Machine Learning.

Sandhya P. is an Associate Professor in the School of Computing Science and Engineering at Vellore Institute of Technology, Chennai, India. She has published her works in number of SCOPUS indexed and UGC indexed journals. She has also presented her paper in international conferences at Las Vegas, USA and Vietnam. She has won best paper award for her work on web services. She has also won distinguished Engineering award for contribution in IoT. She is currently guiding three research scholars. She is a bronze medalist in M.Tech. Her area of interest includes deep learning, SOA, Semantic web and IoT. She has also served as reviewer in ISBCC (Springer) and ICRTAC (IEEE) conferences. She is the head of Semantic web research group at VIT- Chennai Campus. She has attended faculty development programs on Machine Learning, IoT, computer vision, instructional design, etc.

Uma V. received the M.Tech, and PhD degrees in computer science from Pondicherry University in 2007 and 2014 respectively. She was awarded the Pondicherry University gold medal for M.Tech. degree in Distributed Computing Systems. She has more than 10 years of teaching experience at PG level. Her research interest includes Data mining, knowledge representation and reasoning (spatial and temporal knowledge) and sentiment analysis. She has authored and co-authored more than 20 peer-reviewed journal papers, which includes publications in Springer and Inderscience. She has also authored 4 chapters in various books published by IGI Global. She has also authored a book on temporal knowledge representation and reasoning. She received the Best Paper Award in International Conference on Digital Factory in the year 2008.

Wen Zeng is an associate professor and the leader of information theory research group, Research Center for Information Science Theory and Methodology, institute of scientific and technical information of China (ISTIC). She received her Ph. D. in Mechanical and Electronic Engineering in 2009 from Shenyang Institute of Automation Chinese Academy of Sciences. Her fields of interest include information analysis method and technology, information theory and method, Knowledge organization and Management.

Junsheng Zhang is a professor and the leader of data mining and information analysis research group, Research Center for Information Science Theory and Methodology, institute of scientific and technical information of China (ISTIC). He received his Ph. D. in Computer Science in 2009 from Institute of Computing Technology, Chinese Academy of Sciences. His fields of interest include Data and

Information Analysis, Information and Knowledge Management, Semantic Analysis and Computing, Mobile and Cloud Computing.

Index

Ensure Quality Research is Introduced to the Academic Community

Become an IGI Global Reviewer for Authored Book Projects

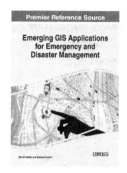

Premier Reference Source

Emerging GIS Applications for Emergency and Disaster Management

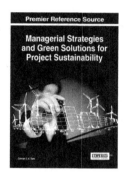

Premier Reference Source

Managerial Strategies and Green Solutions for Project Sustainability

Premier Reference Source

Comparative Approaches to Using R and Python for Statistical Data Analysis

Premier Reference Source

Solutions for High-Touch Communications in a High-Tech World

The overall success of an authored book project is dependent on quality and timely reviews.

In this competitive age of scholarly publishing, constructive and timely feedback significantly expedites the turnaround time of manuscripts from submission to acceptance, allowing the publication and discovery of forward-thinking research at a much more expeditious rate. Several IGI Global authored book projects are currently seeking highly-qualified experts in the field to fill vacancies on their respective editorial review boards:

Applications and Inquiries may be sent to:
development@igi-global.com

Applicants must have a doctorate (or an equivalent degree) as well as publishing and reviewing experience. Reviewers are asked to complete the open-ended evaluation questions with as much detail as possible in a timely, collegial, and constructive manner. All reviewers' tenures run for one-year terms on the editorial review boards and are expected to complete at least three reviews per term. Upon successful completion of this term, reviewers can be considered for an additional term.

If you have a colleague that may be interested in this opportunity, we encourage you to share this information with them.

IGI Global Proudly Partners With
eContent Pro International
Receive a 25% Discount on all Editorial Services

Editorial Services

IGI Global expects all final manuscripts submitted for publication to be in their final form. This means they must be reviewed, revised, and professionally copy edited prior to their final submission. Not only does this support with accelerating the publication process, but it also ensures that the highest quality scholarly work can be disseminated.

English Language Copy Editing

Let eContent Pro International's expert copy editors perform edits on your manuscript to resolve spelling, punctuaion, grammar, syntax, flow, formatting issues and more.

Scientific and Scholarly Editing

Allow colleagues in your research area to examine the content of your manuscript and provide you with valuable feedback and suggestions before submission.

Figure, Table, Chart & Equation Conversions

Do you have poor quality figures? Do you need visual elements in your manuscript created or converted? A design expert can help!

Translation

Need your documjent translated into English? eContent Pro International's expert translators are fluent in English and more than 40 different languages.

Printed in the United States
By Bookmasters